INFORMATION SYSTEMS

Fabio Guilherme da Silva

TAP

Toronto Academic Press

INFORMATION SYSTEMS

Fabio Guilherme da Silva

Toronto Academic Press
4164 Lakeshore Road
Burlington ON L7L 1A4
Canada
www.tap-books.com

Email: orders@arclereducation.com

ISBN: 978-1-77956-317-0

ABOUT THE AUTHOR

Fabio Guilherme da Silva is an academic, analyst, and software developer with over 25 years of experience in the field. He obtained a Bachelor's in Mathematics (with a specialisation in Informatics) from the State University of Rio de Janeiro (UERJ) in 1994, and began working as a software developer and business analyst right away. He worked on projects for numerous companies in Brazil, including giants such as TV Globo, Halliburton, UBS, and the government of the State of Rio de Janeiro. In 2010, he obtained his Master's in Information Systems from the Federal University of the State of Rio de Janeiro (UNIRIO), and in 2015, a Doctorate in Computer Science from the Pontifical Catholic University of Rio de Janeiro (PUC-Rio). His research was dedicated to the use of artificial intelligence in games and interactive storytelling, and for both of these latest two degrees, he was awarded a full scholarship from the Brazilian government. During his doctoral degree, he worked as a researcher at ICAD/IGames/VisionLab at PUC-Rio, producing reports that helped win some game copyright infringement cases in court, including one for Zynga. In 2012, he was awarded an Honourable Mention (Interactivity) by the International Telecommunication Union (ITU) for his work. He then worked as a lecturer at PUC-Rio and FUCAPE Business School before leaving Brazil in 2018 to work for companies in Argentina, Germany, the USA, and the UAE. He currently lives in Portugal where he works as a researcher and assistant professor at the European University of Lisbon, focusing his research and teaching on Artificial Intelligence, Games, and Programming Languages. In addition to his pursuits in Computer Science and IT, Fabio also holds a diploma in International Relations and is fluent in eight languages. In his free time, he enjoys travelling, sports and playing music, having already toured and played in multiple countries in Europe and the Americas.

Table of Contents

List of Figures

List of Tables

PREFACE

In the past, when a company received a customer order, whether for a service or a product, the order had to navigate a cumbersome paper-based workflow, moving from inbox to inbox across various departments. This process often involved retyping the order at multiple stages, significantly increasing the likelihood of human error. Furthermore, there was no accurate method to track the order's status, as no centralized tracking system existed to alert each department of updates. Consequently, customers frequently had to contact the company's warehouse to manually research their order status, leading to inefficiencies and frustration.

Today, the inaccuracies of paper-based tracking have been eradicated by the implementation of Enterprise Resource Planning (ERP) systems. According to a recent study by Panorama Consulting Solutions, 63% of companies use their ERP software to eliminate inefficiencies in processes such as order tracking. Unlike standalone computer systems, ERP systems operate through a unified program that links various functional departments, including finance, HR, manufacturing, warehouse, planning, purchasing, inventory, sales, and marketing. While each department may use its own set of software modules, these modules are interconnected, allowing seamless information sharing throughout the organization. When one department finishes updating and processing an order, it is automatically routed to the next department, ensuring that everyone is immediately aware of any changes made.

In the context of the global market, many businesses are increasingly engaging internationally, seeking greater revenue and broader business opportunities. The global information systems market has witnessed consistent demand from numerous businesses, each facing unique challenges based on their size. For smaller businesses, controlling operations and storing information are relatively straightforward. However, as businesses expand, particularly those with global interactions, information systems become crucial for managing operations accurately without the need to significantly increase the number of employees. By leveraging ERP systems, businesses of all sizes can efficiently manage their operations, reduce manual errors, and improve overall productivity, positioning themselves competitively in the global market.

The adoption of ERP systems represents a significant advancement in business operations, streamlining processes, and enhancing efficiency. By automating and integrating various departmental functions, these systems enable businesses to operate more effectively, reduce errors, and provide better service to their customers. As companies continue to expand globally, the role of ERP systems in managing complex operations and facilitating seamless communication across departments will only become more critical. The purpose of this book is to analyze and investigate the strategic role of information systems in modern enterprises.

Contents/Structure of the Book

"Information Systems" is a comprehensive book presenting the critical role of information technology in contemporary business environments. The book is divided into ten chapters, each providing a detailed exploration of different facets of information systems and their applications.

Chapter 1 introduces the fundamental concepts of information systems. It covers the basics of how information systems support business operations, decision-making, and competitive strategies. The chapter also discusses the various types of information systems and their roles in different organizational contexts.

Chapter 2 focuses on Management Information Systems (MIS), exploring how they help organizations manage their operations more efficiently. It explains the components of MIS, including data collection, processing, and dissemination, and how these systems aid in decision-making processes by providing timely and accurate information.

Chapter 3 addresses the crucial aspects of acquiring software and hardware for businesses. It discusses the strategic considerations for selecting and implementing technology solutions, including cost, scalability, compatibility, and vendor evaluation. The chapter also touches on the procurement processes and best practices for successful technology integration.

Chapter 4 deals with database systems and the significance of big data in today's data-driven world. It explains the fundamentals of database management systems (DBMS), data modeling, and database design. The chapter also explores big data technologies and analytics, highlighting their importance in extracting valuable insights from large datasets.

Chapter 5 focuses on Decision Support Systems (DSS) and their role in enhancing organizational decision-making. It covers the components of DSS, including data, models, and user interfaces, and illustrates how these systems support complex decision-making processes through data analysis, simulations, and what-if scenarios.

E-commerce is the focus of chapter 6, which examines the principles and practices of conducting business online. The chapter explores various e-commerce models, digital payment systems, and the technological infrastructure needed to support online business activities. It also discusses the challenges and opportunities associated with e-commerce.

Chapter 7 explores the concepts of networks and cloud computing. It explains the architecture and components of computer networks, including LANs, WANs, and the internet. The chapter also delves into cloud computing, discussing its benefits, deployment models, and the impact on business operations.

Chapter 8 covers Business Intelligence (BI) and analytics, emphasizing their importance in strategic decision-making. It explains the tools and techniques used in BI, such as data mining, predictive analytics, and dashboards. The chapter also highlights how businesses can leverage analytics to gain a competitive edge.

Information security is the focus of chapter 9, which discusses the strategies and technologies used to protect information assets. It covers topics such as cybersecurity threats, risk management, encryption, and access controls. The chapter also emphasizes the importance of developing a robust security policy to safeguard sensitive data.

The final Chapter 10 examines the relationship between information technology and organizational structure. It discusses how IT can influence organizational design, culture, and processes. The chapter also explores the role of IT in fostering innovation, improving efficiency, and enabling organizational change.

Through these ten chapters, "Information Systems" provides a thorough understanding of the critical role that information technology plays in modern businesses, offering valuable insights for students, professionals, and anyone interested in the field of information systems.

Audience

This book will be of interest to students, professionals, and academics who are interested in the field of information technology and its applications in various business and organizational contexts. This book serves as a comprehensive guide for undergraduate and graduate students pursuing degrees in computer science, information systems, business administration, and related disciplines. It is also a valuable resource for IT professionals, system analysts, and managers who seek to understand the strategic role of information systems in enhancing business processes, improving decision-making, and driving innovation. Additionally, researchers and educators in the field of information systems will find this book useful for its in-depth analysis of current trends, technologies, and methodologies. By covering a wide range of topics, from the fundamentals of information systems to advanced concepts like data analytics and cybersecurity, this book aims to equip its readers with the knowledge and skills needed to excel in the dynamic and ever-evolving landscape of information technology.

Learning Features

- Start-of-chapter learning objectives
- Key terms in each chapter
- Summary Points at the end of each chapter
- Review Questions at the end of each chapter
- Case Studies and Activities in each chapter for solving real problems
- References at the end of each chapter

CHAPTER

1 Information Systems: An Overview

LEARNING OBJECTIVES

After studying this chapter, you will be able to:

- Understand information systems: definitions and components;
- Identify six major types of information systems;
- Discuss about acquiring information systems and services;
- Explain information systems security and control;
- Identify impacts of information systems;
- Describe information technology.

KEY TERMS FROM THIS CHAPTER

Complex system
Enterprise resource planning
Information security
Open-source software
Software-as-a-service (SaaS)
Decision support system
Information
Management information system (MIS)
Organization
Transaction process system (TPS)

INTRODUCTION

An information system is a cohesive group of parts used to gather, store, process, and distribute data as well as knowledge and digital goods. Information systems are necessary for businesses and other organizations to run their operations, communicate with suppliers and customers, and fight in the market. Electronic markets and interorganizational supply chains are managed by information systems. Businesses use information systems, for example, to handle their human resources, process financial accounts, and market to prospective consumers online. Information systems are the foundation of many large businesses. These include the mostly auction-based eBay; the growing electronic mall and cloud computing services provider Amazon; the business-to-business e-marketplace Alibaba; and the search engine giant Google, which makes the majority of its money from keyword advertising on Internet searches. Governments use information systems to offer citizens services at a reasonable cost. Information systems are used to deliver digital products like software, video products, and electronic books as well as online services like social networking and gaming. People conduct a large portion of their personal lives through information systems, most of which are Internet-based: socializing, studying, shopping, banking, and entertainment.

Over the millennia, significant new technologies for information recording and processing emerged, giving people new capabilities and increased power. Just two examples are Blaise Pascal's mechanical calculator invention in the 17th century and Johannes Gutenberg's printing press invention in the middle of the 15th century. These innovations brought about a significant revolution in the gathering, analyzing, sharing, and retrieving of data and knowledge. Consequently, this resulted in more profound alterations to personal lives, corporate structures, and human governance.

The census tabulator designed by Herman Hollerith was the first large-scale mechanical information system created to process the 1890 U.S. Hollerith's machine, which was used for the census, was a significant advancement in automation and served as a model for the creation of computerized information systems.

A pioneer in this type of information processing was the UNIVACI, which was set up at the U.S. Bureau of the Census for administrative purposes in 1951 and at General Electric for business purposes in 1954. Personal computers began to make some of the benefits of information systems available to individuals and small businesses in the late 1970s. Early in the decade, the Internet started to grow into a worldwide network of networks. The World Wide Web, created by Tim Berners-Lee in 1991 as a way to access the linked data kept in the widely scattered computers connected by the Internet, went live and started serving as the main service on the network. The widespread use of the Internet and the Web has made it possible for people to access information and other resources, as well as to build relationships between individuals and organizations on a never-before-seen scale. The development of electronic commerce over the Internet has led to a sharp increase in the distribution of products (software, music, e-books, and movies), business transactions (buying, selling, and advertising on the Web), and digital interpersonal communications (via e-mail and social networks). Information systems have expanded to accommodate mobility as the default human state with the global proliferation of smartphones, tablets, laptops, and other computer-based mobile devices, all of which are connected by wireless communication networks.

Information systems had a significant impact on society as they made it possible for people to engage in a wider range of activities. These systems altered the structure and makeup of organizations, sped up daily tasks, made it easier for people to form and maintain new, frequently more fulfilling relationships, altered the kinds of products that were purchased, and altered the nature of work. Knowledge and information have become essential economic resources. However, the reliance on information systems also brought new risks in addition to new opportunities. While attempting to contain the threats, intensive industry innovation and academic research continuously create new opportunities.

1.1. INFORMATION SYSTEMS: DEFINITIONS AND COMPONENTS

A collection of various devices used in the distribution of information is referred to as an information system (IS). An information system (IS) consists of the following components: hardware, software, computer system connections and data, information system users, and the system housing.

1.1.1. Information System

Two perspectives have been used to define information systems: one pertains to their function, while the other addresses their structure. An information system is a technologically implemented medium that is used to record, store, and distribute linguistic expressions and to facilitate the making of inferences. This is the functional definition of an information system. From a structural standpoint, an information system is made up of a variety of components, including people, procedures, data, models, technology, and partially formalized language. These components work together to form a coherent structure that fulfills a specific organizational function.

From a conceptual standpoint, the functional definition is beneficial because it highlights the actual actions that users take while utilizing the information system. They converse with specialists in order to resolve a specific issue. It is evident from the structural definition that IS are socio-technical systems, i.e., systems made up of people, behavioral guidelines, and conceptual and technical objects.

Technically speaking, an information system is a collection of connected parts that support organizational decision-making and control by gathering, processing, storing, and distributing information (or retrieving it). Information systems can aid managers and employees in problem analysis, the visualization of difficult concepts, and the development of new products in addition to supporting decision making, coordination, and control.

An information system generates the data needed by organizations for decision-making, operations control, problem analysis, and the development of new goods and services through three processes. Input, processing, and output are these tasks. Raw data is captured or gathered by input from sources either inside the company or outside of it. This raw input is transformed into a more meaningful form through processing. The information that has been processed is transferred to the intended recipients or users through output. Feedback is another essential component of information systems; it is output that is sent back to the relevant members of the organization for their assessment or correction of the input stage (Figure 1.1).

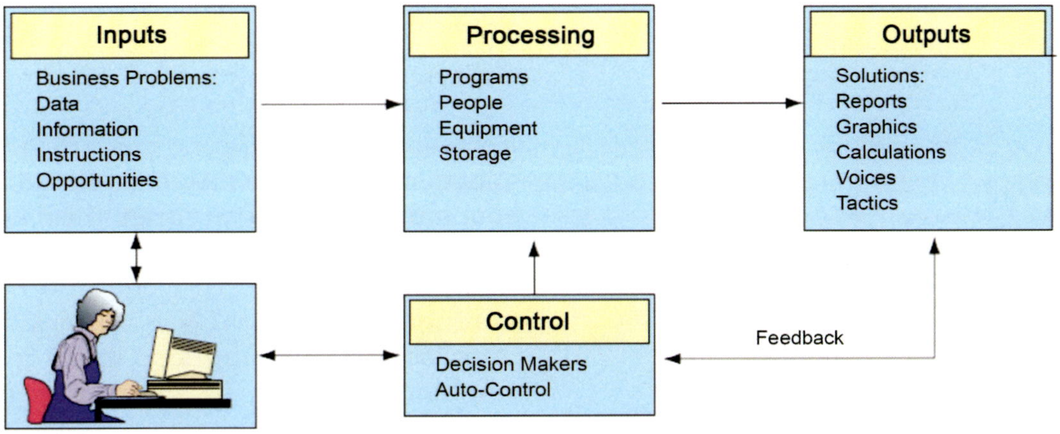

Figure 1.1. *Functions of an information system.*

Source: https://si12650138.wordpress.com/wp-content/uploads/2013/04/whats-information-system.png.

The study of complementary networks of hardware and software that individuals and organizations use to gather, filter, process, create, and distribute data is known as information systems (IS). Information systems are created by people and consist of hardware, software, and communications networks. They are usually used in organizational settings to gather, produce, and distribute useful data. Information systems consist of interconnected components that collaborate to gather, process, store, and distribute information to facilitate decision-making, coordination, control, analysis, and visualization within an organization.

1.1.2. Computer-Based Information System

An information system that uses computer technology to carry out part or all of its intended tasks is known as a computer-based information system (CBIS). A personal computer and some software can be the only components of such a system. Alternatively, it might consist of thousands of computers of different sizes along with hundreds of plotters, printers, and other devices, as well as databases and wired and wireless communication networks. People are typically a part of an information system as well.

1.1.3. Components of Information Systems

Computer hardware and software, telecommunications, databases and data warehouses, human resources, and procedures are the main parts of an information system. Information technology (IT) is the hardware, software, and telecommunications that are integrated into the management and operations of businesses today (Figure 1.2).

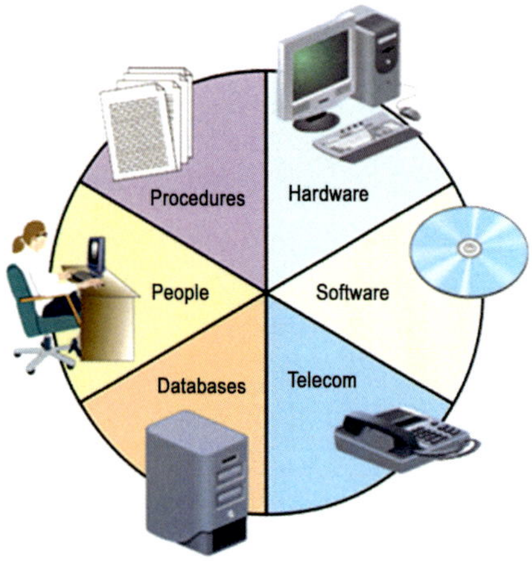

Figure 1.2. *Computer based information systems.*

Source:https://1.bp.blogspot.com/-RJK_tZSQV2c/Wpet4th9V8I/AAAAAAAAHeg/Lio5-bwfmy0IE_iHSrU6kUYyTpoTNKjoQCK4BGAYY Cw/s1600/komponen-sistem-informasi.png.

1.1.3.1. Computer Hardware

In today's global landscape, even the smallest businesses and many households around the world own or rent computers. People may have multiple devices such as smartphones, tablets, and wearables. Large organizations use distributed computer systems, with powerful servers in data centers, personal computers, and mobile devices all integrated into their information systems. Sensors are now widespread, collecting data and controlling systems through devices called actuators. This hardware, along with peripherals like storage disks and input-output devices, make up the essential components of information systems. The cost of hardware has decreased, while processing speed and storage capacity have increased thanks to Moore's law. Despite these advancements, concerns about power consumption and environmental impact are being addressed by designers. More and more, computing and storage services are being delivered from the cloud, accessible through telecommunications networks.

1.1.3.2. Computer Software

System software and application software are the two main categories of computer software. The operating system is the main piece of system software. In addition to managing the data, program files, hardware, and other system resources, it gives the user control over the computer, usually through a graphical user interface (GUI). Applications are programs made to manage particular tasks for users. People now frequently use smartphone apps to access information systems. Additional examples include "vertical" applications that cater to a particular industry sector, such as an application that plans, routes, and monitors package deliveries for an overnight carrier, as well as general-purpose application suites with their word-processing and spreadsheet programs. Larger businesses develop other applications internally or externally and use licensed applications created and maintained by specialized software companies, tailoring them to their particular needs. Applications provided as software-as-a-service (SaaS) from the cloud via the Internet are also available to businesses. Open-source software, which can be downloaded for free and modified under a license that guarantees its continued availability, is posing a threat to proprietary software, which is sold by and supported by its suppliers.

1.1.3.3. Telecommunications

Information is transmitted and computer systems, wearables, and portable devices are networked together via telecommunications. Either wired or wireless media are used to establish connections. Fiber optics and coaxial cable are examples of wired technologies. Mobile computing is supported by wireless technologies, which are primarily based on the transmission of radio waves and microwaves. With computing devices integrated into a wide range of physical objects, ubiquitous information systems have emerged. For instance, products that are moving through the supply chain can have sensors, like radio frequency identification devices (RFIDs), attached to them to track their location and monitor their condition. Massive volumes of data can be generated by wireless sensor networks that are connected to the Internet and utilized for environmental monitoring or the pursuit of increased productivity.

Different computer network configurations can be made based on an organization's requirements. Local area networks, or LANs, link computers at a specific location, like a campus or office building. Smart cities rely on metropolitan area networks (MANs) as their electronic infrastructure, which serves a restricted and densely populated area. Wide area networks (WANs) link widely separated data centers, often owned and operated by various companies. Peer-to-peer networks allow for widespread content sharing since they lack centralized control. Billions of computers across every continent are connected by the Internet, which is a network of networks. Through networking, users can connect with others and access information resources like big databases as well as people who may be colleagues, clients, friends, or people who have similar interests in their personal or professional lives. Different intranets that are accessible via a browser can offer internet-like services to an organization and for its exclusive use; an intranet could be set up as an access portal to a shared corporate document base, for instance. Extranets are created by encrypting the messages to create so-called virtual private networks (VPNs), which allow business partners to communicate with each other privately and securely over the Internet.

With sensors and actuators widely dispersed throughout the physical world and providing data, like the blood pressure of an individual or the acidity of a square yard of soil, a massive Internet of things has emerged. The availability of such data facilitates sustained decision-making based on processing of the vast amount of accumulated data as well as quick response when needed. Large-scale networking infrastructure facilitates the expanding trend of cloud computing by allowing multiple businesses to share information system resources, which improves utilization efficiency and gives data center locations more flexibility. Telecommunications networks can be easily controlled by software-defined networking thanks to algorithms that can adapt to changing demands and resource availability in real time.

1.1.3.4. Databases and Data Warehouses

Database-stored data is primarily delivered by many information systems. A database is an arranged collection of linked data that can be retrieved individually or in groups to meet different needs. Product catalogs and employee records are common instances of databases. An enterprise's management and operations are supported by databases. Archival data that has been gathered over time and can be mined for information to create and promote new products, provide better customer service to current clients, or connect with prospective clients is stored in data warehouses. Anybody who has ever made a credit card purchase—online, in person, or through mail order—is covered by these data collections.

Big data is a broad initiative that refers to the massive collection and processing of textual data that is frequently gathered on the Web as well as quantitative, or structured, data. Making decisions based on the information provided by big data can have many advantages. Examples include the use of resources sparingly as a result of preventing waste, evidence-based medicine, and recommendations for new products (like movies or books) based on user interests. Big data makes creative business models possible. For instance, a for-profit company uses cellphones all over the world to crowdsource (gather information from multiple independent individuals) the prices of goods. Aggregated data allows for more responsive decision making than was previously possible by providing early information on price movements.

Processing textual data, like user reviews and opinions posted on blogs, social networks, and discussion boards, enables automated sentiment analysis for use in new product development, competitive intelligence, marketing, and other decision-making processes.

1.1.3.5. Human Resources and Procedures

An essential element of any information system is qualified personnel. Technical staff members include database administrators, programmers, computer security specialists, business analysts, development and operations managers, and computer operators. Additionally, every employee in a company needs to receive training on how to make the most of information systems. Through their use of the Web, billions of people worldwide are gaining knowledge about information systems.

An information system's operating and maintenance procedures are included in its documentation. To run a payroll program, for instance, protocols must be set up, encompassing when to run the program, who can run it, and who can access the output. The autonomous computing initiative involves the increasingly automatic operation of data centers through software embedded with the procedures.

1.1.4. Difference between Computers and Information Systems

Computers are an essential component of an information system because they offer efficient and successful means of processing data. But an IS is much more than just a computer system.

Understanding the business and the environment it operates in is essential for the effective implementation of an information system (IS).

For example, it is required to comprehend the processes involved in purchasing and selling stocks, bonds, options, and so forth, as well as any relevant government regulations, in order to develop an IS that supports transactions carried out on the New York Stock Exchange.

Therefore, knowing computers alone is insufficient when learning about information systems. Computers are just one component of a larger system that needs to be planned, run, and maintained. An example can be found in a city's public transportation system. Although buses are an essential component of the system, more are required. Planning bus routes, stops, schedules, and other aspects necessitates a thorough understanding of consumer demand, traffic patterns, local laws, safety regulations, and similar factors. Similar to buses, computers are only one part of a larger, intricate system.

1.2. SIX MAJOR TYPES OF INFORMATION SYSTEMS

Six information systems, each supporting a distinct organizational level, are found in a typical organization. Among these systems are the operational level's transaction processing systems (TPS), the knowledge level's office automation systems (OAS) and knowledge work systems (KWS), the management level's decision support systems (DSS) and management information systems (MIS), and the strategic level's executive support systems (ESS) (Figure 1.3).

Figure 1.3. *Types of information systems.*

Source: https://c8.alamy.com/comp/2AGAY7A/types-of-information-systems-2AGAY7A.jpg.

1.2.1. Transaction Processing Systems

To carry out their regular business operations, every company needs to process transactions. Any action or event that has an impact on the organization is referred to as a transaction. Transactions may vary from one organization to another based on the nature of the business. Order entry, goods receipt, shipping, and other transactions are examples of transactions that occur in a manufacturing unit. Transactions that take place in a bank include cashing checks, making deposits and withdrawals, etc. Nonetheless, certain activities, such as placing orders, billing clients, employing staff, maintaining employee records, etc., are shared by every organization. Organizations use transaction processing systems (TPS) to support the processing of business transactions.

1.2.2. Office Automation Systems

An office automation system (OAS) is a group of computers, communication devices, and employees to carry out administrative duties. It facilitates official activities at all organizational levels and carries out office transactions. These tasks can be separated into managerial and clerical categories.

Office automation systems facilitate a variety of clerical tasks, such as writing documents, typesetting, printing, mailing, setting up meetings, and maintaining calendars. Office automation systems support conference calls, message and report creation, performance management, and organizational performance. An office automation system incorporates a number of applications, including word processing, email, and electronic filing.

1.2.2.1. Word Processing

Documents such as memos, reports, letters, and other electronically printable materials are prepared using word processing. Text is input via the keyboard and shown on the computer's display panel. With the aid of word processor commands, this text can be altered, saved, and replicated. Spell checking, grammar checking, and counting (characters, lines, pages, etc.), header and footer, index creation, and automatic page numbering are all features of word processors

1.2.2.2. Email

Email, also known as electronic mail, makes it easier to transfer documents or messages using a computer and communication lines. This speeds up mail delivery and lowers the time and expense associated with sending paper mail. Email allows you to send text messages as well as a variety of other types of data, including images, audio, and video.

1.2.2.3. Voice Mail

One useful call service that lets you record and store phone messages in the computer's memory is voice mail. These messages are always retrievable by the intended recipient.

1.2.3. Knowledge Work Systems

A knowledge work system (KWS) is a specialized system designed to ensure that technical skills and knowledge are appropriately integrated into business operations and to encourage the creation of new knowledge. By giving them access to analytical, graphic, communication, and document management tools, it supports knowledge workers in producing and disseminating new knowledge.

The knowledge workers must also look outside the company for knowledge. As a result, knowledge work systems need to make external databases easily accessible. Knowledge work systems should also have an intuitive user interface to make it easier and faster for users to find the information they need. Financial workstations, virtual reality platforms, and computer-aided design (CAD) systems are a few instances of knowledge work systems.

1.2.3.1. Computer-aided Design (CAD) Systems

These systems automate the use of computers and graphics software for the creation and revision of designs. Tooling and manufacturing process design specifications can be obtained through CAD software.

During the manufacturing process, this saves a significant amount of time and money.

1.2.3.2. Virtual Reality System

These systems are more capable of rendering, simulating, and visualizing than CAD systems. They create computer-generated simulations that nearly seem real by using interactive graphics software. They can be applied to business, scientific, and educational endeavors.

1.2.3.3. Financial Workstations

They are employed to merge a variety of data from both external and internal sources. Research reports, market data, and contact management data are some examples of this data. Financial workstations make it easier to quickly analyze vast amounts of financial data and trading situations. Additionally, portfolio management makes use of it.

1.2.4. Management Information Systems

In particular, middle managers' planning, controlling, and decision-making tasks are supported by management information systems. A management information system (MIS) gathers transaction data from underlying transaction processing systems (TPSs), reports, displays, and other information products.

These information products offer data that complies with managers' and supervisors' requirements for making decisions. Managers can make decisions for which the process for arriving at a solution has been predetermined thanks to management information systems, which use straightforward procedures like summaries and comparisons.

The format of reports generated by MIS is typically pre-established. A summary report, like one on the quarterly sales made by each sales representative in the company, is a typical MIS report. An example of a different kind of management information system report is an exception report, which details the exceptional circumstances under which a sales representative's sales fall well short of expectations. Reports are typically generated by management information systems on a monthly, quarterly, or annual basis. On the other hand, managers can view the hourly or daily data thanks to MIS. Additionally, they give managers online access to the organization's historical records and current performance.

1.2.5. Decision Support Systems

An interactive computer-based information system called a decision support system (DSS) is used at the management level of an organization, much like MIS. On the other hand, it processes data to assist managers in making decisions, which sets it apart from MIS. It gives middle managers the knowledge necessary for them to make wise choices. For example, a bank manager can determine the annual targets by analyzing changing trends in loans and deposits with the help of a decision support system.

Decision support systems are made to help managers solve particular managerial issues or tasks. In general, they support managers in reaching logical conclusions through semi-structured decision-making. They occasionally can, however, also assist in making difficult decisions. They make use of data produced by TPSs and OASs in order to justify such decisions. Statistical power is higher in decision support systems than in other information systems. They use a wide range of decision models to analyze data or condense enormous amounts of data into a format (often tables or charts) that facilitates managers' comparison and analysis of data. They offer an interactive environment so that users can ask new questions, add or modify data as needed, and collaborate with them directly.

1.2.6. Executive Support Systems

An extension of MIS, an executive support system (ESS) is a computer-based information system that facilitates top-level organizational decision-making. The executive support system assists in making non-routine decisions that impact the entire organization, necessitating discernment and judgment.

ESSs provide more efficient display options, better telecommunications, and more general computing capabilities than DSSs. Senior executives can solve a wide range of problems with the aid of charts and graphs that are displayed using sophisticated graphics software. They use external data about events like new competitors and tax laws, along with summarized internal data from MIS and DSS, to make informed decisions. High-importance data is filtered, compressed, and tracked before being made available to strategic-level managers.

1.3. ACQUIRING INFORMATION SYSTEMS AND SERVICES

Despite their high cost, information systems are a valuable corporate asset due to their many advantages. In order to acquire information systems and services that will support business initiatives, organizations must make long-term plans. Businesses must, however, react quickly to new opportunities. Priorities are set for projects based on long-term corporate plans, individual needs, and requirements of data workers, top management, and other stakeholders. For instance, some projects might need to be completed right away in order to comply with a new government reporting requirement or to communicate with the information system of a new client. Due to their strategic importance or larger anticipated benefits, other projects might be assigned a higher priority.

After a particular information system is determined to be necessary, it must be purchased. Usually, the firm's current information systems architecture is taken into consideration when doing this. Either internal development or modification or external sourcing may be used in the acquisition of information systems. In the highly developed IT market of today, businesses typically purchase information systems and services from specialized vendors. Information systems specialists' main responsibilities include customizing applications to meet the needs of their employers and integrating applications to produce a cohesive systems architecture for the company. Internally, only smaller applications are typically developed. The end users themselves may create some more individualized applications.

1.3.1. Acquisition from External Sources

Purchasing an information system from outside the company can be done in a few main ways. An increasing number of businesses are outsourcing their information systems. The process of outsourcing involves assigning the primary functions of a company's systems and operations, like data centers, telecommunications, software development, and maintenance, to a specialized business that performs these functions under long-term contracts that outline the service levels (i.e., the extent and caliber of services to be rendered). Moving the services overseas is a requirement of outsourcing in certain situations outsourcing in an effort to take advantage of cost or skill advantages. The outside company is then in charge of acquiring new applications. In other instances, the business might contract out just the creation or upkeep of its information systems, with the external business acting as a systems developer. The use of cloud computing as a source of information services is growing. It provides on-demand Internet access to services provided by an organization that maintains data centers equipped with the required software and additional resources. Three levels of service provision are possible: the services can be offered as software-as-a-service (SaaS) that the company can use over the network, as the platform for creating new applications, or as the infrastructure for running current applications. SaaS in particular has emerged as an affordable option for using business systems. Although some businesses create their own private clouds to share resources that staff members can access over the network from a variety of devices, frequently including smartphones, cloud computing is typically supplied by outside vendors. The main benefits of public clouds are their scalability and avoidance of capital expenditures; the partial loss of control is a disadvantage.

Businesses can opt to obtain an application by renting a proprietary package under license from a vendor, and having the vendor or an outside contractor customize the software either internally or externally. This is how enterprise systems are typically leased. Using an open-source application is an alternative; its program code is freely available for modification by anybody under a different kind of license that guarantees the application's perpetual openness. Technical support from specialized vendors is typically included in the costs associated with using open-source software.

1.3.2. Internal Information Systems Development

One of two main approaches is utilized when an organization develops an information system internally: rapid application development (RAD) or life-cycle development. Software providers employ similar techniques in order to offer more universal and adaptable systems. The development and upkeep of large organizational systems, like enterprise systems, typically follow a methodical process called a system life cycle that comprises six stages: installation, operation and maintenance, system analysis, design, programming and testing, and feasibility study. The actual system development process takes place over the first five stages, with long-term exploitation coming at the end. After a certain amount of time (with necessary maintenance), the information system may be upgraded or phased out. A significant update puts the system into a new development life cycle (Figure 1.4).

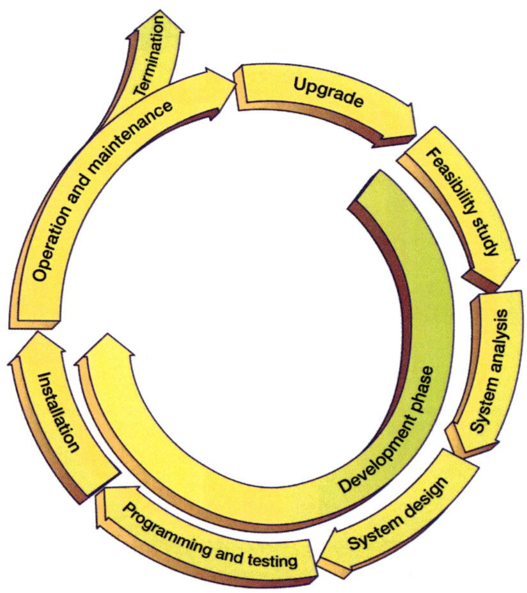

Figure 1.4. *Information system life cycle.*

Source: https://cdn.britannica.com/67/65067-050-8C1E0FC9/Information-systems-life-cycle-development-phase-information.jpg.

Determining whether the system is desirable in light of long-term plans, strategic initiatives, and a cost-benefit analysis is the main goal of a feasibility study. The next step, system design, produces a comprehensive blueprint for how the new system will be organized, while system analysis offers a detailed response to the question, what will the new system do? The system's individual software modules are created, tested, and integrated into a functional system during the programming and testing phase. Additional testing phases guarantee ongoing quality control. Installation entails transferring organizational operations to the new system, integrating it with existing systems, and conducting the last testing of the system in the workplace. The system's implementation activities, such as user training and organizational process modifications, are part of the later stages of development. Life-cycle development is often criticized for its lengthy development timelines, extensive documentation requirements, and, occasionally, for not meeting the user's requirements at the end of a protracted development process. RAD is displacing life-cycle development more and more. Prototypes, or early working versions of applications, are created fast and cheaply using a variety of Rapid Application Development (RAD) approaches, despite their imperfections. After presenting this prototype to the users, feedback is gathered, suggested changes are implemented, and eventually the system as a whole is developed from the various prototype iterations. Certain companies have implemented joint applications development (JAD), which is a formal process for system developers and users to collaborate. Sometimes life-cycle development and rapid application development (RAD) are combined: during the first system analysis phase, a prototype is created to ascertain user requirements, and then life-cycle development takes over. Agile development, a variation of RAD, attempts to do away with the idea of a prototype by building an initial version of the system, releasing it to users, and then making frequent changes as needed.

Systems development has adopted industrial software production and reuse techniques. As a result, reusable software components are created, examined, and categorized in preparation for their eventual integration into information systems.

The use of Web services, which are software objects that deliver a specific function (like looking up a customer's order in a database) and can be stitched together into inter-organizational information systems enabling business partners to cooperate, is a particularly significant component-based development technique.

System maintenance is the process of making significant changes to an installed system over the course of its useful life after it is turned over to its users and operations staff. Generally speaking, a large system will be used and maintained for five to ten years, if not longer.

The majority of maintenance consists of adapting the system to new hardware, software, and the organization's evolving needs. However, occasionally, mistakes in design must be fixed, and software "bugs" must be eliminated as soon as they are found.

1.4. INFORMATION SYSTEMS SECURITY AND CONTROL

Information security issues have taken center stage in concerns about the well-being of the world community since information systems were made available to the public on the Internet and were deeply ingrained in the infrastructure of daily life worldwide as well as in the operations and management of governmental and commercial institutions.

1.4.1. Information Systems Security

The integrity and safety of system resources and operations fall under the purview of information systems security. In developed nations, the majority of organizations rely on their information systems to operate securely. In actuality, this security is frequently essential to the very fabric of societies. It is essential to many infrastructure systems, such as those that provide power, water, and healthcare. Air traffic control systems and critical care units rely heavily on information systems. A complete failure of financial institutions' information systems would not last more than a day or two. Massive sums of money that exist only as electronic signals sent over networks or as spots on storage disks are handled by electronic funds transfer systems (EFTS). Information systems must be subject to stringent controls, such as ongoing countermeasures and frequent audits, to guarantee that they remain safe from various threats. Figure1.5 illustrates how security measures relate to one another.

It is estimated that human error causes greater losses in information systems operation, even though cases of computer crime and abuse receive a lot of media attention. Disaster recovery planning, which is a component of a corporate business continuity plan, is specifically concerned with disasters like earthquakes, floods, and fires. It is also essential to have a backup plan in case software, servers, or telecom networks malfunction.

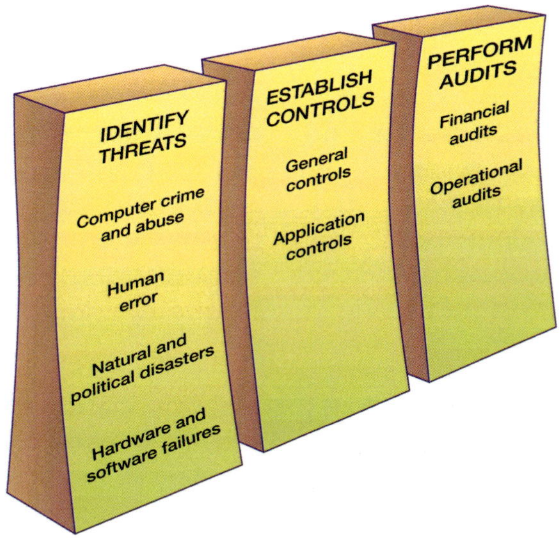

Figure 1.5. *Information system security measures.*

Source: https://cdn.britannica.com/68/65068-050-7EEC7DAD/step-Information-systems-security-measures-information-system.jpg.

1.4.2. Computer Crime and Abuse

Every year, computer crime—illegal activities where computers are the main tool—causes billions of dollars' worth of losses to the global economy. Although it doesn't qualify as a crime, computer abuse still involves using a computer in an unethical manner. The goals of so-called information system hacking include sabotage, cyberwar, governmental and commercial espionage, vandalism, and consumer information theft. Phishing and the planting of malware, such as Trojan horses, logic bombs, computer viruses, and worms, are two of the more popular forms of cybercrime.

Phishing entails using deception to obtain a legitimate user's login password and other personal information by sending messages purporting to be from a reputable organization, like a bank or government agency. Identity theft, or the impersonation of a user to obtain access to the user's resources, may occur after a successful phishing raid to obtain the user's information. One type of attack that is particularly common is computer viruses. These are program instructions with the ability to propagate to other computer systems by inserting copies of themselves into other programs in addition to carrying out malicious deeds. Worms are entire computer programs that spread via telecommunications networks, much like viruses. Viruses and worms have the capacity to spread quickly and extensively, which allows them to cause enormous harm. Damage can come from denial-of-service attacks, which involve flooding systems with erroneous requests, or from hacking into databases containing large amounts of data, such as credit card numbers.

The malefactor hides unauthorized instructions inside a legitimate program in a Trojan horse attack. A logic bomb is made up of concealed instructions, frequently introduced using the Trojan horse method, that remain dormant until a particular occasion, at which point they become active. In a well-known instance, a logic bomb was planted in the human resources system of an insurance company in Fort Worth, Texas, in 1985 by a programmer. The entire employee database was destroyed when the programmer was fired and his name was removed from it. Once one system on the Internet is compromised, it can be used to take control of numerous others and assemble them into what are known as "botnets," which are capable of launching large-scale attacks against other systems in order to steal data or interfere with their functionality. An increasing number of people are worried that computer-controlled items like TVs and refrigerators could be used as botnet targets in the "Internet of things." It is challenging to keep devices safe from malware because of their variety.

1.4.3. Information Systems Controls

An organization implements controls, which are a collection of technological measures and procedural guidelines, to guarantee the safe and effective operation of information systems. Application and general controls work together to protect information systems. All information system activities within an organization are subject to general controls. Controlling access to computer systems and the data they store or send over telecommunications networks is one of the most crucial general control mechanisms. Administrative measures that limit employee access to only those procedures directly related to their jobs are examples of general controls. These safeguards therefore restrict the harm that a single employee or employee impersonator can cause. Installed in high-stress environments like stock exchanges or medical facilities, fault-tolerant computer systems are made to manage and isolate issues so that the system can keep running. In the event that the primary information system fails, backup systems, which are frequently located in remote areas, may be triggered.

Application controls are unique to each application and consist of steps like verifying input data, recording system access, routinely archiving copies of different databases, and making sure that only authorized users can access information.

1.4.4. Securing Information

As wide area networks (WANs) and the Internet in particular proliferated, controlling access to information systems became increasingly challenging. Users can access systems from any unattended computer within an organization or from almost anywhere via the Internet, as can intruders. Every authentic user has a different name and a password that is changed on a regular basis as a security precaution. Requiring some sort of physical authentication, such as a smart card or physical token, or a personal trait like a fingerprint, retinal pattern, hand geometry, or signature, is another security measure. Many systems combine these kinds of security measures. For example, automatic teller machines use a combination of an identity card and a personal identification number (PIN). Firewalls are security measures positioned between an organization's internal networks and the Internet. The incoming and frequently outgoing data traffic is continuously filtered by these hardware and software combinations.

Data encryption is an alternative method of preventing access to information, and it has become increasingly important in electronic commerce. In such transactions, public key encryption is frequently employed. Communications encrypted with the addressee's public key can only be decrypted by the intended recipient, who possesses the private key required to maintain confidentiality. Moreover, digital signatures—an extra code appended to a message to confirm its origin—and digital certificates—digital certificates granted to each party by a reliable third party—allow for the authentication of both parties in an electronic transaction. To identify corruption, a particular kind of anti-tampering code can also be appended to a message. Comparable methods exist to guarantee that participants in an electronic transaction cannot subsequently withdraw their involvement. Certain messages need extra characteristics. For instance, a payment made with electronic cash functions similarly to physical cash and is protected by encryption to guarantee the buyer's anonymity. Intrusion detection systems are used to keep an eye on information systems continuously. They identify unusual occurrences and record the data required to generate reports and identify the origin and type of any potential intrusion. When an intrusion is detected in real time, more proactive systems also make an effort to stop it.

1.4.5. Information Systems Audit

An information systems audit is used to assess how well controls are in place within an information system. The purpose of an audit is to determine whether information systems are protecting company assets, preserving the accuracy of data that is communicated and stored, successfully advancing company goals, and running smoothly. It is a component of a wider financial audit that confirms the accuracy of an entity's financial statements and accounting records. Information systems are made to allow for the tracing of each and every financial transaction. Stated differently, every transaction needs to have an audit trail that traces its origin and processing steps. In addition to financial audits, technological audits confirm that information technologies are properly selected, set up, and applied, and operational audits assess the efficacy and efficiency of information systems operations.

1.5. IMPACTS OF INFORMATION SYSTEMS

Computerized information systems have had a significant impact on businesses, economies, and societies, as well as on the people whose lives and activities are carried out in these social aggregates. This has been especially true since the introduction of the Web and mobile computing.

1.5.1. Organizational Impacts of Information Systems

Information systems facilitate or improve key organizational capabilities. These systems support company operations, decision-making by individuals and groups, innovation through the development of new products and processes, relationships with partners, suppliers, and customers, the pursuit of competitive advantage, and, in certain situations, the business model itself (e.g., Google). Information systems open up new possibilities for how businesses collaborate and compete, how organizations are set up, and how workspaces are designed. In general, the use of Web-based information systems can improve the coordination of supply chains or webs at a reasonable cost and dramatically reduce the costs of communication between employees and businesses. This has caused a lot of organizations to focus on their core skills and contract out other aspects of their value chain to specialized businesses. The implementation of flatter organizational structures with fewer hierarchical layers is a result of the ability to communicate information effectively within a company.

However, not all information systems result in increased revenue. Success hinges on the ability to use information systems skillfully as well as how well they integrate with other company resources, like strong business partnerships or in-depth industry knowledge. New organizational structures are made possible by the use of information systems. Specifically, there have been the emergence of so-called virtual organizations, which do not depend on traditional organizational charts and physical offices. The network organization and the cluster organization are two prominent types of virtual organizations. Long-term business partners provide products and services to a central hub firm in a network organization. When a group of comparatively small businesses work together, they can give the impression of being a large corporation. In fact, the main force behind such an organization might be no more than a lone business owner assisted by a small team of workers. As a result, network organization creates a dynamic ecosystem of businesses centered on Web-based information systems for their establishment and operation. Teams of people with complementary skills, both permanent and temporary, make up the main work units in a cluster organization. Web resources, corporate intranets, and collaboration systems are a big help to team members, who are often scattered all over the world, in their work. Global virtual teams can operate around the clock by electronically "following the sun" with their knowledge work. Information systems made available via mobile platforms have made it possible for staff members to work almost anywhere, not just outside of company buildings. The newly emerging workplace adopted the slogan, "Work is the thing you do, not the place you go to." Home offices, local work hubs, client locations, and mobile offices of individuals like insurance adjusters are examples of virtual workplaces. Teleworkers are employees who work remotely from the headquarters of their employer.

Because of the Web, consumers now play a different role. They can actively collaborate with the producers to co-create value rather than just being the passive consumers of goods. The users of massively multiplayer online games and virtual worlds have largely created their own value. Online reviews and opinions serve as electronic word-of-mouth that has the power to make or break products. Through sponsored co-creation, businesses draw in clients to help with ideation and assessment, joint product development, and marketing of already-available goods and services. For these reasons, online virtual customer communities are established.

1.5.2. Information Systems in the Economy and Society

The expansion of multinational businesses and corporations has been aided by network-based information systems as well as the world's transportation infrastructure. Numerous industries have demonstrated a correlation between increased productivity and the implementation of information systems when these systems are used in conjunction with other corporate resources. Many business-to-business and individual relationships and transactions have been transferred to the Internet and Web by electronic commerce, opening up new opportunities and improving efficiency. Due to the growth of the Internet-based ecosystem, open-source software, cheap hardware and telecoms, and widespread access to mobile phones worldwide, there has been a surge in entrepreneurial activity and the rise to prominence and substantial market value of several businesses based on novel business models. Electronic malls, online gaming companies, electronic auction companies, and search engine companies are a few examples. A worldwide redistribution of work has been occurring as a result of the numerous opportunities for transferring work containing data, information, and knowledge in electronic form to the most economical venue.

A number of societal and ethical issues came to light as information systems became widely used in advanced economies and society at large. The most crucial ones are those pertaining to personal privacy, property rights, open communication and universal access, accuracy of information, and quality of life. The ability to manage one's personal data is essential to maintaining one's right to privacy. Even though most people view privacy invasion as an unwanted loss of autonomy, government and commercial entities must gather data to support administrative functions and take advantage of sales and marketing opportunities. Because personal data is routinely gathered and possibly shared in an essentially unregulated way, electronic commerce poses a unique privacy risk. One privacy issue that needs to be resolved by a combination of market forces, industry self-regulation, and possibly government regulation is the ownership and control of the personal profiles, contacts, and communications on social networks. The absence of an international legal standard makes it more difficult to prevent invasions of privacy.

Patents, trade secrets, and copyrights provide some, but not perfect, protection for intellectual property, which includes software, books, music, and films. These intangible commodities, however, are readily duplicated and electronically transmitted over the Internet for unauthorized use and duplication. Laws and technological protections, such as electronic watermarks and encryption against piracy, are combined, but user ethics play a major role in preventing abuse. In the information age, the tools of protection themselves—like patents—have a significant impact. However, there are concerns about the protection of business methods (such as Amazon's patenting of one-click ordering) and there are several obstacles to the worldwide enforcement of intellectual property protection.

Having access to information systems through the Web is essential for complete engagement in today's society. It is important to prevent any disparities in access to the Internet between countries, regions, and social or ethnic groups. The ability to freely use the Web for communication and to share knowledge is highly valued. Many believe that freedom of speech is a fundamental human right, and the Internet is considered to be the most accessible platform to exercise this right. However, there are valid concerns about safeguarding children online without restricting freedom of speech. Technological tools, like filtering software for blocking inappropriate content, have had some success in addressing these concerns.

Everyone is concerned about the security and accuracy of data found in databases and data warehouses, whether it be in government files, credit bureau records, or health and insurance data. This is because improper disclosure of privileged or false information can have a negative impact on one's daily activities, livelihood, and personal safety. Organizations must guarantee proper security, access to, and use of such files, and individuals must collaborate in reviewing and correcting their files. Information systems have an impact on people's personal and professional lives. Information systems can be used in the workplace to reduce laborious tasks and offer employees more autonomy, or they can be used carelessly to eliminate jobs and expose the remaining workforce to constant electronic surveillance. Customers can use the Internet for networking, shopping, and entertainment, but they run the risk of dealing with computer viruses, credit card number interception, and spam (unsolicited e-mail).

Through electronic elections, referendums, and polls, information systems can increase the involvement of common citizens in government. They can also offer electronic access to government services and information, enabling the electronic filing of taxes, the direct deposit of government checks, and the viewing of both current and past government documents, among other things. By making the public's access to government data searchable and user-friendly, more transparent and advantageous government operations can be achieved. The Internet allows the public realm of discussion and self-organization to grow and gives people a voice. Information systems, however, have also evoked Orwellian visions of corporate intrusion into personal life and government monitoring. It is still up to society to strengthen its legal, social, and technological frameworks in order to fully utilize information systems.

Job markets and professions have been impacted by the exponentially increasing power of computers, which is fueled by Moore's law, and the development of ever-more-sophisticated software, particularly systems that use artificial intelligence (AI) techniques.

Some job opportunities are lost due to affordable and flexible robotics. Cognitive computing has emerged as a rival to human professionals. It consists of systems that use AI techniques, such as computer learning, pattern recognition in various media, and massive amounts of stored information.

Concerns regarding the caliber of employment have been raised by the "on-demand economy" that has emerged thanks to information system platforms. Instant access to services, like transportation, is made possible by platforms (like Uber and Lyft) that link those in need of a service with those who supply it—usually individuals. These business models provide flexibility, greater independence for suppliers, and convenience for demanders, despite the claim that they undermine stable workplaces.

1.5.3. Information Systems as a Field of Study

The field of study known as information systems is typically found in business schools. The development and study of information technology theories, practices, and systems for managing and operating businesses and bolstering their market offerings is the primary goal of the field. By using a sociotechnical approach, the field situates the study of information technology within the framework of organizations, management, and society. Information systems were first studied academically in the 1960s. The Association for Information Systems (AIS) is the academic society advancing the field's development.

1.6. INFORMATION TECHNOLOGY

The field of information technology (IT) encompasses all aspects of computing, including hardware, software, telecommunications, and other systems that aid in communication as well as information transmission.

Information technology (IT) is the creation, processing, storing, securing, and exchanging of all types of electronic data through the use of computers, networking, storage, and other physical devices, infrastructure, and procedures.

Unlike personal or recreational technologies, IT is typically used in the context of enterprise operations. IT is used for business purposes that include both phone and computer technology.

The Harvard Business Review first used the term "information technology" to distinguish between general-purpose computers that could be programmed for a variety of tasks and purpose-built computers intended to carry out a specific range of tasks. Transistors and integrated circuits were a part of the IT industry's evolution starting in the middle of the 20th century. As computing power increased, device costs and energy consumption decreased, a cycle that is still in place today as new technologies are developed.

1.6.1. IT Software and Hardware

IT consists of multiple layers of operating systems, applications (software), virtualization, management, and automation tools, as well as physical hardware and operating systems. The IT domain can include user devices, peripherals, and software, such as laptops, smartphones, or even recording equipment. IT can also refer to the methods, architectures, and laws controlling how data is used and stored.

Databases like SQL Server, transactional systems like real-time order entry, email servers like Exchange, Web servers like Apache, CRM software, and enterprise resource planning software are examples of business applications. For business purposes, these applications carry out preprogrammed instructions to manipulate, aggregate, distribute, or impact data in some other way.

Business applications are run on computer servers. Through one or more business networks, servers communicate with client users and other servers. Any type of technology that stores data is referred to as storage. Data can be in any format, including multimedia, file-based, phone-based, Web-based, sensor-derived, and future formats. Volatile random-access memory (RAM), solid-state flash drives, hard drives, and non-volatile tape are examples of storage media.

Virtualization and cloud computing, where physical resources are abstracted and pooled in various configurations to meet application requirements, are examples of how IT architectures have evolved. Clouds can be deployed in a corporate data center, dispersed throughout locations and shared with other IT users, or in a hybrid manner combining the two.

1.6.2. IT Education and Job Functions

The company's IT assets and infrastructure are deployed and managed by a group of administrators and other technical staff members. To support tools, apps, and operations, IT teams require a broad range of specialized information and technology skills and knowledge. The IT team is augmented by third-party contractors and IT vendor support staff. IT professionals have a wide range of specializations available to them, including network architecture, desktop support, server or storage administration, hardware, software development, and application management. Businesses often look for IT specialists with a variety of overlapping or mixed skill sets.

1.6.3. Common IT Careers

- **Chief Information Officer**: This individual is in charge of the IT and computer systems that help the business achieve its objectives.
- **Chief Technology Officer**: This individual establishes all organizational technology goals and policies.
- **IT Director**: This individual is in charge of making sure that all of the company's technological tools and procedures run smoothly. This position is often referred to as an IT leader or manager.
- **Systems Administrator**: An environment with multiple users is configured, managed, supported, and troubleshooted by this individual. This role may be divided into smaller sub-roles within an organization based on the technology involved, such as server, desktop, network, virtualization, or other component-specific administrators or teams.
- **Application Manager**: The provisioning and administration of a high-value business application, like Exchange, is the main responsibility of this individual.
- **Developer**: This individual or group writes, modifies, and tests program code to satisfy internal or external business goals.
- **Architect**: To support the business as best they can, this person looks over and modifies IT functions.

1.6.4. Issues and Challenges in Information Technology

1. Data overload is becoming a more serious problem for many IT professionals as computing systems and capabilities continue to grow globally. Large amounts of processing power, complex software, and human analytical

abilities are needed to process massive amounts of data efficiently and generate actionable business intelligence.

2. The majority of businesses now depend on teamwork and communication skills to handle the complexity of IT systems. Many IT professionals work with business users who are interested in using IT as a tool to complete tasks more quickly, but who are not trained in computer networking or other information technologies.
3. Many business executives are particularly concerned about system and network security issues because any security incident has the potential to harm a company's reputation and incur significant financial costs.

1.6.5. Strategic Uses of Information Technology in Business

When it comes to adding value to a company and facilitating organizational change, information technology is crucial. In order to do that, chief information officers have evolved into important contributors to board groups that create and implement business-focused strategic solutions. The goal is to increase an organization's competitiveness through the alignment of IT and business strategies.

1.6.5.1. Support Innovation

Cloud computing can expedite the process for organizations looking to enhance their innovation capabilities and create new goods or services for the market. Instead of investing in fixed resources, cloud computing allows organizations to pay for additional IT resources on a pay-as-you-go basis during the development project. The extra resources can be used by organizations to expedite development or conduct pilot projects. This gives the company a significant competitive advantage by allowing it to launch new products faster than the competition.

1.6.5.2. Improve Responsiveness

Organizations can swiftly scale up their IT resources in response to shifting market conditions thanks to cloud computing. Businesses that provide goods and services online might struggle to manage a spike in traffic, which could cost them customers. Adding cloud resources gives them a competitive edge by allowing them to adapt to demand fluctuations, boost sales, and keep customers happy.

1.6.5.3. Increase Collaboration

Collaboration-enhancing IT solutions can give a company a significant competitive edge. For example, equipping field service teams with smartphones allows service engineers to serve customers more quickly and effectively. Instead of postponing a repair, engineers working at a customer site can arrange audio or video conferences with technical or product experts at headquarters to discuss and work through a complex problem. By setting a company apart from rivals, providing exceptional customer service gives an organization a competitive edge.

1.6.5.4. Enhance Customer Insight

A strategic advantage can be obtained by gathering and evaluating data to learn more about the requirements and preferences of customers. Organizations can create personalized communications and tailored offers that boost customer satisfaction and promote loyalty by utilizing robust analytics software.

1.6.5.5. Introduce New Business Models

IT can be used by organizations to strategically alter their business models. A business that has historically sold its goods through physical stores could use IT to create an online storefront that would allow it to reach a larger market, cut costs associated with delivery, and provide customers with a more convenient experience.

1.6.6. Information Technology and Information Systems

Information technology can be broadly defined as an organization's use of a collection of computer systems. In its strictest sense, information technology refers to an information system's technological component. Databases, networks, software, hardware, and other electronic devices are all included. It can be thought of as an information system's subsystem. However, information systems and information technology can also be used interchangeably at times.

In its widest meaning, information technology (IT) refers to the group of information systems within an organization, the people who utilize them, and the management team in charge of them.

IT plays a big part in facilitating organizational processes and activities. With time, that role will grow in significance. As a result, it is imperative that managers and other professional staff members gain knowledge of IT not only in their respective fields of expertise but also throughout the entire company and in cross-organizational contexts. It goes without saying that knowing how effective information systems are created, utilized, and maintained will make you more successful in your chosen field of work. Additionally, you'll be more productive if you can identify and steer clear of failing strategies and systems. In many respects, being comfortable with information technology will also help you to benefit from new IT systems and products as they are developed, both in your personal and professional life. Finally, you should become knowledgeable about information technology (IT) as this can lead to more job opportunities. Computerization reduces employment in some areas but increases employment in others.

There is a significant demand for traditional IT professionals, such as programmers, systems analysts, and designers. Additionally, many exciting opportunities are emerging in new fields like multimedia design, document management, network security, object-oriented programming, m-commerce, the Internet, and e-commerce. According to a study by the U.S. Bureau of Labor Statistics, all seven of the top fastest-growing professions through 2010 were related to computers or information technology. These are the top seven professions:

1. Computer software applications engineers;
2. Computer support specialists;
3. Computer software systems engineers;
4. Network and computer systems administrators;
5. Network systems and data communications analysts;
6. Desktop publishers;
7. Database administrators.

It is recommended to have a college degree in computer science, computer information systems (CIS), management information systems (MIS), electronic commerce, or e-business in order to take advantage of the lucrative opportunities in information technology. Many universities have begun offering e-business or e-commerce degrees in the past few years. Numerous educational institutions provide graduate degrees with an emphasis on information technology.

1.6.7. Computer Networking and Information Technology

Information technology and business computer networking are often closely related since networks are essential to the operations of many businesses.

Networking trends that play a key role in IT include:

- **Network Capacity and Performance**: The demand for network bandwidth on IT networks and the Internet has skyrocketed due to the popularity of online video. More sophisticated software programs that facilitate more detailed graphics and intricate computer interaction also often result in higher data volumes and increased network traffic. IT departments need to make the right plans for both the present and future expansion of their business.
- **Mobile and Wireless Usages**: Nowadays, IT network administrators are responsible for managing a variety of smartphones and tablets, in addition to the usual PCs and workstations. They need to ensure that the wireless hotspots in the IT environment are of high performance and have roaming capability. In larger office buildings, deployments are meticulously planned and tested to avoid dead spots and signal interference.
- **Cloud Services**: IT shops have moved to cloud computing environments where data is maintained by third-party hosting providers, instead of maintaining their own server farms for email and business databases as in the past. The traffic patterns on a company network are drastically altered by this shift in the computing model, but educating staff members on these new applications also takes a lot of work.

There have been numerous revolutions in the world. The world has improved and grown thanks to the information system. The business sector has benefited greatly from the revolution in many ways, particularly in the area of management, which has been able to increase operational efficiency in numerous ways. The ability to store and retrieve information has greatly improved, which has led to an increase in operational and business efficiency. It is not even feasible to predict where the system will be in ten years due to the dynamic nature of technology, which is expected to continue changing over time.

CASE STUDY

INFORMATION SYSTEMS AT MCDONALD'S

McDonald's Corporation (McDonald's), a US-based global hamburger and fast food restaurant chain, had installed several Information Systems to for the operational convenience of its employees and to help them in their decision making. It had implemented these information systems to store and leverage customer information, provide quick service to the customers, impart training to its employees, etc. These systems were used to make it more convenient for customers to buy food through electronic payments. Also, an effective customer relationship management strategy was implemented to retain customers.

As of 2017, McDonald's was one of the world's largest restaurant chains. The company had its roots in a small fast food joint started by two brothers named Richard James McDonald and Maurice James McDonald in San Bernardino, California in 1940. A businessman Ray Croc was associated with the rapid growth of the fast food retail chain in the US and globally in the subsequent years. It took 33 years for McDonald's to open its first 10,000 restaurants. While it touched the 20,000-restaurant mark in mid-1996, the total surpassed 23,000 by the end of 1997. McDonald's celebrated its 50th anniversary on April 15, 2005.

McDonald's controlled many of its self-operated and franchised restaurants globally, managing the marketing, restaurant operations, HR, real estate development training, as well as quality control. As a consequence, the network was huge, and the amount of information was massive. The company encountered many challenges in developing and preserving the information needed for effective decision making. To solve this problem, McDonald's developed Information Systems to maintain and leverage the customers' information across the globe.

Challenges

Analysts felt that erratic electric power supply would pose a challenge to the functioning of the McDonald's restaurants as the total information systems relied on power supply. Another challenge was the staff lacking technical knowledge in case of information system failure.

The Road Ahead

McDonald's used Information Systems to increase efficiency and deliver quality food to its customers with advanced technology so that the food would be fresher, tastier, and hotter each time they delivered it. The Information System was also leveraged to decrease the effort, cost, and time involved in the procedures.

CLASS ACTIVITY

DATABASE DESIGN WORKSHOP

An Information Systems (IS) class activity can be designed to engage students in hands-on learning experiences that reinforce key concepts, develop practical skills, and foster critical thinking. Here's a sample class activity focused on database design and management:

Objective

To provide students with hands-on experience in designing and implementing a relational database system.

Materials Needed

- Computers with database management software installed (e.g., MySQL, Microsoft Access, PostgreSQL).
- Projector or screen for demonstration purposes.
- Handouts or slides outlining the database design process and key concepts.
- Sample data sets for practice exercises.

Activity Steps

- **Introduction:**
  - Provide an overview of the importance of database design and management in Information Systems.
  - Introduce the basic concepts of relational databases, including tables, relationships, keys, and normalization.
- **Database Design Exercise:**
  - Divide students into small groups and assign each group a hypothetical scenario (e.g., a university course registration system, an online bookstore inventory).
  - Instruct each group to design a relational database schema to represent the data requirements of their scenario.
  - Encourage students to identify entities, attributes, relationships, and constraints, and to normalize the database schema to eliminate redundancy and improve efficiency.
  - Circulate among the groups to provide guidance and answer questions as needed.

- **Database Implementation:**
  - After completing the database design phase, instruct each group to implement their database schema using the database management software provided.
  - Guide students through the process of creating tables, defining relationships, and setting up constraints such as primary keys and foreign keys.
  - Encourage students to populate their database with sample data to test its functionality and integrity.
- **Query and Reporting Exercise:**
  - Once the databases are implemented, introduce a set of sample queries or reporting requirements related to the scenarios assigned to each group.
  - Challenge students to write SQL queries to retrieve specific information from their databases (e.g., list all courses offered in a given semester, calculate the total sales revenue for a specific product category).
  - Discuss the results of the queries and demonstrate how to generate reports or visualizations using SQL or reporting tools.
- **Wrap-Up and Reflection:**
  - Reconvene as a class to discuss the challenges and insights gained from the activity.
  - Encourage students to reflect on the importance of database design principles in creating efficient and scalable information systems.
  - Provide resources for further learning, such as recommended readings, online tutorials, or additional practice exercises.
- **Key Takeaways:**
  - Hands-on experience in designing and implementing relational databases.
  - Understanding of database design principles such as normalization and entity-relationship modeling.
  - Proficiency in writing SQL queries to retrieve and manipulate data.
  - Appreciation of the role of databases in supporting organizational operations and decision-making.

This activity can be adapted and customized based on the specific learning objectives and resources available in the classroom.

SUMMARY

- An information system (IS) refers to a collection of multiple pieces of equipment involved in the dissemination of information.
- A computer-based information system (CBIS) is an information system that uses computer technology to perform some or all of its intended tasks.
- An office automation system (OAS) is a collection of communication technology, computers and persons to perform official tasks.
- A knowledge work system (KWS) is a specialized system built to promote the creation of knowledge and to make sure that knowledge and technical skills are properly integrated into business.
- Management information systems are especially developed to support planning, controlling, and decision-making functions of middle managers.
- A decision support system (DSS) is an interactive computer-based information system that, like MIS, also serves at the management level of an organization.
- An executive support system (ESS) – an extension of MIS – is a computer-based information system that helps in decision making at the top-level of an organization.
- Information systems are a major corporate asset, with respect both to the benefits they provide and to their high costs.
- There are several principal ways to acquire an information system from outside the organization. Many firms have resorted to outsourcing their information systems.
- Information systems security is responsible for the integrity and safety of system resources and activities.
- Computer crime—illegal acts in which computers are the primary tool—costs the world economy many billions of dollars annually.
- To ensure secure and efficient operation of information systems, an organization institutes a set of procedures and technological measures called controls. Information systems are safeguarded through a combination of general and application controls.
- A collection of various devices used in the distribution of information is referred to as an information system (IS). An information system (IS) consists of the following components: hardware, software, computer system connections and data, information system users, and the system housing.
- An information system that uses computer technology to carry out part or all of its intended tasks is known as a computer-based information system (CBIS). A personal computer and some software can be the only components of such a system.
- Computer hardware and software, telecommunications, databases and data warehouses, human resources, and procedures are the main parts of an information system.

- Computers are an essential component of an information system because they offer efficient and successful means of processing data. But an IS is much more than just a computer system. Understanding the business and the environment it operates in is essential for the effective implementation of an information system (IS).
- Six information systems, each supporting a distinct organizational level, are found in a typical organization. Among these systems are the operational level's transaction processing systems (TPS), the knowledge level's office automation systems (OAS) and knowledge work systems (KWS), the management level's decision support systems (DSS) and management information systems (MIS), and the strategic level's executive support systems (ESS).
- In order to acquire information systems and services that will support business initiatives, organizations must make long-term plans. Businesses must, however, react quickly to new opportunities. Priorities are set for projects based on long-term corporate plans, individual needs, and requirements of data workers, top management, and other stakeholders.
- The process of outsourcing involves assigning the primary functions of a company's systems and operations, like data centers, telecommunications, software development, and maintenance, to a specialized business that performs these functions under long-term contracts that outline the service levels (i.e., the extent and caliber of services to be rendered).
- Information security issues have taken center stage in concerns about the well-being of the world community since information systems were made available to the public on the Internet and were deeply ingrained in the infrastructure of daily life worldwide as well as in the operations and management of governmental and commercial institutions.
- Phishing entails using deception to obtain a legitimate user's login password and other personal information by sending messages purporting to be from a reputable organization, like a bank or government agency.
- Computerized information systems have had a significant impact on businesses, economies, and societies, as well as on the people whose lives and activities are carried out in these social aggregates. This has been especially true since the introduction of the Web and mobile computing.
- Information technology (IT) is the creation, processing, storing, securing, and exchanging of all types of electronic data through the use of computers, networking, storage, and other physical devices, infrastructure, and procedures.

REVIEW QUESTIONS

1. What is an information system? Describe the components of information systems.
2. What is a computer-based information system? Explain.
3. Differentiate between computers and information systems.
4. What are the various types of information systems? Explain.

5. Discuss about information system infrastructure and architecture.
6. Describe the organization of information services.
7. Explain information systems security and control.
8. What do you understand by information technology? Discuss common IT careers.

REFERENCES

1. Alter, S. (2013). Work system theory: Overview of core concepts, extensions, and challenges for the future. *Journal of the Association for Information Systems, 14*(2), 72–121.
2. Aram, M., & Neumann, G. (2015, July 1). Multilayered analysis of co-development of business information systems. *Journal of Internet Services and Applications, 6*(1). https://doi.org/10.1186/s13174-015-0030-8.
3. Avgerou, C. (2000). Information systems: What sort of science is it? *Omega, 28*, 567–579. https://doi.org/10.1016/s0305-0483(99)00072-9.
4. Bynum, T. W. (2008). Norbert Wiener and the rise of information ethics. In J. van den Hoven & J. Weckert (Eds.), *Information technology and moral philosophy*. Cambridge University Press. ISBN 978-0-521-85549-5.
5. Casalino, N., & Mazzone, G. (2008). Externalization of a banking information systems function. Features, regulatory, and critical aspects. In A. D'Atri, M. De Marco, & N. Casalino (Eds.), *Interdisciplinary aspects of information systems studies* (pp. 89–96). Physica-Verlag Springer. https://doi.org/10.1007/978-3-7908-2010-2_12.
6. D'Atri, A., De Marco, M., & Casalino, N. (2008). *Interdisciplinary aspects of information systems studies*. Physica-Verlag Springer. https://doi.org/10.1007/978-3-7908-2010-2 ISBN 978-3-7908-2009-6.
7. Dostal, J. (2007). School information systems (Skolni informacni systemy). In *Infotech 2007 – modern information and communication technology in education* (pp. 540–546). Votobia. ISBN 978-80-7220-301-7.
8. Gitta, C., & South, D. (2011). *Southern Innovator Magazine Issue 1: Mobile phones and information technology*. United Nations Office for South-South Cooperation. ISSN 2222-9280.
9. Kedar, S. (2009). *Database management systems*. Technical Publications. ISBN 978-81-8431-584-4.
10. Khurshudov, A. (2001). *The essential guide to computer data storage: From floppy to DVD*. Prentice Hall. ISBN 978-0-130-92739-2.
11. Kock, N., Gray, P., Hoving, R., Klein, H., Myers, M., & Rockart, J. (2002). Information systems research relevance revisited: Subtle accomplishment, unfulfilled promise, or serial hypocrisy? *Communications of the Association for Information Systems, 8*(23), 330–346.
12. Mansour, O., & Ghazawneh, A. (2009). Research in information systems: Implications of the constant changing nature of IT capabilities in the social computing era. In J. Molka-Danielsen (Ed.), *Proceedings of the 32nd Information Systems Research*

Seminar in Scandinavia (IRIS 32) (pp. 89–96). Molde University College. ISBN 978-82-7962-120-1.

13. Neumann, G., Sobernig, S., & Aram, M. (2014). Evolutionary business information systems. *Business and Information Systems Engineering, 6*(1), 33–36. https://doi.org/10.1007/s12599-013-0305-1.
14. Orlikowski, W., & Iacono, C. (2001). Research commentary: Desperately seeking the "IT" in IT research—a call to theorizing about the IT artifact. *Information Systems Research, 12*(2), 121–134. https://doi.org/10.1287/isre.12.2.121.9700.
15. Proctor, K. S. (2011). *Optimizing and assessing information technology: Improving business project execution*. John Wiley & Sons. ISBN 978-1-118-10263-3.
16. Ward, P., & Dafoulas, G. S. (2006). *Database management systems*. Cengage Learning EMEA. ISBN 978-1-84480-452-8.

CHAPTER

2

Management Information Systems

LEARNING OBJECTIVES

After studying this chapter, you will be able to:

- Understand management information systems (MIS) concept;
- Describe physical view of MIS;
- Explain role of management information systems in an organization;
- Identify impact of MIS on an organization;
- Describe the context of public sector reform;
- Understand management reporting system;
- Review transaction processing system.

KEY TERMS FROM THIS CHAPTER

Business Intelligence (BI)
Data Processing
Distributed system
Domain knowledge
Operations management
Management reporting system
Data Mining
Data Storage
Documentation
Information
Strategic Planning
Management Information System (MIS)

INTRODUCTION

A concept from the last two or three decades is the Management Information System (MIS). There are several ways to understand and describe it. It goes by several other names, including computer-based information system and information and decision system.

- A system that supports organizational decision-making with information is known as a management information system, or MIS.
- A management information system (MIS) is an integrated human-machine system that provides information to support an organization's operations, management, and decision-making processes.
- A management information system (MIS) is characterized as a system that is built upon an organization's database and is intended to supply information to its members.

Despite the fact that there are several definitions, they all lead to the same place, i.e., the MIS is a system that aids in the organization's decision-making processes. The distinction is in how the MIS's components are defined. MIS, on the other hand, is a computerized business processing system that produces information for individuals within an organization to meet their information needs and aids in decision-making to accomplish the organization's corporate goal. In the public sector, MIS is also intended to provide services to citizens.

Organizations need information from management information systems (MIS) to manage themselves effectively and efficiently. Computer systems used for organization management are commonly referred to as management information systems. Hardware, software, data (information for decision making), procedures (design, development, and documentation), and people (individuals, groups, or organizations) are the five main parts of MIS.

The fact that management information systems are used to analyze and support strategic and operational activities sets them apart from other types of information systems. Scholarly usage of the term encompasses the investigation of how individuals, teams, and institutions assess, plan, execute, oversee, and employ information-generating systems to enhance the efficacy and efficiency of decision-making. These systems may include decision support, expert, or executive information systems.

2.1. MANAGEMENT INFORMATION SYSTEMS (MIS) CONCEPT

Over time, the idea of the management information system (MIS) has expanded to include a wide range of organizational functions. MIS is required in every organization. The original idea behind MIS was to process the organization's data and deliver it on a regular basis as reports. From data collection through processing, the system was mainly able to manage the information.

Because each person had to select the processed data and use it according to his needs, it was more impersonal. When the difference between data and information was established, this idea underwent additional modification. The result of data analysis is information. This idea is comparable to a raw material and its final form. However, there are numerous methods for analyzing data that result in varying degrees of detail and product specifications. Because every person may have a different orientation toward the information, it was necessary that the system concept be individual-oriented.

This idea was expanded upon to include the idea that the information should be presented by the system in a way that influences the user and prompts them to take action, such as opening a file or conducting research. Later on, it was discovered that although such an impact was a welcome change, analysis and reporting still required a selective approach. Thus, exception reporting became ingrained in MIS. The organization needed to change the standard for an exception. The idea held true until and to the extent that the standard for an exception continued to be true and functional. Fixing the norm for an exception becomes a pointless endeavor because the environment is always changing and becoming more competitive, at least for those in higher positions within the company. Subsequently, the idea that the system ought to be able to manage need-based exception reporting emerged. This need may pertain to a single person or to a collection of people. This required that all data be kept in one location and organized so that it can be accessed by anyone and processed to meet their needs. The idea is that although the data is one, different people may perceive it in different ways.

During the course of these conceptual developments, the idea of end-user computing with multiple databases began to take shape. This idea transformed MIS fundamentally. Decentralization of the system and the information user's independence from computer experts were the changes. As this came to pass, the idea of MIS evolved into a decision-making system. The computer department's responsibility is to oversee the information resource and delegate information processing to the user. Today's definition of MIS is a system that manages databases, gives users access to computing resources, and offers a range of tools for making decisions. It also allows citizens and beneficiaries to connect with organizations and use MIS from outside sources.

The idea behind MIS places a great value on the person and his aptitude for using data. MIS uses data analysis to provide information. Many academic disciplines are used in the data analysis process. These contribute to the effectiveness and utility of MIS by incorporating ideas, concepts, and theories from the fields of management science, psychology, and human behavior. MIS is designed using these academic disciplines, which also help to evolve the modeling and decision-making decision support tools. The fundamentals of management and its procedures form the basis of MIS. If the idea of a management information system is developed after methodical planning and design, it can be developed for a particular goal. Analysis of the company, management policies and viewpoints, organizational culture, and management style are all required. In this situation, information should be produced that is helpful for running the company. Only when it is envisioned as a system with a suitable design is this feasible. Because of this, MIS mainly draws on systems theory to provide solutions for the intricate input and output flow scenarios. It makes use of communication theories to develop system designs that can handle data inputs, processes, and outputs while transferring information from a source to a destination with the least amount of noise or distortion. It makes use of Viz's system design principles the capacity to continuously modify or correct the system in accordance with changes in the operating environment of the MIS. Such a design aids in maintaining the MIS in tune with the demands of the company's business management. Thus, the idea is a synthesis of management, information, and system principles, theories, and practices that results in a single product known as the Management Information System (MIS).

2.1.1. History of MIS

The five eras of Management Information System evolution corresponding to the five phases in the development of computing technology: (i) Mainframe and minicomputer computing, (ii) Personal computers, (iii) Client/server networks, (iv) Enterprise computing, and (v) Cloud computing.

IBM and its mainframe computers dominated the first era of computers, which included minicomputers. IBM provided the hardware and software for these machines, which frequently occupied entire rooms and required teams to operate. These computers' cost decreased as a result of their increased capacity and ability to handle more data as technology developed.

When microprocessors began to rival mainframes and minicomputers in 1965, the decentralization of computing power from large data centers to smaller offices accelerated, ushering in the second era of personal computers. Small computer technology gave way to personal computers in the late 1970s, and these relatively inexpensive machines were becoming mass-market staples. This allowed companies to give their workers access to computing power that would have cost lakhs of rupees just ten years earlier.

The third era, known as client/server, emerged when computers on a shared network access shared data on a server, as a result of growing enterprise information sharing requirements and falling costs. Thousands or even millions of people can access data at once thanks to this. High-speed networks brought about the fourth era of enterprise, which connected every facet of the business and provided rich information access that covered the entire management structure. Every computer is put to use. The most recent, known as the fifth era (cloud computing), uses networking technology to deliver data storage and applications regardless of the hardware's location, configuration, or type. Managers can now access the MIS remotely using laptops, tablets, and smartphones thanks to increased mobility brought about by high-speed cellular and Wi-Fi networks.

2.1.2. Components of Management Information Systems

In order to provide decision makers with the information they require, Management Information Systems must be equipped with all the components required to gather, process, store, and retrieve data as needed.

These systems employ the following four elements to accomplish this:

1. **Information System:** Infrastructure, staff, hardware, and software are all involved in this. This part facilitates the gathering of data for the MIS's storage. Computers, network devices, printers, and scanners are examples of hardware. Enterprise software used by the business and any other software required for the operation of the network are included in the software elements. Because of this component, information can be gathered by enabling employee interaction with the system.
2. **Database Management System:** Computer programs that aid in data storage and retrieval make up the majority of this component. Naturally, it also refers to the actual physical databases that hold the data after it has been collected. Management Information Systems can make use of a variety of database management systems. The volume of data that must be processed and stored in the system will determine how suitable the systems are. While some database management systems are small enough to run on a home computer, others require larger, more sophisticated devices, such as mainframe computers. Study up on database technologies.
3. **Intelligence System:** The processing of the gathered data and its clear presentation are the responsibilities of this component. Top executives are intended to have an easy time making business decisions, and this is reflected in every aspect of data processing and display. It is also known as business intelligence, which is the process of storing human knowledge and applying logic to quickly solve problems in the future when patterns emerge.
4. **Research System:** This part focuses on determining the organization's primary management issues and formulating substitute choices that might have worked in a given circumstance. This makes it easier to make the best choice by ensuring that all of the options are considered and examined. Not always is the right choice the most apparent one. Even in those situations, this Management Information Systems component guarantees that the optimal choice is made.

2.1.3. Role of Management Information Systems in Business

Reporting on business operations to support decision-making is the primary function of management information systems. This is to guarantee that the company is run more effectively and efficiently in order to realize its full potential and obtain a competitive edge.

Let's examine a few additional functions that management information systems perform within a company which includes:

- **To Provide Information Readily to Company Decision Makers:** Managers require rapid access to information in order to make wise decisions that will improve the performance of the company, regardless of the issue at hand—be it marketing, financial, or operational. Management Information Systems improve this by systematically keeping a plethora of company data in one place that managers can readily access via a network. Because managers from various departments will have access to the same information, they will be able to make decisions that will help the company solve its problems as quickly as possible.
- **Management Information Systems Also Help in Data Collection:** Data from sources outside the company is combined with data gathered from routine business operations. This makes it possible for distributors, retailers, and any other supply chain participants to have positive and productive relationships. Since all MIS members can access a central database containing production and sales data, it also aids in maintaining accurate performance monitoring. Having access to this data also makes it more likely that issues will be identified early, and decisions will be made promptly based on the most recent data.
- **To Promote Collaboration in the Workplace:** Every large organization has numerous scenarios where decisions must be made after consulting with multiple people or departments. These choices can be made slowly if there is no effective means of communication. Even with effective channels of communication, the process would encounter several obstacles before it is finished if the various stakeholders did not have access to all the data that was available. Even if the members of the decision-making group are working from different physical locations, Management Information Systems guarantee that they have access to all the data needed to make the decision.
- **To Run Possible Scenarios in Different Business Environments:** Many precautions must be taken before making a decision that could impact on the company's reputation as a whole. It is imperative to ensure that the decision will not negatively impact the company. With the help of management information systems, executives can perform "what-if" scenarios to see how decisions will impact key business metrics. The information is displayed in reports and graphs that are simple to read and interpret. For instance, a human resource manager can predict the effects of cutting staff in a manufacturing department on revenue, production, sales, and even profit. An additional illustration would be how a shift in price affects profitability. It is simpler for executives to make

wise choices that won't throw the business into disarray once they can determine whether or not a given choice will benefit the organization.

- **Management Information Systems Give Accurate Projections of the Company's Standing in the Short and Long Term:** The majority of the choices made by senior managers within organizations impact the strategies of the companies. Because of this, some of them might require adjustments to the company's objectives or plans. The majority of management information systems have trend analysis features that let you forecast how a business will perform in its current configuration and how it will change after any changes you are thinking about are put into place. Even without the trend analysis feature, management information systems can still give you enough data to accurately perform the analysis with third-party tools.
- **Management Information Systems Help Track the Implementation of Particular Decisions in a Company:** Executives utilize these systems to project what they expect from a given decision before making it. In the event that they choose to move forward with the changes, performance will need to be continuously observed to determine whether you are on course to meet your goals. Management Information Systems provide thorough reports and suggestions to ensure that the goals are evaluated efficiently. You receive information indicating whether your choices have had the intended outcome. If not, you'll be able to get back on track by taking the appropriate corrective action as soon as possible.
- **To Improve the Company's Reporting.** Executives utilize these systems to project what they expect from a given decision before making it. In the event that they choose to move forward with the changes, performance will need to be continuously observed to determine whether you are on course to meet your goals. Management Information Systems provide thorough reports and suggestions to ensure that the goals are evaluated efficiently. You receive information indicating whether your choices have had the intended outcome. If not, you'll be able to get back on track by taking the appropriate corrective action as soon as possible.

2.1.4. Advantages of Management Information Systems

Implementing Management Information Systems has numerous advantages. While the organization as a whole benefit from all of these advantages, management finds some of them easier to use.

Let's examine more closely to discover the benefits that a MIS can offer you are:

- All parties involved in the business have access to a single database that contains all the information required for regular business operations. When the MIS is utilized for project management, high levels of transparency can be attained by the contractor, client, and consultant, making it simple to build trust. Additionally, because data collection tools like forms and questionnaires will be standardized and information will always be easily accessible, operations will run more smoothly.

- Because a significant portion of their time is saved by the more effective information system, employees and other stakeholders in the company will have more time to devote to productive tasks. Otherwise, this time would have been used to retrieve or set up conventional file systems and information recording systems. Because of this, the business can reduce its labor expenses and increase output in a set amount of time while doing so in a more efficient manner.
- The ability of data processing tools to greatly enhance the caliber of decisions made within the organization is another advantage of management information systems. Most management information systems come with integrated data processing tools that can make decisions based on inputs from various sources. This facilitates the creation of more effective plans for the distribution of labor, material handling, and even project execution as a whole.
- Since employees can record progress in smaller milestones throughout the day on mobile devices rather than all at once at the end of the day, management information systems ensure a higher degree of accuracy in data collection. This is made possible by the flexibility that comes with using mobile devices, such as smartphones and tablets, to provide information about the progress of any process within the organization. The availability of the most recent information allows management to gain a better understanding of the progress.
- These systems log all inputs and modifications. For future reference, the time the change was made is also recorded. Because each action can always be traced back to the specific people who started it, the company is able to achieve a higher level of accountability. As a result of the system's constant availability and clear presentation of data, including production numbers for each shift and sales reports, it will also be simple to identify the top-performing workers.
- Because management information systems have a central database that is accessible via the corporate network, they assist departments in handling less paperwork. This implies that the business can go paperless while simultaneously lowering its carbon footprint and streamlining and speeding up processes. Due to the substantial decrease in the need for supplies like plain paper, ink, and toner cartridges, the bills also decrease. Since there will be no need to send documents back and forth for approval and signatures, transportation costs are also decreased. We'll save shelf space and use it for other things. Going paperless will also cut down on waste for the company.
- Companies can quickly determine their strengths and weaknesses in completing a variety of tasks thanks to reports. Management Information Systems (MIS) offer a wealth of reports, including

revenue, employee performance, expense tracking, and many more. Businesses can enhance their operations by utilizing these reports.

- Top executives can gain a general understanding of the company's financial situation with the aid of management information systems. These systems can also provide general project status reports for particular initiatives inside the company. Top managers and executives can now quickly determine whether the business is on track to meet its objectives thanks to this.
- The majority of management information systems give consumers a way to gather and store important customer data and feedback. With this data, businesses can more easily modify their marketing campaigns and product offerings to better meet the needs of their target audience and increase sales.
- A company can obtain a competitive edge by implementing management information systems, which facilitate faster and more seamless operations, leading to more efficient and timely results. Employee motivation will increase as most tasks will become easier with improved data access, and customers will be satisfied with the service delivery because they will receive the answers they seek faster.
- Repetitive roles can be eliminated with the aid of MIS: superfluous components of a system can be found when information is stored effectively. As a result, any efforts that were redundant are removed, allowing the business to make better use of its resources.

2.1.5. Challenges When Applying Management Information Systems in Business

Companies implementing Management Information Systems in their operations are likely to encounter a number of difficulties despite the many advantages includes:

- One of the primary obstacles to implementing a Management Information system in a large organization is the expense of the equipment required. Devices that will be used by executives and staff to interact with the system must be purchased. These gadgets consist of desktops, laptops, tablets, and server computers. To ensure that the system functions properly, the business must also make an investment in a high-quality network that will link these devices.
- When using management information systems in a business, employee training may also become a concern. To fully benefit from the system, one must have a thorough understanding of how it operates. As a result, the business must make sure that managers and staff members are properly trained to use the system. This exercise can be costly and time-consuming.
- The cost of the systems is high since each organization has different needs, and management information systems must be tailored to fit each one. This implies that before developing the system, vendors

must have brainstorming meetings with management representatives to better understand the needs. Consequently, the system's cost increases, making it unaffordable for small and medium-sized businesses.

- As was previously mentioned, every business has different requirements when it comes to Management Information Systems, and many of them wind up investing in systems that don't have the features they really need. Investing in a system that isn't designed for your business will give you better access to information that won't help you run your business more efficiently. Consequently, you won't be able to obtain the optimal return on investment.
- Additionally, skilled workers are required to maintain the system's functionality at all times. Management information systems, like any other system, require regular maintenance to function at their best. This implies that your business will require the addition of specialized staff to handle system maintenance. Without these individuals, utilizing the system will be difficult since mistakes won't be fixed, which will lead to operational inefficiencies.
- Large company changes have a significant impact on management information systems. For this reason, you should always think about how changes will affect the information system before making any changes to the way the business is run. The existence of the system becomes a limitation when certain changes become impossible to implement without altering the Management Information Systems. But a decent MIS should be able to easily incorporate the majority of minor adjustments.
- Many employees will lose their jobs as a result of management information systems: Since some office messenger and traditional registry clerk duties will be completed automatically by the system, these positions will need to be reduced or eliminated after it is implemented. These workers will not be pleased with the changes, and when many workers are laid off, it may easily lead to lawsuits or other issues with trade unions.

2.1.6. Levels of Management and Their Information Requirements

Information management is the activity that unites all other management functions. These days, managing a tonne of data is a must for managers who want to be able to report on it and use it to make decisions that have an immediate impact.

A marketing manager would only attempt to fine-tune a sales strategy after thoroughly examining a wealth of pertinent data regarding the market, customer, product, and pricing strategies of competitors.

In a similar vein, a human resource manager would gather a great deal of information about the job profile, the candidate's suitability for the position, the dynamics of the labor market, etc. before attempting to hire someone. The competitive environment of today makes management an even more difficult task. Decisions must be made quickly and after thorough data analysis. These very reasons explain why information technology (IT) intervention is becoming more and more common in contemporary management functions. But technology-assisted information management has also changed significantly over time.

It has evolved from merely being a supporting role to becoming an essential tool for obtaining a competitive edge.

As they become more convinced of the advantages of making such significant investments, more and more companies are spending money to acquire the newest management information system tools, such as enterprise resource planning (ERP), customer relationship management (CRM), knowledge management (KM), decision support system (055), business intelligence (81) suites, and data warehouse (OW) facilities.

2.1.7. Information Needs for the Different Levels of Management

Although management as a whole may have similar overarching goals, such as maximizing shareholder value, it is by no means a monolithic organization. There are various levels of management, as has already been mentioned, and each one serves a particular function. The strategic level is at the top, tactical issues are at the middle level, and operational issues are at the bottom level. Strategic decisions are made at the top level, tactical decisions are made at the middle level, and operational decisions are made at the entry level. It will now be necessary to provide contextual information in order to make such decisions (Table 2.1).

Table 2.1. *Information Needs of Different Levels of Management*

Levels of Management	Problems Handled/ Decisions Made	Type of Information Required
Top level	Unstructured problems.	Strategic information from within the organization and outside.
Middle level	Decisions are based on situations not/rarely handled in the past.	Information about likely scenarios. Information that can be analyzed in different ways.
	Decision-making variable not clearly defined.	
		Exception reports
	Semi structured/structured problems.	Regular summarized reports.
	Decisions on regular issues.	Information that can be drilled deeper for insight.
	Decisions on tactical issues.	
Operational level	Structured problems	Information to help find out exceptions so that they can be reported to top management
	Structured decision-making	
		Operational information
	Decision-making on the basis of set rules	Rule based information, guidelines, handbook level information

Source: https://ecomputernotes.com/mis/information-and-system-concepts/levelsofmanagement.

Strategic factors like labor costs, market accessibility, and potential for long-term growth are taken into account by a top-level manager when choosing where to locate the company's new factory. He or she is not concerned with the operational details at the shop floor level, such as the cause of an employee's absence. With a strategic perspective, he or she will only require information that will enable them to make the best decisions. For him, information is only a resource if it can raise the caliber of his strategic judgment. Information is only a resource at other levels if it can be used to obtain benefits.

2.1.8. The Responsibilities of MIS to Management Functions

In most businesses, the Management Information Systems (MIS) department assists other departments with their technological requirements. Information is provided to other departments, including accounting, marketing, human resources, and operations, by this crucial function. Additionally, MIS offers computer support, reports, forms, information, and electronic records to your company. Reports on marketing analysis, accounting records, and documentation for the HR system are typical outputs.

2.1.8.1. Accounting Function

MIS is responsible for many aspects of the accounting function. The MIS department's primary responsibilities include tax accountability, payroll processing, and reporting. Furthermore, MIS is responsible for all payroll and tax-related reporting and documentation. Reporting to management on a weekly, monthly, quarterly, and annual basis is another crucial task for MIS. Your MIS department also needs to make sure that all federal, state, and local agencies are being followed, and that management and other governmental bodies are receiving reports.

2.1.8.2. Human Resources Function

Your MIS department is crucial to Human Resources. The responsibility for implementing and monitoring all benefits information rests with the MIS department, from program administration to 401K duties. Furthermore, through their learning management systems, the training and development department uses MIS to enroll and track participants in their training program. Your MIS department must also handle salary administration and performance reviews. Every employee's report is also a significant responsibility for the MIS team.

2.1.8.3. Marketing Function

For numerous crucial tasks, your marketing function relies on MIS. Your MIS department is required to generate daily sales and product analysis information. Product details are generated from ordering information, which must be received by MIS associates promptly and accurately. The work of MIS reports results in decisions about marketing tactics and product placement. All significant decisions in marketing management are made following data analysis by your MIS team.

2.1.8.4. Operational Functions

Operations is arguably the department that depends on your MIS department the most. For your business to run well, you need to receive sales and profit information at least once a day. Reports produced by your MIS department serve as the basis for staffing decisions, including scheduling assignments. Operations must receive financial statements from your MIS associates on a monthly, quarterly, and annual basis in addition to information regarding expense reporting. In this fiercely competitive environment, operations are essentially flying blind without MIS input.

2.2. PHYSICAL VIEW OF MIS

The organization's databases serve as the foundation for the physical view of the MIS, which is comprised of multiple subsystems assembled together. Data collection, transaction processing, validation, processing, analysis, and database storing are some of these subsystems.

A corporate level or a functional level could be the subsystem. The information that they provide is developed for functional or operational management. It also offers corporate management information and conducts systematic data analysis and provision to governments for the purpose of designing welfare programs.

As a result, MIS is a dynamic idea that is frequently altered in response to modifications in the business management process. It constantly communicates with the business's internal and external environments and offers a system correction mechanism to ensure that the system can effectively meet the evolving information needs. Hence, MIS is a dynamic design whose main goal is to supply information for decision-making. It is created with the organizational structure in mind, taking into account the individuals who make up the management functions, managers, and managerial control.

2.3. ROLE OF MANAGEMENT INFORMATION SYSTEMS IN AN ORGANIZATION

The function of a company's MIS is comparable to that of the body's heart. MIS is the heart, and the information is the blood. The heart's function in the body is to pump clean blood to every part of it, including the brain. When necessary, the heart pumps out more blood more quickly. It processes the incoming impure blood, controls it, and delivers it to the required location in the required amount. It provides the blood that the human body needs both normally and during emergencies.

MIS functions as a crucial component within the organization, serving to collect data from various sources, process it, and distribute it to those who require it. It is designed to meet the information needs of individuals, groups, management staff, managers, and top executives. Utilizing a range of systems including Query Systems, Analysis Systems, Modeling Systems, and Decision Support Systems, MIS supports activities such as Strategic Planning, Management Control, Operational Control, and Transaction Processing.

In summary, MIS supports middle management with planning, goal-setting, and business function control. Planning and control are two management tools that are used to support it. Top management benefits from MIS in goal-setting, strategic planning, and the evolution of business plans and their execution. MIS facilitates communication, generates information, identifies problems, and aids in decision-making. As a result, MIS is essential to an organization's management, administration, and operations.

2.4. IMPACT OF MIS ON AN ORGANIZATION

The functions, performance, and productivity of the organization are all impacted by the MIS, which is why it is so crucial to it. The management of marketing, finances, production, and staff all improve in efficiency with strong support. It becomes simple to track and monitor the functional targets. The functional managers are kept up to date on the developments, successes, and shortcomings in the likely trends in the different business domains. This aids in long-term perspective planning and forecasting. A situation that is extraordinary is brought to the manager's attention, prompting him to act or make a decision. All members of the organization can access structured data and a knowledge base thanks to a well-managed information reporting system. The manager can save valuable time by utilizing the information immediately or by combining it with analysis, thanks to its readily available format.

Another effect that MIS has on the organization has to do with how well the business is understood. The definition of a data entity and its properties is where MIS starts. It makes use of a data, entity, and attribute dictionary that is intended for use in the organization's information generation process. Since every information system in the company uses a dictionary, there is a shared vocabulary and understanding of terms, which facilitates clear communication and a shared understanding among all members of the organization. In order to create an affective system design, MIS requires that the business operations be systemized.

The effectiveness of management is impacted by a well-designed system that puts the manager first. An informed manager is inspired to employ a range of management tools by the wealth of information available. He finds that using activities like modeling and experimentation is helpful. He is able to use tools and techniques that are not possible to use manually thanks to the use of computers.

The mundane nature of clerical work is transferred to computerized systems by the MIS, freeing up human intelligence for more productive work, since it operates on fundamental systems like databases and transaction processing. Within the organization, a significant amount of labor is seen to be involved in this activity. Seventy percent of the time is spent on recording, searching, processing, and communicating, according to a study on how people use their time. This represents a significant overhead for the company. This overhead is directly impacted by MIS. It makes the organization's work culture information-based.

2.4.1. MIS: A Support to the Management

range of choices are made at every stage of the management process, including organizing, staffing, directing, coordinating, and controlling. If management can articulate the decisions that must be made, MIS facilitates decision-making. Information support for decision-making in the management process is the aim of the MIS. It assists in a way that maximizes efficiency in achieving business objectives. Since decision-making is not limited to a specific level, management at all levels is expected to rely on MIS to support them in carrying out business operations. MIS is useless to the company unless it turns into a management tool.

2.4.2. Factors Contributing to the Success of MIS in PSUs

A MIS needs each and every one of the features stated below in order to succeed are:

- Management Information Systems (MIS) are embedded within the managerial functions to establish specific goals that help prioritize the business's key issues. Sufficient resources are allocated to support the development of MIS, while obstacles related to people and organization are eliminated to facilitate progress.
- The MIS users choose the appropriate information processing technology needed to satisfy their needs for data processing and analysis.
- The needs of the user guide the orientation, definition, and design of MIS, and its operational viability is guaranteed.
- Because MIS is constantly monitored, its open system architecture can be adjusted to meet evolving information requirements.
- MIS emphasizes the causes and explanations for non-achievement while concentrating on the objectives and results.
- It is not permitted for MIS to become a hub for generating information while ignoring noise in the communication and information systems.
- Since MIS acknowledges that managers are human, all human behavioral aspects must be taken into account by the systems during the management process.
- MIS acknowledges the necessity of meeting the various information requirements for various objectives. Information becomes too abundant and useless when it is globalized without consideration for the various goals.
- Because MIS is simple to use, it has features in its design that contribute to its user-friendly nature.
- MIS acknowledges that new needs arise and that information needs become outdated. As a result, MIS design has the fundamental capacity to promptly satisfy evolving information needs.
- The focus of MIS is on creating the information support needed to manage important success factors. It focuses on the applications that are vital to the needs of upper management.

2.4.3. Factors Contribution to MIS Failure in PSUs

A MIS breakdown occurs frequently in PSUs. The following is a list of common factors that contribute to this includes:

- Although management may not always need the information that MIS provides, it does tend to provide the information that is typically required for the function. MIS is designed to be a data processing tool, not an information processing tool. MIS turns into an impersonal system in this situation.

- Implementation issues arise from the business systems' complexity being underestimated and not taken into account in the MIS design.
- The MIS lacks sufficient checks and controls as a result of inadequate attention being paid to the quality control aspects of the inputs, the process, and the outputs.
- The organization's transaction processing systems are not streamlined during the development of MIS, and stakeholders are not properly trained in MIS failing to recognize that the producers of the data and the users of the information are two different groups and that each must have a significant and accountable role in the MIS.
- Certain important and crucial needs of its users are not met by MIS, including reliance on system staff, lack of user-friendliness, processing tasks that cannot be completed in a specific way, and database query response.
- Incomplete and inaccurate information is produced when there is a belief that computerized MIS can handle every management issue related to business planning and control, as well as when there is a lack of administrative discipline in adhering to standardized systems and procedures.

2.4.4. MIS in Public Sector Organizations

The use of MIS in government and PSU public administration has evolved significantly in recent years. A framework known as the "stage of growth" is created and employed to explain the relationships between different government agencies and the usage of MIS over time. When this framework was used on a particular sizable public sector organization, it was discovered that the PSUs' use of information systems had not kept up with the demands and advancements of the organization over the previous few years. Any organization's lifeblood is information and communication. Without them, no managerial process—not even design or planning—can be carried out. Communication can be defined as the process of exchanging information between members of an organization and the decision-making centers within the organization.

Government agencies are currently overloaded with data and information that comes from external sources or is produced by internal government transactions. The government needs these kinds of data and information in order to plan future welfare programs. Government representatives need to prepare themselves for the phenomenon of the explosion of information so they are not overwhelmed by unnecessary information. They have to manage information, which means they have to create a structure or system to gather, arrange, process, and distribute the appropriate information to the appropriate person at the appropriate time. It is imperative that this need be taken into consideration when developing MIS for public sector organizations. Technology is not only changing how government agencies operate and carry out their operations, but it is also rapidly redefining the systems already in place within the bureaucratic structure.

In the next ten years, the majority of citizens will possess IT skills, requiring public sector units (PSUs) to adapt their services accordingly. Management Information Systems (MIS) have evolved into vital tools for financial transactions, online service delivery, and auditing within PSUs. Staff members must now utilize MIS for various tasks, relying on it to provide crucial information for decision-making and facilitating communication. As the need for communication between head and regional offices grows, MIS will play an increasingly important role in maintaining an efficient work environment.

PSUs can use IT as a resource in their organizational procedures and operations. However, this is where IT and other technologies diverge.

IT has a wide range of potential applications in the public sector, unlike other technologies that are typically limited to particular fields and clearly defined operational domains. IT is applicable to PSU management and operational procedures.

There are an estimated 5870 public sector companies in the nation, all of which receive funding from state or federal governments, either entirely or in part. This enormous number ought to have significantly boosted the PSU MIS market, but instead, PSU MIS is still in its early stages of expansion. Small local software developers lead this niche market, which is dominated by in-house implementations and customized solutions. The Indian market lags well behind its counterparts in China, South Korea, Singapore, and Malaysia when it comes to adopting new technologies. Without a doubt, Indian PSUs have been slow to recognize the benefits of information technology. Low MIS penetration in PSUs can be attributed to a number of factors, including a lack of knowledge, a low priority placed on financing IT-related investments, a lack of appropriate solutions, and a lack of professional decision-making.

1. **Low Priority to Spending on IT by PSUs:** Compared to their private sector counterparts, PSUs in India place a very low priority on IT budgeting. PSUs are fine with shelling out hundreds of crores of rupees for infrastructure, but they have serious reservations about investing in IT.
2. **Lack of Professional Decision Making:** The PSU's top bureaucrats, IT personnel, and domain experts should ideally make up the team that makes decisions about the selection of MIS. However, in PSUs, the people in charge of overseeing IT projects are either IT managers or CIOs, neither of whom has functional domain expertise.
3. **Lack of Suitable Solutions:** The majority of government PSUs since appropriate MIS suitable for PSUs are not currently available in the market, of India have opted for in-house solutions or built a customized one from software agencies.
4. **Lack of Awareness:** Many PSUs are still unaware of the significance of MIS implementation and the way it boosts productivity. They view IT as a capital-intensive venture with negligible to no yield. This lack of interest in MIS has turned out to be a significant deterrent. PSUs create in-house or customized solutions that fall short of their expectations and fail to deliver the intended outcomes for MIS projects, all while operating on shoestring budgets. The majority of PSUs that have adopted MIS do not offer training to all stakeholders. PSUs in India have undertaken a number of significant IT initiatives. These

programmes, though, have only applied to Nava Rathna PSUs. The field of MIS will grow significantly as more medium-sized and small PSUs see the benefits of implementing MIS and increase their IT budgets. This will enable PSUs to provide more creative and superior services to the public.

2.4.5. Centralized Versus Decentralized Management of Public Information Systems

Public sector organizations have eight primary areas of responsibility when it comes to information systems: planning, development, acquisition, training, and technical support; data management; organizational structures and staffing; computing and data management architecture; data management; and information systems development. Although there are significant obstacles to be overcome, taking on these tasks in a centralized manner can increase efficiency. While using a decentralized approach can aid in the distribution of computing within the company, it is frequently inefficient. For public information systems, a "core-periphery" strategy that combines both central and local action is therefore thought to be the most successful.

2.4.6. MIS and Public Sector Accountability

Accountability in public sector reform can be defined as a desire to make public sector staff more accountable for their decisions and actions (Figure 2.1).

There is a broad set of accountabilities in the public sector, including:

- Managerial accountability;
- Political accountability;
- Financial accountability.

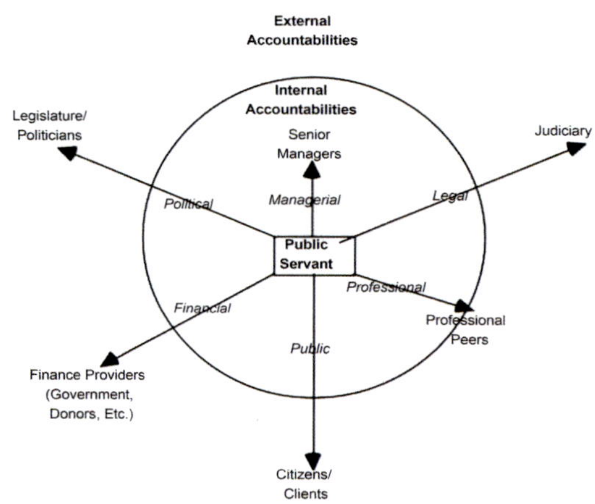

Figure 2.1. *Accountabilities in public sector.*

Source: https://www.researchgate.net/profile/Tolga-Demirbas/publication/306929917/figure/fig1/AS:401410530267136@1472715136334/Accountabilities-in-Public-Sector.png.

2.4.7. Accountability Outcome Associated with the New Computerized Information Systems in PSUs

Three main accountability impacts of information systems—especially computerized information systems in PSUs—are illustrated here with evidence from several cases.

- Essential support for accountability;
- Alteration of the balance of accountabilities; and
- Undermining of accountability.

Information systems that only have a monitoring mechanism enable reporting; recipients are informed about choices and results but are unable to assess them. Openness is merely supported by those who have monitoring and comparison tools; recipients are able to assess whether choices and results adhere to acceptable performance standards, but they are powerless to take further action based on this information. Information systems that enable recipients to take actions that impact the source decision maker—that is, those that offer mechanisms for monitoring, comparison, and control—are the only ones that can be considered to genuinely support accountability.

2.5. THE CONTEXT OF PUBLIC SECTOR REFORM

In general, public sector reform refers to adjustments made within public sector organizations (PSOs) with the aim of enhancing their efficiency. Because of this, public sector reform has been a continuous process since the establishment of organizations that we can now refer to as the "public sector."

- **Increased Efficiency**: Enhancing the public sector's input-to-output ratio; the goal of these reforms is to solve the enormous amount of money spent on it and/or the inefficiencies of many of its procedures.
- **Decentralization:** the shifting of decision-making to lower, more localized levels of the public sector; the goals of these reforms are to make decision-making more flexible and responsive while also lowering the costs associated with centralized decision-making.
- **Increased Accountability**: increasing the accountability of public sector employees for their choices and deeds. Such reforms are justified by the need to put more pressure on employees to deliver quality work, increase their responsiveness to recipient groups, and curtail dishonest or ineffective practices.
- **Improved Resource Management**: optimizing the allocation of financial, human, and other resources. From their definition, it is evident why these reforms are necessary. Refocusing the planning, measuring, and management of these resources' performance is frequently part of it.
- **Marketization**: Expanding the application of market forces to encompass interactions within government, citizen-government relations, and public-private sector relationships and boundaries. These reforms are justified by the idea that improved market relations will reduce costs and boost the efficacy and/or efficiency of service delivery.

2.6. MANAGEMENT REPORTING SYSTEM

Business information is provided by a management reporting system, which is a component of a management control system. Reports and/or statements may be used to present this information. The system is made to help managers by giving them access to relevant information in a timely manner.

2.6.1. Need for Effective Management Reporting System

Systems for management reporting assist in gathering the data managers require to operate a successful company. Information could be about finances, the number of employees, clients, accounts, goods, client assets under custody, investment performance, etc. A management reporting system can do a lot of things. Nonetheless, an organization requires an efficient management reporting system for the following six reasons:

- Constant need of reports for decision making and analysis of trends;
- Reports being unavailable with the right stakeholders at the right time;
- Lack of visibility and a single holistic view of the enterprise performance;
- Data redundancy, duplication of data leading to data management and quality issues leading to error prone reports;
- High value resources;
- Changing a global report to fit local needs.

An effective management reporting system helps:

- Improve decision making;
- Improves management effectiveness;
- Improves responsiveness to issues;
- Improve efficiency of resources in the delivery of organizational services.

MR systems were traditionally limited to information retrieval. But over time, the system has experienced significant change, becoming a strong platform for management and reporting. Technology has advanced to the point where it can now provide both non-financial and financial information, enabling management to take the appropriate action to control their business activity.

Thanks to IT advancements, traditional bookkeeping tasks can now be automated. The system is more important in assisting management in making wise business decisions. It is beneficial in:

- Identifying the problem;
- Evaluate alternate solutions;

- Implement the best solution;
- Review implementation.

2.6.2. Five Essentials of an Effective Management Reporting System

Reports produced by an MR system ought to be of high quality, with appropriate information flow, timely generation, and proper formatting.

- The system ought to possess sufficient flexibility to conform to every need expressed by the user. If there are any deviations from predetermined standards or estimates, it should also offer insights. It should accomplish all of these while saving the company money. Report localization contributes to their simplicity. Businesses ought to focus more on localizing their MR systems because it makes reporting easier. This facilitates the making of better decisions for every field or area.
- One expects an accurate MR system. There ought to be no disparities in the reporting. These systems must be accurate because they assess a company's performance at any given time. Senior management, especially C-level executives, will use the reports that the systems generate, so accuracy is crucial!
- Only when a management reporting system produces reports quickly can it be considered effective. A management reporting system is useless if it cannot generate reports when required. With today's technology, businesses can get information more frequently and more quickly.
- The cost-effectiveness of a management reporting system is an essential component. The process of compiling reports from this system should never be too challenging. They ought to be able to defend their expenses as well. An organization's decision to use an MR system may be influenced by cost.
- In the end, the management should be able to make educated decisions with the assistance of the reports that the system generates. In other words, the reports have to be specific enough to inform management of the need for the next adjustment.
- Executives will always need to get the most up-to-date information in the most convenient and detailed manner. Therefore, new reports should be proactively created based on the constantly changing parameters, or the existing reports themselves must be modified as needed.
- A key element in an MR system's success is the automated delivery of reports, both dynamic and static, based on the organizational hierarchy levels.
- In conclusion, a proficient management reporting system ought to uphold a superior degree of uniformity concerning the appearance and feel of the reports, as well as the technology, instruments, and procedures employed for each report.

2.6.3. Characteristics of Management Reporting Systems

Management reporting systems, known as MRS, are the most sophisticated information systems geared towards management. The primary goal of MRS is to supply lower and middle management with printed or electronic reports as well as inquiry capabilities to assist in maintaining operational and management control within the enterprise.

Characteristics of MRS include:

- Instead of being developed quickly by creating a simpler prototype system and then making adjustments based on user experience, they are typically created over a long period of time by information systems professionals rather than by end users. They also typically use life cycle oriented development methodologies.
- These systems are designed to operate in scenarios where the information needs are reasonably well-established and should not change significantly.
- MRSs do not provide direct assistance in the process of making decisions, which involves identifying potential solutions to issues and choosing which one to apply.
- Rather than attempting to forecast the future, MRSs are focused on reporting on the past and present.
- In general, MRSs are not very good at analysis. Instead of being based on complex models, they rely on data extraction from databases using predetermined criteria and data summarization.
- Rather than reporting information from outside the company, MRSs focus primarily on reporting on internal operations.

2.6.4. Reporting by Management Report Systems

A transaction processing system's collected and maintained database or databases that have been split off from the main database specifically for this purpose can both be used by MRSs to generate reports. There are various reasons why distinct spin-off databases might be established, including:

1. Avoiding interference and delays in transaction processing;
2. Maintaining the security of central databases; and
3. Economizing by using local databases accessible to local managers to counter heavy telecommunications costs of working with a central database.

MRSs provide the following types of reports:

- **Scheduled (Periodic) Reports:**
  - Are furnished on a daily, weekly, biweekly, or other regular basis depending on the decision-making need.
  - The format and the informational content of scheduled reports are fixed in advance. However, it is crucial to identify the essential informational needs of various managers to facilitate each manager's decision making and to prevent information overload.
  - The concept of responsibility reporting is generally applied managers receive reports within their specific areas of responsibility.
  - A hierarchy of performance

reports arises, with each report including only the items that the manager can control.

- **Exception Reports:**
  - produced only when pre-established out of bounds@ conditions occur and containing only the information regarding these conditions. Exception reporting helps managers avoid perusal of incident figures and concentrate on deviations from the norm and on unusual events.
- **Demand (Ad Hoc) Reports:**
  - The ability of a manager to request a demand report or screen output as needed enhances the flexibility of MRS use and gives the end user the capability to request the information and format that best suit his or her needs. Query languages provided by DBMSs make data accessible for demand reporting.

2.6.5. Keys to Ensure Your Management Reporting System Can Carry You Forward

A growing business experiences an increase in volume and variety of transactions, a division and delegation of responsibilities, and a complexity and criticality in working capital management as more people become involved. When that occurs, you will require management reporting tools that are able to grow with the company.

You will need to switch to more sophisticated management reporting systems in order to accomplish this, from simple accounting systems.

To make sure your reporting system fulfills your needs, follow these three suggestions are:

- **Be Proactive:** Pay special attention to G.O.I. to start the transition process early on and avoid implementing aggressive growth strategies that will be impeded by insufficient systems.
- **Look for Clues:** Make a change if you find that your system's user count or transaction volume is impeding its performance. Additionally, try not to apply too many band-aid solutions.
- **Adapt to Growth:** The reporting system's main function will change as your business expands from keeping simple accounting records to turning into an operational tool. These reports should provide more targeted information that is summarized and distributed to all managers and departments in an easily understood format.

2.7. TRANSACTION PROCESSING SYSTEM

An information and document generation system that gathers, enters, stores, retrieves, and processes pertinent information about business events is called a transaction processing system (TPS). It records the work completed and is therefore a subset of the organization's operational subsystem.

There are two main purposes for the data collected and stored by a TPS. Firstly, it is used to support daily operations by making it available to relevant parts of the organization and external entities. Secondly, the data is utilized to generate management reports that assess the efficiency and effectiveness of operations. Transaction data is not only valuable for day-to-day tasks but can also be used for historical reference, forecasting, trend identification, and performance measurement. Understanding a TPS involves looking at it from both external and internal perspectives, as well as considering its logical and physical components. While the primary focus of a TPS is on daily operations, it also plays a crucial strategic role within an organization. If a TPS malfunctions, it can negatively impact external relationships with customers and suppliers.

Any organization, regardless of size, sector, or focus on profit, exists to add value to the resources it receives from its external environment in order to serve its clientele. The tasks that consistently add value to the organization's output are carried out at the operational level. The activities that compare achieved results with management-set goals constitute the management control level. The purpose of this comparison is to find and address any potential discrepancies between the two. A TPS collects and stores data for two reasons. First, in order to facilitate regular, day-to-day operations, they should be made available to relevant organizational departments as well as external stakeholders. Secondly, to generate performance reports regarding the efficacy and efficiency of the operations and feed them into the management reporting system. Whichever function it fulfills, a TPS keeps the information it collects in a database for later use. Since the TPS and the management reporting system are separated by the database, it serves as a buffer between the TPS now and the TPS later on (Fig. 2 2). Trans means "beyond," as in transatlantic. A transaction is the action that an entity performs beyond itself, i.e., on another entity. Hence a transaction, at the simplest level, can be defined as an event involving the action of one entity on another. The word exchange is often used to characterize a transaction (Figure 2.2).

Information technology was not required in simpler, earlier days when small-scale business operations were conducted to obtain precise status updates on business processes. To act as a mediator between the users and the physical reality they were attempting to measure or alter, no technology was required. For example, in a matter of seconds, a clerk could go to the storage room, check on the availability of a particular item, and then report back to the customer when a customer walked into the store with that question. This organization's warehouse grew in size in tandem with its continued expansion. It would take too long to manually check the item availability after a certain point.

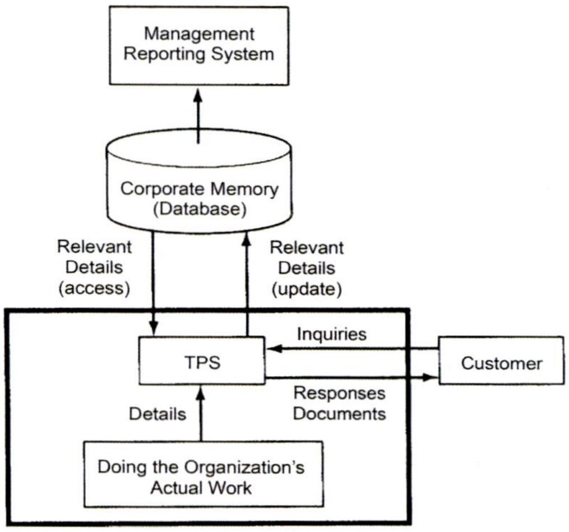

Figure 2.2. *The larger framework of TPS.*

Source: https://zimmer.fresnostate.edu/~sasanr/Teaching-Material/MIS/TPS/TPS.pdf.

This is where technology steps in to act as a mediator between people and the reality they are attempting to manipulate (Fig 2.3). In an environment where computers are used, all pertinent information about sales and shipments is input into a computer system. The amount of any item sold or bought is then automatically updated by the computer system. As a result, the previous scenario would be repeated as follows: The clerk would have to use the computer to check the availability of an item when a customer walks into the store and inquires about its availability. Stated differently, the clerk now uses the computer as a window into the outside world. The only useful method for understanding what is going on in the world is to use the system's representation of it. Only what the system declares to be true can be taken as true.

The aforementioned image makes clear how crucial it is to document events that have an effect on other areas of the company and must be retrieved later. Yet, an event has a wide range of characteristics. It is only necessary to record and store the attributes that will be useful for later retrieval and use. This serves as the foundation for the definition of a transaction, which is defined as a business event that requires the recording of pertinent information both externally—for a customer, supplier, business partner, etc.—and internally—in the corporate database.) because of the potential effects this information may have on the organization's other operations and stakeholders. As a transaction, it occurs within a specific time frame. It is always time- and date-stamped. Because management can later measure performance down to any desired unit of time, this is significant for reporting purposes. ("How many Big Macs are sold per hour?") (Figure 2.3).

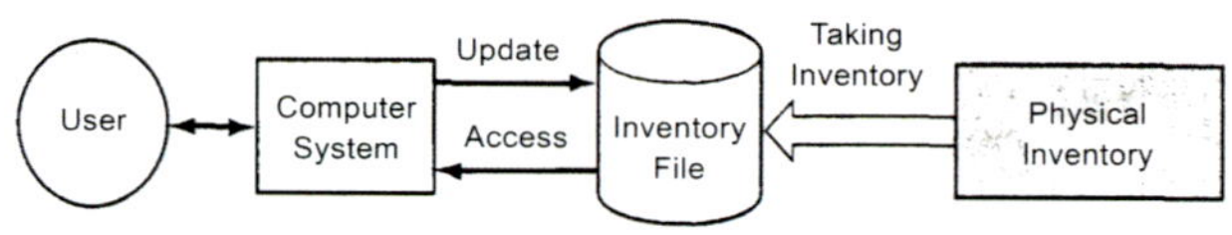

Figure 2.3. *The computer system mediating between the humans and physical reality in an inventory application.*

Source: https://zimmer.fresnostate.edu/~sasanr/Teaching-Material/MIS/TPS/TPS.pdf.

Updates brought about by a transaction are of three types:

- Adding a new record, such as when a new customer signs up;
- Changing an existing record, such as changes in credit available for a customer when that customer makes new purchases or returns already purchased products; and

- Deleting a record, such as when a product is discontinued.

When interpreted in this way, transactions date back to the invention of writing. Archaeologists have discovered clay tablets with cuneiform writing in the Fertile Crescent that document business dealings like the sale of slaves. These tablets date back thousands of years.

What matters more and more in a world where the virtual is seen as the representation of the physical is not what actually occurred but rather what the system recorded as having occurred. There are four distinct scenarios in Table 2.2:

1. Something happened, and it was documented. In this instance, the virtual and physical are perfectly reflected.
2. Something occurred, but it was never documented. Think about a client complaint that either never got recorded or got recorded but was later removed (intentionally or not). This incident was not documented, so it would not be remembered by the group as a whole (i.e., the database), thereby failing to initiate the appropriate steps that a customer complaint should, like sending the customer a letter of apology and looking into the internal procedures that led to the complaint (bad product, rude employee, etc.). This information wouldn't be used because the company forgot about it, unless the customer complained once more.
3. A nonexistent event was inadvertently documented as having taken place. This may occur as a result of fraud or forgery, but improper processing is more likely to be the cause. As a result, products may be in stock even though the computer system indicates they are not. Therefore, while a salesperson is checking inventory online, they might inadvertently view an item as unavailable and pass up a sale even though the item is in stock.
4. Nothing was recorded about an event that never happened. Once more, the virtual and physical are perfectly reflected in this instance.

Table 2.2. *What Happened Versus What was Recorded. The Event: Returning a Rental Item (e.g., a Videotape) on Time*

	It was recorded	It was not recorded
It really happened	1. Ok Example: A rental item is returned on time and is recorded as having been returned on time.	2. It did "not happen" Example: A rental item is returned on time but is mistakenly stamped as having been returned late.
It really did not happen	3. It 'happened' Example: A rental item is returned late but is mistakenly stamped as having been returned on time.	4. Ok Example: A rental item is returned late and it is stamped as having been returned late.

Source: https://zimmer.fresnostate.edu/~sasanr/Teaching-Material/MIS/TPS/TPS.pdf.

In short, in the TPS mind-set, if it was not recorded, it did not happen; if it was, it did.

There are three key points regarding the transaction concept that need to be addressed. A subtlety of the concept of an event is that it can occasionally refer to certain occurrences that are expected to occur but do not. For example, it might be considered a nonevent if a customer forgets to pay with his credit card by the due date. However, that non-event will turn into an event and result in finance charges on the subsequent account cycle because it is anticipated that the payment will be received by the deadline.

Relevance is the concept that is linked to the second nuance. It is possible to distinguish between two types of relevance: operational and managerial. Transactions capture the relevant attributes of events, but relevant to what?

The operational relevance of an event is derived from other operations in the organization that use the data captured about this event. The simplest way to bring out the operational relevance of an attribute of an event is to ask. "What operations in the organization will later use this piece of information, and how?" For instance, consider the business event in which a salesperson takes a prospective customer to lunch. The amount spent would be relevant because it will be used to later reimburse that salesperson.

The controls implemented by management to ensure that everything proceeds as planned determine an event's managerial relevance. Going back to the previous example, the amount spent on lunch would also be relevant to management because it should not go over a cap set by management. However, the managerial significance of the lunch's goal is more important. In the event that piece of information is not recorded, how will management determine whether that expense was worthwhile?

The managerial type of relevance can be extended beyond control to include strategic objectives. It used to be that as soon as a customer walked through the door of the corner shop, the proprietor knew who he was and what he wanted. With the scale of business operations increasing immensely over time, organizations have become more impersonal. Strategic conceptions of TPS aim at bringing those days back. Retailers are trying to bring back the "personal touch" using technology to compensate for impersonal contact. Regardless of the scale of an organization's operations, it is good business to know who the organization's customers are and what they want.

Big businesses struggle because they don't even know who their clients are. A big-box store may be able to tell you how many units of a certain item it sold at a given time, but it typically has far less information about the customers. When properly designed, TPS enables micro-marketing—the capacity to pinpoint specific niche markets or even individual consumers and either sell them a product they require or encourage them to purchase one by offering a personalized discount. Special-privilege cards that grant discounts on specific items are one way to recognize and reward loyal customers. The supermarket employees greet the customer by name as soon as he swipes his card through the machine and sees his name appear on the monitor.

The idea of update versus access is the subject of the third nuance. Since there is no database update involved, accessing a database to run a query or generate a report is typically not considered a transaction. But if a query is designed to be tracked, then it counts as a transaction. For example, a read/access operation would typically be triggered when a customer asks about the availability of an item. Eventually, though, management might notice that the questions are actually a means of monitoring demand. Each inquiry would then be monitored with regard to the requested items and their availability. An item's high degree of unavailability would alert management to place an order for more of it or increase production.

2.7.1. Features of Transaction Processing Systems

Reliable transaction processing is essential to the success of commercial businesses because it guarantees timely fulfillment of customer orders and payment to suppliers and partners. As a result, transaction processing has grown to be an essential component of efficient company management. Transaction processing systems provide businesses with the ability to handle transactions quickly, ensuring that data flows freely and that processes advance smoothly across the entire organization. A TPS will usually show the following traits.

2.7.1.1. Rapid Processing

In light of evolving technology and consumer demands for prompt service, the ability to process transactions quickly is essential to any business' success. TPS systems are built to handle transactions almost instantly, guaranteeing that customer data is accessible to the processes that need it.

2.7.1.2. Reliability

In the same way, customers have a low tolerance for errors. TPS systems need to be created with the goal of preventing any transactions from being missed and ensuring the systems remain reliable at all times. TPS systems are built to include multiple protective measures and plans for recovering from disasters. These strategies help to maintain a failure rate that meets acceptable levels.

2.7.1.3. Standardization

To optimize efficiency, transactions must be handled consistently. TPS interfaces are made to collect the same data for every transaction, regardless of the customer, in order to guarantee this.

2.7.1.4. Controlled Access

Access to TPS systems must be limited to those employees who need them, as they can be extremely effective as business tools. Employees lacking the necessary skills and abilities to control the system are prevented from influencing the transaction process by limiting their access to it.

2.7.1.5. Transactions Processing Qualifiers

The ACID test must be passed by system transactions before they can be classified as TPSs. The four requirements listed below are mentioned in the ACID tests:

2.7.1.6. Atomicity

A transaction is said to be atomic when it is either fully completed or not at all. For instance, a transfer of money between accounts is only considered a bona fide transaction if both the withdrawal and the deposit are made. It is not considered a transaction if one account is debited and the other is not credited. Transaction processing systems (TPS) guarantee the completion of transactions.

2.7.1.7. Consistency

TPS systems function within a framework of integrity constraints, also known as operating rules. Any transaction with a negative value would be rejected if an integrity constraint required all database transactions to have a positive value.

2.7.1.8. Isolation

Transactions need to look as though they happen alone. For instance, it must appear as though the debiting of one account and the crediting of another occur simultaneously when money is transferred between two accounts. Before money is debited from one account, it cannot be credited to another.

2.7.1.9. Durability

Transactions cannot be reversed once they are finished. A log will be made to record all completed transactions in order to guarantee that this will remain the case even in the event of a TPS failure.

These four requirements guarantee that transactions are completed by TPS systems in a systematic, dependable, and standard manner.

2.7.2. Types of Transactions

Every organization needs a customized transaction process that fits with its business strategies and procedures, even though standardizing the transaction process is necessary to maximize efficiency. Consequently, there are two main categories of transactions:

2.7.2.1. Batch Processing

Data is stored for processing at predetermined times via batch processing, a transaction type that conserves resources. For businesses that need to process a lot of data with few resources, batch processing is helpful.

Batch processing is commonly used for credit card transactions, where transactions are processed on a monthly basis instead of immediately. This method allows for the transactions to be grouped together and processed all at once, which ultimately saves IT resources that would otherwise be spent on processing individual transactions.

2.7.2.2. Real Time Processing

Speed is often the most important factor. For instance, in order for the bank and the customer to both be able to monitor funds.

It is imperative that when a bank customer withdraws a significant amount of money from their account, the transaction be completed and the account balance updated as soon as possible.

2.7.3. Characteristics of Transaction Processing System

There are 4 characteristics in every single transaction processing system.

1. **Rapid Response:** TPSs are updated to process transactions instantly in order to guarantee that the data will be available in the shortest amount of time, thereby reducing the users' waiting times.
2. **Reliability:** The reliability of TPS is essential when handling cash transactions. TPS must be designed to prevent transactions from slipping through undetected while also ensuring continuous operation. The failure rate must be kept within acceptable levels,

and comprehensive safeguards and disaster recovery systems should be integrated into the design of TPS.

3. **Inflexibility:** As soon as the steps change, mistakes or errors may happen. Transactions must be processed in the same order in order to optimize TPS efficiency. In light of this, TPS interfaces must be created such that the same data may be obtained for every transaction.

4. **Controlled Processing:** A transaction processing monitor is located at each end of the computer system to guarantee accurate transaction input. It still needs to be under human control. TPSs can even be used to falsify transactions and alter data. Because of this, access to the system must be limited to those in positions of authority.

2.7.4. TP System Architecture

The computer system that houses the transaction programs, both hardware and software, is known as a TP system. A TP system's software components are typically organized in a unique way. Within each of these components, various portions of the application run which includes:

1. **End-user Device:** A person who requests that a transaction be carried out, such as a bank customer or an online retailer, is referred to as an end user. A physical device, like a gas pump or register, could be considered an end-user device. Alternatively, it might be a desktop web browser on a PC or other desktop device. If the device is dumb, all it does is send data that the user types in and display data that is sent to it. In the event that it is a smart device, the front-end program, or application code, is executed.
2. **Front-End Program:** An application code that communicates with the end-user device is called a front-end program. Typically, it transmits and receives forms and menus to give the user a choice of transactions to complete and to get input from the user. The front-end program is typically an application run by a web server that interacts with the browser over HTTP, and the device is typically a web browser. After verifying the user's input, the front-end program sends a request message to the other system component whose responsibility it is to carry out the transaction.
3. **Request Controller:** Messages from front-end programs are sent to a request controller, which then converts them into one or more calls to the appropriate transaction programs. Calling a local program is all that is required in a centralized system to accomplish this. Sending the message to a system where the program is present and able to run is necessary in a distributed transfer protocol system. It follows the request's progress as it moves between programs if more than one is required.
4. **Transaction Server:** A transaction server refers to a process that executes the specific portions of the transaction program that carry out the tasks requested by the user. Usually, this involves reading and writing data from a shared

database, potentially making calls to other programs, and potentially providing a response that is sent back to the device that submitted the original request.

5. **Database System:** A database system maintains shared data that an application needs in order to function.

For instance, a user submits orders using a web browser in an Internet-based order processing application. A web server, which reads, writes, and possibly maintains a shopping cart, controls the front-end program. Requests are forwarded by a request controller from the web server to the transaction server so that it can handle the user's requested order. In order to process the order, the transaction server must gain access to the database that records orders, catalog data, and warehouse inventory. It may also need to get in touch with another transaction server in order to charge a credit card.

A restricted set of transaction programs, such as those for order shipping and money transfers, are available on the server and correspond to actual business processes. There are usually no more than a few hundred, and usually only a few dozen. Applications that are bigger than this are typically divided up into smaller, independent apps. Typically, each of these programs performs a modest amount of labor. The average size of a transaction program varies depending on the application, so there is no universally accepted definition. However, depending on how dispersed it is, a typical transaction may have zero to thirty disk accesses, a few thousand to a few million instructions, and at least two messages, but frequently many more. It might be dispersed if various application services are required to process it or if handling the application load requires multiple machines. It is typically expected that the program will run in a single or two seconds to provide the user with a prompt response. We'll see a second, more technical justification for short transactions later on, and it has to do with locking conflicts.

In many cases, database systems have a greater impact on transaction programs' support than do the application programs themselves. The database is typically much larger than that, even though it can occasionally be small enough to fit in main memory. Certain databases for Transaction Processing demand a high quantity of nonvolatile storage devices, like solid state or magnetic disks, straining the capabilities of database system software and storage technologies to their limits. The database may be divided into multiple machines or replicated in order to scale even further.

Over the past fifteen years, transactional middleware product categories have undergone rapid evolution. Transactional middleware products were known as TP monitors or on-line TP (OLTP) monitors prior to the World Wide Web (WWW). Application server products were first released in the middle of the 1990s to assist application developers in addressing new issues brought about by the Web, such as integrating with web servers and web browsers.

Application servers first served as a link between the Internet and already-in-use commercial systems that were overseen by TP monitors. The functionality of TP monitors and application servers converged in a comparatively short period of time. Object request brokers and message-oriented transactional middleware gained popularity at the same time.

Enterprise application integration systems are a product category that was built on message-oriented middleware.

The enterprise service bus is an additional transactional middleware product that resulted from the adoption of Web Services, which are standard Internet-based protocols for application communication. In conclusion, workflow products have gained popularity as a means of assisting users in defining and overseeing lengthy business processes. While most transactional middleware products are marketed as a comprehensive environment for creating and running TP applications, users occasionally put together their own TP environments by assembling components from different transactional middleware products.

2.7.5. Transaction Processing Modes

Transaction processing may be accomplished in one of two modes:

1. On-line mode;
2. Batch mode.

Characteristics of on-line transaction processing:

1. Each transaction is completely processed immediately upon entry;
2. OLAP is the most common mode of used today;
3. More costly than batch processing;
4. Database is always up to date;
5. Require the use of fast secondary storage such as magnetic disks.

Characteristics of batch transaction processing:

1. Relies on accumulating transaction data over a period of time and then processing the entire batch at once;
2. Batch processing is usually cyclic: daily, weekly, or monthly run cycle is established depending on the nature of the transactions;
3. Cheaper than on-line processing;
4. Easier to control than on-line processing;
5. Database is constantly out of date;
6. Batch processing is now being captured using disk files.

2.7.6. Transaction Processing Subsystems in a Firm

Data processing, or overall transaction processing, is a term that describes how a company conducts its main business operations. A company's main transaction processing subsystems are those that assist:

1. Sales;
2. Production;
3. Inventory;
4. Purchasing;
5. Shipping;
6. Receiving;
7. Accounts payable;
8. Billing;
9. Accounts receivable;
10. Payroll;
11. General ledger.

2.7.7. Transaction Processing Activities

Naturally, the nature of each transaction influences how it is processed to some extent. Among the fundamental components of transaction processing are:

1. Data capture and validation;
2. Transaction – dependent processing steps;
3. Database maintenance.

2.7.7.1. Date Capture

Automating source data is a common method of using direct data entry. Electronic data interchange is becoming more and more important to transaction processing systems (EDI).

These systems enable computer-to-computer communication without repetitive data entry by substituting formatted transaction data transmitted over telecommunications networks for paper documents. While some companies use EDI internally, its main purpose is to facilitate intercompany communication.

2.7.7.2. Data Validation

Validation tests usually involve verifying that valid codes, valid values, and missing data items are present. Authorization of the transaction based on the inventory that is available and the customer's record may constitute more thorough validation.

2.7.7.3. Processing Steps Dependent on the Transaction and on Processing Mode

The following processing steps can be carried out depending on the type of transaction and whether the system runs in batch mode or online:

1. **Classification:** The system classifies incoming transactions to select further processing steps.
2. **Sorting:** Transaction records are arranged in order of the value of the data item(s) that uniquely identifies each of them.
3. **Data Retrieval:** The purpose of an inquiry transaction is retrieval of data from the database. Other transactions may involve data retrieval as well.
4. **Calculation:** The calculations required depend on the nature of the transaction.
5. **Summarization:** Usually performed to obtain simple reports offered by TPS, this step computes summaries across all or some of the transactions.

2.7.7.4. Database Maintenance

Updates must be made to databases or system files following any transaction other than an inquiry. In this way, the information gathered by TPSs provides management-focused information system components with a source of detail.

2.7.8. Transaction Documents

Purchase orders, payroll checks, invoices, and other transaction documents are produced by a large number of TPSs. Action documents and information documents are the two categories into which these transaction documents generated by TPS can be separated.

1. Action documents specify how something should be done. Turnaround documents start the process and are given back to the agency making the request once it is finished. As a result, they can also be used as input documents in other transactions.
2. Documents containing information verify the occurrence of a transaction or provide details about one or more transactions. Transaction documents need to be

handled manually and sometimes distributed in multiple copies. It's an expensive procedure that could result in discrepancies if one copy doesn't make it to its intended location.

2.7.9. Query Responses and Reports

Though far less complex than management reporting systems, TPS do provide some basic reporting and querying features. The majority of searches yield a large screen of data. But inquiries also frequently result in reports being written.

TPSs, in contrast to management reporting systems, usually offer a small selection of scheduled reports. These reports are generated on time and have their format and content preprogrammed into the TPS software. The TPS reports are frequently very lengthy.

The following report types are produced by TPS:

1. **Transaction Logs:** are listings of all transactions processed during a system run and include purchase order manifests or sales registers.
2. **Error (Edit) Reports:** error reports list transactions found to be in error during the processing. They identify the error and sometimes also list the corresponding master file or database records.
3. **Detail Reports:** detail reports are extracts from the database that lists records satisfying particular criteria.
4. **Summary Reports:** typical summary reports produced by TPSs include financial statements.

CASE STUDY

MANAGEMENT INFORMATION SYSTEM AT DELL

Management information system involves the information system and the organization. MIS begins where computer science ends. Computer scientists deserve accolades for developing and delivering even more advanced forms of information technology: hardware technology; software technology; and network technology. Yet because no technology implements itself, there is more to MIS than just information technology. MIS has dimensions. The four interrelated dimensions of MIS are as follows: First, MIS involves not just information technology, but also its instantiation; second, MIS involves, as reactive and inextricable elements, both an information system and its organizational context; third, MIS involves information technology as a form of intellectual technology; and fourth, MIS involves the activities of a profession or corporate function which are integral to the essence of what MIS.

Dell Computer Corporation: Company Background

Dell Computer Corporation is a major manufacturer of personal computers, computer peripherals, and software. Among the leading producers of computers in the world, Dell sells its products directly to customers through the Internet and mail-order catalogs rather than through retail outlets. The company is based in Round Rock, Texas. At Dell Computers, customers are brought into the product planning and manufacturing processes, with all employees encouraged having contact with customers. Through effective collaboration across boundaries, ideas can be shared about product designs and value propositions. The result is faster and more customer-focused product and service innovation. To produce the capacity for this, considerable attention must be placed on organizational structures, processes, skills and culture. Such elements may need a radical overhaul in established companies. Dell was founded in 1984 by Michael Dell. In 1983, during his freshman year at the University of Texas, he bought excess inventory of RAM chips and disk drives for IBM personal computers from local dealers. He resold the components through newspaper advertisements at prices far below retail cost. By 1984, his sales totaled about $80,000 a month. In April 1984, Dell dropped out of school to launch his company.

The new company soon began manufacturing its own IBM-compatible computers under the name PCs Limited. Because Dell sold computers directly to users through advertisements in magazines and catalogs, the company could price its machines lower than those sold through retail stores. Sales reached nearly $6 million during the company's first year, climbing to $34 million the following year. By 1987, Dell was the leading mail-order computer company in the United States. In that year, it created a sales force to target large corporations and began adding international offices to capture the direct-mail market outside the United States. While the company continued to grow rapidly;

Dell experienced a series of setbacks that hurt profits. In 1990, the company began selling computers through retail stores, an effort it abandoned in 1994. In 1991, Dell launched a line of notebook computers, but quality problems and inadequate production planning forced the company to stop selling for a year. In 1994, Dell launched a new line of notebook computers and expanded efforts to increase overseas sales. Dell also began focusing on the market for servers, which used the computers to run local area networks. By the late 1990s, Dell was firmly in place as the world's number one direct seller of computers. More than 50% of the company's computer sales transactions took place via its website, which generated worldwide sales in excess of $40 million a day.

Information Processing Tools

Information processing or Data processing is the analysis and organization of data. It is used extensively in business, engineering, and science and an increasing extent in nearly all areas in which computers are used. Businesses use data processing for such tasks as payroll preparation, accounting, record keeping, inventory control, sales analysis, and the processing of bank and credit card account statements. Engineers and scientists use data processing for a wide variety of applications, including the processing of seismic data for oil and mineral exploration, the analysis of new product designs, the processing of satellite imagery, and the analysis of data from scientific experiments.

Data processing is used extensively in business, engineering, and science and to an increasing extent in nearly all areas in which computers are used. Data processing is divided into two kinds of processing: database processing and transaction processing. A database is a collection of common records that can be searched, accessed, and modified, such as bank account records, school transcripts, and income tax data. In database processing, a computerized database is used as the central source of reference data for the computations. Transaction processing refers to interaction between two computers in which one computer initiates a transaction and another computer provides the first with the data or computation required for that function. Most modern data processing uses one or more databases at one or more central sites.

Transaction processing is used to access and update the databases when users need to immediately view or add information; other data processing programs are used at regular intervals to provide summary reports of activity and database status. Examples of systems that involve all of these functions are automated teller machines, credit sales terminals, and airline reservation systems. The information processing tools that Dell uses include computers, the internet, maps, spreadsheets, models, and databases. For the operational level of Dell, the most appropriate tool for information processing is maps. Through the said information processing tool, decisions on how to operate the organization can be initialized and made. Maps can be used to determine which country/place information will be acquired from, it can also assist in determining the demographic level of people and information will be gathered. Maps can be in the form of charts that can also provide necessary information. The information gathered in turn can assist in helping to decide how an organization will be operated. For the tactical level of Dell, the most appropriate tool for information processing is databases. Through the said information processing tool, the records that can assist in finding out the strength and weakness of the company can be used to determine the tactic that will be used by the organization. For the strategic level of Dell, the most appropriate information processing tool is the internet or World Wide Web. Through the internet, trends and strategies by other companies can be known. After analyzing the trends and strategies used by other companies, an appropriate strategy can be formulated to use by the organization.

Inventory Control Systems

Individual businesses need, first and foremost, an efficient inventory control system. This implies the minimum amount of inventory that will provide the consumers with what they need whenever and wherever they need it. Effectiveness of the inventory system means basically having an inventory mix that is most likely successful in satisfying consumer needs (Samli & Sirgy, 1995). The inventory control systems used by Dell is up to date and reliable to prevent problems to arise. The inventory system of Dell makes sure that anything the consumer needs will be available to them at any given time. It is also what the company uses to know if certain products are still available or misuse of the inventory system may cost problems for the company.

Conclusion

Management information system involves the information system and the organization. Dell benefits a lot from the management information system. The system helps the company create strategies that will help the company conquer any problems and threats from competitors. The system also assists the company in processing the needed information. Management Information Systems also helps a company to create or update its inventory control system.

Recommendations

Since the MIS of a company is a vital part of its operations and its survival in the modern world, it must be well updated and it must compete well with MIS's competitors. The MIS of a company should be created from high standards so that it can be of stiff competition against its counterparts. The MIS system should help the company to achieve its goals and assist the company in reaching its potential.

Case Study Questions

1. Comment on the MIS in Dell and suggest the positives and negatives of MIS in Dell?

2. Dell directly sells its computers to the customer whether it will give them good and reliable information or they are lacking in information system due to this move?
3. Develop the information flow diagram for dell and suggest some improvement in the same.
4. MIS is a combination of Management, Information and System of the three parts of the information system in which area does the Dell lacking?

CLASS ACTIVITY

MIS IMPLEMENTATION

Objective: To analyze a real-world case study of MIS implementation and its impact on organizational performance.

Materials Needed

- Case study on MIS implementation (select a relevant and recent case study from a reputable source).
- Projector or screen for displaying the case study.
- Handouts or slides summarizing key concepts related to MIS and its role in organizations.
- Whiteboard or flipchart for group discussions.

Activity Steps

1. **Introduction**

- Provide an overview of Management Information Systems (MIS) and their significance in organizations.
- Explain the purpose of the activity: to analyze a case study of MIS implementation and evaluate its effectiveness in addressing organizational challenges.

2. **Case Study Presentation:**

- Present the selected case study to the class, highlighting the organization's background, challenges, goals, and the MIS solution implemented.
- Emphasize key aspects such as the selection process for the MIS, implementation timeline, challenges faced during implementation, and outcomes achieved.

3. **Group Discussion:**

Divide students into small groups and assign each group specific discussion questions related to the case study.

Encourage groups to discuss the following topics:

- How did the organization's MIS address its business needs and challenges?
- What were the key success factors and challenges during the MIS implementation process?
- What were the outcomes and impacts of the MIS implementation on organizational performance, efficiency, and decision-making?
- What lessons can be learned from this case study regarding the effective implementation and management of MIS?

4. **Group Presentations:**

- After the discussion, invite each group to present their findings and insights to the class.
- Encourage groups to share their perspectives, analysis, and recommendations based on the case study.
- Facilitate a brief Q&A session after each presentation to allow for further discussion and clarification.

5. **Reflection and Wrap-Up:**

Conclude the activity by summarizing the key takeaways from the case study analysis.

- Encourage students to reflect on the importance of MIS in organizational decision-making and problem-solving.
- Discuss how the lessons learned from the case study can be applied to future MIS projects and organizational initiatives.

6. **Key Takeaways:**

- Understanding of the role of MIS in addressing organizational challenges and supporting decision-making.
- Insights into the factors influencing the success of MIS implementation projects.
- Critical thinking skills in analyzing real-world case studies and drawing conclusions.
- Application of theoretical concepts in MIS to practical business situations.

This activity provides students with a hands-on opportunity to apply their knowledge of MIS concepts to real-world scenarios, fostering a deeper understanding of the role of MIS in organizations

SUMMARY

- Over time, the idea of the management information system (MIS) has expanded to include a wide range of organizational functions. MIS is required in every organization. The original idea behind MIS was to process the organization's data and deliver it on a regular basis as reports.
- In order to provide decision makers with the information they require, Management Information Systems must be equipped with all the components required to gather, process, store, and retrieve data as needed.
- Reporting on business operations to support decision-making is the primary function of management information systems. This is to guarantee that the company is run more effectively and efficiently in order to realize its full potential and obtain a competitive edge.
- The organization's databases serve as the foundation for the physical view of the MIS, which is comprised of multiple subsystems assembled together. Data collection, transaction processing, validation, processing, analysis, and database storing are some of these subsystems.
- The Management Information System (MIS) assists clerical employees with processing transactions and answering any questions they may have about transaction data, record status, and document references. MIS aids junior management by offering operational data to assist with planning, scheduling, and control, as well as helping with decision-making at the operational level to address any issues that may arise.
- Public sector organizations have eight primary areas of responsibility when it comes to information systems: planning, development, acquisition, training, and technical support; data management; organizational structures and staffing; computing and data management architecture; data management; and information systems development.
- Business information is provided by a management reporting system, which is a component of a management control system. Reports and/or statements may be used to present this information. The system is made to help managers by giving them access to relevant information in a timely manner.
- Systems for management reporting assist in gathering the data managers require to operate a successful company. Information could be about finances, the number of employees, clients, accounts, goods, client assets under custody, investment performance, etc.
- An information and document generation system that gathers, enters, stores, retrieves, and processes pertinent information about business events is called a transaction processing system (TPS). It records the work completed and is therefore a subset of the organization's operational subsystem.

REVIEW QUESTIONS

1. 1Explain the concept of management information systems.
2. What are the components of management information systems?
3. Discuss the levels of management and their information requirements.
4. What is the importance of management information systems?
5. What is the impact of management information system?
6. How can management information systems improve business?
7. What is management reporting system?
8. Elaborate the transaction processing system.

REFERENCES

1. Chalotra, V. (2011). Warehouse management information system: A new perspective in supply chain management. *Indian Journal of Applied Research, 1*(9), 29–30. https://doi.org/10.15373/2249555x/jun2012/12.
2. Costa, A., Ferreira, C., Bento, E., & Aparicio, F. (2016). Enterprise resource planning adoption and satisfaction determinants. *Computers in Human Behavior, 63*, 659–671. https://doi.org/10.1016/j.chb.2016.05.090.
3. Joshi, G. (2013). *Management information systems*. Oxford University Press. ISBN 978-0-19-808099-2.
4. Magno-Tan, M. J., Crisostomo, A. V., Villaflor, B., & Faller, J. C. (2014). Cloud-based college management information system for universities. *International Journal of Information and Education Technology, 4*(6), 508–512. https://doi.org/10.7763/ijiet.2014.v4.460.
5. Oliveira, J. F. de, Fernandes, M. E., & Lima, C. R. C. (2013). Information technology management system: An analysis on computational model failures for fleet management. *Journal of Information Systems and Technology Management, 10*(3), 577–596. https://doi.org/10.4301/s1807-17752013000300007.
6. Palchuk, O., Kononenko, L., & Mytsenko, V. (2020). Information support of innovation management in the accounting system. *Central Ukrainian Scientific Bulletin. Economic Sciences, 4*(37), 228–235. https://doi.org/10.32515/2663-1636.2020.4(37).228-235.
7. Peret, P. (2022). Risks management. In *Information system audit* (pp. 193–214). CRC Press. https://doi.org/10.1201/9781003230137-10.
8. Polyakov, M., Khanin, I., Bilozubenko, V., Korneyev, M., & Nebaba, N. (2020). Information technologies for developing a company's knowledge management system. *Knowledge and Performance Management, 4*(1), 15–25. https://doi.org/10.21511/kpm.04(1).2020.02.
9. Sej-Kolasa, M. (2010). An environmental management system as an information system. *Economics & Sociology, 3*(1a), 101–118. https://doi.org/10.14254/2071-789x.2010/3-1a/8.

10. Sivaranjini, P., & Praveena, S. (2011). Knowledge management system for organisational development information technology. *Indian Journal of Applied Research, 3*(6), 363–364. https://doi.org/10.15373/2249555x/june2013/120.

11. Usmonov, T. U. (2020). Optimization of global information flows in transport system management. *Journal of Advanced Research in Dynamical and Control Systems, 12*(SP7), 2024–2032. https://doi.org/10.5373/jardcs/v12sp7/20202319.

12. Weik, M. H. (2000). Information management system. In *Computer science and communications dictionary* (p. 776). Springer. https://doi.org/10.1007/1-4020-0613-6_8939.

13. Wiederhold, R. (1992). Integrated information management system. *Prehospital and Disaster Medicine, 7*(2), 161–166. https://doi.org/10.1017/s1049023x00039418.

CHAPTER 3

Acquisition of Software and Hardware

LEARNING OBJECTIVES

After studying this chapter, you will be able to:

- Understand specification of hardware;
- Perform software configuration management;
- Explain reliability, availability, and maintainability.

KEY TERMS FROM THIS CHAPTER

Access Management Services
Computer Hardware
Computer Programmers
Computer Software Licensing
Educational Technology
Information Services
Mainframe Computer Maintenance
Software Acquisition
Computer Cabinet Maintenance
Computer Hardware Maintenance
Computer Security
Computer Software Rental
Hardware Maintenance
Software Licensing
Public Utilities Services
Software Coding

INTRODUCTION

The process of acquiring a computer system, be it a desktop, laptop, server, or other computing device, is referred to as computer acquisition. This procedure entails locating, evaluating, acquiring, and configuring the hardware and software components required to satisfy particular demands or specifications. It can be carried out for a variety of reasons by businesses or individuals, such as office work, gaming, scientific research, data analysis, and more. The process of purchasing a computer includes every step, from selecting the right form factor and specifications to installing and setting up the system.

Purchasing hardware and software is an essential component of contemporary technology management for individuals, companies, or organizations. Getting the physical and digital tools required to support different operations, tasks, and goals is part of this process. The acquisition process is complex and involves careful consideration of factors like functionality, compatibility, cost-effectiveness, and long-term sustainability. It involves everything from necessary software applications to complex hardware infrastructure.

Acquisitions of software and hardware are essential in today's digital environment for increasing productivity, optimizing workflows, fostering innovation, and accomplishing strategic objectives. The choices made during the acquisition phase can have a big influence on overall performance and competitiveness, whether it's buying the newest hardware to boost computational capabilities or software to optimize business processes.

With the goal of assisting people and organizations in making wise decisions, this chapter offers best practices, useful steps, and insights into the software and hardware acquisition process. Stakeholders can successfully navigate the complexities of technology procurement by knowing the specifics of software and hardware acquisition. This will help to ensure that investments are in line with goals and provide real value.

3.1. SPECIFICATION OF HARDWARE

The term "hardware" describes every component that makes up a computer system. This includes the main processor unit, a display screen, a keyboard, a mouse, and occasionally a printer for a traditional desktop computer. Frequently included are speakers, a webcam, and an external hard drive for backup storage. Even though a computer's technical specifications aren't as important as they were even a few years ago, it's still always helpful to have a basic understanding of hardware terminology. It goes without saying that having this knowledge is helpful when buying or upgrading a computer and/or associated peripherals to make sure everything will work properly and connect.

The bare minimum hardware needed to run a particular piece of software (like an operating system or application program) is frequently the basis for decisions regarding hardware specifications. In fact, many users still find it most sensible to choose or upgrade their hardware based on the software they need or want to run.

In general, a computer's performance is determined by four things: the amount of random access memory (RAM), the graphics system, the internal hard drive's speed and capacity, and the CPU's speed and architecture. The majority of users will also find the Internet connection's specifications to be significant. The majority of computer users should consider what kind of storage device they will need to store and backup all of their important data, especially if they work with a lot of photos, music files, or videos.

3.1.1. Processor Speed and Architecture

The fastest current processors run at up to 4.7GHz. The speed of a computer's processor chip, also referred to as its clock speed, is measured in gigahertz (GHz). Nonetheless, any processor operating at 1GHz or higher is still more than adequate for the majority of computing tasks, such as emailing, word processing, spreadsheet work, and web browsing.

Applications like video editing, 3D graphics work, and (for most power users) computer gaming are examples of where higher processor speeds become more significant. In these cases, a faster processor is generally preferable. Having said that, those who require a very powerful computer should be aware that CPU performance is now based on much more than just speed. When Intel unveiled their processor numbering scheme, it was very clear what it meant. These show the clock speed of a processor along with information about its architecture, cache, and front side bus (FSB) speed.

The most crucial factor influencing a processor's performance, after clock speed, is its architecture, which describes the intricacy and fundamental design of the device. Certain processors are just more advanced than others. Intel, for instance, produces both more powerful processors under the Core processor family and more basic processors called Celerons and Pentiums. The most powerful of these are the Core 7 and later models include the Core 2, Core i3, Core i5, and Core i7.

Every Intel Core processor has multiple cores, or more specifically, multiple physical processors made from a single component. For instance, Core 2 Quad processors have four processor cores, whereas Intel's Core 2 Duo chips have two processor cores on a single chip. Multi-core processors are typically far more powerful than conventional single-core processors in most scenarios. This is essentially because they have multitasking abilities. Thus, multi-core processors can be significantly more powerful even when they operate at slower speeds than single-core processors. For instance, a 2 GHz Core 2 processor typically yields far higher productivity than a 3 GHz Pentium processor with a single core. Hopefully, all of this clarifies why clock speed alone is no longer a reliable measure of processor power and that the processor's architecture, particularly its number of cores, now plays at least as big a role.

Today's most powerful business workstations and servers are powered by Intel chips, which also produce very-high-specification chips called Xeons and Itaniums. Intel's Celeron, Pentium, and Core processors are all found at the core of new desktop and laptop computers. If it seems like there are a lot of options, that's because Intel has turned to a variety of processor section wizards to try and explain its processor ranges on its own website.

In addition, Intel provides a line of low-power processors known as Atoms, which further broadens the company's selection and complexity of processors. These were initially designed to be used in mobile computers, such as netbooks, and are incredibly energy-efficient. On the other hand, modern desktop computers are progressively incorporating the newest dual core Atom processors. Many people will find that a computer equipped with the newest 1.66GHz or 1.88GHz dual core Atom processor can handle any computing task they throw at it, and it will likely use at least four times less energy than a computer with a Celeron, Pentium, or Intel Core based system.

A computer's total power is determined by its architecture, clock speed, cache, and front side bus (FSB) speed of the processor. To put it briefly, cache is a type of extremely quick memory that is built into the processor chip and is used to store instructions, or work, so that the processor doesn't have to slow down too much in between tasks. Megabytes (MB) are the unit of measurement for cache; high-end Itanium processors can have up to 24MB, while low-end Celeron processors can have as little as 0.25MB (256KB). The short answer is that more cache is better, but there is still a significant cost associated with high cache levels.

The speed at which a microprocessor communicates with the motherboard, or main circuit board of a computer, to which it is physically connected, is known as front side bus (FSB) speed. Once more, higher measurements equate to better overall performance. FSB speeds currently range from 533MHz, which is still more than enough for the great majority of applications, to 1600MHz.

3.1.2. Random Access Memory (RAM)

The temporary storage area that a computer loads software programs and user data into while it is operating is called random access memory, or RAM. All RAM technologies available today are volatile, meaning that if a computer's power is cut off, everything stored there is lost. A computer will function faster and more efficiently in general if it has more RAM. In order to function, computers with low RAM must constantly move data to and from their hard drives. This usually causes them to become not just generally slow but also obnoxious sporadically slow.

RAM comes in gigabytes (GB) and megabytes (MB) of measurement. The software that a computer must have in order to function properly determines how much RAM it needs. With 1GB of RAM, a Windows XP computer will typically run smoothly, but with twice this amount (i.e., 2GB) is a reasonable minimum for Windows 7 computers. The majority of mobile computers typically have much less RAM, and in some cases, even desktop computers with smaller operating systems can function quite well with as little as 128MB of RAM.

3.1.3. Graphics System

The graphics system of a computer dictates how well it functions with visual output. Graphics systems can be plugged in as a separate video card or integrated into the motherboard of a computer. With the exception of video editing and gaming, graphics systems built into motherboards, or "onboard graphics," are becoming very strong and capable of supporting the demands of most software applications. High-resolution color images can now be seen on any standard-sized display screen, or any monitor up to roughly 19 inches in size, using any type of modern computer graphics system. The ability of a computer to handle high definition video playback and the speed and quality at which 3D scenes—including games—can be rendered are now determined by the more advanced graphics cards. The ability for most separate graphics cards to connect multiple display screens to a computer is another important feature. Others allow video recording as well.

With their own CPU chips and RAM devoted to 3D rendering and video decoding, modern graphics cards have essentially evolved into stand-alone computers. It should come as no surprise that the more RAM and the faster, more advanced processors that are available on a graphics card, the better for overall performance. Nevertheless, high-end graphics cards can reach several thousand or pounds in price. Generally speaking, there's not much use in going with anything else than onboard graphics these days unless a computer is going to be used for 3D graphics processing or a large amount of video editing or recording. If a computer with onboard graphics ever needs to be upgraded, swapping it out for a new graphics card is also a fairly simple process. Graphics cards are connected to either an AGP or PCI Express slot on the motherboard of a computer. The more advanced and potent PCI Express standard calls for the use of two PCI Express slots, which are necessary for the best graphics cards. In order to maintain stable operation, a PC that has upgraded from onboard graphics may also need to have its power supply upgraded.

3.1.4. Hard Drive Speed and Capacity

The large capacity storage units found inside computers that hold user data and software are called hard disk drives. A computer's internal hard disk(s) have a capacity measured in gigabytes (GB), just like the majority of other modern storage devices. These days, a new Windows 7 computer's hard drive must have a minimum capacity of 40GB; if more than office software will be installed, a much larger drive is advised.

A second internal hard disk devoted solely to video storage is highly recommended for stable operation in cases where a computer will be used for video editing on a regular basis. Indeed, Adobe now advises that a PC have at least three internal hard drives for professional video editing with a program like Premiere Pro CS5. Furthermore, if you want your computer to function properly, you shouldn't disregard this advice lightly!

The majority of computers are set up to store temporary files on a portion of the internal hard drive. An effective computer depends on having a swap file, which implies that a computer's hard drive must always have some free space in order to function. Hard disk capacity, however, won't affect system performance as long as it's big enough to hold the necessary software and user data without filling up to more than 80% of its capacity. However, the speed of a computer's primary internal hard disk has a major impact on overall system performance. This is merely due to the fact that a computer will operate more slowly the longer it takes to read data and software from the disk and to access temporary files.

The speed of conventional, spinning hard disks is determined by two important parameters. The physical disk's rotational velocity is the first. Revolutions per minute (rpm) can be 4200, 5400, 7200, 10000, or 15000 at this time. Data can be read from or written to a disk more quickly the faster it spins, so the faster the disk, the better. While most laptop hard drives run at 4200 or 5400 rpm, most desktop hard drives run at either 5400 or 7200 rpm. But switching to a 10000 or 15000 rpm disk—like a Western Digital Velociraptor—can end up being one of the least expensive ways to improve a desktop computer's responsiveness and performance.

The interface that connects a conventional internal hard drive to the motherboard of the computer is the second important component that affects its performance. There are three different types of interfaces: IDE (also known as UDMA), slower and more traditional; SATA, the newest and most common type found on most new PCs; and SCSI, the oldest and fastest disk interface standard found in its most recent iteration. Having said that, SATA's introduction has rendered SCSI virtually obsolete in desktop computing environments because it offers a relatively fast interface at a significantly lower cost and complexity than SCSI.

3.1.5. Input Devices

Although the specifications of the parts that make up a computer's system case are important, most users now place much more value on the variety of computer peripherals they have access to, or more specifically, the input and output hardware that enables them to interact with the digital world. The majority of people have found that the most significant developments in the last five years have been the startling shifts in the methods that people can now generate, output, and handle computer data.

Keyboards continue to be the primary method used to enter most text and numerical data into computers. Over the previous few decades, there hasn't been much of a change in computer keyboards either. The addition of an increasing number of unique function keys, wireless technologies, and enhancements to support health and safety regulations for display screen equipment are among the most common developments. For example, early IBM PC keyboards were incredibly durable, but because of their sturdy keyboard switches, many users who typed on them all day long experienced problems with repetitive strain injuries. Modern keyboards, on the other hand, call for a far lighter touch.

The other common type of computer input device, in addition to keyboards, is a mouse or pointing device. In the 1960s, the Stanford Research Institute created the first mouse using wood. Even now, the fundamental idea of navigating a compact, buttoned device to position and choose using a pointer on a computer screen is still the same. The range of rodents that are currently accessible has changed. While some have developed into trackballs or pads integrated into laptop computers, many are now wireless. Many people now prefer graphics tablets for precise graphics work, like photo retouching, where a pen or other tool is used on a special surface. These days, a lot of mobile computing devices have touchscreens, which enable a pen or finger to be placed right in front of the display to operate a computer. Nowadays, nearly all tablets and smartphones, as well as numerous point-of-sale systems and Wacom's gorgeous Cintiq, come with touchscreens.

Over the past ten years, webcams and digital cameras have also greatly expanded how a large number of people use and think about computers. These days, digital photography is ubiquitous. Images are typically uploaded to a PC for printing, sharing online, or sending by email. Every type of digital camera is still becoming more similar. The main purposes of webcams are still to record videos straight into a PC or to facilitate desktop video conferences. Nevertheless, a lot of digital stills cameras can double as webcams. While many digital video cameras can take still images, many digital stills cameras can also record video clips. Naturally, mobile phones have these same features. In the future, it will also be much simpler to share still and moving images between computers and a variety of mobile devices thanks to innovations like Microsoft's Surface computer.

In addition to cameras, inexpensive scanners have made it simple for millions of people to take pictures and documents and upload them straight to computers. Conversely, printers and scanners are becoming more similar, with multi-function devices (MFDs) frequently containing a printer, scanner, photocopier, and occasionally a fax machine. When paired with optical character recognition (OCR) software, scanners enable the capture of editable text in addition to images. In conclusion, digital data capture commonly employs microphones and audio recorders on the input side. It goes without saying that microphones are required for online audio and video conferencing. On the other hand, there is currently a rise in the usage of portable audio recorders. These sound recorders support a number of file types, such as MP3, WAV, and BWF. Most people agree that Fostex is the top producer of upscale digital audio recording gear.

3.1.6. Output Devices

With the majority of newly designed desktop displays being flat panels measuring between 15" and 19" inches diagonally, display screens continue to be the most common type of computing output peripheral. However, some people still prefer the much bulkier cathode ray tube (CRT) monitors for high-end graphics work where precise color control is necessary. Video projectors are now also widely used for other types of visual output, particularly in training and education. Although TFT (thin-film transistor) LCD (liquid crystal display) technology currently powers the majority of flat computer displays, OLED (organic light emitting diode) screens, which are already found in some media players and mobile phones, are expected to replace these over the course of the next ten years.

Printers are the other widely used type of computer output hardware, even though the paperless office dream is still just that—a dream.

These days, the majority of printers are either laser or inkjet. High-quality color output is now possible with both of these technologies, with inkjet technologies still slightly superior for photo printing. Compared to laser printers, inkjet printers are less expensive to purchase but more costly to operate. These days, many printers are also scanners and fax machines in one, which is why they are sometimes called multi-function devices (MFDs). MFDs can print, scan, photocopy, and send faxes.

Additionally, printing is no longer merely a 2D, flat process. Although 3D printers are not yet widely used in homes, they are now offered by businesses like 3D Systems, Solid Scape, and ZCorp. These enable a computer to produce a tangible three-dimensional object in different materials, such as plastics, resins, or even organic tissue! Other hardware for computer output comprises speakers and other gadgets like iPods and other music players, which are used by millions of people to take music off their PC and listen to it somewhere else.

Similar to digital cameras, this represents a huge paradigm shift since many of our most frequently used hardware devices are only ever momentarily connected to personal computers, which are quickly evolving into digital hubs. Conversely, it could be argued that we carry our computers around with us more and more in the form of hardware that we carry around with us but that functions only when it interacts with a PC or, more often, a website.

3.1.7. Connection Technologies

In the context of hardware explanation, the variety of connection technologies that are utilized to connect various input, output, and storage devices to a computer is the last item that truly cannot be disregarded. Nowadays, the following physical connection technologies are widely used:

Nowadays, USB ports are almost commonplace. USB, or the universal serial bus, was first introduced in 1996, and is now used to connect a wide range of devices, including digital cameras, printers, modems, scanners, and many storage devices. There are now three USB standards available: USB 1.1, USB 2.0, and USB 3.0.

Only older computers have USB 1.1 ports, which have a 12 Mbps (megabits per second) data transfer speed. The most widely used ports are USB 2.0, which has a speed of 480 Mbps, which is ten times faster. With a theoretical maximum data transfer speed of 4,800 Mbps, or 4.8 Gbps (gigabits per second), USB 3.0 was just introduced.

The physical appearance of USB 1.1, USB 2.0, and USB 3.0 ports is essentially the same. To support faster data transfers, USB 3.0 connectors have an additional set of pins. These fit into the back of a typical Type A plug. To accommodate the additional set of pins, the larger plugs and sockets on all other USB 3.0 connectors have been redesigned. This means that USB 2.0 cables can be used with USB 3.0 devices if they are used at USB 2.0 speeds, but USB 3.0 cables cannot be used with USB 2.0 and USB 1.1 peripherals. All USB cables and connectors are color-coded bright blue for convenience of identification.

Computers and display screens are connected via VGA or DVI ports. The more recent standard is DVI. Nevertheless, there are adapters that let VGA screens connect to DVI ports and vice versa, so practically speaking, the only thing that matters when buying a screen is that you get the correct cable. Accordingly, for the crispest and most stable image when using a high resolution display (a 19-inch or larger monitor at any resolution higher than 1024x768), a DVI connection should be used whenever at all possible. This is a result of the VGA port's outdated analog design, which was never meant to support the high display resolutions of today.

There are still printers that connect to the parallel port on computers. The lack of a parallel port on many new PCs is beginning to cause issues, so make sure to check this if you're buying a new PC and don't want to swap out your printer.

Finally, E-SATA and firewire ports are widely used. For various legal reasons, firewire ports—also referred to as i-link or 1394 ports—are most frequently used to connect external hard drives and digital cameras to computers. External hard drives and other external storage devices, like DVD writers, are connected to E-SATA ports.

3.1.8. Online Hardware

Hardware resources are now being delivered over the Internet, a new phenomenon brought about by cloud computing and high-speed Internet access. Initially, this innovation was referred to as Hardware as a Service, or HaaS. However, Platform as a Service, or PaaS, and Infrastructure as a Service, or IaaS, are now the two sub-divisions of this term in common usage.

These days, a number of major cloud computing providers provide data storage and processing power online. Elastic Compute Cloud, or EC2, is an IaaS product that Amazon, for instance, currently offers. This enables customers to buy computer processing power from Amazon online. These online hardware resources are bought in instances, each of which has a predetermined amount of RAM, storage, and processing power. As an illustration, an EC2 small instance presently has 160 GB of storage, 1 EC2 compute unit, and 1.7 GB of memory. Data transmission is billed by the gigabyte, while computing instances are billed by the instance hour used.

Online hardware rentals come with a lot of benefits. For instance, Amazon emphasizes the qualities of EC2's elastic (users can increase or decrease requirements in a matter of minutes), flexible (users can customize the specifications of each individual computing power instance), affordable (no dedicated capital investment is needed), and dependable (EC2 leverages Amazon's established data centers and network infrastructure).

3.2. SOFTWARE CONFIGURATION MANAGEMENT

Organizations frequently utilize software configuration management (SCM), a discipline within software engineering, to manage changes made to their software products. SCM consists of standard procedures and techniques. SCM facilitates version selection, control, baselining, tracking of changes, and identification of individual components and configurations. Another name for SCM is software control management. The goal of version control and reliable version selection in software version management (SCM) is to manage changes made to large, complex software systems.

SCM is the systematic management, organization, and control of changes in documents, code, and other entities throughout the Software Development Life Cycle. The main objective of SCM in software engineering is to enhance productivity and reduce errors.

3.2.1. Why Do We Need Configuration Management?

Implementing a software configuration management system is primarily motivated by:

- The software is being updated continuously by a number of people.
- A software project may involve several versions, branches, and authors, and the team may be geographically dispersed and working simultaneously in this scenario.
- It is necessary to adapt to changes in user requirements, policies, finances, and schedule.

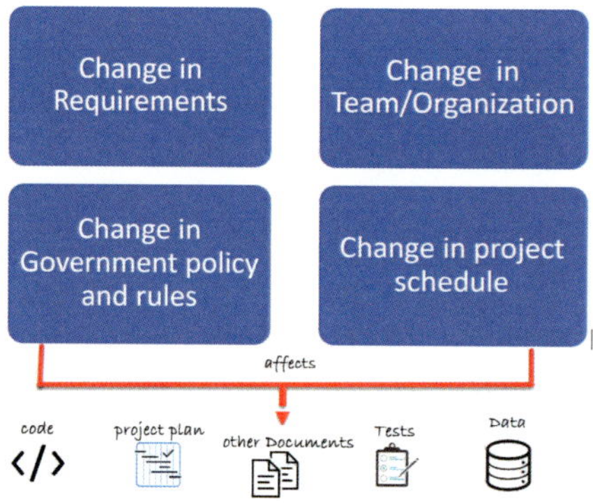

Figure 3.1. *Software configuration management.*

Source: https://www.guru99.com/images/1/051818_1048_SoftwareCon1.png.

- Programs ought to function across a range of hardware and operating systems.
- Helps to develop coordination among stakeholders.
- The SCM process is helpful in managing the expenses related to system modifications (Figure 3.1).

3.2.2. Tasks in SCM Process

- Configuration Identification;
- Baselines;
- Change Control;
- Configuration Status Accounting;
- Configuration Audits and Reviews.

3.2.2.1. Configuration Identification

One way to ascertain the software system's scope is through configuration identification. This step gives you the ability to manage or control something, even if you are unsure of what it is. It is a description that includes the project identifier, version information, and the CSCI type (Computer Software Configuration Item).

Activities during this process:

- Configuration items such as test cases, source code modules, and requirements specifications are identified.
- CSCIs within the SCM repository are identified through the application of object-oriented techniques.
- Basic objects are the first to be grouped into aggregate objects in the process.
- Each object has unique characteristics that make its identity clear to all other objects.
- A list of the necessary resources, including the file, the document, the tools, etc.

3.2.2.2. Baseline

An officially recognized version of a software configuration item is called a baseline. It is assigned and fixed during the SCM process at a particular time. Only official change control procedures can be used to make changes to it.

Activities during this process:

- Facilitate construction of various versions of an application.
- Defining and choosing the procedures for handling different iterations of these work products.
- The system requirements that have been reviewed align with the functional baseline.
- Widely used baselines include functional, developmental, and product baselines.

In simple words, baseline means ready for release.

3.2.2.3. Change Control

Change control is a methodical process that guarantees consistency and quality when modifications are made to the configuration object. The software configuration manager receives the change request in this step.

Activities during this process:

- To create a stable environment for software development, control ad hoc changes. Modifications are entered into the repository.
- The request's technical viability, potential negative effects, and overall impact on other configuration objects will all be taken into consideration.
- It handles changes and ensures that configuration items are accessible throughout the software lifecycle.

3.2.2.4. Configuration Status Accounting

Throughout the SCM process, configuration status accounting keeps track of every release. Monitoring the features of each version and the modifications that led to this version are part of this step.

Activities during this process:

- Maintains a log of every modification made to the prior baseline in order to arrive at a new baseline.
- Identify all items to define the software configuration.
- Monitor status of change requests.
- Complete listing of all changes since the last baseline.
- Allows tracking of progress to next baseline.
- Allows to check previous releases/ versions to be extracted for testing.

3.2.2.5. Configuration Audits and Reviews

Software Configuration audits confirm that every software product meets the minimum requirements. It guarantees that what is constructed will be completed.

Activities during this process:

- Auditors carry out configuration auditing by verifying that established procedures are being followed and that the SCM objectives are being met.
- To confirm adherence to standards for configuration control reporting and auditing the modifications made.
- Additionally, SCM audits guarantee that traceability is upheld throughout the procedure.
- Ensures that modifications to a baseline align with the configuration status reports.
- Validation of completeness and consistency.

3.2.3. Participant of SCM Process

Following are the key participants in SCM (Figure 3.2).

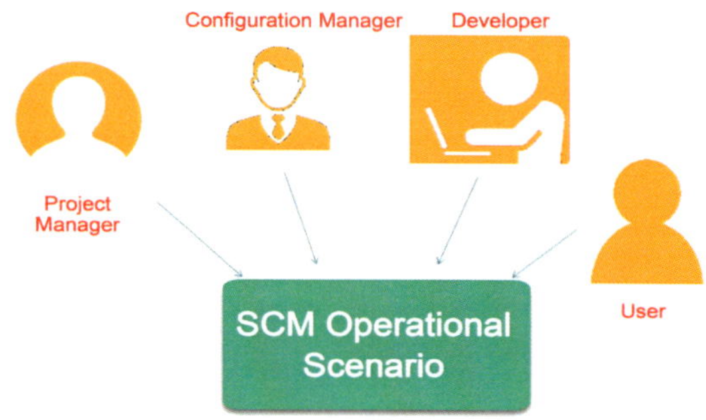

Figure 3.2. *SCM process.*

Source: https://www.guru99.com/images/1/051818_1048_SoftwareCon2.png.

1. **Configuration Manager:**

- Config item identification falls under the purview of the Configuration Manager;
- CM ensures team follows the SCM process;
- He/She needs to approve or reject change requests.

2. **Developer:**

- The developer must modify the code in accordance with standard development practices and any change requests. Their responsibilities also include managing the code configuration.
- Conflicts should be resolved and changes verified by the developer.

3. Auditor:

- SCM audits and reviews are the auditor's responsibility.

- It is necessary to guarantee the release's completeness and consistency.

4. Project Manager:

- Make sure the product is developed in the allotted time.
- Tracks the development's progress and identifies problems with the SCM procedure.
- Provide reports regarding the software system's status.
- Ensure that procedures and guidelines for developing, modifying, and testing are followed.

5. **User:** To make sure he has the most recent version of the software, the end user should be familiar with the essential SCM terminology.

3.2.4. Software Configuration Management Plan

Early in a project's lifecycle, the SCMP (Software Configuration Management Planning) process planning is initiated. The SCM plan is the product of the planning phase and may be expanded upon or altered as the project progresses.

- The SCMP may adhere to an organization-specific standard or a public standard such as IEEE 828.
- It outlines the kinds of documents that need to be managed as well as their names. Test_v1 Example.
- The SCMP identifies the individual in charge of creating baselines and overseeing the entire SCM process.
- Fix policies for version management & change control
- Describe the tools that are available for use in the supply chain management process.
- Database for configuration management used to store configuration data.

3.2.5. Software Configuration Management Tools

The three essential features listed below should be present in any change management software.

1. **Concurrency Management:** Concurrent operation refers to the simultaneous execution of two or more tasks. In the context of SCM, concurrency refers to multiple people editing the same file at the same time. Concurrency can lead to a number of urgent problems if it is not properly managed with SCM tools.
2. **Version Control:** SCM archives all file changes or uses an archiving method. In the event of problems, the previous version can be rolled back with the aid of the archiving or save feature.
3. **Synchronization:** Users have the option to check out the entire repository or multiple files. After working on the necessary file, the user returns the modified version to the repository. To remain up to date with the modifications made by other team members, they can synchronize their local copy.

Following are popular tools

1. **Git:** Git is an open source, free tool that facilitates version control. It is made to work quickly and effectively on any kind of project.
2. **Team Foundation Server:** A collection of technologies and tools called Team Foundation allow the team to plan and work together to develop a product.
3. **Ansible**: It is a tool for managing software configuration that is open source. In addition to configuration management, it provides task automation and application deployment.

3.3. RELIABILITY, AVAILABILITY, AND MAINTAINABILITY

Systems engineers, logisticians, and users are highly interested in three system attributes: reliability, availability, and maintainability (RAM). Collectively, they have an impact on a system's utility and economic life-cycle costs. For systems engineers, logisticians, and users alike, reliability, maintainability, and availability (RAM) are three system attributes that are highly valuable. When combined, they have an impact on a system's or product's life-cycle costs as well as its utility. Reliability engineering as it exists today has its roots in World War II. Electronic and mechanical components were the discipline's initial areas of concern. However, current trends indicate a sharp increase in the number of consumer, industrial, and military products with integrated computing capabilities. Reliability in these rapidly expanding domains requires consideration of both hardware and software due to the widespread integration of computers into systems and products used by industry, government, and the military.

Models of maintainability pose some intriguing difficulties. The total amount of time needed for an item's evacuation, diagnosis, resource assembly (parts, bays, tools, and mechanics), repair, inspection, and return is the amount of time needed to repair it. Timeframes for repairs can also be impacted by administrative delays, like holidays. Frequently, the minimum time required for these sub-processes to finish is not zero, which means that the distribution utilized to simulate maintainability has a threshold parameter. The minimum probable time to repair is the definition of a threshold parameter. Queuing effects can further complicate maintainability estimation by producing non-independent repair times. This dependency often leads to intractable analytical solutions for maintainability-related problems and encourages the use of simulation to support analysis.

3.3.1. Basic Definitions

- **Reliability:** It is defined as the likelihood that a system or system component will operate as intended under specified circumstances and for a predetermined amount of time without experiencing any problems. The function, the setting, the time frame, and the definition of failure must all be precisely described in a precise definition. It can be unexpectedly challenging to define each as precisely as one would like.
- **Maintainability:** It is described as the likelihood that a system or system component can be fixed in a given setting and within a given time frame.

Shorter repair times are implied by increased maintainability.

- **Availability:** The probability that a repairable system or system element will function under specific environmental conditions at a given time.

Any instance in which an item or component of an item fails or refuses to function as intended is referred to as a failure. The physical, chemical, electrical, thermal, or other process that leads to failure is known as the failure mechanism. In an electronic system, an internal error may have occurred prior to the failure, and the fault may have been caused by a software defect. The method or outcome of the mechanism through which an item fails is known as the failure mode. The extent of the failure mode's impact determines its severity.

3.3.2. Probability Distributions used in Reliability Analysis

The likelihood that a component will survive until time t can be used to conceptualize reliability. The chance of failure prior to or at time t is its complement. Then, if the time t to failure is defined as a random variable T.

$$R(t) = P(T > t) = 1 - F(t)$$

the failure probability is the cumulative distribution function (PDF) of a mathematical probability distribution, where R(t) is the reliability and F(t) is the failure probability. For this, continuous distributions like the exponential, Weibull, log-normal, and generalized gamma are used. The expected number of failures or the single probability of success are computed using discrete distributions, such as the Poisson, Bernoulli, and Binomial.

Although the interpretation differs, maintainability can be measured using the same continuous distributions that are used for reliability (i.e., probability that a failed component is restored to service prior to time t). Predictions of maintainability, however, can be very complex since they may need to take into consideration procedures like staffing, sparing, travel time, and administrative delays. Since the probability distributions used in reliability and maintainability estimation only offer estimates of the actual failure and restoration of the items under review, they are referred to as models.

The parameters in these models should ideally have estimated values based on operating experience or life testing. It can be expensive to carry out these tests or to gather reliable operational data after the items are deployed. Consequently, engineering judgment, approximations using data from similar systems, and other techniques are occasionally used. This means that estimates derived from scant data may be wildly inaccurate.

3.3.3. RAM Considerations during Systems Development

RAM are built-in features of a system or product that need to be taken into account at every stage of development. Many models of the development process have been proposed by authors of textbooks, reliability standards, and other groups. This section's discussion is based on a standard that the US and the Electronic Industry Association jointly developed and embraced by the United States. The Department of Defense outlines four processes: comprehending the needs and limitations of the user; designing for reliability; producing for reliability; and monitoring during use and operation.

3.3.3.1. Understanding User Requirements and Constraints

To comprehend user requirements, information regarding functional requirements, constraints (e.g., mass, power usage, spatial footprint, life cycle cost), as well as requirements that align with RAM specifications. These lead to the emergence of system requirements, each of which should be dependent on the anticipated operating environments and include requirements for availability, maintainability, and reliability. Just as defining general functional requirements is difficult as it is crucial to the success of development, so too is defining RAM requirements.

3.3.3.2. Design for Reliability

It is then possible to formulate and assess system designs that are based on user requirements and system design alternatives. During this stage, reliability engineering works to improve system resilience by implementing features like built-in testing, diversity, redundancy, advanced diagnostics, and modularity to facilitate quick physical replacement. Additionally, by taking steps like using stronger materials, using better components, reducing extreme environmental conditions, or shortening maintenance, inspection, or overhaul intervals, it might be possible to lower failure rates. Thermal analyzes for mechanical and electrical components, mechanical stress, corrosion, and radiation analyzes for mechanical components, and electromagnetic interference (EMI) measurements or analyzes for electrical components and subsystems are examples of design analyzes.

Since the hardware in the majority of computer-based systems has a mean time between failures of hundreds of thousands of hours, software will typically be the focus of system design measures to increase system reliability. The most obvious approach to increase software reliability is to increase its quality through more methodical testing and development. Techniques for achieving this fall under the purview of software engineering and are outside the purview of this section. However, architectural diversity, independence, and redundancy can also increase availability and reliability. Redundancy needs to be combined with managed failure detection and switchover, as well as steps to guarantee data consistency. Retries, restarts, input and output validity checks, watchdog timers, flow control, data integrity checks (like hashing or cyclic redundancy checks), and retries can all be used in software architecture to improve reliability and failure detection coverage.

RAM is also impacted by analyzes conducted during design time by related disciplines. To make sure that operators and maintainers can interact with the system in a way that minimizes failures and the restoration times when they do occur, human factor analyzes are required. RAM and cyber security in computer-based systems are also closely related. Defensive measures, on the one hand, lessen the frequency of malicious event-related failures. However, hardware like firewalls, policy enforcement tools, and access/authentication servers (sometimes referred to as "directory servers") can also turn into performance bottlenecks or single points of failure that lower system availability and reliability.

3.3.3.3. Production for Reliability

RAM production has a lot of quality-related problems. The most crucial ones are making sure that production procedures are consistent and repeatable and that all supply chain items have clear and comprehensive specifications. The others have to do with designing for storage, transportation, and manufacturing. Problems with configuration management, installation testing, and integration testing impact large software-intensive systems information systems. Data on failures and improvements to correct failures are captured through testing and recording of failures in the FRACAS or the Problem Reporting and Corrective Action Systems (PRACAS). This might be the same system as used during the design, or it might be a different system depending on organizational factors.

3.3.4. Monitoring During Operation and Use

After systems are deployed, their availability and dependability are evaluated to determine whether the product or system has achieved its RAM goals, to spot unforeseen failure modes, to document fixes, to evaluate the use of maintenance resources, and to evaluate the operating environment. For this, you could use a maintenance management database or the FRACAS. Maintaining a precise log of operating time and the length of outages, in addition to failures, is essential for evaluating RAM. Systems that only report on incidents involving repairs and outages might not be adequate for this use. In order to fully understand the interaction between logistical and RAM issues, an organization should have an integrated data system that enables reliability data to be taken into account with logistical data, such as parts, personnel, tools, bays, transportation and evacuation, queues, and costs. To enable the organization to benefit from full situational awareness with regard to RAM, these issues in turn need to be integrated with management and operational systems.

3.3.5. Reliability and Maintainability Testing

During a product's or system's lifetime, reliability testing can be done at the component, subsystem, and system levels. Several categories of reliability testing that are related to hardware include.

- **Reliability Life Tests:** They are conducted to empirically determine the time until failure for products and systems that cannot be repaired, as well as the intervals between failures for systems that can be restored. The decision to end these tests can be based on a predetermined time frame or number of failures. Techniques are used to account for any failures that are censored or units that are still functioning, which helps to provide a more precise estimation of reliability.
- **Accelerated Life Tests:** In order to conduct accelerated life testing, items under test (typically electronic parts) are heated to temperatures significantly higher than those expected for operation, and results are then extrapolated using the Arrhenius relation.
- **Highly Accelerated Life Testing/Highly Accelerated Stress Testing (HALT/HASS):** They identifies failure modes, margins, and design flaws by subjecting test units—components or subassemblies—to severe temperature and vibration tests.

- **Parts Screening:** It is not a test, but rather a process in which components are operated for a prolonged period after the infant mortality period. This allows for less durable items to fail, leaving only the more durable parts to be assembled into the final product or system.

System level testing examples include the following, which cover both software and hardware.

- **Stability Tests:** These tests involve assessing the performance of integrated hardware and software systems through life tests. The main objective is to determine the failure rate of the system and evaluate its operational suitability. Test conditions should accurately replicate the operating environment and workload, and provide a method for identifying and documenting any failures that occur.
- **Reliability Growth Tests:** They involve the testing of items during the development and early production stages to evaluate the increase in reliability as a result of improvements in manufacturing processes for hardware or software quality for software products.
- **Failure/Recovery Tests:** By calculating the probability of switchover for redundant systems, such testing evaluates a system's fault tolerance. The ability of the hardware and software to recognize a failure and adjust the system so that it continues to function is tested through the simulation of failures.
- **Maintainability Tests:** By mimicking hardware or software failures that necessitate maintainer intervention for restoration, these tests evaluate the system diagnostics capabilities, physical accessibility, and maintainer training offerings.

Reliability testing should be integrated into the overall system engineering effort due to its potential to affect schedule and cost. The quantity of test units, testing duration, testing environment, and failure detection methods are all factors to be taken into account when planning a test.

3.3.6. Data Issues

Accurate RAM models for a system are typically unknown, so data is assumed or collected to select a distribution for the model and fit the parameters. This approach is different from traditional statistics courses, as the normal distribution is rarely used due to its limitations for life distribution. Reliability data is unique as it is often censored, biased, observational, and lacks information on covariates like environmental conditions. Testing data is expensive, leading to small sample sizes and requiring complex strategies to address these issues. Consequently, estimates based on limited data can be highly imprecise. To sum up, choosing computer hardware and software for the company is a crucial management choice that can boost productivity and business performance while cutting down on wasteful spending. For a number of reasons, including the high cost of new computer components, the fact that IT is now essential to an organization's success, and the requirement that the components meet the needs of the organization and be powerful enough to handle the growing demand from users in the future. The managers and IT specialists of an organization must decide whether to use external technology service providers or own and maintain technology assets, as well as the new technological requirements for electronic commerce and digital firms. They must also ascertain the total cost of technology assets and choose computer hardware and software. A business can expand by making wise choices when it comes to computer hardware and software. The money of investors and businesses will be burned by bad ones. The company will fail once these funds are gone.

CASE STUDY

HARDWARE AND SOFTWARE COMPANY

Company Overview

$7+ million, 35-year-old, privately held hardware and software company who was a regional player with virtual sales team members located across the East coast. The company focuses on a non-profit market space, dominated by international players selling their proprietary software and hardware offerings.

Business Problem

The firm's revenues were flat and sales and marketing costs were increasing as their technology offerings' price entered into the decline stage of their product life cycle. Additionally, their market potential was diminishing in their existing market zones due to their long-term geographic presence.

Client Solution

Value Forward did a complete 360° Business Success Assessment of their entire company including technology, sales, marketing, strategy, operations and financial statements and then supplied written business model recommendations to the CEO. Upon review and acceptance by the CEO, we worked with him one-on-one to implement the suggestions and trained his sales team on the Value Forward method.

Client Results

The client revenues increased 85% and they sold their biggest deal in the company's history beating their number one competitor. Additionally, the client expanded U.S. wide and reduced their selling costs by implementing our Sales and Marketing 2.0 Success System for revenue capture. Sales team members now only travel for the largest client opportunities and their sales cycle selling time is 40% less. The company is now using us to help them plot out their continued growth and evaluate strategic acquisitions to build out the client's offerings.

CLASS ACTIVITY

Software and Hardware Acquisition Simulation

Objective: To simulate the process of acquiring software and hardware for an organization, considering various factors such as requirements, budget constraints, and vendor evaluation criteria.

Materials Needed

- Case study scenario outlining the organization's needs, budget, and objectives.
- List of software and hardware options available for acquisition.
- Evaluation criteria worksheet for assessing software and hardware options.
- Projector or screen for displaying the case study and evaluation criteria.
- Whiteboard or flipchart for group discussions.

Activity Steps

1. **Introduction:**

- Present the case study scenario to the class, describing the organization's background, objectives, and requirements for software and hardware acquisition.
- Explain the purpose of the activity: to simulate the procurement process and evaluate different options based on specified criteria.

2. **Software and Hardware Evaluation:**

- Divide students into small groups and assign each group the task of evaluating software and hardware options based on the provided criteria.
- Provide students with a list of available options and the evaluation criteria worksheet.
- Instruct groups to discuss and assess each option's suitability based on factors such as functionality, compatibility, scalability, cost, vendor reputation, and support services.

3. **Vendor Presentations:**

- Invite representatives from software and hardware vendors to present their products to the class.
- Allow vendors to showcase the features, benefits, and pricing of their offerings.
- Encourage students to ask questions and gather additional information to inform their decision-making process.

4. **Decision Making and Justification:**

- After evaluating the options and vendor presentations, instruct each group to make a final decision on the software and hardware to acquire.

- Ask groups to prepare a brief presentation justifying their decision, highlighting the reasons for their choice and how it aligns with the organization's needs and objectives.
- Encourage groups to consider trade-offs and discuss any challenges or concerns they encountered during the evaluation process.

5. **Group Presentations and Discussion:**

- Invite each group to present their decision and justification to the class.
- Facilitate a discussion on the different approaches taken by each group, the factors influencing their decision-making, and any lessons learned from the activity.
- Encourage students to share insights and perspectives on the software and hardware acquisition process.

6. **Reflection and Wrap-Up:**

- Conclude the activity by summarizing the key takeaways and insights gained from the simulation.
- Encourage students to reflect on the complexities and considerations involved in acquiring software and hardware for organizations.
- Discuss the importance of strategic planning, vendor evaluation, and budget management in the procurement process.

7. **Key Takeaways:**

- Understanding of the software and hardware acquisition process.
- Application of evaluation criteria to assess options and make informed decisions.
- Collaboration and teamwork skills in group decision-making and justification.
- Appreciation of the challenges and trade-offs involved in procurement decisions.
- This activity provides students with a hands-on experience in evaluating software and hardware options and making strategic decisions aligned with organizational objectives.

SUMMARY

- The term "hardware" describes every component that makes up a computer system. This includes the main processor unit, a display screen, a keyboard, a mouse, and occasionally a printer for a traditional desktop computer. Frequently included are speakers, a webcam, and an external hard drive for backup storage.
- The fastest current processors run at up to 4.7GHz. The speed of a computer's processor chip, also referred to as its clock speed, is measured in gigahertz (GHz). Nonetheless, any processor operating at 1GHz or higher is still more than adequate for the majority of computing tasks, such as emailing, word processing, spreadsheet work, and web browsing.
- The temporary storage area that a computer loads software programs and user data into while it is operating is called random access memory, or RAM. All RAM technologies available today are volatile, meaning that if a computer's power is cut off, everything stored there is lost.
- The graphics system of a computer dictates how well it functions with visual output. Graphics systems can be plugged in as a separate video card or integrated into the motherboard of a computer.
- The large capacity storage units found inside computers that hold user data and software are called hard disk drives. A computer's internal hard disk(s) have a capacity measured in gigabytes (GB), just like the majority of other modern storage devices.
- Software Configuration Management (SCM) is the systematic management, organization, and control of changes in documents, code, and other entities throughout the Software Development Life Cycle. The main objective of SCM in software engineering is to enhance productivity and reduce errors.
- Early in a project's lifecycle, the SCMP (Software Configuration Management Planning) process planning is initiated. The SCM plan is the product of the planning phase and may be expanded upon or altered as the project progresses.
- Systems engineers, logisticians, and users are highly interested in three system attributes: reliability, availability, and maintainability (RAM). Collectively, they have an impact on a system's utility and economic life-cycle costs.
- To comprehend user requirements, information regarding functional requirements, constraints (e.g., mass, power usage, spatial footprint, life cycle cost), as well as requirements that align with RAM specifications.

REVIEW QUESTIONS

1. What do you understand by hardware?
2. What is software configuration management?
3. Why do we need configuration management?
4. Write a short note on baseline.
5. Discuss reliability, availability, and maintainability. What probability distributions are used in reliability analysis?

REFERENCES

1. Aiello, R. (2010). *Configuration management best practices: Practical methods that work in the real world* (1st ed.). Addison-Wesley.
2. Beebe, N. H. F. (2017). Chapter I – Integer arithmetic. In *The mathematical-function computation handbook – Programming using the MathCW portable software library* (1st ed., pp. 969–1035). Springer International Publishing. https://doi.org/10.1007/978-3-319-64110-2.
3. Berczuk, A., & Appleton, B. (2003). *Software configuration management patterns: Effective teamwork, practical integration* (1st ed.). Addison-Wesley.
4. Department of Defense, USA. (2001). *Military handbook: Configuration management guidance (rev. A) (MIL-HDBK-61A)*. http://www.everyspec.com/MIL-HDBK/MIL-HDBK-0001-0099/MIL-HDBK-61_11531/ (accessed on 5th January 2010).
5. Evans, C. L. (2018). *Broad band: The untold story of the women who made the internet*. Portfolio/Penguin.
6. Fuegi, J., & Francis, J. (2003). Lovelace & Babbage and the creation of the 1843 'notes.' *Annals of the History of Computing, 25*(4), 16–26. https://doi.org/10.1109/MAHC.2003.1253887.
7. Scott, J. A., & Nisse, D. (2001). Software configuration management. In *Guide to Software Engineering Body of Knowledge*. http://www.computer.org/portal/web/swebok/htmlformat (accessed on 5th January 2010).
8. Shapiro, F. (2000). Origin of the term software: Evidence from the JSTOR electronic journal archive. *IEEE Annals of the History of Computing, 22*(2), 69–71. https://doi.org/10.1109/MAHC.2000.887997.

CHAPTER

4

Database System and Big Data

LEARNING OBJECTIVES

After studying this chapter, you will be able to:

- Understand data fundamentals;
- Discuss on data modeling and database characteristics;
- Explain Relational database management systems (RDBMS);
- Learn about Big data.

KEY TERMS FROM THIS CHAPTER

Big data
Data Analytics
Data management
Data Visualization
Database management system (DBMS)
Graph Database
Computer system
Data hierarchy
Data modeling
Database
Entity
Relational Database

INTRODUCTION

All that constitutes a database is a well-structured set of connected information, usually kept on disk and available to numerous users at once. Generally speaking, databases are divided into application areas. For instance, data related to human resources (employees and payroll), sales, accounting, and so forth, might be contained in different databases. A DBMS is used to manage databases.

Data is stored in a database management system so that it can be more easily retrieved, altered, and produced.

Data management has evolved from a crucial skill to a crucial differentiator that can distinguish market winners from losers for businesses of all sizes. Government agencies and Fortune 1000 companies are beginning to reap the rewards of the web pioneers' innovations. In order to investigate how they can use Big Data to revolutionize their industries, these companies are formulating new plans and reassessing current tactics. They are discovering during this process that big data is not limited to a single technology, method, or project. Instead, it is a general trend in many business and technological domains.

Big Data is the term for projects and technologies involving data that is too large, too diverse, or too rapidly evolving to be effectively addressed by traditional skills, infrastructure, or technologies. Put another way, there is too much data in terms of volume, velocity, or variety.

However, modern technologies enable the extraction of value from big data. Retailers, for instance, can monitor user web clicks to spot behavioral trends that enhance their stocking, pricing, and campaigns. In order to forecast outages and encourage more energy-efficient consumption, utilities can measure the amount of energy used in households. Through social media signals, governments and even Google are able to identify and monitor the emergence of disease outbreaks. By using the sensor output from their drilling equipment, oil and gas companies can make safer and more effective drilling decisions.

The term "Big Data" refers to data sets that are too big and complicated to handle with conventional software tools.

4.1. DATA FUNDAMENTALS

Any collection of characters that have been compiled and translated for a purpose—usually analysis—is generally referred to as data. Any character is acceptable, including text, numbers, images, sounds, and videos. Data has no effect on either humans or computers if it is not contextualized (Figure 4.1).

Figure 4.1. *Big data analytics solutions.*

Source: https://www.oakridgeit.com/wp-content/uploads/2016/09/Big-Data-Applications.jpg.

Data in a computer's storage is a set of numbers presented as bytes made up of bits, which are binary digits with values of either one or zero. The CPU processes data using logical operations to generate new data (output) based on the original data (input).

4.1.1. Data Defined

Basic values or facts are called data. It should be noted that the scientific community views the term "data" as plural, as in "the data are collected," not "the data is collected." Nevertheless, not everyone adheres to this, so occasionally you'll see data used as singular.

Every operation a computer performs involves some sort of data processing. A computer would not be very useful without data. Thus, it's critical to comprehend data representation and organization.

4.1.2. Analog Versus Digital Data

Data can be represented in two general ways: digitally and analogically. Continuous, or "analogous," to the real facts they represent, are analog data. Digital data are discrete and composed of a finite set of constituents. Computers are digital, but nature is analog.

There is continuity in many aspects of the natural world around us. Consider the color spectrum, for instance. There are an endless number of shades in this continuous rainbow. Conversely, computer systems are finite rather than continuous. Binary digits are used to store all data, and the amount of data that can be represented is limited. For instance, the number of colors in a computer color image is finite, even though it may be very large.

Let's take a closer look at the color example. Essentially, the first monitor displays were monochromatic text terminals. Text in white or light green was displayed against a black backdrop. More colors were used by more recent monitors, though still not nearly enough to depict simple images. Millions of colors and a much more natural appearance characterize modern displays. Nevertheless, there are only so many colors.

4.1.3. Hierarchy of Data

Data Hierarchy refers to the systematic organization of data, often in a hierarchical form. Data organization involves fields, records, files and so on (Figure 4.2).

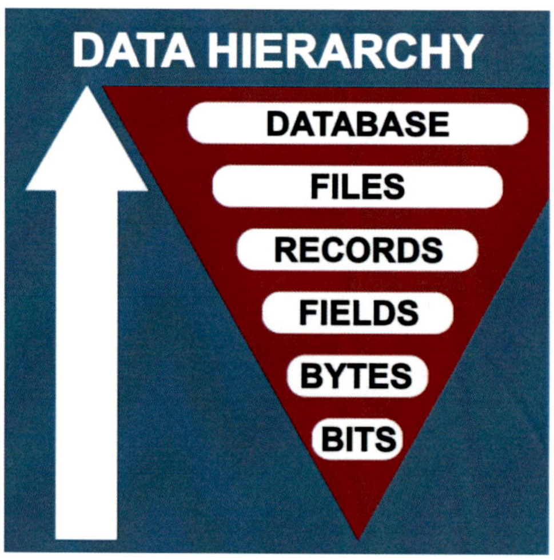

Figure 4.2. *A data hierarchy is a series of ordered groupings in a system, beginning with the smallest unit to the largest.*

Source: https://ecampusontario.pressbooks.pub/app/uploads/sites/2109/2021/11/data_hierarchy-1.png.

4.1.3.1. Bit

Binary digits or bits are used to store all data in a computer's memory or storage devices. A bit can indicate 1 or 0 by being either "ON" or "OFF."

4.1.3.2. Byte

A BYTE is an 8-bit group. A byte can represent a single character or, depending on the situation, additional data like a sound, a portion of an image, etc.

4.1.3.3. Field

FIELD is a group of characters. e.g., data held about a person may be split into many fields including ID Number, Surname, Initials, Title, Street, Town, etc.

4.1.3.4. Record

RECORD is a group of fields holding all the information about one person or item.

4.1.3.5. File

FILE a collection of records. A stock file will contain a record for each item of stock, and so on.

4.1.3.6. Database

DATABASE may consist of many different files, linked in such a way that information can be retrieved from several files at once.

4.1.4. Types of Data

The last ten years have seen a rise in the creation of digital data due to the expansion of the web and smartphones. Data now includes web activity records, logs, and text, audio, and video information. That contains a lot of unstructured data.

Data that is at least one petabyte in size has been referred to as "big data." Big data is summed up in three words: volume, variety, and velocity. Big data-driven business models, which view data as an asset in and of itself, have emerged in tandem with the growth of web-based e-commerce. These developments have also led to an increased focus on data privacy and its social applications (Figure 4.3).

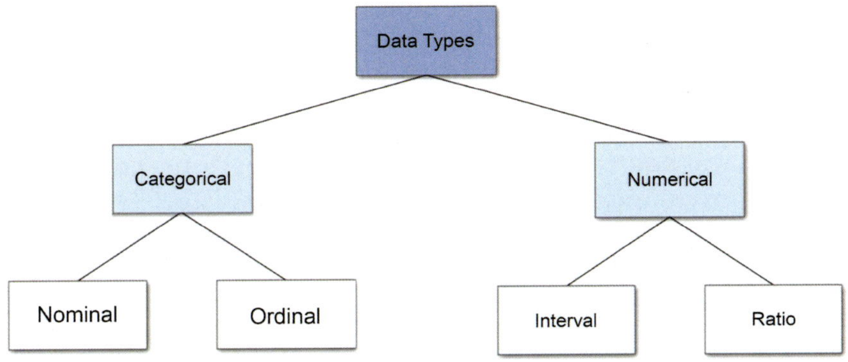

Figure 4.3. *Data types.*

Source: https://cdn-images-1.medium.com/max/1600/1*dvvxoZTdewLFs3RyZTJreA.png.

Data has meaning beyond its use in computing applications oriented toward data processing.

For example, in electronic component interconnection and network communication, the term data is often distinguished from "control information," "control bits," and similar terms to identify the main content of a transmission unit. Moreover, in science, the term data is used to describe a gathered body of facts. That is also the case in fields such as finance, marketing, demographics and health.

4.1.5. Database Approach to Data Management

Multiple applications with multiple users can share data thanks to database approaches to data storage. Databases are organized in ways that are significant to a company. There would be a link in the database between the suppliers and the geographic areas, for instance, if an organization kept records on the suppliers and the areas they service. Redundant data is lessened by databases.

The software that manages all database accesses is called a Database Management System (DBMS).

A DBMS gives users a logical perspective of the data. Users cannot see how this data is saved or retrieved. A database management system (DBMS) limits who can access which data and guarantees data consistency throughout the database.

4.1.6. Data Management and Use

Organizations now have a lot of data, so it's important to make sure that data quality is maintained by minimizing duplication and making sure that the most recent, accurate records are used. Modern data management involves many steps, such as extract, transform, and load (ETL) procedures for integrating data and data cleansing. Data for processing has come to be complemented by metadata, sometimes referred to as "data about data," that helps administrators and users understand database and other data.

Combining structured and unstructured data into analytics has become valuable as businesses look to profit from this knowledge. Systems for these kinds of analytics are designed to process data streams for instantaneous use in operations and to handle incoming data consumed at high ingestion rates, as they increasingly aim for real-time performance.

The concept of a database for transactions and operations has evolved over time to include databases for reporting and predictive data analytics. One prominent example is the data warehouse, which is designed to handle operational queries from business analysts and executives. Data mining techniques have developed as a result of an increasing focus on identifying patterns and forecasting business outcomes.

4.2. DATA MODELING AND DATABASE CHARACTERISTICS

Data modeling is the act of developing a data model that will be used for storing information in a database. This model serves as a visual representation of the data.

- Data objects;
- The associations between different data objects;
- The rules.

In addition to enforcing government policies, business rules, and regulatory compliances on the data, data modeling aids in the visual representation of data. Data models guarantee the quality of the data while guaranteeing consistency in naming conventions, default values, semantics, and security.

Rather than focusing on the operations that must be done on the data, data models highlight what data is required and how it should be arranged. A data model aids in the development of a conceptual model and establishes the relationships between data items, much like an architect's building plan.

4.2.1. Characteristics and Benefits of a Database

The database approach is different from the file-based system or approach in a number of ways. The advantages (and features) of the database system are covered in this section.

4.2.1.1. Self-describing Nature of a Database System

The term "self-describing" refers to a database system that includes metadata, or definitions and descriptions of the data and relationships between tables in the database, in addition to the database itself. The DBMS program uses this data, as do database users when necessary. A database system differs greatly from a traditional file-based system in that it separates data and information about the data, with the data definition being a part of the application programs.

4.2.1.2. Insulation between Program and Data

If a user wishes to modify a file's structure, it may be necessary to modify all the programs that access that file in a file-based system because the application programs define the structure of the data files.

However, the data structure is kept in the system catalogue rather than the programs when using the database approach. Thus, all it takes to alter a file's structure is a single change. Program-data independence is another term for this barrier that separates the programs from the data.

4.2.1.3. Support for Multiple Views of Data

Multiple data views can be supported by a database. A view is a portion of the database that has been defined and reserved for specific system users. Different users of the system may perceive it in different ways. Only the information that a user or group of users find interesting may be included in each view.

4.2.1.4. Sharing of Data and Multiuser System

The database systems in use today are made to support numerous users. In other words, they facilitate simultaneous access to the same database by numerous users. Concurrency control strategies are the features that allow for this kind of access. These tactics guarantee the accuracy of the data accessed and the preservation of data integrity.

Compared to older multiuser database systems that only allowed one user at a time, the design of contemporary databases is far more user-friendly.

4.2.1.5. Control of Data Redundancy

Every data item in the database approach should ideally be kept in a single location within the database. Data redundancy may still be necessary in some circumstances to enhance system performance, but it is managed by application programming and is minimized by introducing the least amount of redundancy feasible during database design.

4.2.1.6. Data Sharing

There are numerous benefits to an organization's data being integrated into a database system. Initially, it permits sharing of data between staff members and other system users. Second, it allows users to produce more information than they could have without the integration out of a given amount of data.

4.2.1.7. Enforcement of Integrity Constraints

In order to guarantee that users enter accurate data and preserve data integrity, database management systems need to have the capacity to define and enforce certain restrictions. A database constraint is a limitation or guideline that specifies what can be added to or changed in a table, such as the format required for a postal code or the addition of a legitimate city in the City field. Constraints on databases come in various forms. For example, data type establishes what kind of data is allowed in a field—numbers only, for example. The primary key and other data uniqueness measures make sure that no duplicate entries are made. Limitations may be basic (found in fields) or intricate (found in programming).

4.2.1.8. Restriction of Unauthorized Access

Different users within a database system will possess varying levels of access privileges. As an illustration, one user may only have read-only access (i.e., one person may have read-only access (that is, the capacity to read a file but not edit it), while another person may have read-write access (that is, the capacity to read and edit a file). This is why a security subsystem should be included in a database management system in order to establish and manage various user account kinds and prevent unwanted access.

4.2.1.9. Data Independence

The ability to have independent data is another benefit of a database management system. Put differently, the application programs and the descriptions of the system data, or data describing data, or metadata, are kept apart. This is made possible by the fact that the database management system handles data structure modifications rather than having the program itself do so.

4.2.1.10. Transaction Processing

Concurrency control subsystems are an essential component of a database management system. This feature makes sure that even if multiple users update the same piece of information, the data is valid and consistent throughout the transaction processing process.

4.2.1.11. Provision for Multiple Views of Data

A DBMS by definition allows multiple users to access its database at the same time or separately. Users need not care about the location and method of storing the data they access.

4.2.1.12. Backup and Recovery Facilities

You can prevent data loss by using backup and recovery techniques. The database system offers a different procedure for data recovery and backup than a network backup. The only way to recover a database in the event of a hard drive failure that prevents access to the database stored on the hard drive is via a backup (Figure 4.4).

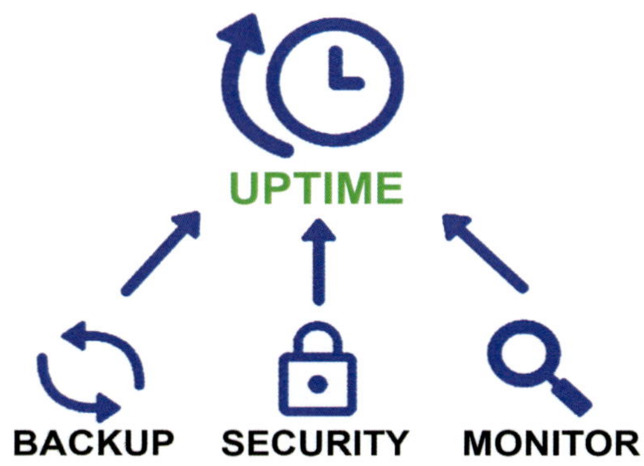

Figure 4.4. *Backup and recovery facilities.*

Source: https://infotelsystems.com/wp-content/uploads/Up-Time-Graphic.png.

The recovery subsystem is in charge of ensuring that the database is returned to its initial state in the event that a computer system malfunctions in the middle of an intricate update procedure. These are a database management system's two additional advantages.

4.2.2. Types of Database Models

There are many kinds of data models. Some of the most common ones include:

- Hierarchical database model;
- Relational model;
- Network model;
- Object-oriented database model;
- Entity-relationship model;
- Document model;
- Entity-attribute-value model;
- Star schema;
- The object-relational model, which combines the two that make up its name.

Depending on a number of variables, you can use any one of these to describe a database. The most important thing is to find out if the database management system you're using supports a specific model. Though some do support multiple models, the majority of database management systems are designed with a specific data model in mind and demand that their users adhere to it.

Furthermore, various models are applicable at different phases of the database design process. The most effective way to map out relationships between data in a way that people can understand is through high-level conceptual data models. Conversely, record-based logical models more closely mimic the ways in which the data is kept on the server.

When choosing a data model, you should also consider how well a given model fits your database's strengths, be they speed, cost-effectiveness, usability, or some other factor. Let us examine some of the most widely used database models in more detail.

4.2.2.1. Relational Model

The most popular model, the relational model, groups data into tables, or relations, which are made up of rows and columns. An attribute of the entity in question, such as the price, zip code, or birthdate, is listed in each column. A relation's attributes collectively are referred to as its domain. When an attribute or set of attributes is selected to serve as a primary key that can be referenced in other tables, it is referred to as a foreign key.

Every row, also referred to as a tuple, contains information about a single instance of the relevant entity, like a specific employee.

One-to-one, one-to-many, and many-to-many relationships are among the relationship types between those tables that are taken into consideration by the model. Here is one instance (Figure 4.5):

Student ID	First name	Last name
52-743965	Charles	Peters
48-209689	Anthony	Sondrup
14-204968	Rebecca	Phillips

ProviderID	Provider name
156-983	UnitedHealth
146-823	Blue Shield
447-784	Carefirst Inc.

Student ID	ProviderID	Type of plan	Start date
52-743965	156-983	HSA	04/01/2016
48-209689	146-823	HMO	12/01/2015
14-204968	447-784	HSA	03/14/2016

Figure 4.5. *Relational model.*

Source: https://d2slcw3kip6qmk.cloudfront.net/marketing/pages/chart/seo/database/discovery/relational-model.svg.

Tables in the database can be normalized, or made to adhere to rules for normalization, which gives the database scalability, flexibility, and adaptability. Each piece of data is atomic, or divided into the smallest feasible pieces, after it has been normalized.

Structured Query Language is commonly used to write relational databases (SQL). "It was E.F. Codd who introduced the model in 1970."

4.2.2.2. Hierarchical Model

Data is arranged using the hierarchical model into a structure resembling a tree, with a single parent or root for each record. Records that are siblings are arranged in a specific order. That arrangement serves as the database's physical storage order. For describing many relationships in the real world, this model works well (Figure 4.6).

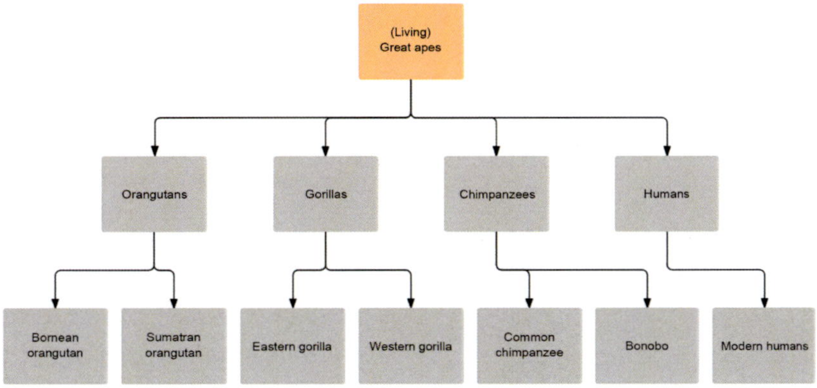

Figure 4.6. *Hierarchical model.*

Source: https://d2slcw3kip6qmk.cloudfront.net/marketing/pages/chart/seo/database/discovery/hierarchical-model.svg.

Due to certain operational inefficiencies, IBM's Information Management Systems, which were primarily used in the 1960s and 1970s, are no longer commonly found.

4.2.2.3. Network Model

By permitting many-to-many relationships between linked records, which implies multiple parent records, the network model expands upon the hierarchical model. The model is built using sets of related records, drawing on the principles of mathematical set theory.

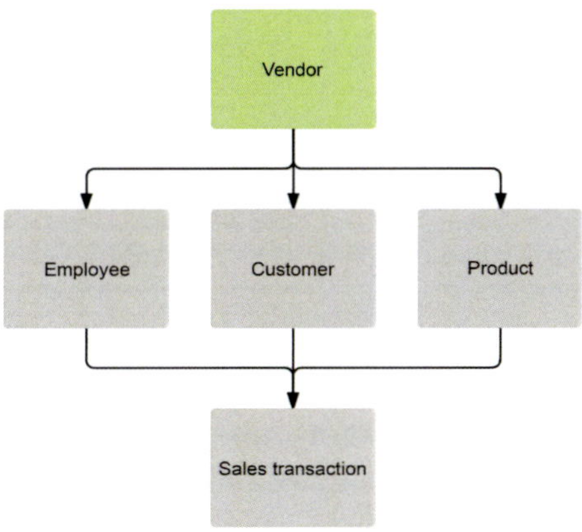

Figure 4.7. *Network model.*

Source: https://d2slcw3kip6qmk.cloudfront.net/marketing/pages/chart/seo/database/discovery/network-model.svg.

One owner or parent record and one or more member or child records make up each set. This model allows for the representation of complex relationships because a record can be a member or a child in multiple sets. The Conference on Data Systems Languages (CODASYL) officially defined it, and that is when it became most popular in the 1970s (Figure 4.7).

4.2.2.4. Object-oriented Database Model

A database is described in this model as a group of objects, or reusable software components, with related features and operations. Object-oriented databases come in various varieties: Images and other types of media that are not compatible with relational database storage are included in multimedia databases. Anything can link to anything else using a hypertext database. It's not the best option for numerical analysis, but it works well for organizing a large amount of dissimilar data.

Since it includes tables but isn't restricted to them, the object-oriented database model is the most well-known post-relational database model. Hybrid database models are another name for these types of models (Figure 4.8).

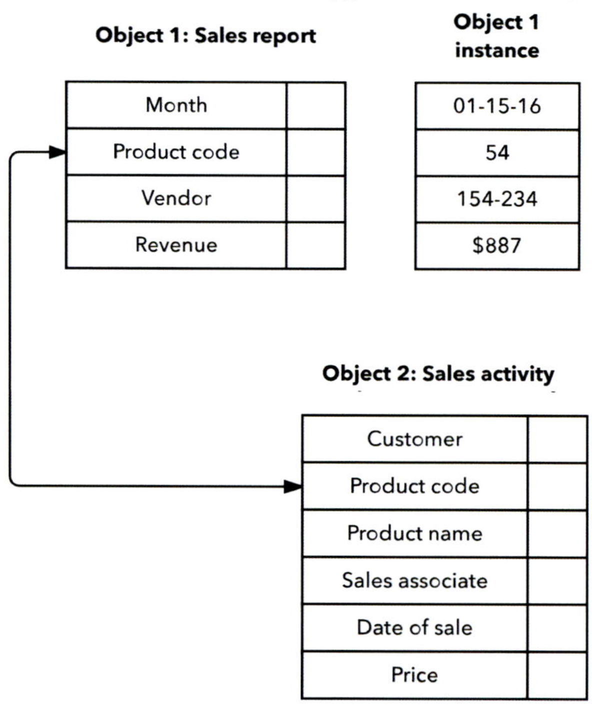

Figure 4.8. *Object-oriented database model.*

Source: https://d2slcw3kip6qmk.cloudfront.net/marketing/pages/chart/seo/database/discovery/object-oriented-model.svg.

4.2.2.5. Object-relational Model

This hybrid database model blends some of the more sophisticated features of the object-oriented database model with the ease of use of the relational model. Essentially, it lets designers add elements to the well-known table structure. Vendor languages, SQL3, ODBC, JDBC, and proprietary call interfaces are examples of languages and call interfaces that are extensions of those utilized by the relational model.

4.2.2.6. Entity-relationship Model

Although it isn't as closely related to the actual structure of the database, this model, like the network model, captures the relationships between real-world entities. Rather, it's frequently employed for conceptual database design. The people, places, and objects that are the subject of data points are referred to as entities in this context.

These entities are composed of specific attributes that collectively form their domain. Additionally mapped are the cardinality, or relationships between entities (Figure 4.9).

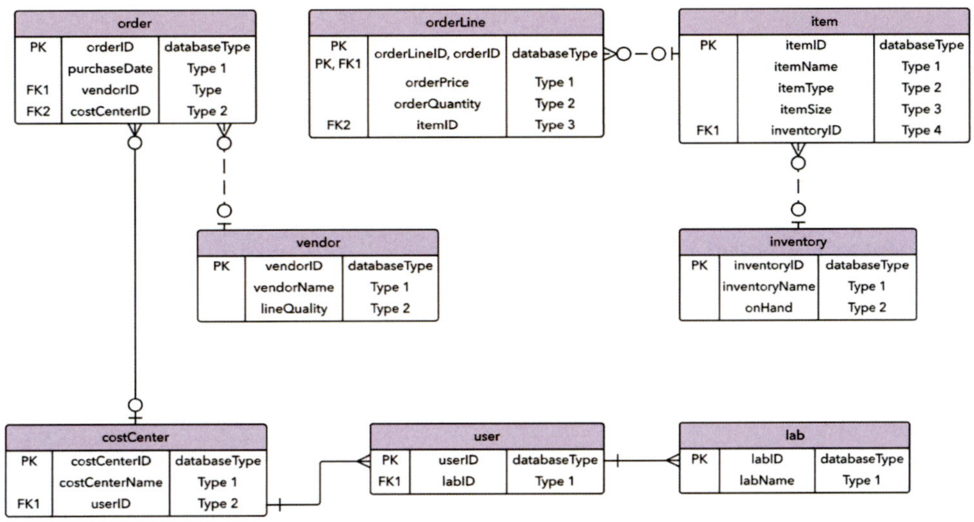

Figure 4.9. *Entity-relationship model.*

Source: https://d2slcw3kip6qmk.cloudfront.net/marketing/pages/chart/seo/database/discovery/er-diagram.svg.

The star schema, in which a central fact table links to multiple dimensional tables, is a popular variation of the ER diagram.

4.2.2.7. Other Database Models

A variety of other database models have been or are still used today.

4.2.2.7.1. Inverted File Model

The purpose of a database constructed with an inverted file structure is to enable quick full text searches. Under this model, the location of the related files is indicated by the values of a lookup table's keys, which are used to index the data content. For example, this structure can offer almost real-time reporting in analytics and big data. Software AG's ADABAS database management system has been using this model since 1970, and it is still supported today.

4.2.2.7.2. Flat Model

The earliest and most basic data model is called the flat model. All of the data is merely listed in a single table with rows and columns. This model is inefficient for all but the smallest data sets because the computer must read the entire flat file into memory in order to access or manipulate the data.

4.2.2.7.3. Multidimensional Model

The purpose of this relational model variation is to enable better analytical processing. Although the relational model is intended for online analytical processing (OLAP), it is optimized for online transaction processing (OLTP).

The dimensions that the database is tracking are detailed in each cell of a dimensional database. As opposed to two-dimensional tables, it looks like a collection of cubes.

4.2.2.7.4. Semi-structured Model

In this model, the data itself is embedded with the structural data that is typically found in the database schema. The line separating data and schema in this case is, at best, hazy. Systems that we treat as databases but are unable to constrain with a schema, like some Web-based data sources, can be described by this model. It's also helpful for explaining how different databases interact with one another when they don't follow the same schema.

4.2.2.7.5. Context Model

When necessary, this model can integrate components from other database models. It assembles components from network, Semi-structured, and object-oriented models. All of the data points in this model are divided according to whether they represent an association or an entity. According to this model, an association is something that only exists in connection to another thing, whereas an entity is anything that exists on its own.

The associative model structures the data into two sets:

- A set of items, each with a unique identifier, a name, and a type;
- A collection of links, every one having its own unique identifier along with the source, verb, and target's unique identifiers. The three identifiers can all point to either an item or a link, and the stored fact is related to the source.

Other, less common database models include:

- Semantic model, which includes information about how the stored data relates to the real world;
- XML database, which allows data to be specified and even stored in XML format;
- Named graph;
- Triplestore.

4.2.2.7.5. NoSQL Database Models

In addition to the object database model, other non-SQL models have emerged in contrast to the relational model:

The graph database model, which is even more flexible than a network model, allowing any node to connect with any other.

The multivalue model, which breaks from the relational model by allowing attributes to contain a list of data rather than a single data point.

The document model, which is designed for storing and managing documents or semi-structured data, rather than atomic data.

4.2.2.8. Databases on the Web

A database of some sort is used by the majority of websites to arrange and display data for users. When a user utilizes these websites' search features, their search terms are translated into queries that a database server can handle. Middleware typically serves as the link between the database and web server. Due to their widespread use, databases can be found in practically every industry, from microtargeting a specific voter group during a political campaign to online shopping. Airlines and automakers are among the industries that have established their own standards for database design.

4.3. RELATIONAL DATABASE MANAGEMENT SYSTEMS (RDBMS)

A relational database management system (RDBMS) is a database engine/system based on the relational model specified by Edgar F. Codd—the father of modern relational database design—in 1970. Most modern commercial and open-source database applications are relational in nature. The most important relational database features include an ability to use tables for data storage while maintaining and enforcing certain data relationships (Figure 4.10).

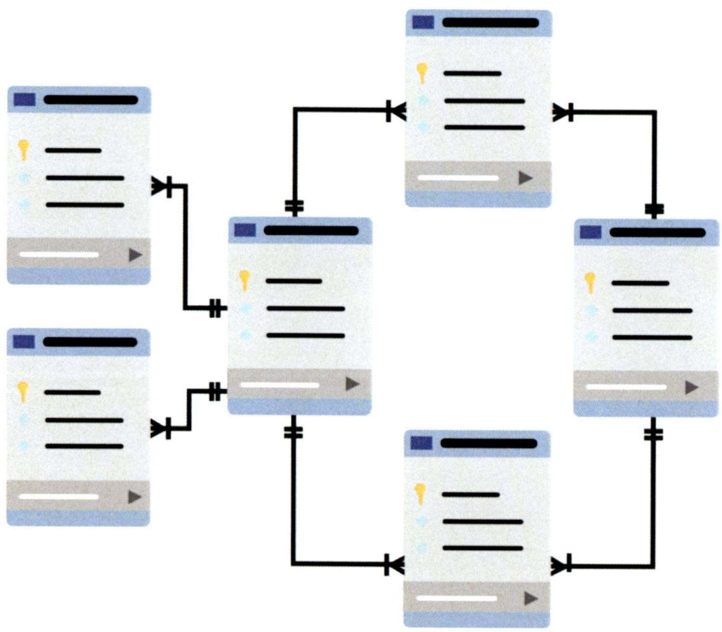

Figure 4.10. *Relational database management systems (RDBMs).*

Source: https://png2.kisspng.com/20180330/rwe/kisspng-relational-database-management-system-database-sch-database-5abe2d1b472559.1726668015224128272914.png.

In 1970, Edgar F. Codd, a British computer scientist with IBM, published "A Relational Model of Data for Large Shared Data Banks." At the time, the renowned paper attracted little interest, and few understood how Codd's groundbreaking work would define the basic rules for relational data storage, which can be simplified as: Data must be stored and presented as relations, i.e., tables that have relationships with each other, e.g., primary/foreign keys. To manipulate the data stored in tables, a system should provide relational operators – code that enables the relationship to be tested between two entities. A good example is the WHERE clause of a SELECT statement, i.e., the SQL statement SELECT * FROM CUSTOMER_MASTER WHERE CUSTOMER_SURNAME = 'Smith' will query the CUSTOMER_MASTER table and return all customers with a surname of Smith.

Codd later published another paper that outlined the 12 rules that all databases must follow to qualify as relational. Many modern database systems do not follow all 12 rules, but these systems are considered relational because they conform to at least two of the 12 rules.

Most modern commercial and open-source database systems are relational in nature and include well-known applications, e.g., Oracle DB (Oracle Corporation); SQL Server (Microsoft) and MySQL and Postgres (open source).

4.3.1. Functions of Relational Database Management Systems

It is difficult to separate the fundamental relational database from the components of the relational database management system that underpin it in real-world operations.

The most fundamental RDBMS operations are those that deal with the create, read, update, and delete (CRUD) operations. They serve as the cornerstone of a system that is well-organized and encourages the consistent handling of data.

Typically, the RDBMS offers metadata collections and data dictionaries that are helpful for handling data. These provide well-defined data structures and relationships programmatically. One common RDBMS capability is data storage management, which has come to be defined by data objects, which can be anything from stored procedures to binary large object (blob) strings. These kinds of data objects can be handled in a variety of ways across different RDBMSs and expand the capabilities of basic relational database operations.

SQL is the most widely used method for RDBMS data access. Statements in the Data Definition Language (DDL) and Data Manipulation Language (DML) make up its primary linguistic components. For development projects that combine the use of SQL with popular programming languages like Java, .NET, and COBOL (Common Business-Oriented Language), extensions are available.

RDBMSs employ sophisticated algorithms to enable numerous users to access the database concurrently while preserving data integrity. An additional overlay service that the RDBMS offers for the basic database as it is used in enterprise settings is security management, which enforces policy-based access.

Database administrators (DBAs) are responsible for overseeing and managing database activity; RDBMSs help them in their work. Tools facilitate the automation of database backup and data loading. Log files that monitor system performance based on predetermined operational parameters are managed by RDBMSs. This makes it possible to measure query performance in particular, as well as database capacity and usage. RDBMSs give DBAs access to graphical interfaces that make database activity easier to see.

Relational technology's ACID compliance is a feature that has shown to be crucial in enterprise computing, though it is not exclusive to RDBMSs. These qualities—

which stand for atomicity, consistency, isolation, and durability—have made RDBMSs especially well-suited for managing commercial transactions.

Key applications like online retailing, travel reservation systems, and banking ledgers rely heavily on relational database management systems. As RDBMSs have developed, they have attained ever-higher degrees of query optimization and have also emerged as essential components of business reporting, analytics, and data warehousing applications. RDBMSs are the backbone of the majority of master data management (MDM) systems and are essential to the operation of many enterprise applications.

4.3.2. RDBMS Product History

As word of the relational data model spread in the early 1970s, numerous competing relational database management systems emerged. E. F. Codd, an IBM researcher, initially theorized this and related techniques, putting forth a logical organization for databases as opposed to the physical organization that was prevalent at the time.

At a time when such equipment could be unaffordable for businesses, Codd's work saved file space on storage disk drives through the concept of data normalization.

What could be referred to as the RDBMS era was preceded by file systems and database management systems. These systems were mostly powered by mainframe computers. Even though RDBMSs were also used on mainframes (IBM's DB2 is a notable example), UNIX midrange computer deployments were largely responsible for their rise to prominence in the enterprise. The distributed architecture of client/server computing, which linked groups of standalone PCs to file and database servers, relied heavily on the RDBMS.

Client/server computing led to the emergence of numerous RDBMSs. Oracle, Ingres, Informix, Sybase, Unify, Progress, and other companies were among the rivals. Three RDBMSs eventually came to rule commercial implementations. Despite persistent challenges from rival technologies, Oracle, IBM's DB2, and Microsoft's SQL Server—which was built on a design initially licensed from Sybase—found significant favor throughout the client/server computing era.

With the end of the 20th century came the rise in popularity of less expensive, open-source RDBMSs, especially for web applications. PostgreSQL and MySQL were among these systems.

RDBMSs eventually faced competition from NoSQL systems as distributed computing gained traction and cloud architecture was used more frequently.

These systems were sometimes created specifically for large-scale cloud distribution and high scalability, sacrificing full consistency in the SQL sense in favor of what is known as eventual consistency of data.

However, RDBMSs must exist in some capacity even in the most varied and intricate cloud systems due to the requirement for some level of guaranteed data consistency. RDBMS versions have also undergone substantial restructuring in order to support cloud replication and parallelization.

4.3.3. Popular Relational Database Management Systems

The RDBMS you are using will determine how slightly the SQL syntax is different. The following is a synopsis of well-known RDBMSs:

4.3.3.1. SQLite

A well-known open source SQL database is called SQLite. A whole database can be kept in one file. Not needing to connect your database to a server, all of the data can be stored locally, which is one of the biggest benefits this offers.

SQLite is a commonly used database option for cellphones, PDAs, MP3 players, set-top boxes, and various other electronic gadgets. The SQL courses available on Codecademy utilize SQLite in their teachings (Figure 4.11).

Figure 4.11. *SQLite.*

Source: https://www.mathworks.com/matlabcentral/mlc-downloads/downloads/submissions/58433/versions/4/screenshot.jpg.

4.3.3.2. MySQL

The most widely used open source SQL database is MySQL. It is frequently accessed using PHP and is generally used for developing web applications.

Some of the key benefits of MySQL include its user-friendly interface, cost-effectiveness, long-standing reputation (established in 1995), and robust community support for troubleshooting and guidance.

Among the drawbacks are that it lacks some sophisticated features that developers might be accustomed to, has a history of experiencing poor performance when scaling, and open source development has slowed down since Oracle acquired MySQL (Figure 4.12).

Figure 4.12. *MySQL.*

Source: http://sqlbackupandftp.com/blog/wp-content/uploads/2015/01/mysql-logo_2800x2800_pixels1.png.

4.3.3.3. PostgreSQL

A free and open-source SQL database, PostgreSQL is not governed by any business. Development of web applications is the usual use for it.

Numerous benefits of MySQL are also present in PostgreSQL. It features an extensive developer community, is affordable, dependable, and simple to use. Additionally, it offers a few more features like support for foreign keys without the need for complicated configuration.

PostgreSQL's primary drawback is its slower performance in comparison to other databases, like MySQL. In addition, PostgreSQL instances are harder to find hosts or service providers that offer managed versions of the database because it is not as widely used as MySQL.

4.3.3.4. Oracle DB

The Oracle Database is owned by Oracle Corporation, and its source code is not publicly available.

The Oracle DB system is well-suited for large-scale applications, with a particular focus on the banking industry. Many of the leading banks worldwide rely on Oracle applications due to their robust technology and wide range of pre-integrated business applications, which include specialized features designed specifically for banking operations. The primary drawback of utilizing Oracle is that, unlike its open source rivals, it is not available for free and can be highly costly (Figure 4.13).

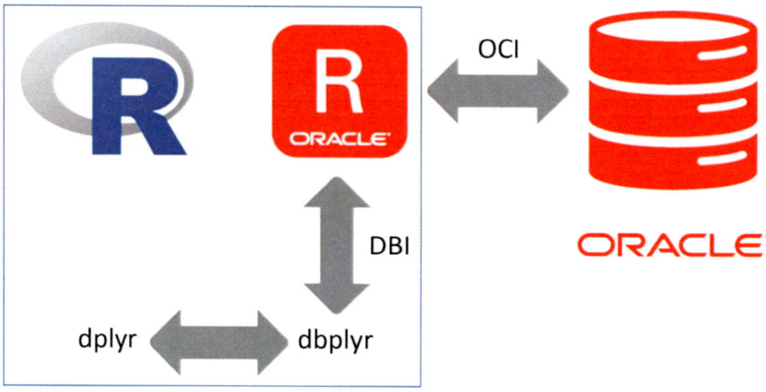

Figure 4.13. *Oracle DB.*

Source: https://i1.wp.com/technology.amis.nl/wp-content/uploads/2017/08/oracloe-and-r-sized.png?fit=1404%2C672&ssl=1.

4.3.3.5. SQL Server

Microsoft owns SQL Server. Like Oracle DB, the code is close sourced. Most large enterprise applications primarily rely on SQL Server. The notable distinction between Oracle and SQL Server is that SQL Server is limited to the Windows Operating System. Microsoft provides an Express version that is free of cost at first, but as your application grows, it can become quite costly.

4.3.4. Benefits of Relational Databases

An excellent option for designing a scalable and adaptable data storage system that facilitates the management of large amounts of data is the relational database.

- **Manageability:** To begin with, an RDB is simple to work with. It is possible to update one data table without affecting the others. Additionally, you can grant one group access to some data sets while restricting their access to others, such as private employee data.
- **Flexibility:** Updating your data is now easier than ever with the ability to make changes only once. No more tedious task of altering multiple files individually. Extending your database is a simple process as well. As your records increase, a relational database can easily scale up to accommodate your growing data.
- **Avoid Errors:** In a relational database, errors are non-existent since they can be readily verified by cross-referencing the data with other sections of the records.

Additionally, the issue of outdated data obscuring the picture is eliminated because all information is kept in one location.

4.3.5. Challenges of Relational Databases

- **Scalability:** Due to the fact that single servers are used to build relational databases. This implies that you will require more costly hardware with greater power, storage, and memory in order to scale.
- **Performance:** More complex relationships result from the rapid growth of data in terms of volume, velocity, variety, and complexity. Performance can be slowed down by relational databases' propensity to struggle to keep up.
- **Relationships:** Since relationships between elements are not actually stored by relational databases, understanding the connections between your data depends on other joins.

4.4. BIG DATA

Large or complex data sets for which conventional data processing tools are insufficient are referred to as "big data." Big Data is essentially made up of data creation, analysis, sharing, storage capacity, analysis, visualization, querying, privacy, and data capture.

4.4.1. Definition

- Big Data is a collection of sizable datasets that are too big to handle with conventional processing methods. Big data is now more than just data; it's an entire field with its own set of tools, methods, and frameworks.
- The term "big data" refers to the volume of organized and unstructured data that is used in regular business settings. What matters is how organizations use these and the data that's relevant.
- Big data facilitates the analysis of complex ideas for more informed choices and strategic actions made for the organization's growth.

4.4.2. The Evolution of Big Data

Even though the phrase "big data" is relatively new these days, the process of compiling and archiving vast amounts of data for later analysis is not. When industry analyst Doug Laney defined big data as falling into three categories in the early 2000s, the concept was born.

- **Volume:** Businesses, social media, sensor or machine-to-machine data, and business transactions are just a few of the relevant sources from which organizations gather data. Storage used to be a major problem, but as new technologies like Hadoop have developed, the load has decreased.
- **Velocity**: Data streams have improved on time and at a velocity that is unmatched. The need to handle massive amounts of data in real-time operations is being driven by RFID tags, sensors, and smart metering.
- **Variety**: Data can be found in many different forms, including unstructured text documents, email, video, audio, stock ticker data, financial transactions, and structured, numerical data stored in traditional databases. In SAS, we take into account two more big data dimensions.

4.4.3. The Categories Which Come Under Big Data

The data generated by different devices and their applications is what big data uses. Listed below are a few of the disciplines that fall under the big data umbrella.

- **Black Box Data:** It is integrated by flight crafts, which hold a lot of data, including crew member conversations and any other communications (such as orders or alert messages) sent by the technical grounds duty staff.

- **Social Media Data:** Millions of people worldwide post information and opinions on social networking sites like Facebook and Twitter.
- **Stock Exchange Data:** It contains data (all specifics of in- and out-of-business transactions) regarding the decisions made by customers regarding the "buyer" and "seller" in terms of share between various companies.
- **Power Grid Data:** The data stored in the power grid primarily contains the information used by a specific node with respect to base stations.
- **Transport Data:** It contains information on the model, capacity, availability, and distance of vehicles from a variety of transportation sectors.
- **Search Engine Data:** Numerous data sets are retrieved by search engines from various database sources.

4.4.4. Big Data for the Enterprise

Businesses of all sizes can save costs, increase revenue, and accomplish a host of other goals by utilizing big data databases.

- **Build New Applications:** With the help of big data, a business may be able to instantly repackage billions of real-time data points about its resources, customers, and products in order to improve customer service or resource efficiency. For instance, a sizable US city is utilizing MongoDB to gather and analyze geospatial data in real-time from more than thirty departments in order to reduce crime and enhance municipal services.
- **Improve the Effectiveness and Lower the Cost of Existing Applications:** Big data technologies can provide a standard solution running on commodity hardware in place of highly customized, costly legacy systems. Furthermore, compared to proprietary technologies, big data technologies can be implemented far more affordably because many of them are open source. For instance, a Tier 1 bank significantly decreased the licensing and hardware expenses linked to the proprietary relational database it formerly operated by moving its reference data management application to MongoDB. This also improved the application's compliance with regulatory standards.
- **Realize New Sources of Competitive Advantage:** Businesses that use big data can respond more quickly to changes than their rivals by acting more nimbly. For instance, one of the biggest providers of Human Capital Management (HCM) solutions was able to quickly develop mobile applications that combined data from numerous unrelated sources thanks to MongoDB.
- **Increase Customer Loyalty:** Businesses and other organizations are better able to react to customer demand quickly and accurately when there is greater data sharing within the organization and faster updates. For instance, MetLife, one of the top 5 worldwide insurance companies, used MongoDB to quickly compile client data from more than 70 sources and present it in a single, quickly updated view.

4.4.5. The Importance of Big Data

The importance of big data is how you utilize the data which you own. Data can be fetched from any source and analyze it to solve that enable us in terms of

1. Cost reductions;
2. Time reductions;
3. New product development and optimized offerings; and
4. Smart decision making.

Combination of big data with high-powered analytics, you can have great impact on your business strategy such as:

- Finding the root cause of failures, issues and defects in real time operations.
- Generating coupons at the point of sale seeing the customer's habit of buying goods.
- Recalculating entire risk portfolios in just minutes.
- Detecting fraudulent behavior before it affects and risks your organization.

4.4.5.1. Banking

With vast volumes of data coming in from various sources, banks need to come up with novel and creative ways to handle big data. It's critical to assess client needs, deliver services in accordance with those needs, reduce risk and fraud, and uphold regulatory compliance. Financial institutions must work with big data to take advanced analytics one step further.

4.4.5.2. Government

Government organizations have made significant improvised strides in managing utilities, operating agencies, addressing traffic congestion, and reducing the impact of crime when they apply analytics to their big data. In addition to its benefits in Big Data, governments also deal with privacy and transparency concerns.

4.4.5.3. Education

Teachers' perspectives on big data have a big influence on curriculums, students, and school systems. They can identify students who are at risk, guarantee the progress of the students, and establish a makeshift system for evaluating and assisting principals and teachers in their instruction by analyzing large data.

4.4.5.4. Health Care

In terms of patient records related to healthcare. Plans for treatment details about prescription drugs, etc. everything must be completed precisely, promptly, and with sufficient transparency in some areas to comply with strict industry regulations. Good health care is the outcome of effective management, which also reveals untapped opportunities to enhance patient care.

4.4.5.5. Manufacturing

In today's fiercely competitive market, manufacturers can enhance their output and quality while reducing waste, as processes are considered critical components. Many manufacturers are developing analytics so they can make more nimble business decisions and solve problems more quickly.

4.4.5.6. Retail

The largest challenge facing the retail sector is maintaining customer relationships, which is best handled by managing big data. Retailers need to come up with original marketing concepts to draw in customers, figure out the best way to handle transactions, and use improvised strategies to apply creative Big Data ideas to grow their business.

4.4.6. Utilizing Big Data in Businesses

The conversion of big data into information nuggets makes things very simple for the majority of business enterprises. We now know what their customers want, which products are selling quickly, what end users expect from customer service, how to expedite the marketing process, how to cut costs, and how to create economies of scale in a highly effective way. Big Data is therefore in high demand in the IT industry since it offers enormous benefits to businesses.

1. **Big Data Technologies:**
   - Precise examination conducted using big data that facilitates cost savings, lowers risks associated with business operations, and increases and optimizes operational efficiencies.
   - To fully benefit from big data, infrastructure must be able to handle massive amounts of both structured and unstructured data in real time, while also guaranteeing data security and privacy.
   - There are numerous technologies on the market from various suppliers, such as Microsoft, IBM, Amazon, and so forth in order to handle big data. In order to master a specific technology, one must study its classes, which include the following areas.
2. **Operational Big Data:**
   - It comprises programs like MongoDB, which offers functionalities for real-time and interactive workloads where data is typically collected and saved.
   - NoSQL big data systems are made to take advantage of new cloud computing architectures, allowing for the reasonable and effective execution of large-scale computations. Thus, this makes managing big data workloads much simpler, more affordable, and quicker to implement.
3. **Analytical Big Data:**
   - Its systems include MapReduce, which offers analytical capabilities for collective and complex analysis, and Massively Parallel Processing database systems.
   - Based on a system called MapReduce, which can be scaled up from single servers to thousands of high-end and low-end machines, MapReduce offers a new technique for data analysis that showcases the capabilities offered by SQL.

4.4.7. Selecting a Big Data Technology: Operational Versus Analytical

Two types of technology dominate the Big Data landscape: those that offer analytical capabilities for complex, retrospective analysis that may touch all or most of the data, and those that offer operational capabilities for real-time, interactive workloads where data is primarily captured and stored. These technological classes work well together and are commonly used in tandem.

Big Data operational and analytical workloads present conflicting requirements, and systems have developed to meet each of these demands independently and in very different ways. The development of new technological architectures has been fueled by each. Operational systems, like NoSQL databases, are designed to handle large numbers of concurrent requests with minimal latency for responses based on extremely strict access controls. Conversely, analytical systems prioritize high throughput; queries in these systems can be extremely complex and touch most, if not all, of the system's data at once. Both systems typically manage tens or hundreds of terabytes of data across billions of records across numerous servers running in a cluster.

4.4.7.1. Operational Big Data

In the realm of operational Big Data tasks, NoSQL Big Data systems like document databases have become popular for a wide range of applications. Other specialized architectures, such as key-value stores, column family stores, and graph databases, are designed for more specific uses. NoSQL technologies were created to overcome the limitations of relational databases in today's computing world, offering faster performance and more cost-effective scalability.

Crucially, NoSQL Big Data systems are made to capitalize on the novel cloud computing architectures that have appeared in the last ten years, enabling the efficient and low-cost execution of massive computations. This results in far simpler management of operational Big Data workloads that can be implemented more quickly and affordably.

Most operational systems require real-time intelligence on active data in addition to user interactions.

For instance, in a multi-user game or financial application, users are presented with aggregates of user activities or instrument performance to guide their decisions. Some NoSQL systems can offer insights into patterns and trends using real-time data with minimal coding, eliminating the need for data scientists and extra infrastructure.

4.4.7.2. Analytical Big Data

Conversely, when it comes to handling Analytical Big Data workloads, MPP database systems and MapReduce are often utilized.

These technologies have emerged in response to the constraints of traditional relational databases which struggle to expand beyond the capacity of a single server. Additionally, MapReduce offers a fresh approach to data analysis that complements the functionalities offered by SQL.

Retrospective analytical workloads offer significant business value as applications become more popular and users produce larger amounts of data.

MapReduce has become the go-to solution for Big Data analytics when these workloads require algorithms that go beyond basic aggregation.

Certain NoSQL systems come with built-in MapReduce capabilities, which makes it possible to conduct analytics on live operational data. On the other hand, data from NoSQL systems can be transferred to analytical platforms like Hadoop for MapReduce (Table 4.1).

Table 4.1. *Overview of Operational Versus Analytical Systems*

	Operational	Analytical
Latency	1 ms – 100 ms	1 min – 100 min
Concurrency	1000 – 100,000	1 – 10
Access Pattern	Writes and Reads	Reads
Queries	Selective	Unselective
Data Scope	Operational	Retrospective
End User	Customer	Data Scientist
Technology	NoSQL	MapReduce, MPP Database

Source: https://www.ijltemas.in/DigitalLibrary/Vol.2Issue11/66-71.pdf.

4.4.8. Considerations for Decision Makers

Although some Big Data technologies are mature enough for mission-critical production use, the field is still in its early stages in some aspects. Consequently, the path ahead may not always be straightforward. When organizations are creating Big Data strategies, they should keep in mind several factors to consider when choosing technology partners, such as:

- Online Versus Offline Big Data;
- Software Licensing Models;
- Community;
- Developer Appeal;
- Agility;
- General Purpose Versus Niche Solutions.

4.4.8.1. Online Versus Offline Big Data

Big Data is available both offline and online. Data created, ingested, transformed, managed, and/or analyzed in real-time to support operational applications and their users is referred to as online big data. Big Data originated on the internet. For these applications to meet SLAs and user expectations for modern application performance, latency must be extremely low and availability must be high. This covers a wide range of applications, such as sophisticated CRM programs, real-time ad servers, analytics, social networking news feeds, and more. MongoDB and other NoSQL databases are a couple of examples of online Big Data databases. Applications that ingest, transform, manage, and/or analyze Big Data in a batch setting are referred to as offline big data. Usually, they don't produce any new data. Response times for these applications may be sluggish—up to hours or days—but this kind of use case is frequently acceptable. Given that they typically generate a static (Versus operational) output, like a dashboard or report, they can even momentarily go offline without affecting the final objective or outcome. Workloads based on Hadoop, contemporary data warehouses, extract, transform, load (ETL) applications, and business intelligence tools are a few examples of offline Big Data applications. When deciding which Big Data technologies to implement, organizations should take their intended use of the data into account. An operational data store like MongoDB is required for developers wishing to create apps that support operational use cases in real-time. Offline solutions like Hadoop can be a useful tool for people who need a place to carry out lengthy analyzes offline, possibly to support decision-making procedures. Businesses who are interested in both use cases have the option to pursue them concurrently, and they occasionally discover connections between offline and online Big Data technologies. MongoDB, for example, offers Hadoop integration.

4.4.8.2. Software License Model

There are three general types of licenses for Big Data software technologies:

- **Proprietary:** A software company owns and controls the software product. Licensees cannot access the source code. Typically, customers purchase a perpetual license for the product, which grants them unlimited use, along with yearly maintenance fees for software updates and support. Databases from Oracle, IBM, and Teradata are a few examples of this model.
- **Open-Source:** The source code and software product are both freely downloadable. Businesses make money off of software by charging for subscriptions and related goods that have extra features, like support services and management tools. This model is exemplified by MongoDB (by MongoDB, Inc.) and Hadoop (by companies other than Cloudera).
- **Cloud Service:** The service is provided over the public Internet and hosted in a cloud-based environment apart from the data centers of the customers. The most common form of business is metered (i.e., either subscription-based or pay-per-use. Amazon Elastic MapReduce and Google App Engine are two instances of this model.

The use of cloud-based solutions is restricted for many Fortune 1000 companies due to internal data privacy policies and regulations. Thus, the majority of Big Data projects are powered by on-premises technologies. The majority of the pioneers of Big Data are web companies that created robust hardware and software and made it open-sourced for the greater community. As a result, open-source software is typically utilized for Big Data projects.

4.4.8.3. Community

There is a chance to pick up knowledge from others in these early days of big data. Businesses should take into account the number of other projects that have similar goals and are utilizing the same technologies. Organizations should take into account the following to comprehend the adoption of a particular technology:

- The number of users;
- The prevalence of local, community-organized events;
- The health and activity of online forums such as Google Groups and StackOverflow;
- The availability of conferences, how frequently they occur and whether they are well-attended.

4.4.8.4. Developer Appeal

Talent in Big Data is in high demand. The best engineers and data scientists in the country frequently work for Google and Facebook, two organizations renowned for being magnets for the brightest brains and for exposing employees to cutting edge technology. Businesses need to provide something more than just cash in order to compete for this talent. By providing developers with challenging projects and utilizing popular technologies with active developer communities and promising futures, organizations can draw in top talent. Opting for user-friendly technologies that appeal to developers can also broaden the pool of potential candidates. Additionally, technologies that are attractive to developers can lead to more efficient teams that feel empowered by their tools, resulting in quicker time to market and decreased development expenses.

4.4.8.5. Agility

Big Data solutions that facilitate agility should be used by organizations. Technologies that clear the path and let teams concentrate on what they can do with their data rather than how to set up new infrastructure and apps will be beneficial to them. This will facilitate rapid iteration in response to shifting business requirements and the exploration of numerous avenues and hypotheses for obtaining value from the data.

In this context, agility comprises three primary components:

- **Ease of Use:** A technology that is user-friendly for developers, with a well-structured architecture and ample tools and resources, can facilitate quick initiation and value realization in Big Data projects. Conversely, technologies that are difficult to learn and have limited educational support will lengthen the project execution process.
- **Technological Flexibility:** When teams come up with new discoveries and adjust to internal and external demands, the product should make it reasonably simple to change requirements on the fly, including how data is modeled, which data is used, where data is pulled from, and how it is processed. Scalability and dynamic data models, or schemas, are desirable qualities to look for.
- **Licensing Freedom:** Teams can start using free community versions of open-source software quickly, which makes them easier to adopt. From a licensing perspective, they are typically easier to scale as well because teams can purchase additional licenses as needed. In contrast, proprietary software vendors frequently demand sizable upfront license purchases, which hinders teams' ability to grow both now and down the road.

4.4.8.6. General Purpose Versus Niche Solutions

Organizations are consistently striving to streamline their use of technologies in order to decrease complexity, enhance proficiency in preferred tools, and optimize vendor relationships. It is important for organizations to evaluate whether integrating a Big Data technology will support one specific objective or multiple objectives. General-purpose technologies allow for the distribution of expertise, infrastructure, skills, integrations, and other investments from the initial project across multiple projects. While niche technologies may be suitable for individual projects, a more universal tool may be more beneficial for the organization overall.

4.4.9. Barriers

Barriers that are imposed on big data are as follows:

- Capture data;
- Storage Capacity;
- Searching;
- Sharing;
- Transfer;
- Analysis;
- Presentation.

CASE STUDY

BIG DATA CASE STUDY IBM

International Business Machine (IBM) is an American company headquartered in New York. IBM is listed at # 43 in Forbes list with a Market Capitalization of $162.4 billion as of May 2017. The company's operation is spread across 170 countries and the largest employer with around 414,400 employees.

IBM has a sale of around $79.9 billion and a profit of $11.9 billion. In 2017, IBM holds most patents generated by the business for 24 consecutive years.

IBM is the biggest vendor for Big Data-related products and services. IBM Big Data solutions provide features such as store data, manage data and analyze data.

There are numerous sources from where this data comes and accessible to all users, Business Analysts, Data Scientist, etc. DB2, Informix, and InfoSphere are popular database platforms by IBM which supports Big Data Analytics. There are also famous analytics applications by IBM such as Cognos and SPSS.

IBM's Big Data Solutions are as below:

1. **Hadoop System:** It is a storage platform that stores structured and unstructured data. It is designed to process a large volume of data to gain business insights.
2. **Stream Computing:** Stream Computing enables organizations to perform in-motion analytics including the Internet of Things, real-time data processing, and analytics
3. **Federated discovery and Navigation:** Federated discovery and navigation software help organizations to analyze and access information across the enterprise. IBM provides below listed Big Data products which will help to capture, analyze, and manage any structured and unstructured data.
4. **IBM® BigInsights™ for Apache™ Hadoop®:** It enables organizations to analyze a huge volume of data quickly and in a simple manner.
5. **IBM BigInsights on Cloud:** It provides Hadoop as a service through the IBM SoftLayer cloud infrastructure.
6. **IBM** Streams: For critical Internet of Things applications, it helps organizations to capture and analyze data in motion.

CLASS ACTIVITY

DATABASE SYSTEMS VERSUS BIG DATA DEBATE

Introduction

Provide an overview of database systems and big data, explaining their definitions, characteristics, and applications.

Introduce the purpose of the debate: to compare and contrast database systems and big data technologies in terms of their features, benefits, challenges, and applications.

Debate Preparation

- Divide the class into two groups: Team Database Systems and Team Big Data.
- Assign specific debate topics or questions to each team, covering various aspects such as data volume, velocity, variety, storage, processing, scalability, and analysis.
- Instruct teams to research their assigned topics, gather evidence, and prepare arguments to support their positions.

Debate Rounds

- Conduct multiple rounds of debates, with each round focusing on a specific topic or question.
- Allocate a set amount of time (e.g., 5–7 minutes) for each team to present their arguments.
  - Encourage teams to use examples, case studies, and statistics to strengthen their arguments.
  - Allow time for rebuttals and counterarguments from the opposing team.
- Facilitate a respectful and constructive discussion, ensuring that all students have the opportunity to participate.

Audience Participation

- After each debate round, invite audience members to ask questions or provide comments on the arguments presented.
- Encourage students to critically evaluate the merits of each position and engage in meaningful discussions.
- Facilitate a balanced exchange of perspectives and insights from both sides.

Wrap-Up and Reflection

- Conclude the debate by summarizing the key points and insights from each team's arguments.
- Facilitate a class discussion on the strengths and weaknesses of database systems and big data technologies, as well as their respective applications and challenges.
- Encourage students to reflect on their own understanding of the topic and how the debate influenced their perspectives.

Key Takeaways

- Understanding of the differences and similarities between traditional database systems and big data technologies.
- Appreciation of the applications, benefits, and challenges associated with each approach.
- Development of critical thinking, research, and communication skills through debate participation.
- Insights into real-world scenarios where database systems and big data technologies are used to manage and analyze large volumes of data.

This activity provides students with an engaging and interactive way to explore the complex and evolving landscape of database systems and big data technologies, fostering a deeper understanding of their role in contemporary information management and analytics.

SUMMARY

- Any collection of characters that have been compiled and translated for a purpose—usually analysis—is generally referred to as data. Any character is acceptable, including text, numbers, images, sounds, and videos. Data has no effect on either humans or computers if it is not contextualized.
- Data can be represented in two general ways: digitally and analogically. Continuous, or "analogous," to the real facts they represent, are analog data. Digital data are discrete and composed of a finite set of constituents. Computers are digital, but nature is analog.
- Data Hierarchy refers to the systematic organization of data, often in a hierarchical form. Data organization involves fields, records, files and so on.
- Data that is at least one petabyte in size has been referred to as "big data." Big data is summed up in three words: volume, variety, and velocity. Big data-driven business models, which view data as an asset in and of itself, have emerged in tandem with the growth of web-based e-commerce. These developments have also led to an increased focus on data privacy and its social applications.
- Multiple applications with multiple users can share data thanks to database approaches to data storage. Databases are organized in ways that are significant to a company. There would be a link in the database between the suppliers and the geographic areas, for instance, if an organization kept records on the suppliers and the areas they service. Redundant data is lessened by databases.
- A relational database management system (RDBMS) is a database engine/system based on the relational model specified by Edgar F. Codd—the father of modern relational database design—in 1970.
- The most fundamental RDBMS operations are those that deal with the create, read, update, and delete (CRUD) operations. They serve as the cornerstone of a system that is well-organized and encourages the consistent handling of data.
- Big Data is essentially made up of data creation, analysis, sharing, storage capacity, analysis, visualization, querying, privacy, and data capture.
- Big Data operational and analytical workloads present conflicting requirements, and systems have developed to meet each of these demands independently and in very different ways. The development of new technological architectures has been fueled by each.

REVIEW QUESTIONS

1. What is the primary function of a graph database?
2. What is the primary function of a data lake?
3. What are the differences between primary keys and foreign keys in a database?
4. Explain the concept of indexing in databases. How does it improve query performance?

5. Describe the ACID properties in the context of database transactions.
6. What is a data warehouse? How does it differ from a traditional database?
7. Explain the role of data visualization in big data analysis.

REFERENCES

1. Assuncao, M. D., Calheiros, R. N., Bianchi, S. C., Netto, M. A. S., & Buyya, R. (2015). Big data computing and clouds: Trends and future directions. *Journal of Parallel and Distributed Computing, 79–80*, 3–15.
2. Curry, E., Metzger, A., Berre, A. J., Monzón, A., & Boggio-Marzet, A. (2021). A reference model for big data technologies. In E. Curry, A. Metzger, S. Zillner, J. C. Pazzaglia, & A. García Robles (Eds.), *The elements of big data value* (pp. 109–136). Springer. https://doi.org/10.1007/978-3-030-68176-0_6.
3. Demchenko, Y., Ngo, C., & Membrey, P. (2013). Architecture framework and components for the big data ecosystem. *SNE Technical Report*, University of Amsterdam.
4. Demirkan, H., & Delen, D. (2013). Leveraging the capabilities of service-oriented decision support systems: Putting analytics and big data in cloud. *Decision Support Systems, 55*(1), 412–421.
5. Gandomi, A., & Haider, M. (2015). Beyond the hype: Big data concepts, methods, and analytics. *International Journal of Information Management, 35*(2), 137–144.
6. Kang, J., Kim, K., & Suk, S. (2015). Personal information access control scheme for secure NFC integrated payment. In *Computer Science and its Applications* (pp. 263–268). Springer. https://doi.org/10.1007/978-3-662-45402-2_39.
7. Li, X., & Yang, T. (2015). Signal processing oriented approach for big data privacy. In *2015 16th International Symposium on High Assurance Systems Engineering* (pp. 1149–1176). IEEE. https://doi.org/10.1109/HASE.2015.23.
8. McAfee, A., & Brynjolfsson, E. (2012). Big data: The management revolution. *Harvard Business Review, 90*(10), 60–68.
9. Paakkonen, P., & Pakkala, D. (2015). Reference architecture and classification of technologies, products and services for big data systems. *Big Data Research, 2*(3), 166–186.
10. Westerlund, M., Hedlund, U., Pulkkis, G., & Bjork, K. (2014). A generalized scalable software architecture for analyzing temporally structured big data in the cloud. *New Perspectives on Information Systems and Technology, 1*, 559–569.

CHAPTER 5

Decision Support Systems

LEARNING OBJECTIVES

After studying this chapter, you will be able to:

- Understand concept of decision support system (DSS);
- Describe the decision making models;
- Discuss the models of managerial decision making.

KEY TERMS FROM THIS CHAPTER

Administration
Customer relationship management (CRM)
Decision-making
Executive information system (EIS)
Management information
Recognition-primed decision (RPD)
Communication
Decision making process
Effective management
Interpersonal communication
Psychology

INTRODUCTION

An electronic program used to assist decisions, assessments, and actions within a company or organization is known as a decision support system (DSS). Massive data sets are sorted through and analyzed by a DSS, which then compiles detailed information that can be utilized in decision-making and problem-solving. A decision support system compiles, evaluates, and synthesizes data to generate extensive information reports. This is how a DSS differs from an ordinary operations application, which has the sole purpose of gathering data, as an informational application. The DSS can run entirely on computers or on human power. It might occasionally combine the two. The best systems evaluate data and take action on behalf of the user. They enable human users to make decisions more quickly and with greater knowledge, at the very least.

An information system that facilitates organizational or business decision-making is called a decision support system (DSS). DSSs support people in making decisions about issues that may be dynamic and difficult to define in advance, such as unstructured and semi-structured decision problems. They are typically used by mid- and upper-level management, operations, and planning departments within an organization. Systems for making decisions can be entirely computerized, entirely human-powered, or a hybrid of the two. Before decision support systems, organizational leaders made careful use of the advanced insights produced by a data analytics platform by relying primarily on their professional training and experience. By collecting, evaluating, and presenting organizational data for use in business decision-making, decision support systems systematize that. With this DSS approach, it is possible to make analysis recommendations and simulate the results of various scenarios using powerful augmented analytics or modeling. Different factors allow for more accurate outcome prediction and the making of business decisions based on the best information available. DSS thus facilitates both prescriptive and predictive analytics.

5.1. CONCEPT OF DECISION SUPPORT SYSTEM (DSS)

Decision Support Systems (DSS) use current and historical data from external sources and internal information systems to assist executives in making better decisions. They offer a much better source of information to use in the decision-making process by fusing vast volumes of data with complex analytical models and tools and simplifying the system. A class of computerized information systems called Decision Support Systems (DSS) is designed to assist in making decisions. DSS are interactive computer-based systems and subsystems designed to assist decision makers in effectively utilizing data, documents, knowledge, and/or models in conjunction with communications technologies to accomplish decision process tasks.

Although most businesses have integrated decision support systems into their daily operations, many still view these systems as specialized parts of a company. For example, a lot of businesses download and analyze sales data, budget sheets, and forecasts on a regular basis.

They then update their strategy after assessing and analyzing the current outcomes. Although decision support systems in businesses have a set structure, the data they are used to make decisions are actually dynamic and ever-changing (Figure 5.1).

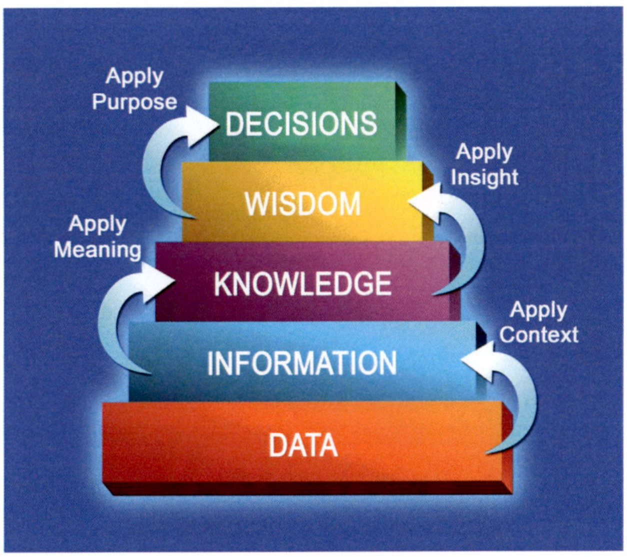

Figure 5.1. *Decision support systems.*

Source: https://dssmis.wordpress.com/wp-content/uploads/2015/02/dst-pyramid1200x10671.jpg.

5.1.1. Programmed and Non-programmed Decisions

Decisions can be classified as either non-programmed or programmed.

Programmed decisions are essentially automated processes that involve carrying out general routine tasks.

- These decisions have been taken several times.
- These decisions follow some guidelines or rules.

One example of a programmed decision is deciding on the inventory reorder level.

Unusual and unaddressed circumstances give rise to non-programmed decisions, so –

- It would be a new decision.
- There will not be any rules to follow.
- These decisions are made based on the available information.
- The manager makes these choices based on perception, judgment, instinct, and discretion.

Purchasing new technology, for instance, is a non-programmed choice. Most decisions made with decision support systems are not preprogrammed. As a result, these systems will not have a specific report, content, or format. Reports are produced instantly.

5.1.2. Attributes of a DSS

- Adaptability and flexibility;
- High level of Interactivity;
- Ease of use;
- Efficiency and effectiveness;
- Complete control by decision-makers;
- Ease of development;
- Extendibility;
- Support for modeling and analysis;
- Support for data access;
- Standalone, integrated, and Web-based.

5.1.3. Benefits of DSS

- Improves efficiency and speed of decision-making activities.
- Improves the organization's capacity for futuristic decision-making and its level of control and competitiveness.
- Facilitates interpersonal communication.
- Encourages learning or training.
- It presents novel strategies and provides fresh evidence for an uncommon decision because it is primarily applied to non-programmed decisions.
- Helps automate managerial processes.

5.1.4. Classification of DSS

Diverse approaches exist for categorizing DSS. DSS is categorized by Hoi Apple and Whinstone as follows:

- **Text Oriented DSS:** It includes information that is textually represented and may influence a decision. It makes it possible to electronically create, edit, and view documents as needed.
- **Database Oriented DSS**: A database is essential in this situation because it holds well-structured and organized data.
- **Spreadsheet Oriented DSS:** Spreadsheets containing data that enable the creation, viewing,

and modification of procedural knowledge as well as commands the system to carry out independent tasks are included. The most widely used tools are Lotus 1-2-3 and Excel.

- **Solver Oriented DSS:** Its foundation is a solver, which is an algorithm or process designed to carry out specific computations and work with a specific kind of program.
- **Rules Oriented DSS**: It follows certain procedures adopted as rules.
- **Rules Oriented DSS**: In a rules-oriented DSS, procedures are adopted. The example is the export system.
- **Compound DSS**: It is built by using two or more of the five structures explained above.

5.1.4.1. What Can a DSS Analyze?

The DSS is an information application that generates thorough data. An operations application, on the other hand, would be the one to gather the data initially.

Mid-to upper-level management is the main users of a DSS, which is essential for comprehending vast volumes of data. A DSS, for instance, could be used to forecast a business's income for the following six months in light of revised product sales projections.

This is not an easy calculation that can be completed manually because there are a lot of factors that surround the estimated revenue figures. Based on the company's historical product sales data and present variables, a DSS can integrate multiple variables and produce an outcome as well as alternative outcomes.

5.1.4.2. How Can a DSS Present the Information?

Providing customers with information in an understandable manner is the main goal of utilizing a DSS.

One of the advantages of a DSS system is that it can be configured to produce a wide range of reports according to user requirements. A DSS can produce written reports or graphically represent projected revenue in the form of bar charts or other charts.

5.1.4.3. Where Can a DSS Be Used?

Data analysis is no longer restricted to big, heavy mainframe computers as technology develops.

A DSS can be installed on the majority of computer systems, including laptops, as it functions primarily as an application. Some DSS applications can be accessed via mobile devices as well.

For users who travel often, the DSS's flexibility is quite helpful. This enables them to have access to information at all times, enabling them to make the best decisions for their business and clients at any time.

5.1.4.4. Test Your Skills with Trading Challenges

Use our FREE Stock Simulator to test your trading abilities. You can submit trades in a virtual environment with $100,000 in cash before you start risking your own money, making it the perfect platform to get your feet wet in the markets.

Enroll now to communicate with traders of all experience levels and backgrounds, and gain insight from their trading strategies to become a more astute investor.

5.1.5. Types of Decision Support Systems (DSS)

- **Data-Driven DSS** extract valuable information from the vast volumes of data made available by the company's TPS and MIS systems so that executives can utilize it to make better decisions. They are able to "free-flow" the data instead of requiring a theory or model. A Data-Driven DSS is the first general kind of decision support system. These systems include Executive Information Systems (EIS), Spatial Decision Support Systems, Data Warehousing and Analysis Systems, File Drawer and Management Reporting Systems. Systems for business intelligence are another type of data-driven DSS. Data-Driven DSS places a strong emphasis on gaining access to and manipulating sizable structured data databases, particularly time series of internal business data and occasionally external data. The simplest kind of functionality is offered by straightforward file systems that can be accessed by retrieval and query tools. Additional functionality is provided by data warehouse systems that enable data manipulation using computer tools designed for a particular task and environment or by more general tools and operators. Data-Driven DSS, in conjunction with Online Analytical Processing (OLAP), offers the most advanced functionality and decision support associated with the examination of extensive historical data sets.
- **Model-Driven DSS:** Systems that employ representational models, optimization models, and accounting and financial models fall under a second category known as "Model-Driven DSS." Model-Driven DSS places a strong emphasis on using and modifying models. The most basic level of functionality is provided by straightforward statistical and analytical tools. Certain OLAP systems that facilitate intricate data analysis could be categorized as hybrid DSS systems that offer modeling, data retrieval, and data summarization features. Model-Driven DSS are typically less data-intensive, but they do use decision-makers' parameters and data to help them analyze a situation. For Model-Driven DSS, very large databases are typically not required. Model-Driven DSS were mainly utilized for the standard what-if analysis and were kept apart from the organization's main information systems. These systems heavily rely on models to help executives understand the impact of their decisions on the company, its suppliers, and its customers. That is, what if we increase production of our products and decrease the shipment time?
- **Knowledge-Driven DSS**: The terminology for this third category of DSS is still developing, with the current preferred term being Knowledge-Driven DSS. By adding the modifier "driven" to the word knowledge, it maintains consistency within the framework and emphasizes the importance of the knowledge base. Knowledge-Driven DSS have the ability to suggest or recommend actions to managers. These DSS are computer systems with specialized problem-solving capabilities, encompassing

knowledge about a specific domain, an understanding of problems within that domain, and proficiency in solving these problems. A related concept is Data Mining, which involves analytical applications that search for patterns within databases. Data mining is the process of extracting data content relationships from large amounts of data.

- **Document-Driven DSS**: A new form of DSS called a Document-Driven DSS or Knowledge Management System is developing to assist managers in organizing and accessing unstructured documents and Web pages. This type of DSS integrates various technologies for storing and processing information to enable comprehensive document retrieval and analysis. Through the Web, users can access vast document databases containing hypertext documents, images, sounds, and videos. Documents that can be accessed through a Document-Driven DSS include policies, product specifications, catalogs, and corporate historical records such as meeting minutes, corporate documents, and important correspondence. A search engine is a key tool associated with a Document-Driven DSS, providing powerful decision-making support.
- **Communications-Driven and Group DSS** While Group Decision Support Systems (GDSS) were the first of their kind, a broader category known as Communications-Driven DSS or groupware has since emerged. This new category encompasses communication, collaboration, and decision support technologies that don't fit neatly within traditional DSS types. It's important to recognize these systems as a distinct category of DSS. A Group DSS combines communication and decision models, making it a hybrid Decision Support System. These systems facilitate problem-solving by allowing decision-makers to work together as a group. Groupware technology supports electronic communication, scheduling, document sharing, and other activities aimed at enhancing group productivity and decision-making. Within this category, we have various technologies and capabilities, such as Group DSS, two-way interactive video, White Boards, Bulletin Boards, and Email (Figure 5.2).

Figure 5.2. *Types of decision support systems (DSS)*

Source: https://assets-global.website-files.com/5ef788f07804fb7d78a4127a/61cc20621f33166101a1472a_decision%20support%20system-min.jpeg.

5.1.6. Components of Decision Support Systems (DSS)

Scholars and MIS personnel have traditionally talked about developing Decision Support Systems in terms of four main components:

- The user interface;
- The database;
- The models and analytical tools; and
- The DSS architecture and network.

This conventional list of elements is still helpful because it highlights the parallels and discrepancies among various DSS categories and types. The primary foundation of the DSS framework is the various emphasizes placed on DSS components during the actual construction of systems.

- **Data-Driven, Document-Driven and Knowledge-Driven DSS:** require specific database elements. A straightforward flat-file database with fewer than 1,000 records may be used in a Model-Driven DSS, but the model component is crucial. There are differences in the design and implementation of Data-Driven, Document-Driven, Model-Driven, and Knowledge-Driven DSS, according to experience and some empirical evidence.
- **Complex Implementation Issues:** They are also brought about by multi-participant systems such as Group and Inter-Organizational DSS. For example, a designer should be particularly concerned about the user's interest in applying the Data-Driven DSS in unexpected or novel situations when putting it into practice. While a DSS's specific task and scope can create significant differences, all Decision Support Systems have similar technical components and a common goal of assisting in decision-making.
- **A Data-Driven DSS Database:** This is an assortment of structured data, both recent and historical, gathered from various sources and arranged for convenience of use and examination. We are extending the data component to encompass knowledge in the form of rules or frames in Knowledge Driven DSS and unstructured documents in Document-Driven DSS. The structured data or documents in a database are made sense of by computerized tools in order to support management decision-making.
- **Mathematical and Analytical Models:** They are the main part of a DSS that is driven by models. Since every Model-Driven DSS has a distinct set of goals, various models are required and applied. Selecting suitable models is a crucial aspect of design. Additionally, the user interface and necessary data management must be handled by the software used to create particular models. Key variables or parameters in Model-Driven DSS are frequently modified to account for possible shifts in supply, production, the market, sales, the economy, costs, and/or other internal and external factors. The decision-maker then examines and assesses the data from the models.
- **Knowledge-Driven DSS:** When processing rules or figuring out relationships in data, apply specific models. How hardware is arranged, how data and software are distributed within the system,

and how the system's components are integrated and connected are all covered by the DSS architecture and networking design component. Currently, a significant debate centers on whether DSS should be accessible via a corporate intranet's Web browser in addition to being available globally via the Internet. Communications-Driven DSS relies heavily on networking.

5.1.7. Advantages of Decision Support Systems (DSS)

- **Time Savings:** Research has shown and validated shorter decision cycle times, higher worker productivity, and faster access to information for decision making for all types of decision support systems. The use of computerized decision support has been shown to save significant amounts of time. However, researchers haven't always shown that decision quality either didn't change or got better.
- **Enhance Effectiveness:** Greater decision-making efficacy and better decisions represent a second advantage category that has received extensive discussion and analysis. However, it can be challenging to track and evaluate the effectiveness of decision-making. Rather than using objective measurements, the majority of studies have looked at subjective metrics like perceived decision quality. In order to enhance decision making, proponents of building data warehouses point out the potential for more and better analysis.
- **Improve Interpersonal Communication:** DSS can improve communication and collaboration among decision makers. In appropriate circumstances, communications- driven and group DSS have had this impact. Model-driven DSS provides a means for sharing facts and assumptions. Data-driven DSS make "one version of the truth" about company operations available to managers and hence can encourage fact-based decision making. Improved data accessibility is often a major motivation for building a data-driven DSS. This advantage has not been adequately demonstrated for most types of DSS.
- **Competitive Advantage:** This benefit is usually mentioned by vendors in relation to web-based DSS, performance management systems, and business intelligence systems. While using computerized decision support to obtain a competitive advantage is possible, it is not likely to happen. Vendors frequently assist with installation and sell rival companies the identical product. The most likely way for an organization to benefit from this is through the implementation of innovative, high-risk, internal decision support systems. It is and will remain challenging to measure this.
- **Cost Reduction:** A number of studies, particularly case studies, have shown that DSS can save costs by reducing labor costs associated with decision-making as well as expenses related to infrastructure and technology. Building DSS does not always aim to achieve this.
- **Increase Decision Maker Satisfaction:** Analysis of this result has been and may remain

complicated by the novelty of using computers. Decision makers may feel less frustrated, believe that better information is being used, or believe that they are making "better" decisions as a result of DSS. Researchers frequently gauge satisfaction with the DSS rather than satisfaction with utilizing a DSS in decision-making because satisfaction is a difficult concept to quantify. Research has compared the level of satisfaction with and without computerized decision support systems. The intricacy and "love/hate" conflict surrounding the use of computers in decision support are suggested by those studies.

- **Promote Learning:** As a result of using a DSS both initially and continuously, learning can happen. It appears that there are two kinds of learning that take place: acquiring new ideas and improving one's factual comprehension of the business and decision-making environment. For new hires, certain DSS act as "de facto" training resources. This possible benefit hasn't been sufficiently investigated.
- **Increase Organizational Control:** Business transaction data is frequently made available for performance monitoring and ad hoc querying through data-driven DSS. These kinds of systems can improve managers' comprehension of how businesses operate, and managers think this is beneficial. The financial benefit from more detailed data is not always obvious.

Sarbanes-Oxley and other regulations frequently set forth reporting requirements, which has a significant impact on the control information that managers are given access to. On a more sinister note, certain DSS offer summaries of choices made, system usage, and system recommendations. When gathering and using decision-related data for organizational control, managers must exercise extreme caution. The advantages of a DSS may be diminished if staff members believe they are being watched or harassed while using it. On these questions, more investigation is required.

5.1.8. Disadvantages of Decision Support Systems (DSS)

Though developing and implementing Decision Support Systems (DSS) can have positive effects in some circumstances, it can also benefit organizations.

- **Monetary Cost:** Implementing a decision support system involves the investment in an information system to gather data from multiple sources and analyze it to aid in decision making. Certain analyzes required for a decision support system necessitate expertise in data analysis, statistics, econometrics, and information systems, which can result in high costs associated with hiring specialists to establish the system.
- **Overemphasize Decision Making:** It is obvious that those of us who are interested in computerized decision support have a focus on making decisions. Putting in place a decision support system could overemphasize decision-making and decision processes while supporting the rational viewpoint. It is imperative to provide managers with education regarding the wider decision-making context and the

social, political, and emotional factors that influence the success of an organization. It is crucial to keep researching the best times and situations to develop and implement decision support systems. We need to keep asking ourselves whether a particular decision support system is still appropriate to use for making or informing a particular decision, as well as whether the decision situation justifies the use of any kind of decision support system at all.

- **Assumption of Relevance:** It is challenging to resist the belief that the things a computer system is capable of handling are the most important ones for the manager to worry about once it has been installed, claim Winograd and Flores. One risk associated with DSS adoption is that managers may misuse them once they become standard in the workplace. The evidence that this happens is not very strong. The only way to prevent this possible issue is to receive training.
- **Transfer of Power:** Developing decision support systems can be interpreted as giving decision-making power to a computer program, particularly knowledge-driven decision support systems. Rather than DSS, this is more of an issue with decision automation systems. Because we want to enhance decision-making while retaining a human decision-maker in the "decision loop," we support the development of computerized decision support systems. The "need for human discretion and innovation" in the decision-making process is generally valued.
- **Unanticipated Effects:** Using decision support technologies could lead to unexpected outcomes. Certain DSS can theoretically and empirically lower the skill required to complete a decision task. Certain decision support systems actually lessen the efficacy of decision making by providing decision makers with an excessive amount of information.
- **Obscuring Responsibility:** People make "bad" decisions; computers don't. Regretfully, some people might assign personal accountability to a DSS. It is imperative to consistently remind managers that the computerized decision support system functions as a middleman between the system developers and end users. The individuals who designed and utilize the DSS bear full accountability for any decisions made with it.
- **False Belief in Objectivity:** It's possible that managers who employ decision support systems make decisions with greater objectivity. Managers can utilize decision support technologies to justify their actions in addition to using computer software to promote more reasoned behavior. Asserting that managers who use a DSS are more objective and logical than those who do not is oversimplifying the situation.
- **Status Reduction:** There are some managers who believe that using a Decision Support System will lower their position and require them to perform menial tasks. This perception can be a drawback of adopting a DSS. Managers and IS

staff who promote the development and use of computerized decision support systems must address any concerns about status that may arise. It is likely that this perception is becoming less prevalent as computer use becomes more widespread and accepted in organizations.

- **Information Overload:** Excess information poses a significant challenge for individuals, with many Decision Support Systems (DSS) only adding to the overload. Despite this issue, DSS can assist managers in structuring and utilizing information effectively. In fact, DSS have the potential to minimize and control the amount of information received by users. Developers of DSS should make an effort to assess the information load generated by the system, while users of DSS should be mindful of their perception of the amount of information being received. The prevalence of handheld, wireless computing devices may worsen this problem and put users at a disadvantage.

In conclusion, in order to obtain a worthwhile investment, businesses should weigh the benefits and drawbacks of decision support systems before making any purchases.

5.1.8.1. Meaning of Decision Making

The process of choosing a course of action from a list of options that is believed to more satisfactorily address the decision problem's goals than the others is known as decision making. It's a deliberate course of action chosen to accomplish a specific goal. A decision is the process that happens before a chosen course of action is actually carried out. When it comes to managerial decision making, it is an act of choice in which a manager chooses one course of action from among the options available to them in a specific circumstance. To determine the best solution for the decision problem, managers use a process of goal-setting, task definition, alternative search, and plan development.

The following are crucial components of a decision-making process:

1. The decision maker;
2. The decision problem;
3. The environment in which the decision is to be made;
4. The objectives of the decision maker;
5. The alternative courses of action;
6. The outcomes expected from various alternatives; and
7. The final choice of the alternative.

These phases describe a logical process for making decisions. In real life, it is impossible to ignore the impact of different behavioral problems. Furthermore, the four steps might overlap rather than happen in a sequential order. Furthermore, decisions are frequently made iteratively, accepting ideas that work and rejecting those that don't. Human filters, resistance to change, and the quality of the information are the three main things that prevent people from making wise decisions. Information might not always be timely, accurate, comprehensive, or consistent. Managers pay selective attention, exhibit a variety of biases, and prioritize certain aspects of the issue while disregarding others. Not to mention, people are reluctant to change. Therefore, rather than choosing the best course of action, decisions frequently involve striking a balance between the firm's many interest groups.

Individual and collective thought processes influence the choices that people make. When options are not well defined, proper data is not gathered, and costs and benefits are not fairly balanced, poor decisions result. Occasionally, the decision-maker's mindset is to blame rather than the decision-making process itself. Managers frequently fail to recognize the different decision-making traps that can arise.

Some common traps include:

- **The Anchoring Trap:** The first piece of information that managers receive is typically given disproportionate weight.
- **The Status Quo Trap:** Even in the face of superior options, people prefer to keep things as they are.
- **The Sunk-Cost Trap:** Businesses frequently repeat their previous mistakes because they are unable to change their course after making significant investments in a particular strategy or choice.
- **The Confirming-Evidence Trap:** Supervisors typically look for data to confirm a preexisting tendency and ignore contrary data.
- **The Overconfidence Trap:** The majority of people overestimate their capacity for situation analysis and future forecasting.
- **The Framing Trap:** The roles that individuals play within an organization affect how problems are framed. A situation or problem is so frequently expressed incorrectly.

5.1.8.2. Characteristics of Decision Making

- Decision-making involves selecting one option from several available choices.
- It's a human endeavor that primarily requires the use of cognitive skills.
- It is the final step that comes before consideration and logic.
- There is always an environmental component to it. In certain situations, a manager might make one choice, and in other situations, a different one.
- Both a time dimension and a time lag are involved.
- It's always got a reason. With that in mind, choosing not to make a decision might be the best option.
- It includes all of the steps that are taken before a decision is made, such as defining the issue and carefully considering and evaluating the available options (Figure 5.3).

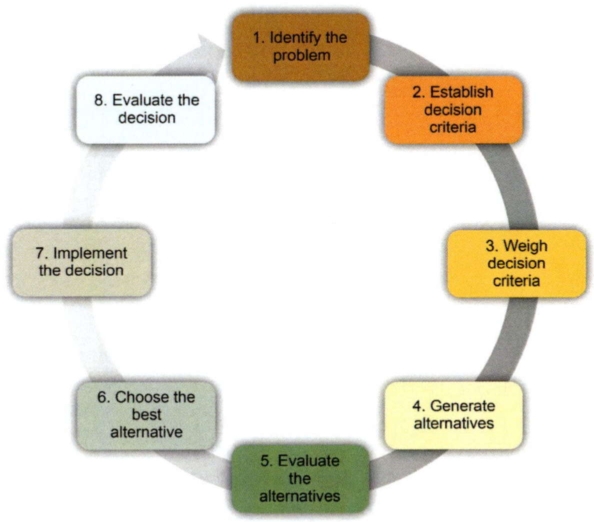

Figure 5.3. *Understanding the decision-making management process.*

Source: https://www.researchgate.net/publication/318730369/figure/fig2/AS:631678498267139@1527615298363/Understanding-the-decision-making-management-process.png.

5.1.9. Elements of Decision Support System

Originally intended to provide strong, adaptable tools for quantitative analysis of management decisions, decision support systems combined mathematical modeling and database management systems. In more recent times, concepts from expert systems and cognitive psychology—which studies how people solve problems and make decisions—have been added to the DSS concept. While data are necessary to make managerial decisions, they are not enough on their own. When making managerial decisions, a number of other factors need to be taken into account.

The sum total factors are:

- Data;
- Decision rules;
- Mathematical models;
- Managerial knowledge;
- Human judgement.

Decisions made using a data base system's set of rules, which are dependent on one particular data item: net profit. It is up to the manager to determine which of the rules applies in these situations, as a traditional data base system is unable to determine whether net profit is normal, above normal, or below normal.

The manager's assessment of whether or not last year's net profit was normal will determine which decision rule is best (though, of course, specific guidelines could be set for this as well).

Because a projection of net profit for the upcoming year is necessary, the set of decision rules is significantly different. Instead of forecasts, the types of data base systems contain historical and current data. Forecasts, of course, are frequently based on statistical or mathematical models that call for historical data.

As a result, the data needed for these projections can be obtained via a database system. The forecasting model is provided by the DSS's modeling component.

However, forecasts based on mathematics are not perfect and might not account for all pertinent variables. Therefore, the forecast needs to be interpreted and adjusted using human judgment. These kinds of managerial decisions are predicated on an understanding of the organization and its surroundings. Data base systems do not contain this knowledge, and computer systems hardly ever contain it at all. In order to make decisions, experts systems attempt to extract expert knowledge from the problem domain, or particular problem area. Similar to the data base in a data base system, knowledge is stored as a distinct entity known as a knowledge base. The data base management system in a data base system is a sophisticated program that works with the data base.

The interference engine in an expert system is a sophisticated program that works with the knowledge base, sometimes referred to as a data base in expert system literature. In a database, most of the data are numerical, though some are also character. Knowledge bases contain more textual or qualitative information, and interference engines may make decisions based on qualitative reasoning as opposed to quantitative models. The creation of decision support systems that combine mathematical models, expert system inference engines, data bases, and knowledge bases into integrated systems for management decision making is already manifestly on the rise. These decision-support tools have enormous potential impact.

5.1.10. Users of Decision Support System

The decision maker is the ultimate user of a decision support system, though he may not be the one who operates it. Alter found four distinct usage patterns based on his analysis of 56 decision support systems.

1. **Terminal Mode:** Through online access, the decision maker uses the system directly.
2. **Clerk Mode:** The decision-maker prepares input on a coding form while utilizing the system directly and offline. The technology used (batch versus online) is the main distinction between this mode and the terminal mode.
3. **Subscription Mode:** Regularly generated reports are sent to the decision maker automatically. This is how management reporting systems are typically used. While this may be the case for certain data analysis systems or accounting models, decision support systems typically do not use them in this manner.
4. **Intermediary Mode:** Through intermediaries who carry out the analysis, interpret, and report the findings, the decision maker makes use of the system. The decision-maker does not have to be aware that the system was utilized by the intermediary to obtain the needed data.

The function of an intermediary is prevalent in the utilization of decision support systems and warrants distinct consideration. Traditionally, the argument has been that managers won't use terminals; thus, decision support systems will face resistance. Chief executive officers have a very diversified job with lots of interruptions. One of the main obstacles to using a system that requires concentration over time is this kind of activity pattern. By using an intermediary, the manager can take advantage of the decision support system without having to carry it out themselves.

There are two kinds of intermediaries, each of which represents a distinct level of manager support.

1. **Expert Tool User:** This individual is proficient in using one or more categories of specialized tools for problem solving. Tasks that the problem solver lacks the knowledge or experience to complete are completed by the expert tool user.
2. **Staff Assistant or Staff Analyst:** This individual possesses specific problem-solving knowledge and some familiarity with decision support technology. When it comes to problem solving, the staff assistant essentially extends the manager's abilities by handling many of the setup, data collection, and initial model building tasks.

The more free-form aspects of the problem-solving process can be the manager's focus. The manager could complete the tasks completed by the staff assistant if they had more time. Even though staff assistants make up the majority of intermediaries, expert tool users are still frequently needed. The systems can be more complex and potent because of the intermediaries. Intermediaries still prefer online interactive systems because they enable faster and more efficient work.

5.1.11. Role of Decision Support System

A unique class of systems called decision support systems helps people make decisions. Decisions must be made at all times, regardless of the situation, just like in an organization. While some decisions are routine and predetermined, others might be strategic and unplanned. However, it is a given that decisions are made at every level of management. Packages used in decision support systems assist managers in making timely and appropriate decisions. A manager or other decision maker uses decision support systems, which use data from the general management information system, to assist in making decisions. The fundamental feature of a decision support system is that it is predicated on a model, technique, or tool. These systems are occasionally used for training, learning, and testing new options. They are also employed for sensing the model's various parameters. All of these scenarios must be considered by the MIS designer when creating the decision support system that will be integrated into the system. If decision-making is done with a well-designed decision support system and is person-independent, the management information system will be more beneficial. These embedded systems all handle the typical range of decision-making scenarios. The decision support system will alert decision makers to the need for action in the event that something beyond the range of possibilities arises. The management information system heavily relies on the decision support system to assist in decision making.

5.1.12. Models of Decision Making

Making decisions, even when they are rational, is a challenging process. All decisions fit into one of the three basic models listed below (Figure 5.4).:

1. The Classical Model.
2. The Administrative or Bounded Rationality Model.
3. The Retrospective Decision-Making Model.

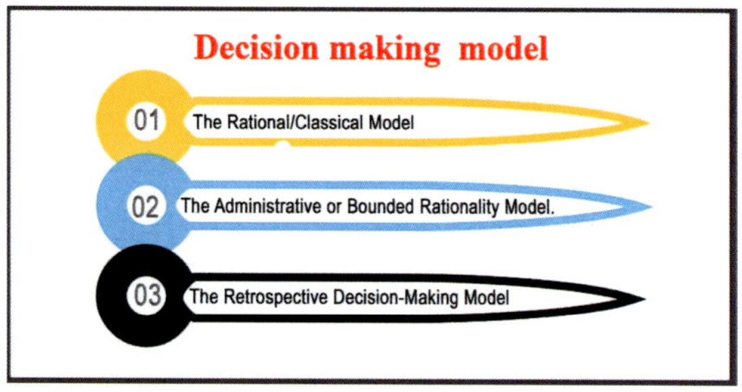

Figure 5.4. *Models of decision making.*

Source: https://miro.medium.com/v2/resize:fit:1400/0*UoPlxMPVVMAlwXaF.

Understanding the nature of decision-making processes in businesses or organizations can benefit from the application of all models. Every model relies on specific presumptions to inform the decisions made.

5.1.12.1. The Classical Model

The first attempt to understand the decision-making process was the rational model. Some people view it as the traditional method of comprehending the decision-making process. The classical model provided a number of previously discussed decision-making steps.

Features of Classical Model:

- Problems are clear.
- Objectives are clear.
- People agree on criteria and weights.
- All alternatives are known.
- All consequences can be anticipated.
- Decision makes are rational.
- They are not biased in recognizing problems.
- They are capable of processing ail relevant information

- They anticipate present and future consequences of decisions.
- They search for all alternatives that maximizes the desired results.

5.1.12.2. Bounded Rationality Model or Administrative Man Model

Achieving an objective is a component of decision-making. In order to make a rational decision, the decision-maker must have a thorough understanding of the various options available to achieve the objectives. Additionally, he should be fully informed and capable of correctly analyzing different alternative courses of action in light of the desired outcomes. Additionally, there should be a desire to choose the best options by going with the one that will fulfill the achievement of the goal.

Horace A. Simon describes rationality as intelligent, objective action. The behavioral nexus between ends and means is what distinguishes it. The choice is reasonable if the right methods are selected to achieve the intended goals.

The idea created by Herbert Simon serves as the foundation for the Bounded Rationality model. This model does not presuppose that each decision-maker is rational. Rather, it makes the assumption that although people might strive for the best answer, they usually make much less because the decisions they face usually require more time, information, and processing power than they have. When making decisions, they accept "limited or bounded rationality." This model is built upon a few fundamental ideas.

1. **Sequential Attention to Alternative Solution:** Instead of listing every potential solution, people typically have a tendency to look at potential solutions one at a time and give up looking for a workable solution—even if it's not always the best—once it's found.
2. **Heuristic:** These presumptions direct the search for alternatives toward fields with a high likelihood of success.
3. **Satisficing:** Selecting a course of action that is satisfactory or "good enough" in the given situation is known as "satisficing," according to Herbert Simon. It is the propensity for decision-makers to settle for the first option that satisfies their minimal standards rather than searching further for the option that yields the greatest outcomes.

When there is little time or when most of the options are nearly identical, satisfying is the preferred option for minor decisions. As a result, although the rational or classic model serves as a prescriptive model that outlines how decisions should be made, it is not entirely effective as a descriptive model when it comes to describing how decisions are actually made.

5.1.12.3. Retrospective Decision Model (Implicit Favorite Model)

This decision-making model focuses on how decision-makers try to justify and rationalize their decisions after they have been made. Per Solberg is the one who developed this model. He observed how graduating business students chose their jobs, noting that implicit preferences—that is, the option they preferred—were frequently identified by the students very early on in the recruitment and selection process. Still, the students persisted in looking for more options, and they soon decided on the best one. The entire procedure is intended to validate an intuitive decision under the pretense of scientific rigor. In this way, the person is persuaded that they are behaving sensibly and making a well-reasoned choice regarding a significant issue.

5.1.12.4. Some Common Errors in Decision-Making

Since the ability to make wise decisions can mean the difference between success and failure, their significance cannot be overstated. Thus, it is essential that every aspect influencing the choice be carefully considered and thoroughly examined. Apart from the quantifiable and analytical technical and operational factors, it is also important to comprehend and give credit to other elements like personal values, personality traits, psychological evaluation, environmental perception, intuition and judgment, and emotional interference. Certain areas where managerial thinking needs to be reevaluated and where some common mistakes are made have been identified by researchers. These should be avoided as they have an impact on the effectiveness of the decision-making process.

Some of the errors are:

1. **Indecisiveness:** Making decisions carries a lot of responsibility. Some people may be reluctant to make a decision because they are afraid of the result. This fear of being wrong could cause a protracted decision-making process and the loss of an opportunity. This is a personality characteristic that needs careful consideration. The managers need to make decisions quickly.
2. **Postponing the Decision Until the Last Moment:** This is a typical trait that leads to rushed decision-making, which usually precludes the possibility of a comprehensive, time-consuming analysis of the issue as well as the identification and evaluation of all available options. When students put off studying until right before their final exams, they typically perform poorly on them.

While some managers may function better under duress, it is typically necessary to give yourself enough time to assess the situation calmly and come to a wise decision. As a result, a plan of action needs to be developed, and deadlines for obtaining data, analyzing it, and choosing a course of action need to be established.

3. **A Failure to Isolate the Root Cause of the Problem:** Treating the symptoms as opposed to the underlying causes is standard procedure. For instance, a persistent emotional issue could be the cause of a headache. A headache medication wouldn't solve the issue. Distinguishing between the causes and symptoms is essential.
4. **A Failure to Assess the Reliability of Informational Sources:** Often, we don't verify the accuracy of the information ourselves because we assume that the other person's opinion is highly trustworthy and dependable. It is common practice to consider the other person's viewpoint in order to assign blame to the source of the information if the decision does not produce the intended outcomes. But this is a bad reflection on the manager's skills and moral character, and the manager has to take responsibility for the decision's result.
5. **The Method for Analyzing the Information May Not Be the Sound One:** Since many information and

factors must be considered when making decisions, especially non-programmed ones, a reliable and sound process must be used to identify, isolate, and select the relevant information. Objectively analyzing more than five or six pieces of information at once is typically not operationally feasible. To help the decision makers, a model that takes into account and manages a large number of variables must be created. Determining the goals, standards, and limitations as early in the decision-making process as feasible will also be desirable. This would help to formalize the procedure so that no requirements or options would be missed. Adhering to established protocols would eradicate the influence of emotions that could skew reasoning and the process.

6. **Do Implement the Decision and Follow Through:** Making a choice is just the start of the process; it's not the end. The real measure of a decision's quality is how it is implemented and the outcomes that follow. Assignment of responsibilities, establishment of deadlines, formulation of an assessment procedure, and advance preparation of backup plans are all necessary. The best outcomes require full implementation of the decisions.

5.2. DECISION MAKING MODELS

Business models are valuable tools for solving problems at work. Decision-making is essential in business, and having models to guide you can be incredibly helpful. In this section, we will discuss decision-making models that can assist you in making smart choices. These models are crucial additions to your operational toolkit. Below are five decision-making models that have proven successful for many businesses. Take the time to familiarize yourself with each model and consider using them the next time you are faced with an important decision.

5.2.1. The Vroom-Yetton-Jago Decision Model

The idea that not all decisions are made equally lies at the core of the Vroom-Yetton-Jago Decision Model. Certain decisions can be made swiftly because they won't have a lasting impact on the business as a whole, but other decisions are very significant and will need input from a wide range of sources. It's critical to comprehend this fundamental idea since not every decision you have to make will be made using the same methodology. This model helps you tailor your decision-making process to the particular circumstances at hand.

This model analyzes the decision that needs to be made using three different factors. These elements are enumerated below:

- **Decision Quality:** In other words, this is the point at which you consider how crucial it is to make the correct choice. Of course, you always want to make the best decision, but in the grand scheme of business, some situations are more crucial than others. It would be inefficient to devote a significant amount of resources to every decision you make because many choices are simply not significant enough to justify such an expenditure. Select carefully which decisions to make and devote a significant amount of time and effort to those that will actually impact the future of your company.
- **Subordinate Commitment:** Your team will be impacted by some of your decisions more than others, depending on how you decide. Take into account the impact that every choice you make will have on your team as well as other people inside and outside the company. You will be more likely to involve your team members in decision-making if you believe that their "buy in" is crucial. If not, you might be able to decide without much help from those in a lower position.
- **Time Constraints:** It goes without saying that the process you can employ to arrive at a decision will be influenced by the timeframe you have available. There will be plenty of time to consult with others, do research, and more if you are

not in a rush to decide. However, if the situation is urgent, you might not have much of an option when asking for assistance from others. Make sure your decision has a well-defined timeline, and indicate when you will have time to gather feedback from different sources.

You ought to have a far better idea of the way forward after holding up the decision you must make to the light provided by each of these three considerations. Next, you'll determine which leadership style is most appropriate for reaching this conclusion. Three options are available to you: collaborative, consultative, and autocratic. For more information on these three, you can read more about the model's details, but their titles generally speak for themselves. This model can help you make an informed decision by helping you consider the elements that go into each decision and the leadership style that works best for that particular situation.

5.2.2. The OODA Loop

It is your responsibility as an owner or manager to make the difficult decisions that lead the company in the right path. You might want to use tools like the OODA Loop to accomplish this. Although this model is comparatively easy to understand and apply, it has great potential for success. It is evident that decision-making is an ongoing process when considering the functioning of your company within the framework of the OODA Loop. This model is called a loop for good reason—it keeps going forever, for as long as the organization in question is in existence.

There are four stages built in to the OODA Loop. Those stages are as follows:

1. Observe;
2. Orient;
3. Decide;
4. Act.

Despite being a simple model, it conveys a lot about how you will approach business decision-making. The first three phases—observe, decide, and act—are fairly simple and are known to all business professionals. However, that second phase—orient—might be alien. The idea here is that in order to make an informed decision, you must correctly orient yourself with the information at hand. You might not make the best choice if you let your personal orientation get in the way, such as by letting memories from the past interfere with the decision at hand.

5.2.3. The Recognition-Primed Decision Model

You don't always have a lot of time in business to make a wise choice. The real world doesn't operate like that, even though it would be wonderful to be able to take some time to sit down in your office and consider all of your options before making a decision. There are moments when you need to take immediate action in light of the information at hand. In such circumstances, you may want to seek help from the Recognition-Primed Decision (RPD) Model.

There are three steps in this model that you will follow in order to arrive at your choice. These procedures are listed below:

1. Experiencing the situation.
2. Analyzing the situation.
3. Implementing the decision.

In the initial phase, it is important to gather as much information as possible about the situation in order to make an informed decision. Actively listen to those directly involved to understand the issue, why it is problematic, and how they believe it can be resolved. Without all the necessary information, a clear and appropriate decision cannot be made.

After gaining a fundamental comprehension of the situation and its significance, you must proceed to the analytical phase in order to initiate the process of finding a resolution. At this point, you can pose a variety of questions to yourself to elicit possible answers based on prior encounters. For instance, what aspects of this scenario are unexpected, and what aspects could you have predicted? Is this a recurrence of a previous event, albeit with a minor variation?

Finally, for a decision to truly take effect, it must be put into action as soon as possible after it has been made. Once you have completed the first two steps of the model, get down to business putting your decision into action. It is of no use to make a decision hastily and then take your time executing it. The implementation phase should be the last thing on your mind as you consider the different options available to you. Ultimately, the efficacy of the decision will be compromised if it cannot be promptly implemented to address the circumstances. The only decisions that will ultimately be successful are those that will function in the real-world application of implementation.

5.2.4. Paired Comparison Analysis

Determining priorities is a crucial component of making wise choices. It makes sense, even if you aren't aware of it at the moment: most of the time, the decisions you make are influenced by your underlying priorities. Making money is, of course, frequently the top priority in business, but it's not always the case. Alternatively put, that doesn't always serve as the benchmark for the choices you have to make. In situations where you are unsure of your priorities, the Paired Comparison Analysis model can be a useful tool for making difficult decisions with a lot of variables to take into account.

To use this model, you must first create a table that will list all of your available options. The chart should list every option you have for the decision that needs to be made, both across the top and down the side. You now possess a chart that enables you to directly compare different options with each other. This is the point at which "paired analysis" becomes relevant. You will evaluate each option in comparison to the others and declare a winner. Continue doing this until every option has been weighed against every other option.

The choice that has prevailed in the most head-to-head matches should ultimately be deemed the victor. Although it won't always be the best tool for making decisions, this one can provide some clarity in cases where there are a lot of conflicting options.

5.2.5. The Ladder of Inference

The Ladder of Inference's purpose is to assist you in avoiding making poor decisions because of biases, prior experiences, or other considerations. When making decisions, your goal should be to put as much of your personal influence aside as possible in order to act in the organization's best interests overall. Seven "rungs" make up the ladder in this model, which is meant to symbolize the common process of thought that goes into making decisions. These are the rungs, arranged as they appear on the ladder, from bottom to top.

1. Reality and facts;
2. Selected reality;

3. Interpreted reality;
4. Assumptions;
5. Conclusions;
6. Beliefs;
7. Actions.

You can see how this theory of human thought processes could be risky when it comes to making business decisions if you consider how it would function in practice. In particular, as your perceptions pass through the "selected reality" and "assumptions" phases, they may become distorted. You risk losing sight of the actual facts that are in front of you when you let your personal beliefs influence the decisions you make. Essentially, employing the Ladder of Inference involves dissecting your own thought processes in order to reconstruct them on a more solid basis. When faced with a novel situation, it is human nature to jump to conclusions, even if those conclusions aren't well grounded in the facts. Thus, by employing this model, you can efficiently search for gaps in your reasoning, fill them in, and then logically climb the ladder once more. Using this tool will ultimately enable you to defend your business decisions, which is something you should always be able to do.

If you haven't used any of the decision-making models on this list before, you'll probably be impressed by what they can accomplish for your company once you put them into practice. It is possible that you will begin to utilize these models on a regular basis for even small decisions, or that you will reserve their application for major decisions. In any event, these models should help you perform better at work.

5.3. MODELS OF MANAGERIAL DECISION MAKING

A range of models and frameworks are used by managers to assess options, assess situations, and make decisions that help the organization reach its objectives. This process is known as managerial decision making.

The models are:

1. Rational Model;
2. Non-Rational Models;
3. Satisficing Model;
4. Incremental Model;
5. Garbage-Can Model.

These models offer various viewpoints on how decisions are made in organizations and offer insightful information about the intricacies of managerial decision making. Managers frequently integrate components from various models based on the situation and type of decision they are making.

5.3.1. Rational Model

The economic theory of the firm serves as the foundation for the rational model of managerial decision making. Economists had a general tendency to assume that managerial decisions would always be in the best interests of their firms' bottom lines when developing theories about the economic behavior of business firms. Many management theorists initially agreed with this assumption. From the perspective of the rational model, managers make perfectly rational decisions. They possess all the pertinent data required to make decisions. They also make logical decisions because they are aware of the various options, consequences, and outcomes. This early 20th-century paradigm has significant shortcomings because it is hard to get all the information needed to make "optimal" decisions in complex situations. Despite its shortcomings, the rational view offers a standard by which real managerial decision-making practices can be evaluated.

5.3.2. Non-Rational Models

In contrast to the rational perspective, a number of non-rational models of managerial decision-making imply that the constraints of information collection and processing make it challenging for managers to reach the best decisions. Researchers have identified three major models of decision-making within the non-rational framework.

These are:

1. Satisficing model;
2. Incremental model; and
3. Garbage-can model.

5.3.3. Satisficing Model

Economist Herbert Simon examined the real actions of managers who made decisions in the 1950s. Simon introduced the idea of bounded rationality based on his research.

This idea implies that managers might not always make the most logical choices. Time constraints and cognitive capacity are two examples of factors that may limit their ability to make decisions. A framework known as bounded rationality was proposed in order to help people comprehend the real process of managerial decision-making. The idea of bounded rationality states that managers' ability to make totally rational decisions is typically constrained by the following factors:

- It's possible that decision-makers don't know enough about the nature of the matter they need to decide. They might also be underinformed about the advantages and disadvantages of potential alternatives.
- Time and money constraints restrict the amount of information that can be obtained about a given decision.
- Decision-makers' opinions regarding the relative importance of different pieces of data may cause them to ignore or overlook important information.
- The ability and intelligence of the decision-maker limits how much they can decide which course of action is best.
- Managers' capacity to make logical decisions is further impeded by their incapacity to retain vast amounts of information.

Simon contends that managers usually settle for a decision that will sufficiently fulfill their needs rather than striving for the best or ideal one. He argues that instead of looking around until they find the best option, managers should settle for the first workable solution they come across. Simon refers to this as "satisficing." According to the satisficing model, managers should only look for alternatives if they find one that appears satisfactory. When the costs of looking for a better option or putting off making a decision outweigh the likelihood of achieving the desired outcome, the satisficing approach may be justified as a suitable method of decision-making.

5.3.4. Incremental Model

An additional method for making decisions is the incremental model. According to the incremental model, managers only make as much of an effort as is necessary to bring the issue down to a manageable level. Here, the manager is more focused on coming up with a quick fix than on choosing a course of action that will enable long-term goal attainment. Managers can make decisions using the incremental model without having to consider a lot of information.

5.3.5. Garbage-Can Model

The garbage-can approach to decision-making suggests that managers make non-programmed decisions in a random manner. This means that decision outcomes are based on chance and are influenced by factors such as the individuals involved in the decision-making process, the specific problems being addressed, the opportunities recognized, and the preferred solutions or strategies frequently utilized by the managers.

The garbage-can strategy is effective in the following situations:

1. When managers do not have a preference for any particular goal;
2. When there is uncertainty about how to achieve objectives; and.
3. When the people taking part in decision-making frequently change. This strategy may have unfavorable effects. When strategic management is lacking, the garbage-can approach is frequently employed.

CASE STUDY

IT SYSTEMS CONVERSION PROGRAM TURNAROUND SAVES MILLIONS IN BUSINESS DISRUPTION COSTS AT MANUFACTURING COMPANY

The program turnaround immediately saved an estimated US $2 million in system support fees by moving applications in-house. But the real value was in the untold millions in revenue saved by preventing manufacturing disruptions and avoiding the opportunity costs of postponing a major sales and marketing campaign.

Company

The client is a global leader in the manufacturing and marketing of pediatric nutritional products and supplements for families throughout the world.

Challenge

To prepare for integration with a new corporate ERP system, the client faced an unmovable deadline for the transfer and conversion of IT Legacy sales, marketing, and manufacturing systems to new software and hardware platforms.

The client was divesting itself from a controlling company, which required them to establish their own data centers to house and run their systems, and which charged approximately US $2 million per year to keep the systems on the controlling company's infrastructure. The move needed to happen quickly and smoothly, as the client's business was at risk: one program was for manufacturing systems without which the company could not make products; another supported the company's web presence, including customer service and ordering.

The original program teams, comprising program and project managers from a third-party vendor, were unable to deliver results and the program was in peril. Planning was inadequate, milestones were missed, and delivery dates were not trusted by the client. Over one-quarter of the projected program time frame had passed with very little progress being made on this business-critical multimillion-dollar program.

Solution

The client's executive leadership council replaced the current vendor-staffed program management team with a new team comprising outside consultants because the requisite experience and knowledge of large-scale IT transformation programs was not present in-house. They selected PM Solutions to perform a quick assessment of the program and provide suggestions for getting it back on track. To achieve the program objectives, PM

Solutions quickly assembled a seasoned team of program managers who reviewed and re-planned all programs and, where necessary, assumed control of day-to-day program operations.

Results

Under the guidance of PM Solutions' onsite team, all individual projects within the program were delivered on time and were ready for integration with the enterprise ERP system.

A structured project process was implemented, and the team was willing to challenge the status quo to simplify the reformulation process. Decisions on direction were made more quickly, and there was clear accountability to ensure work was being completed as planned. Information was communicated with stakeholders on a regular basis, and timelines were met because the program elements were organized, tracked, and measured against an established baseline. This reduced project time from concept to plan to execution by 80%.

The program turnaround led by PM Solutions immediately saved an estimated US $2 million in system support fees by moving applications in-house.

But the real value was in the untold millions in revenue saved by preventing manufacturing disruptions and avoiding the opportunity costs of postponing a major sales and marketing campaign. Best practices were introduced by PM Solutions' expert consultants to ensure continued success in the client's other imminent enterprise programs.

CLASS ACTIVITY

DSS Case Study Analysis

Objective: To analyze a real-world case study of Decision Support Systems implementation and its impact on organizational decision-making.

Materials Needed:

1. Case study on DSS implementation (select a relevant and recent case study from a reputable source).
2. Handouts or slides summarizing key concepts related to Decision Support Systems.
3. Projector or screen for displaying the case study and presentation materials.
4. Whiteboard or flipchart for group discussions.

Activity Steps:

1. Introduction:
- Provide an overview of Decision Support Systems (DSS), explaining their purpose, components, and functions in organizational decision-making processes.
- Introduce the case study scenario, outlining the organization's background, challenges, and objectives for implementing a DSS solution.

2. **Case Study Presentation:**
- Present the selected case study to the class, highlighting the key features, functionalities, and outcomes of the DSS implementation.
- Discuss the challenges faced by the organization, the decision-making process, and the role of the DSS in addressing these challenges.

3. **Group Discussion:**
- Divide students into small groups and assign each group specific discussion questions related to the case study.
- Encourage groups to discuss the following topics:
- How did the organization identify the need for a DSS solution, and what were the key requirements and objectives?
- What were the critical success factors and challenges during the DSS implementation process?
- How did the DSS solution impact organizational decision-making, efficiency, and performance?
- What lessons can be learned from this case study regarding the effective use of DSS in organizations?

4. **Group Presentations:**
- After the discussion, invite each group to present their findings and insights to the class.
- Encourage groups to share their perspectives, analysis, and recommendations based on the case study.
- Facilitate a brief Q&A session after each presentation to allow for further discussion and clarification.

5. **Wrap-Up and Reflection:**
- Conclude the activity by summarizing the key takeaways and insights gained from the case study analysis.
- Encourage students to reflect on the importance of DSS in supporting organizational decision-making and problem-solving.
- Discuss how the lessons learned from the case study can be applied to future DSS projects and organizational initiatives.

6. **Key Takeaways:**

- Understanding of the role of Decision Support Systems in organizational decision-making.
- Insights into the process of identifying requirements, implementing, and evaluating DSS solutions.
- Application of theoretical concepts in DSS to practical business situations.
- Appreciation of the challenges and opportunities associated with leveraging DSS for competitive advantage.

This activity provides students with a practical and engaging way to explore the applications and impact of Decision Support Systems in real-world organizational contexts, fostering critical thinking, analysis, and communication skills.

SUMMARY

- Decision Support Systems (DSS) use current and historical data from external sources and internal information systems to assist executives in making better decisions. They offer a much better source of information to use in the decision-making process by fusing vast volumes of data with complex analytical models and tools and simplifying the system.
- Decisions can be classified as either non-programmed or programmed.
- Originally intended to provide strong, adaptable tools for quantitative analysis of management decisions, decision support systems combined mathematical modeling and database management systems.
- The decision maker is the ultimate user of a decision support system, though he may not be the one who operates it.
- A unique class of systems called decision support systems helps people make decisions. Decisions must be made at all times, regardless of the situation, just like in an organization.
- Business models are valuable tools for solving problems at work. Decision-making is essential in business, and having models to guide you can be incredibly helpful.
- A range of models and frameworks are used by managers to assess options, assess situations, and make decisions that help the organization reach its objectives. This process is known as managerial decision making.

REVIEW QUESTIONS

1. Discuss types of decision support systems.
2. What are components of decision support systems?
3. Describe the characteristics of decision making.
4. Give detail overview on decision making models.
5. Write short notes on management information system.
6. Discuss the role of management information system
7. Learn about MIS functions.
8. Explain the need of management information system (MIS)

REFERENCES

1. Berner, E. S. (Ed.). (2016). *Clinical decision support systems*. Springer International Publishing. http://dx.doi.org/10.1007/978-3-319-31913-1.
2. Fralic, M. F. (1989). Decision support systems. *Nursing Administration Quarterly, 14*(1), 1–8. http://dx.doi.org/10.1097/00006216-198901410-00003.
3. French, S., & Turoff, M. (2007). Decision support systems. *Communications of the ACM, 50*(3), 39–40. http://dx.doi.org/10.1145/1226736.1226762.
4. Greco, S., Mousseau, V., Stefanowski, J., & Zopounidis, C. (Eds.). (2022). *Intelligent decision support systems*. Springer International Publishing. http://dx.doi.org/10.1007/978-3-030-96318-7.
5. Heathfield, H. A. (1995). Decision support systems. *Yearbook of Medical Informatics, 04*(1), 455–457. http://dx.doi.org/10.1055/s-0038-1638034.
6. Loucks, D. P., & da Costa, J. R. (Eds.). (1991). *Decision support systems*. Springer Berlin Heidelberg. http://dx.doi.org/10.1007/978-3-642-76048-8.
7. Moreno-Jiménez, J. M., Linden, I., Dargam, F., & Jayawickrama, U. (Eds.). (2020). *Decision support systems X: Cognitive decision support systems and technologies*. Springer International Publishing. http://dx.doi.org/10.1007/978-3-030-46224-6.
8. O'Sullivan, E. (1985). Decision support systems. *Evaluation Review, 9*(1), 84–92. http://dx.doi.org/10.1177/0193841x8500900105.
9. Olsen, C. R., & Bozeman, W. C. (1988). Decision support systems. *Journal of Research on Computing in Education, 20*(3), 206–212. http://dx.doi.org/10.1080/08886504.1988.10781835.
10. Sànchez-Marrè, M. (2022). *Intelligent decision support systems*. Springer International Publishing. http://dx.doi.org/10.1007/978-3-030-87790-3.
11. Verstam, B. (1997). Decision support and decision support systems. *Radiation Protection Dosimetry, 73*(1), 1–6. http://dx.doi.org/10.1093/oxfordjournals.rpd.a032107.
12. Wallace, M. (2020). *Building decision support systems*. Springer International Publishing. http://dx.doi.org/10.1007/978-3-030-41732-1.
13. Wyatt, J. (1993). Decision support systems. *Yearbook of Medical Informatics, 2*(1), 325–327. http://dx.doi.org/10.1055/s-0038-1637983.

CHAPTER 6 E-Commerce

LEARNING OBJECTIVES

After studying this chapter, you will be able to:

- Explain the features and types of electronic commerce;
- Understand on the strategy of e-commerce technology;
- Focus on mobile commerce;
- Describe internet trading relationship.

KEY TERMS FROM THIS CHAPTER

Comma-separated values
Economic transaction
Electronic Transactions
Local area network
Production design
Trademark dilution
Currency Exchange Rate
Electronic Trading
Inventory
Personal digital assistant
Retail Outlets
Upselling

INTRODUCTION

Businesses and individuals who purchase and sell goods and services online are referred to as engaging in electronic commerce, or e-commerce. Computers, tablets, smartphones, and other smart devices can be used for e-commerce, which is available in a variety of market segments. E-commerce transactions can be used to purchase almost any kind of good or service, including financial services like online banking and stock investing, as well as books, music, and airline tickets. It is therefore regarded as a very disruptive technology.

E-commerce, as mentioned above, is the practice of purchasing and selling physical goods and services through the internet. In order to complete a transaction, multiple parties must exchange data or currency. It is a component of the larger sector of the economy known as electronic business, or e-business, which includes all of the operations necessary to manage a business online.

E-commerce has made it easier for companies, particularly those with limited market penetration like small businesses, to reach a larger audience by offering more affordable and effective channels for distributing their goods and services. Target (TGT) expanded its physical presence by opening an online store where consumers can buy anything from action figures and toothpaste to clothing and coffee makers from the comfort of their own homes.

Offering products and services is more difficult than it first appears. It takes a lot of research on the goods and services you want to offer, the audience, the market, the competitors, and the anticipated costs of running your business. After that's decided, you have to register a legal entity, like a corporation, and choose a name. Next, install a payment gateway on an e-commerce website. If a small business owner owns a dress shop, for example, they can create a website to advertise their clothes and other related products online and accept credit card payments or payments made through a payment processing service like PayPal.

E-commerce has transformed how consumers purchase and use goods and services. An increasing number of individuals are using their computers and smart devices to place orders for easily delivered goods to their homes. As a result, it has altered the retail environment. Due to the significant rise in popularity of Amazon and Alibaba, traditional retailers are being forced to alter their business practices. That's not all, though. Individual sellers have also become more active in e-commerce through their own websites, not to be outdone. Additionally, online markets like eBay and Etsy act as exchanges where a large number of buyers and sellers meet to transact business.

6.1. ELECTRONIC COMMERCE: FEATURES AND TYPES

The electronic purchase and sale of goods and services is known as electronic commerce, or e-commerce. Along with that, it covers other types of online commerce like money transfers. Electronic commerce encompasses both business-to-business and consumer-based transactions. It transcends both space and time. For instance, a customer in one nation can instantly finish a transaction with a company in another.

An example of an electronic commerce transaction would be buying a book online from a company. After making the desired book purchase, the customer loads the item into an electronic shopping cart. Requesting payment and delivery details allows the online bookshop to close the deal with the customer. The online bookshop receives this information from the customer thereafter.

In this case, the online bookshop charges the customer's credit card or accepts another payment method as payment, provided that the customer's payment information is legitimate. The customer gets a notification that the transaction has been completed as well as possibly additional shipment details. After that, the customer receives the book from the online retailer. This virtual bookstore may only be available online, or it may have a physical location where customers can buy books.

Transferring money between bank accounts is another example of electronic commerce. In the event that the customer paid the online retailer for the book with a credit card, money will need to be transferred by the credit card company to cover the cost of the transaction. Instead of mailing a check when the credit card payment is due, the customer can pay for the book and any other purchases made with the card online by transferring money from their account to the credit card company.

When the customer's book is shipped, the online bookshop can complete an additional electronic commerce transaction. The online retailer may arrange for a shipping company to arrange for the book's delivery. The shipping company will pick up the shipment from the online bookstore once it gets notification from the online bookstore that an item is prepared for shipping. The customer may receive notifications about shipments from the online bookshop, along with details on where to find the book while it's being shipped. The online retailer will eventually have to send money to the shipping company in order to cover the cost of the book's delivery.

Additionally, companies can conduct direct electronic commerce with one another. A book publisher will place an order with the online bookstore for a specific quantity of books to be kept in stock. The online bookstore will arrange for a funds transfer to be made to the book publisher. The books will be shipped to the online bookstore's storage facility by the book publisher. To complete the transaction, the book publisher will then need to send money to the shipping company.

6.1.1. Features

Nowadays, e-commerce is all the rage, particularly in developing nations like Brazil, China, and India where computer and internet connections are expanding at a fairly rapid pace. E-commerce differs from the traditional retail business model in that it has certain unique features. These unique features have also greatly contributed to the expansion of e-commerce businesses worldwide. The following are some special characteristics of e-commerce technology.

- **Breaks Geographical Barrier:** Geographical restrictions do not apply to e-commerce, in contrast to traditional retail business. These days, an online retailer can easily sell its goods to customers across the nation.
- **Saves Precious Time:** The most valuable resource in the modern world is time, which e-commerce helps to preserve. Customers can purchase any product they want from the convenience of their home, workplace, or even coffee shop. Customers who choose to shop traditionally would lose a great deal of valuable time, but e-commerce helps them save that time.
- **Power of Accessibility:** Thanks to the internet's power, consumers can purchase anything and everything whenever and whenever they want. This makes e-commerce incredibly accessible today. In reality, a simple impulsive want or slight craving for a product can result in costly shopping, all because e-commerce technology makes shopping accessible.
- **Cuts Supply Chain:** The laborious wholesale and retail supply chains, as well as the over-reliance on sales teams, have been greatly reduced thanks to e-commerce technology. This solely contributes to the product's cost reduction, which ultimately helps the buyer.

6.1.2. Need and Essential Requirements

E-commerce is the practice of conducting business via the internet and the web. Geographical and other barriers have been overcome by e-commerce companies thanks to technology. But an overwhelming lack of in-person interaction combined with an over-reliance on technology has severely damaged consumer confidence in e-commerce businesses.

6.1.2.1. Online Shopping

One of the most common forms of e-commerce is the buying and selling of goods via the Internet. The virtual counterparts of physical retail locations are storefronts made by sellers. Buyers use their mouse to browse and buy products. For instance, even though it did not start online shopping, Amazon.com is undoubtedly the most well-known site for it.

6.1.2.2. Electronic Payments

There must be an online payment method available when making purchases online. Payment gateways and processors enter the picture at this point. The inefficiency involved in writing and mailing checks is decreased when payments are made electronically. It also eliminates a lot of the security risks associated with using cash for payment.

6.1.2.3. Online Auctions

eBay is often the first platform that comes to mind when considering online auctions. While physical auctions have been around longer, the advent of the Internet has made auctions widely accessible to both buyers and sellers. Online auctions are a convenient way to discover prices and many shoppers prefer the thrill of bidding to traditional storefront shopping.

6.1.2.4. Internet Banking

Anybody can now complete the whole range of banking tasks without going to a physical bank branch. The primary force behind e-commerce was the integration of websites with bank accounts and, consequently, credit cards.

6.1.2.5. Online Ticketing

You can book almost any kind of ticket online, including tickets for plays, movies, trains, flights, sporting events, and more. There's no need to stand in line at ticket counters when you purchase tickets online.

6.1.3. Parties to E-commerce Transactions

The primary step in developing an e-commerce solution is building and launching an e-commerce website. Finding the parties to the transaction is the first stage in developing an online store. There are four different models of e-commerce, depending on who is doing the transaction. They are as follows:

1. Business-to-Business (B2B) model;
2. Business-to-Consumer (B2C) model;
3. Consumer-to-Consumer (C2C) model;
4. Consumer-to-Business (C2B) model.

6.1.3.1. Business-to-Business (B2B) Model

The advantages of the B2B model are:

- It is capable of effectively sustaining the flow of the supply chain as well as the procurement and manufacturing procedures.
- Corporate procedures can be automated to provide the appropriate goods and services in a timely and economical manner (Figure 6.1).

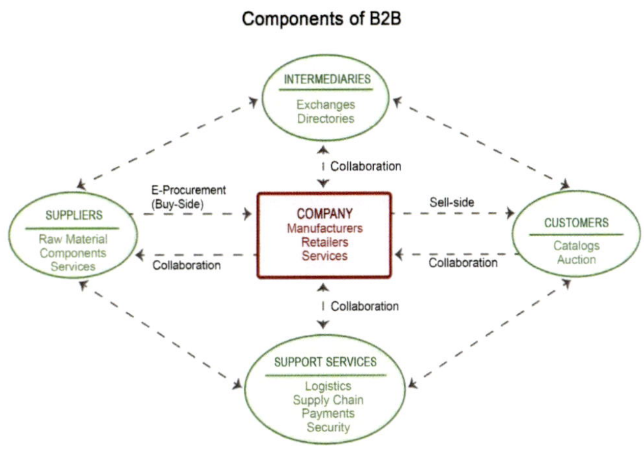

Figure 6.1. *B2B model.*

Source: https://slideplayer.com/slide/4618976/15/images/9/The+Components+of+B2B.jpg.

6.1.3.2. Business-to-Consumer (B2C) Model

The B2C model facilitates transactions between businesses and consumers, specifically those occurring over the Internet.

It is utilized by any business that offers products or services to consumers through online platforms. These businesses typically showcase their products in an online catalog and store related information in a database. Additionally, the B2C model encompasses various services such as online banking, travel booking, and health information dissemination (Figure 6.2).

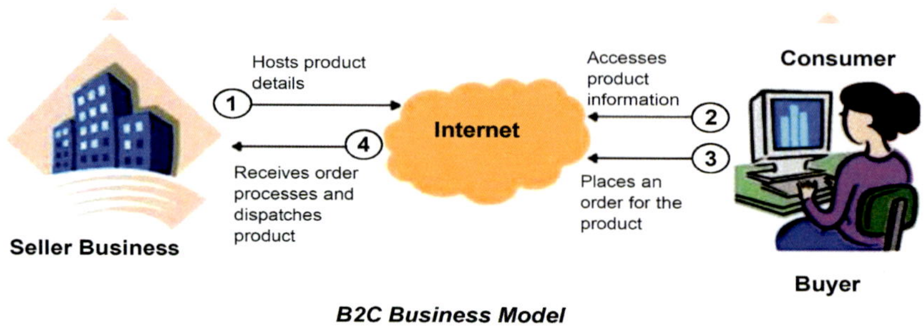

Figure 6.2. *B2C model.*

Source: https://benchpartner.com/bp-content/uploads/2022/04/9-NDtuGg84tUV.jpg.

6.1.3.3. Consumer-to-Consumer (C2C) Model

The C2C model facilitates direct transactions between consumers, where one consumer sells to another. Online auction websites like eBay and Baazee serve as platforms for consumers to advertise and sell their products to each other. Both the seller and buyer must register on the site to participate. Sellers typically pay a fixed fee to list their products, while buyers can bid without any additional fees. These sites bring buyers and sellers together to facilitate transactions (Figure 6.3).

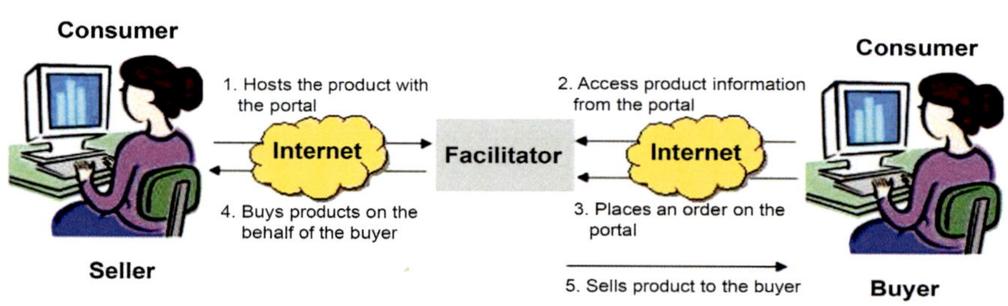

Figure 6.3. *C2C model.*

Source: http://seofiles.s3.amazonaws.com/seo/media/uploads/2017/06/06/c2c-busines-model.PNG.

6.1.3.4. Consumer-to-Business (C2B) Model

A transaction between a business entity and a consumer is the subject of the C2B model. It is comparable to the business-to-consumer (B2C) model; the distinction is that in this scenario, the buyer is the business organization and the seller is the consumer. In this type of transaction, the buyer determines the cost of a specific good instead of the seller. Those who sell goods and services to businesses fall under this category. One website where a customer can post his bio and the services he can provide is monster. com. Any company that would like to use the client's services can get in touch with him and, if appropriate, hire him (Figure 6.4).

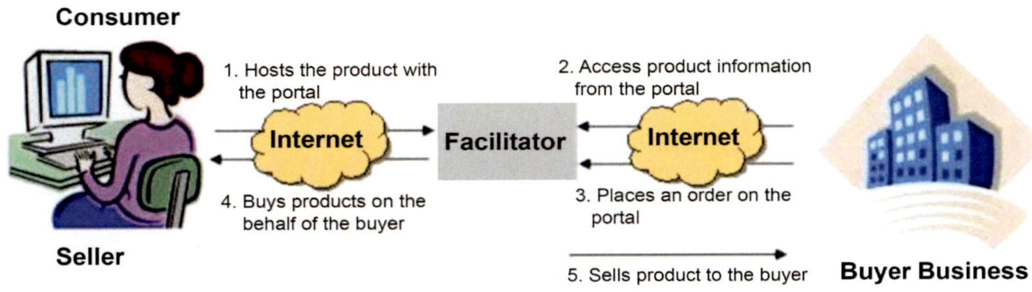

Figure 6.4. *C2B model.*

Source: https://benchpartner.com/bp-content/uploads/2022/04/13-vreQM4C0Ssx.jpg.

6.1.4. Advantages of E-commerce

It makes sense that online shopping is becoming more and more popular given the time and inconvenience associated with visiting different stores in search of a particular item.

The advantages of e-commerce are described as:

- **Gain New Customers with Search Engine Visibility:** The foundation of physical retail is relationships and branding. Search engine traffic is another factor that propels online retail in addition to the first two. Customers frequently click on links from search engine results pages to visit e-commerce websites they are unfamiliar with. For some e-commerce companies, this extra stream of revenue may be the decisive factor.
- **Lower Costs:** The reduced cost is one of the most obvious benefits of e-commerce. A portion of these reduced expenses might be offered to clients in the form of price breaks.
- **Locate the Product Quicker:** Pushing a shopping cart to the appropriate aisle or looking for the desired item are things of the past. Customers using an e-commerce website can quickly refine their product search by using a search box or the user-friendly navigation. Certain websites retain track of users' shopping lists and preferences in order to make repeat purchases easier.
- **Eliminate Travel Time and Cost:** Customers frequently travel great distances to visit their favorite physical store. With a few mouse clicks, they can virtually visit the same store thanks to e-commerce.

6.1.5. Challenges of e-Commerce

The rise of e-commerce is changing the nature of business. It gives businesses new avenues for market expansion, optimizes internal business processes for more effective delivery of goods and services, draws in and keeps consumers in novel and creative ways, and lowers operating expenses. The way suppliers, workers, and customers interact with one another is changing as a result of e-commerce. Organizations are being forced by these changes to develop new strategies and implement them using new techniques. E-commerce is an emerging field that includes transactions involving the buying, selling, and trading of goods and services as well as information electronically. E-commerce has the ability to provide customers with a personalized experience, but understanding its potential requires sound analytics.

6.1.5.1. Challenges

There are a lot of challenges that the current e-commerce shopping portals are facing:

- **Pushy Sales:** Customers eventually become irritated when they search for anything online and are bombarded with pop-up and banner ads. This does not help and will only cause them to visit other websites.
- **Personalization:** The most significant obstacle facing e-commerce and its rivalry with the brick-and-mortar stores of our youth may be personalization. When a store is selling online, it can be challenging to replicate the personal touch and knowledge of the customers' preferences that the owners possess.
- **No-Service Sales:** Although the e-commerce web-store may be visually appealing, the issue arises when customers become lost on the site and are unsure of what to search for or where to navigate. This is a common challenge faced by many e-commerce websites.
- **Choice of Good e-commerce Solution:** Either hosted services or a custom e-commerce website can be created. It can be difficult to choose the right option because there are many available.
- **International Orders:** One of the biggest issues facing global e-commerce is that 40% of e-commerce shopping portals reject orders from outside because most of them lack the systems and logistics necessary to complete the order. Tariffs and duties are additional issues since they make customers reluctant to buy because they are so expensive.
- **Shipping Challenges:** Customers are also irritated by problems with poor supply chain integration, expensive product delivery costs, delivery delays, and, in certain cases, inadequate courier services.
- **Product Return and Refund:** Customers frequently exchange or return products that they are not happy with. This is yet another significant problem that contributes to a general decline in revenue, an increase in shipping costs, and most importantly, a loss of reputation.
- **Currency Challenges:** Specifications for import and export vary amongst nations. This makes online shopping and product delivery less seamless problems with currency exchange

rates and credit card limits. Payment gateways are restricted in some countries, which can lead to issues.

- **International Taxation:** Our world has become a global village, and the internet has genuinely made business boundaries seamless, global, and nonexistent. The problem is that physical boundaries still exist in the world, and they are not going to disappear anytime soon. Every nation has distinct tax laws, as do even its individual states. Their integration into a web fabric presents a significant difficulty.
- **Customer Service:** Electronic marketers prioritize website performance over personal assistance and customer relationships.

6.1.5.2. Solutions to the Challenges

While there are some challenges that business owners are currently unable to control and cannot solve in the near future, there are many others that can be overcome. What can be done is as follows:

- **Personalization:** Although it can be difficult, personalization can make a big difference in how customers interact with brands online if done correctly. Make use of clever tools like web analytics, observe online consumer behavior, and engage with and reward customers. Customers will enjoy shopping more in an online store that offers greater personalization.
- **Segmentation:** Segmenting your customer base is crucial. Not every client should receive the same treatment. To better target offers and marketing campaigns, it is a good idea to segment your customer base into three categories: first-time users, highly valuable active users, and inactive customers. Utilize analytics to target the appropriate clients.
- **Make Site Navigable:** Sometimes users have a tendency to become lost on the website. To make things easier for the customers, the website should have proper navigation. Aim to create a correctly structured e-commerce website.
- **Choosing E-commerce Solution:** It is preferable to conduct research based on particular requirements. Examine the feature lists, check out the demos, and consult reviews from more knowledgeable people. A large community is usually a better option because it will provide more resources such as security audits, third-party plug-ins, themes, help, tutorials, and sample codes, all of which can help an e-commerce webstore become more productive.
- **Delivered Duties Paid:** Taxes and duties are paid by e-marketers on the goods they sell. Selling goods abroad with hassle-free services and all-inclusive prices via international courier services is preferable. Reducing shipping costs and registering the product is another smart move.
- **Shipping:** It is preferable to deliver large quantities at once to a single hub and distribute according to local shipping costs. We refer to this as regionalization.
- **Product Return and Refund:** Ensure that every product description is current and pertinent. Make sure

the goods you're going to deliver come from approved suppliers as well.

- **Multiple Payment Options:** Be accepting of all payment methods, including prepaid cards, e-wallets, and others which will improve cash flow and free clients from credit card debt.
- **Focus on Customer Service:** Online users expect quick answers to their questions, so be proactive in engaging with them through round-the-clock email, phone, and chat support. Encourage customers to interact with you through various channels, including social media. Keep them informed about your latest deals and promotions and gather feedback on their thoughts about them.

6.2. STRATEGY OF E-COMMERCE TECHNOLOGY

E-commerce can help even small businesses that offer personal services, like hair and nail salons, by offering a website where customers can purchase related health and beauty products that are typically exclusive to their local clientele.

E-commerce no longer needs a costly interface or personal security certificate, despite the fact that it once did. Numerous hosting companies and vast online presences provide virtual storefronts as easy-to-use solutions for vendors with minimal or no online experience. The hosting servers come equipped with all the tools required to run a profitable e-commerce website, so the individual merchant doesn't have to reinvent the wheel. The features of these tools include the capacity to accept a range of payment methods, including safe credit card transactions, virtual shopping carts, inventory and sales logs, and more.

6.2.1. Doing Business Over Internet Networks

Computer tools are beneficial to almost any kind of business; word processors and spreadsheet creators, like Microsoft Word and Excel, have become indispensable office software. Even though a single, disconnected computer can be quite strong, one that is part of a network can be much more powerful and beneficial to your company.

6.2.1.1. Does Your Business Need a Network?

Undoubtedly, a business computer network will be required if you want your company to be competitive in the market, whatever that market may be. Just having a computer in your company is insufficient; it also needs to be able to communicate with other computers and systems.

If your company employs more than one person, having a computer network within it can be advantageous. You and your staff will be able to communicate with one another and share documents and office supplies like fax machines, printers, and scanners thanks to a local area network, or LAN.

Linking your company's network to the world's largest network, the Internet, significantly increases the worth and efficiency of your enterprise. Access to vital data and information, email, voice, and video options, as well as global customer access, are all made possible by an internet connection.

6.2.1.2. Business Office Networks

You should set up a local area network to connect your computers, printers, and other equipment, regardless of the size of your company. Creating an office network will let you exchange data amongst employees in your company. Furthermore, you will have the ability to share the equipment you own. For instance, multiple employees can use a single printer. Your company's network is not confined to the one building that it operates out of. A campus network can be set up to connect staff members and resources in each building if there are several buildings nearby. Your business network can be connected by a wide-area network, or WAN, if it is located in multiple cities, states, or even countries.

6.2.1.3. Business Networks and Internet Connections

The Internet serves as the global marketplace, allowing you to connect with suppliers, customers, employees, and other essential individuals for your business. Through online platforms, you can promote and sell your goods and services to a worldwide audience. In addition to providing your company with access to the Internet and World Wide Web, an Internet connection can be used to enable employees to access the business network from off-site locations, like home or while traveling, using a mobile connection. Through the use of a virtual private network, or VPN, staff members can safely access the company network from any location with an Internet connection.

6.2.1.4. Network and Internet Connection Security

Security becomes a major concern when your business is connected to the Internet and a network. Every connected business uses data security, network, and backup systems to safeguard its information.

Although using networks to connect your business carries some risk, the advantages are far greater than the drawbacks.

6.2.2. General Sources for Doing Business on the Internet

- **CommerceNet:** A not-for-profit 501c(6) mutual benefit corporation which is conducting the first large-scale market trial of technologies and business processes to support interoperable electronic commerce via the Internet.
- **comScore**. Comscore is an audience measurement tool that offers publishers cross-platform insights, industry benchmarking, customized insights, advertising validation, and extensive demographic data.
- **Fraud.org (National Consumer League).** The creation of Fraud.org is the result of over 20 years of consumer advocacy and education regarding telemarketing and Internet fraud prevention.
- **Market Segmentation:** A Guide to Information Sources: This Business Reference Service guide from the Library of Congress covers books and other materials that address marketing to specific demographic groups in addition to other sources that are crucial for estimating the size and influence of a given market segment. Books on statistics and other materials with a primary focus on a particular generation, ethnicity, or other group are also included.
- **PeerSpectives (Edward Lowe Foundation):** Designed for the

business owner, the site emphasizes peer-networking and "next-level" thinking, encouraging business owners to anticipate issues the company is likely to encounter at the next level of growth and to understand the organizational changes required to move the company to that level. Includes a plethora of brief articles covering a wide range of subjects, including creating an organization, obtaining and overseeing funds, managing human resources, legal matters, taxes, operations, and technology. Citations to other information sources, such as books, articles, research institutes, trade associations, and websites, can be found in some articles.

6.2.3. Electronic Data Interchange (EDI)

Data transfer between two different systems can be facilitated with the use of an electronic data interchange tool. This kind of data interchange is subject to a number of regulations and procedures that need to be arranged beforehand. Establishing an electronic data interchange system is typically done to give clients or business partners a low-cost, safe means of receiving sensitive information. This kind of data transfer is frequently used in the government, banking, and other sectors of the economy where a high level of detail is necessary.

Regular communication between the supplier and the recipient is necessary to establish an electronic data interchange. It usually takes four to six weeks of consistent effort from both parties to finish this kind of project. A developer or programmer with experience in the software that will be receiving or transmitting the data file should be part of each side's project team. Furthermore, it is frequently necessary for infrastructure or security personnel to ascertain the security protocols that must be followed on both ends and how the information will be shared.

Finding the file's format and layout to be sent is the first step in creating an electronic data interchange. This contains the precise data that will be supplied in the file, the date of implementation, and the frequency of file delivery. For instance, the identification number, quantity, amount, currency, date of purchase, customer account number, and unique file identifier of books that a library has bought from a publisher must all be included in the data file. Although the format varies, it is typically text (TXT) or comma-separated values (CSV).

The next issue that needs to be addressed is file security and access to various systems. The most popular way to accomplish this is to set up a file transfer site, or FTP. Actually, all this website is an Internet-accessible network drive. The sender receives a user name and password, which they can use to upload the file as needed. After being informed that a file is available, the recipient can download it from the website and upload it into the primary system.

6.2.3.1. Choose the Best EDI

When selecting an electronic data interchange, there are a number of things to take into account (EDI). The most crucial ones are the business's size, needs, and budget. Prior to making a purchase, it can be advantageous to take the organization's capacity to support an EDI system into account. Many businesses base their decision about which electronic data interchange system to purchase on the systems used by the businesses they frequently do business with.

When selecting an electronic data interchange system, format is a crucial factor to take into account. A version that requires software and integration with the company's computer system may be purchased by certain businesses. For a larger business with a technical support staff, this is usually a good option. A web-based interface is an option for businesses who would prefer not to download an EDI. For smaller companies, this might be a preferable option.

Another thing to think about when selecting an EDI is the requirements of the businesses that an organization interacts with. Certain companies impose stringent guidelines regarding the format and delivery methods for document transmission. Even though the configuration of electronic data interchanges is typically universal, some details might be unique to particular systems. In addition, if a partner's system has proven to be successful, the company may view it as a validated entity.

When looking for an EDI, budget is an additional consideration. Apart from the initial startup costs, it's crucial to consider the cost of maintenance and upgrades. A financial impact estimate and an assessment of the amount of time technical staff will be interacting with the product may also be helpful.

An additional crucial factor to think about is the interface of an EDI. The staff members who will be using the system may have some technical limitations. Expert staff members might be more inclined to handle a sophisticated system, whereas non-technical professionals might prefer an easier-to-use interface. Taking into account the volume and type of data that will be transferred electronically can also be helpful. The average quantity of documents to be shared—from daily approximations to yearly usage—is a crucial consideration. The decision to purchase the system may also be influenced by the anticipated number of employees using it. If multiple people are anticipated to send documents, using a web interface might be more convenient.

6.2.3.2. Benefits of EDI

The electronic interchange of business data in a standardized format is known as electronic data interchange, or EDI. This process enables businesses to communicate electronically with one another instead of using paper documents. Trading partners are companies that conduct business electronically.

Each term in the definition is significant:

- **Computer-to-Computer**: Email, fax, and postal mail are replaced by EDI. Even though email is an electronic method, people rather than computers still need to handle the documents that are sent and received via email. People getting involved causes errors and slows down the processing of the documents. Alternatively, EDI documents can go directly to the relevant program on the recipient's PC (e.g., processing can start right away (through the Order Management System).

A typical manual process looks like this, with lots of paper and people involvement (Figure 6.5):

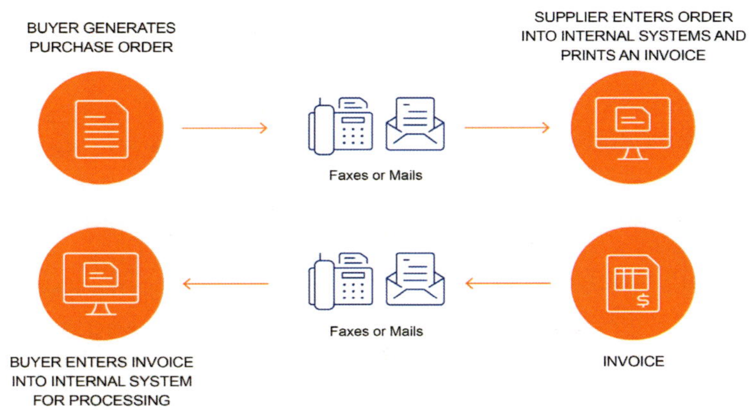

Figure 6.5. *Electronic interchange of business.*

Source: https://www.edibasics.com/wp-content/uploads/Figure-1.1-Manual-Document-Exchange.png.

The EDI process looks like this – no paper, no people involved (Figure 6.6):

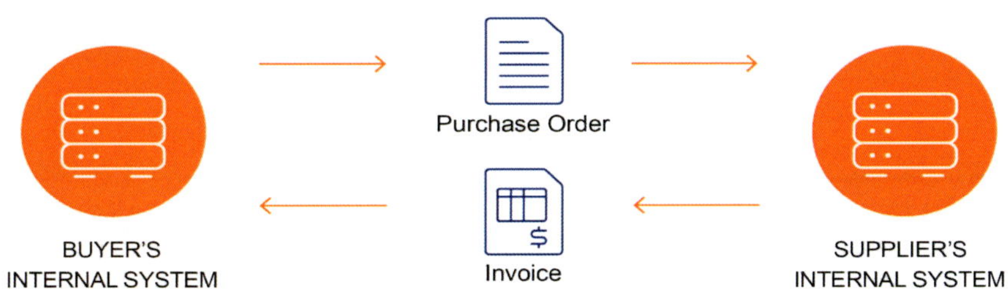

Figure 6.6. *EDI document exchange.*

Source: https://www.edibasics.com/wp-content/uploads/Figure-1.2-EDI-Document-Exchange-1024x340-1.png.

- **Business Documents**: These are any of the documents that companies usually share with one another. Advance Ship Notices, invoices, and purchase orders are the most frequently exchanged documents via EDI. However, there are a ton more, including bill of lading, inventory, customs, and shipping status documents.
- **Standard Format:** In order for computers to read and comprehend EDI documents—which must be processed by computers rather than people—a standard format needs to be followed. Each piece of information is described in a standard format along with its format (e.g., decimal, integer, and mmddyy). A standard format would prevent companies from sending documents in their own company-specific formats, which the recipient's computer system would not be able to understand—just as an English speaker is unlikely to understand Japanese. Today, a number of EDI standards are in use, including XML, TRADACOMS,

EDIFACT, and ANSI. Additionally, there are numerous variations for every standard, e.g., EDIFACT version D12, Release A, or ANSI 5010. Businesses must agree on the precise EDI standard and version before exchanging EDI documents. In order to enable straight through processing of documents and make the data usable by internal applications, businesses usually use an EDI translator, either as in-house software or through an EDI service provider.

- **Business Partners:** Usually, two distinct businesses—referred to as trading partners or business partners—exchange EDI documents. For instance, Company A might purchase products from Company B. Business B receives orders from Company A. Business partners A and B are one another.

6.2.4. Online Payment Technology

An Internet-based approach to handling financial transactions is known as an online payment system. In order to maintain just-in-time inventories, it is common practice for retail stores to maintain direct database connections with their suppliers, which enables vendors to accept payments over the web or other Internet connections. The reach and sales potential of a business are significantly increased by online payment systems.

- **The Facts:** Usually, third-party companies like PayPal, Google, or Click2Pay are in charge of online payment systems. These businesses turn a profit by either accepting a tiny cut of each transaction or by entering into agreements with organizations that require a high volume of transactions.
- **Significance:** It would be impossible for a sizable online retailer like Amazon.com to function without the ability to accept payments online. Due to the fact that all businesses, regardless of size, can accept the same payment methods after registering with third-party payment processors, online payment systems have created a level playing field.
- **Geography:** The Internet and national laws restrict many payment methods, and some vendors and consumers refuse to do business with residents of countries with lax national regulations. Despite this, online payment has a reach as wide as the Internet. Nigeria, for instance, has a notoriously weak fraud protection system, which makes many vendors refuse to accept transactions coming from there.
- **Size:** The United States Census Bureau estimates that $3.7 trillion was transacted in e-commerce in the United States in 2008. This accounted for 16.5% of the US economy and was an increase of 12.1% from the numbers from 2007.
- **Considerations:** Very few companies would not profit from being a part of an online payment system. However, since these transactions are made through independent vendors, no online business should depend solely on one provider. The secret to preventing issues with a single vendor from disrupting a company's cash flow when using online payment systems is diversification.

6.2.4.1. Useful Ways Online Payment Technologies Will Revolutionize Your Business

Many merchants dream of being able to tap into their customers' thoughts. The upcoming wave of payment technology will prioritize providing merchants with greater understanding of the customer experience, particularly at the checkout and payment stages. With data-driven insights, merchants will be able to tailor their services to customers in a more personalized and advanced way, saving time, money, and resources.

We'll go over six strategies in this article that retailers can use to maximize sales and enhance customer satisfaction using payment data without sacrificing operational effectiveness or data security.

6.2.4.1.1. Understanding the Path to Purchase

Better data resources can assist retailers in determining the precise moment in the customer journey when customers abandon their cart, something that many struggle to do. Retailers can make inferences about the reasons behind their customers' non-conversion by understanding when they are leaving the checkout.

6.2.4.1.2. Globalization, Localization and Personalization

Merchants must take into consideration the particular requirements of customers in different locations when pursuing cross-border business. Customers may find it confusing to shop on websites located abroad, particularly if they are unable to use payment methods that are typically accepted in their area.

Simply by determining a customer's location and tailoring the experience accordingly, merchants can enhance the friendliness and comfort of their cross-border shopping experience. Offering appropriate payment options based on the customer's location is one way to do this.

For instance, the retailer can provide a customer experience catered to the local cultural norms, offer promotions that are specifically targeted at that area, and disseminate information about its brand that is pertinent to that community.

When it comes to payment, a lot of customers give up on their carts because the merchant's website does not offer the payment options they would like to use. This is easily fixed by establishing guidelines regarding the payment options that customers can use at various IP addresses or geolocations.

6.2.4.1.3. Protecting Your Consumers from Fraud

Retailers can also foster customer satisfaction and brand loyalty by having the capacity to identify fraud at an early stage and shield consumers from data breaches. Data tools that recognize patterns in consumer behavior, identify irregularities, and flag transactions as possibly fraudulent can be integrated by merchants.

The payment technology can refuse a transaction or flag it for manual review by a company fraud expert if, for instance, a devoted customer who has always shopped with the brand from an IP address in California suddenly starts making payments from an IP address in a fraudulently connected region of China.

6.2.4.1.4. Maximizing Your Payment Rules

Another significant obstacle to the checkout process is back-end inefficiencies, which are readily resolved with increased data transparency. To guarantee higher acceptance rates and eventually higher profits, it is essential to be able to analyze the circumstances surrounding the denial of specific credit cards. With the use of decline rate data, merchants can design unique rules that stop the causes of declines and reroute transactions to save money on transactions. Improved data can assist retailers in detecting, for instance, inaccurate fraud protocols that reject particular card schemes, currencies, or customer locations automatically. In order to avoid these issues, many payment providers currently provide solutions that reroute payments between financial institutions. In order to lower credit card, decline rates and associated cross-border and currency conversion fees, an American retailer may choose to route all payments from European credit cards to European payment providers and all local transactions to its local provider.

6.2.4.1.5. Offering the Omni channel Experience

While maintaining both online and physical stores, many of today's biggest retailers aim to provide customers with an Omni channel experience. However, they lack the necessary tools to ensure a smooth experience across all channels. Modern sophisticated data technologies allow retailers to see the wider picture and comprehend performance across all channels, in addition to analyzing transaction data specific to each retail channel. Merchants are able to better optimize performance across all platforms with this transparency into their payment data.

6.2.4.1.6. The Challenges of Data Maintenance and Storage

Retailers can benefit greatly from data-driven technologies, but there are risks and difficulties associated with using and storing data. Merchants must abide by a number of laws and security procedures, many of which take time to complete and differ from nation to nation, in order to store customer data. However, the majority of payment technologies available today allow retailers to retain compliance and security standards, store data, and view customer information all at the same time. Numerous payment solutions utilize hosted payment fields to address issues related to data management. This approach allows a third-party technology to gather, store, and protect data using white-labeled payment fields that match the design of the merchant's e-commerce site. These fields are hosted on a PCI compliant third-party server. As customers input payment details into these fields, the information is gathered by the technology and kept securely on behalf of the merchant.

6.2.4.1.7. The Possibilities of Big Data

Retailers can design the best checkout experience to satisfy customers by using data intelligence, which provides them with essential knowledge and insight into the customer payment process. Regardless of whether they target local or global consumers, operate in-store, online, or through other channels, or sell physical or digital goods, merchants can use data from customer interactions with the brand to optimize business performance by guiding customers through the checkout process.

6.3. MOBILE COMMERCE

M-commerce, or mobile commerce, refers to the purchasing and selling of goods and services via wireless handheld devices, like PDAs and cell phones. M-commerce, sometimes referred to as next-generation e-commerce, allows users to access the Internet without looking for a place to plug in. Based on the Wireless Application Protocol (WAP), m-commerce is an emerging technology that has advanced significantly more in Europe than in the US. In Europe, mobile devices with Web-ready micro-browsers are far more common than in the US.

Handset makers like Nokia, Ericsson, Motorola, and Qualcomm are collaborating with carriers like AT&T Wireless and Sprint to create WAP-enabled smart phones, which are the industry's equivalent of the Swiss Army Knife, as well as methods of connecting them in order to take advantage of the potential of the m-commerce market. Smart phones, which combine phone, fax, and email functions into one device through Bluetooth technology, are making m-commerce more widely accepted among a workforce that is becoming more and more mobile.

Many believe that m-commerce will overtake wire line e-commerce as the preferred method for conducting digital commerce transactions as content delivery over wireless devices continues to improve in speed, security, and scalability. M-commerce has an impact on the following industries:

- **Financial Services:** brokerage services (where clients can view stock quotes and execute trades from the same handheld device) and mobile banking (where clients use their handheld devices to access their accounts and pay their bills).
- **Telecommunications:** Using a single handheld device, one can perform account reviews, bill payments, and service modifications.
- Service/retail, since customers can make orders and pay for them instantly.
- Services that provide information to a single mobile device, such as traffic updates, sports scores, and financial news.

In an attempt to guarantee m-commerce transaction security, IBM and other businesses are experimenting with speech recognition software.

6.3.1. Opportunities in (or Applications of) M-Commerce

Although still very new, m-commerce has gained popularity and has undergone refinement in recent years. A fundamental instance of mobile commerce involves obtaining sales promotions through a portable electronic device. The most popular use would be for the service provider to text the subscriber with offers of new products, free trials of other services, or other kinds of marketing campaigns. The text message is sent without charge to the subscriber, and they can usually reply with another text message without paying anything. A number of prominent cellular service providers require their users to either consent to this kind of m-commerce or decline to receive the messages.

Offers obtained via mobile commerce can be approved and paid for with the handheld device. If a customer decides to accept an offer, for instance, they typically have a few different ways to pay. The most popular choice is to include a fee in the monthly statement for the rendered services. On the other hand, a lot of m-commerce businesses also provide customers with the option to pay with a credit card that is connected to the SIM card on the portable device.

At the moment, Europe and Asia are the regions where m-commerce is most commonly used. But the idea is starting to catch on in North and South America as well, thanks to the introduction of improved services for cell phones and other mobile devices. At the moment, m-commerce is steadily expanding in the US and Canada, and South America as a whole is leading the way in utilizing this improved technology. M-commerce offers business enterprises the greatest growth opportunities since the dawn of W.W.W., i.e., World Wide Web (WWW is a multi-media system of sound, pictures and video for finding information on the Internet). Through m-commerce, business enterprises can access new customers who would never have used a computer. The scope of possibilities for m-commerce applications is very vast.

Some applications of m-commerce may relate to fields like:

1. Mobile banking;
2. Stock market reports;
3. E-bills;
4. E-salaries;
5. Booking functions;
6. Placing and paying for orders, on fly;
7. Auctions;
8. Retailing;
9. Advertising, etc.

6.3.1.1. Benefits of M-Commerce

Some benefits of m-commerce for business enterprises are:

1. Cost reductions due to streamlined business processes;
2. Reduced sale cycles;
3. Increased revenue streams by accessing new customers;
4. Better customer service;
5. Increase in goodwill, etc.

6.3.1.2. Problems in M-Commerce

Some of the problems which might contain the growth and application of m-commerce are:

1. The existing technology is not best suited for mobile data transfer; as the connections are unstable and data transfer duration is too long.
2. The existing technology is very costly.
3. There is lack of standards relating to mobile phone to network interface; the interfaces between host and mobile platforms and between different mobile platforms.
4. There is a problem of security associated with m-commerce applications. For example, it is not sure what kind of people are behind the billions of mobile devices.
5. The man-machine interface on mobile phone is currently sub-optimal and difficult for mass-market users to manipulate.

6.3.2. Online Portal

A portal is an entrance or door. The World Wide Web and its component webpages are referred to as "online" in this context. A website that serves as a gateway to a variety of resources, including tools, links, and information is known as an online portal, or web portal. There are many uses for an internet portal. Certain portal types are designed to function as a one-stop shop for the majority of needs that certain Internet users may have. A user can save a great deal of time by using an online portal, which provides a variety of the most commonly used information and services, sometimes with the option for personalization. The top current events that are featured in many newspapers, such as headlines and links to significant national and possibly local news, weather forecasts, the day's primetime television schedule, stock market updates, and sports headlines, are among the standard offerings for this kind of portal. A horoscope, trending topics, health and entertainment news, dating and romance advice, links to related websites, a search engine, and occasionally free web-based email are also commonplace.

A company portal, also referred to as an enterprise portal, is another kind of online portal. This kind of web portal serves as the entrance point to an intranet and is typically hosted on a corporate intranet. It contains tools and information that the company's employees will find useful and interesting. Similar to other portals, it might have search engine capabilities, but with an emphasis on internal resources, web-based email access, employee-only content, and, occasionally, more extensive Internet access—possibly to a limited number of websites. Additionally, this kind of portal might have features related to a business dashboard.

An online portal that is specifically designed to represent the needs and interests of the participants in a given industry is called a vortal, or vertical industry portal. All of the information, including tools, forums, data, news, statistics, and research, is therefore connected to the industry that is the focus of the offering. Trade magazines, associations, and special interest groups may host vortals. Vortals can be found in e-commerce as well as industries like advertising, construction, business services, computers, energy, entertainment, and agriculture.

6.3.3. Search Engines

A collection of software tools called search engines are used to look for information in a particular domain and compile it into a database. Though they can also be created for offline content, like a library catalog, the contents of a personal hard drive, or a catalog of museum collections, this term is most frequently used in reference to Internet search engines, which are created expressly to search the Internet. With the aid of these programs, people can arrange and present information so that it is easily accessible.

A search engine's three functions are searching, indexing, and crawling. When a crawl occurs, it searches for newly added content, such as files and web pages that was not there during the previous crawl. Subsequently, the software indexes the data, extracting particular keywords for classification. For instance, indexing on the Internet mainly depends on keywords in web pages and Meta tags that offer details about the page.

After the data has been indexed, a database is created and contains access information. Additionally, some programs "cache" or store data to make it easier to access later. The database returns results that are sorted by relevance when someone searches it.

Despite the fact that all search engines operate similarly, there are many different uses for them. To determine the relevance of their search results, particularly for popular keywords, they mainly rely on intricate algorithms. Consumers are drawn to websites that provide results they find appealing, so search engines such as Google®, Yahoo!®, and Bing® are competing to attract users with features that enhance the relevancy and appeal of their queries.

The act of performing a web search is now so closely linked to Google® that it is frequently referred to as "googling." The business is actually not too happy about this because it thinks that the generic and lower case usage of its name may dilute its trademark. With the ability to learn from their users, a large number of Internet search engines include user activity into their relevancy rankings. To rank search results, they also take into account factors like backlinks from other pages and the reputation of the website, all of which are contained within a small section. Although skilled users can occasionally tamper with search results, a lot of programs adapt and change to help stop this behavior.

6.3.3.1. Search Engines Work

In essence, search engines are computer algorithms that assist users in finding the precise information they seek. While they employ various techniques, they all follow the same fundamental ideas. Creating a local database of the Internet is the first requirement for search engines to operate. Modern versions index every word on every page in addition to a wealth of additional information about the page's relationship to other pages and, in certain situations, all or some of the media that is available on the page. Earlier versions only indexed keywords and page titles. Instead of having to search the entire Internet every time a search query is submitted, search engines should index all of this data so they can conduct searches on it quickly.

These databases are produced by search engines through routine Internet crawls. The majority of pages can now be found by clicking links on other pages; in earlier versions, they frequently needed pages to be submitted to them in order for them to crawl them. These are computer programs designed to index pages, jump from page to page, capture all the information on the page, and follow each link to a new page. They are also known as robots or spiders. Depending on how many spiders they have constantly crawling through the Internet and how quickly they do so, different search engines refresh their indexes at varying intervals. Some search engines work through the Internet every day or two, while others only perform a periodic refresh once a week or month.

The spider makes a note of the words it discovers as it reads through these pages. It keeps track of the frequency with which each word occurs, determines whether the words are weighted according to any particular criteria (like size, location, or HTML markup), and assesses the relevance of the words based on the links that lead to the page as well as the overall context of the page.

The value of each page and the value of each page for the words that appear on it must then be weighted by search engines. The most crucial and challenging step is this one. In its most basic form, it might just keep track of every word on the page and mark it as relevant for searches using that particular keyword. For the majority of users, however, this wouldn't be very helpful because what they want is the most relevant page for their search query. Thus, various engines devise various methods for allocating relative importance.

The algorithms utilized by different search engines are securely guarded to avoid individuals from manipulating pages to improve their rankings, or at least to minimize the extent to which they can do so. This variance is the reason why distinct search engines produce varied results for identical terms. For instance, Google may conclude that a specific page is the most suitable outcome for a search query, while Ask may rank that same page outside of the top 50. These discrepancies are primarily influenced by the importance placed on inbound and outbound links, keyword density, word placement, and various other minor factors.

The latest development in search engines, and probably the direction that search will take overall, is the shift from keyword-based to concept-based searches. With this new type of search, the program attempts to interpret the keywords entered by the user in order to propose pages that may not contain the exact word but are nonetheless relevant to the query, as opposed to restricting the search to the keywords the user enters. Although this field is still in its infancy, it appears to have a great deal of promise for improving the relevancy of searches and making the internet even more user-friendly for finding what you're looking for.

6.3.4. Direct Selling

A salesperson who uses direct selling will typically approach a potential customer face-to-face and with assertiveness, showing them his product or service at their place of business or residence. Direct selling frequently takes the form of door-to-door sales, network marketing, and other independent sales endeavors. A combination of abilities, including presentation, product knowledge, closing, and interpersonal skills, are necessary for successful direct selling.

6.3.4.1. Interpersonal

If your interpersonal communication skills are inadequate, direct selling will not succeed. Customers need to connect with you as a salesperson and have faith in you before you can consistently get them to buy your products. This is particularly true if you sell higher-priced products through direct selling and have to persuade potential customers of their worth. In order to gain access to a person's home or place of business, direct sellers must first establish a friendly and trustworthy manner.

6.3.4.2. Presentation

A lot of direct selling positions require the ability to present. There are occasions when you have to stand in front of potential customers and discuss the benefits of your business, its goods, and services. Tupperware is frequently sold at house parties where guests are invited and the products are presented to them. Product showcases are also frequently held. Vacuum salespeople who knock on doors frequently spend a few hours in a potential customer's home showing them around and outlining the advantages of their product.

6.3.4.3. Product Knowledge

In direct selling, product knowledge is essential. You must establish yourself as the authority in your product category because you frequently sell a single item or a range of related products. In addition to establishing your credibility as a salesperson, this helps uphold the brand you represent. Before making the first call or knocking on the first door, top direct sellers study their products for hours, days, or even weeks.

6.3.4.4. Closing

In direct selling, closing a deal is essential, but it's important in any kind of selling. Some businesses place a strong emphasis on using forceful closing strategies. At this point, you need to convince the prospect to complete the purchase by addressing all of his major concerns and bringing up the close. Effective deal closing requires a certain level of bravery, persuasiveness, and confidence. Certain direct selling companies enforce stringent conversation ratios or quotas on their sellers in order to hold them responsible for closing deals.

6.3.5. E-Business

The term "electronic business" describes transactions involving the purchase and sale of goods and services conducted online. Business-to-business, business-to-consumer, and even consumer-to-consumer sales are all possible in this process. The majority of the time, companies create websites to promote their goods and services and let customers make purchases online. Technological developments on the Internet have made it possible for electronic business, or e-business, to grow to such an extent that very few businesses can compete without making an effort to engage in e-business themselves.

Because of how quickly the Internet has grown, it now has an impact on almost every aspect of modern life. So, it stands to reason that the Internet and all of its applications have permanently changed the way that people conduct business. A modern business is unlikely to succeed by ignoring the global web, with the possible exception of local business. Given this, a large portion of most businesses' attention is currently focused on conducting business electronically.

Electronic business has greatly benefited consumers by providing them with convenience. With just a computer and an Internet connection, individuals can easily complete essential tasks like paying bills, purchasing items, and transferring money with a few clicks. Technological advancements have also improved security measures, giving ordinary people a greater peace of mind when conducting these transactions.

Since almost every step of a business transaction can be completed online, modern businesses frequently focus a large portion of their marketing efforts on their websites and other online applications. Payment can be received and product delivery can occur without the parties physically meeting, whether you're selling to a customer or offering an online service to another company. Although there is no denying the convenience of electronic business, it may not have the same level of trust that comes from face-to-face communication. Via auction and classified websites, customers can also transact electronically with one another when one offers up a product and another connects to make the purchase. Beyond computers, e-business has also expanded, and incredibly sophisticated gadgets like cell phones offer countless opportunities for business uses. In the cutthroat world of business, the ability to reach customers at any time and from any location is a priceless advantage that such technology makes possible.

6.4. INTERNET TRADING RELATIONSHIP

Internet trading has grown significantly in popularity and has greatly aided in the success of many businesses. For instance, trading is the main source of revenue for Internet businesses like eBay and Amazon.com, which have achieved remarkable success in doing so. All big businesses now opt for online trading. Additionally, this implies that brokers and traders who are engaged on the "trading floor" are not allowed to trade. The traders themselves conduct market research and engage in the purchase or sale of capital goods that pique their interest. Internet trading has a lot going for it, including cheap transaction costs, great liquidity, open communication, and narrow spreads. Online trading involves using specialized software to trade contracts over the Internet, a method that is rapidly gaining popularity. Most trading venues are transitioning from the traditional approach of requiring traders to be physically present at a stock exchange or operate through a broker who is physically present. This shift allows individuals to buy assets directly from their trading terminal by providing instructions online.

6.4.1. B2B—Electronic Data Interchange (EDI) and Its Impact on Business

The EDI focuses on e-commerce applications and solutions that increase business trading efficiency while lowering costs. Many businesses all over the world have embraced technology as a means of doing away with the paperwork involved in business transactions, which also helps to do away with errors that arise from manually entering data. Several approaches to EDI use in business have been looked at. An organization must further automate and integrate EDI across all of its other information in order to further reduce costs, boost revenues, and provide higher levels of service. EDI is the foundational technology for developing a highly collaborative operating and service environment. A collaborative implementation is necessary for an organization to function at its peak efficiency. Information is created and expanding at an exponential and uncontrollable rate in the Internet and mobile era. Organizations need a strong standard like EDI to properly harness the sea of data in order to deal with it in a disciplined, automated, controlled, and meaningful manner. EDI, along with its more recent protocols and standards, is a truly comprehensive solution that has withstood the test of time.

6.4.2. B2C—Intra-Organizational E-Commerce

In a large corporation, e-commerce implementation is very challenging. A new area of study called "intra-organizational e-commerce" makes it easier for information to be gathered and shared within organizations so that everyday people's complaints can be quickly resolved.

The advantages are:

- Facilitating faster decision-making by improving departmental employee communication capabilities.
- Tends to decrease record maintenance by doing away with traditional record keeping methods.
- Information collection is a top priority for government agencies, and digital information storage offers effective means of exchanging knowledge and ideas.
- Greater customer satisfaction because all information can be accessed without leaving the office with just a mouse click.

Applications used within a single company are known as intra-organizational e-commerce, and these kinds of projects help with productivity in the sales force, e-publishing, and workgroup communications. B2C e-commerce focuses on transactions, and these projects facilitate social interaction, personal finance management, and the purchase of products and information. Within this framework, the definition for "businesses" can apply to governments as well. Intra-organizational e-commerce includes streamlining efforts within governments; and B2C e-commerce includes government-to-citizen applications and projects.

6.4.3. Supply Chain Management

E-commerce, an advanced transaction method based on computer networks, has become popular worldwide due to the widespread use of computer networks, communication technology, and the internet.

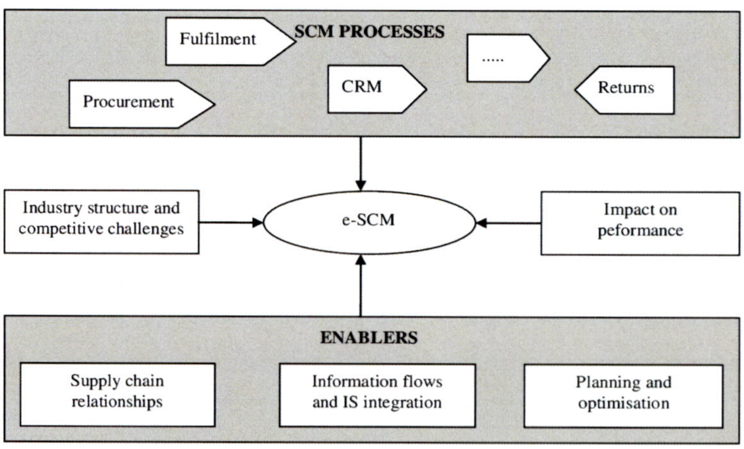

Figure 6.7. *A framework of e-SCM.*

Source: https://d3i71xaburhd42.cloudfront.net/f2f4552df2bd37f138ff614a64f9b8773f5ba835/8-Figure1-1.png.

E-commerce and supply chain management (SCM) are combined in the context of e-commerce, or e-SCM. It prioritizes the needs of the consumer, integrates the entire supply chain process, fully utilizes outside resources, enables quick response times, and significantly lowers stock levels. The growth of e-commerce creates favorable conditions for supply chain management implementation, but it also raises more demands. As a result, e-SCM will genuinely take the lead in enterprise supply chain management and become increasingly widely used by businesses. In addition to being a key area of focus for international business management, e-SCM is becoming a crucial tool for businesses looking to increase their competitiveness and flexibility (Figure 6.7).

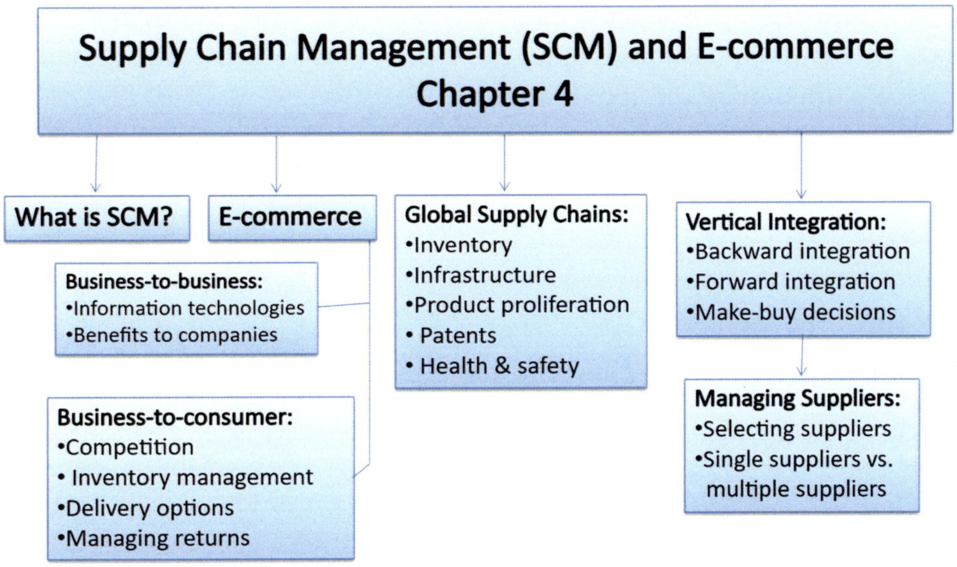

Figure 6.8. *The SCM with e-commerce retail.*

Source: https://slideplayer.com/slide/6228440/20/images/3/Supply+Chain+Management+%28SCM%29+and+E-commerce+Chapter+4.jpg.

The SCM is in charge of overseeing a web of linked companies that provide the final product and service bundles that end users need. SCM includes all transportation and storage of raw materials, completed goods, and inventory of goods in process from the point of origin to the point of consumption. The SCM links disparate enterprise groups in an effort to find the optimal pairing. It symbolizes the idea that system management is fundamentally complex, dynamic, integrative, win-win, and nature cross. The great majority of online sales are made through business-to-business (B2B) e-commerce, which also dominates international supply chain networks (Figure 6.8).

A large amount of content is included in the SCM, such as production design and control, stock control, purchase, sales, logistics, forecast requirements, customer management, partner evaluation and selection, and so forth. It is, in essence, the management of fund, material, and information flow. Thus, utilize the flow of these three flows to elucidate the fundamental ideas of supply chain management.

6.4.4. E-commerce Versus Traditional Commerce

A growing number of conventional small businesses are viewing e-commerce as a legitimate and successful sales channel as a result of the growing acceptance and accessibility of Internet access. E-commerce and traditional commerce differ greatly, though, so it's critical to consider these distinctions carefully when determining whether going e-commerce would be a wise business decision or simply an expensive mistake. In online shopping:

- Everything is digital.
- Less overhead costs.
- Elimination of the middleman.
- Financial transactions on the internet can actually be more secure than in traditional retail environments.
- Speed.
- Empowerment.
- Personalization.

6.4.4.1. Traditional Commerce

Conventional commerce involves the exchange of goods, services, or information through physical means, most likely through a physical store. When referring to shopping, it means going to a physical store rather than shopping online.

It's possible that traditional commerce began before history was written, when our ancestors first chose to specialize their daily tasks. Rather than being reliant on cultivating crops, obtaining food, and crafting tools, families acquired expertise in one of these domains and exchanged a portion of their output for other necessities. Bartering was the original method, but as time went on, the use of money made transactions easier to settle. Nonetheless, trade's fundamental workings remained the same. The differences are described as:

6.4.4.1.1. Direct Interaction

Face-to-face interaction is frequently the foundation of traditional commerce. In order to guarantee a positive transaction, the customer has the opportunity to ask questions, and the sales team can assist them. These frequently present salespeople with the chance to upsell, or persuade the customer to purchase an expensive item or a pair of related items, boosting the store's earnings. However, until features like related items or live chats are added, e-commerce is unable to provide this advantage.

6.4.4.1.2. Lower Costs

E-commerce is typically far less expensive than keeping a physical store open in a similarly prominent area. For instance, starting an online store can be done for less than $50 per month, which is a fraction of the cost when compared to expenses like commercial space rent. For small business owners without the initial capital to hire employees and rent premium retail space so they can sell their products, this can be extremely helpful.

6.4.4.1.3. Reach

With an online store, one can conduct business with anyone who resides in a nation they can send mail to, as opposed to traditional commerce, which is limited to customers who physically visit the store. Additionally, this makes a wide range of other online marketing strategies possible, many of which increase sales and even foot traffic to the store. One can have as many customers as the stock will allow in an online store, which has no capacity restrictions.

6.4.4.1.4. Returns Rate

In a conventional brick-and-mortar store, customers have the advantage of being able to physically experience and inspect products before making a purchase. This helps to minimize the likelihood of returns or complaints stemming from discrepancies between the item and its description in a catalogue or promotional materials. Conversely, when transitioning to online retail, businesses should anticipate a higher rate of returns, as customers may order products to try at home and easily return them via mail without any face-to-face interaction.

6.4.4.1.5. Credit Card Fraud

Because e-commerce is remote, it is much harder to detect fraud, which means that businesses may suffer financial losses as a result of fraud. Even though traditional commerce is not completely secure, it is simpler for a salesperson to confirm that the customer making a purchase is the true credit card holder by requesting a picture ID. Nonetheless, the battle against credit card fraud is well under way, with banks and conscientious online retailers cooperating to ensure that all credit card transactions are authentic.

Selling online involves mastering new customer service techniques, marketing strategies, and order fulfillment processes, but the advantages are significant. By operating online, one can reduce costs, reach a larger customer base, and conduct business around the clock, freeing up time to enhance products and services and improve the overall customer experience.

Certain products, like jewelry, are more suitable for online selling compared to items like houses or cars. Nevertheless, having an online store can also drive traffic to physical stores, as customers can easily discover and explore the products available (Figure 6.9).

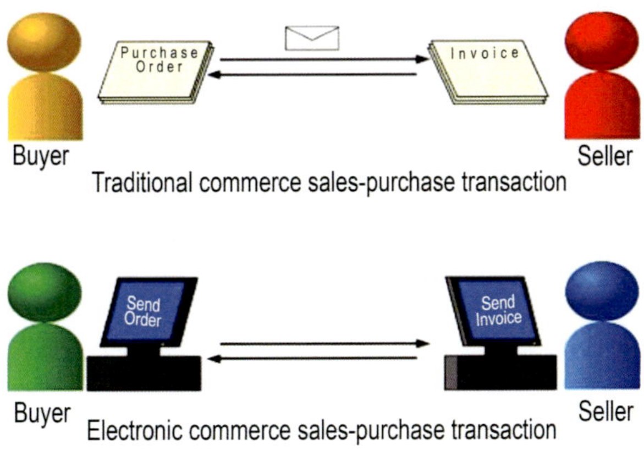

Figure 6.9. *Traditional commerce and e-commerce sales-purchase transaction.*

Source: https://image.slidesharecdn.com/ecommerce-160218092357/75/E-commerce-8-2048.jpg.

The main points of difference between traditional commerce and e-commerce are as (*See* Table 6.1):

Table 6.1. *E-commerce Versus Traditional Commerce*

SL. No	Traditional Commerce	E-Commerce
1	It refers to the commercial transactions and exchange of information, making payment, buying and selling of products and services between two people using the internet.	In e-commerce every transaction, communication, buying and selling of products and services, sending and receiving payments are all done via electronic mode using the internet.
2	In traditional commerce, establishing and maintaining standard practices is difficult.	In E-commerce, establishing and maintaining standard practices is easy.
3	In traditional commerce, a direct interaction between buyer and seller is possible.	In e-commerce, communication between buyer and seller is done indirectly
4	Traditional commerce is carried out by face to face4, telephone lines, and mail systems.	E-commerce is carried out by the internet
5	In traditional commerce, transactions are processed in a manual way.	In e-commerce, Transactions are processed automatically.
6	In traditional commerce, goods are received instantly	In e-commerce, the delivery of goods takes time.
7	In traditional commerce, accessibility to products is for a limited time	In e-commerce, products and services are accessible 24*7
8	Traditional commerce is done where the digital network is unavailable	Using e-commerce a lot of time and money is saved
9	Traditional commerce is an older method of doing business	E-commerce is the latest technology for doing business
10	Its resource focuses on the supply side.	Its resource focuses on the demand side.
11	In traditional commerce, Customers can touch and see the products and also can judge the quality of a product by checking it	In eCommerce, customers are not allowed to check the product physically before getting it.
12	Traditional business has the limitation of reaching people	There is no boundation in reaching people. E-commerce can be done worldwide.

Source: https://www.wdptechnologies.com/difference-between-traditional-commerce-and-e-commerce/.

Today's businesses must constantly innovate to meet the changing needs and desires of consumers for better, faster, and more affordable products and services. Adapting to new technology and consumer trends is crucial for success and survival in the competitive market. E-commerce is rapidly growing in importance for businesses as technology advances, and it should be utilized and integrated into business strategies.

The opportunities for businesses and consumers have expanded exponentially since the advent of the Internet and e-commerce increasing options for customers and providing businesses with more avenues for growth and profit. Like anything else, e-commerce has drawbacks, such as consumer uncertainty, but these are manageable and preventable with wise decision-making and sound business practices.

When launching an online store, a number of aspects and variables must be taken into account and chosen. Among them are various e-commerce platforms, marketing tactics, and a host of other things. A company can operate successfully and profitably in an e-commerce environment if the right procedures and guidelines are followed.

CASE STUDY

CISCO: TRANSFORMATION OF ENTIRE SUPPLY CHAIN INTO AN EXTENDED ENTERPRISE SYSTEM

Cisco Systems of San Jose, California, is a company that develops networking devices such as switches, routers, network management software, and dial- up access servers. By the mid-1990s, realizing that growth depended on our ability to scale manufacturing, distribution and other supply chain processes quickly, Cisco managers decided to reinvent its business model and turn itself into a Web-enabled company. An 'ecosystem' which in fact transformed the entire supply chain into an extended enterprise system based on internet technology was created in order to links customers, prospects, partners, suppliers and employees in a multi-party, multi-location electronic network.

E-Business can be defined as all electronically mediated information exchanges, both within an organization and with external stakeholders supporting the range of business processes. It links internal employees with external customers, suppliers through technology like Internet, intranets, and extranets. E-commerce, conceived as a subset of e-business, can be categorized as buy-side e-commerce which are equivalent to upstream supply chain and sell-side e-commerce which equate to downstream supply chain. A 'supply chain' is a network of facilities and distribution options that performs the functions of procurement of materials, transformation of these materials into intermediate and finished products, and the distribution of these finished products to customers. An effective supply chain management can improve efficiency throughout e-business.

Cisco estimated that in financial year 2000, a total of US$695 million would be saved by adopting this interconnected supply chain. These solid figures prove the potential benefits e-business can bring into Cisco are enormous. Broadly speaking, it is argued that there are at least two primary ways in which the application of e-business technologies can improve the efficiency of a supply chain. First is known as disintermediation, which organization eliminates the communication and coordination costs associated by eliminating links in the supply chain. The second way is by lowering the cost of communication and coordination among the various members of supply chain. In this case, Cisco adopted the second way by using information technology to communicate, which enable faster, more accurate, and lower cost information exchanges with its trading partners.

Upstream Issues (Buy-Side)

Upstream supply chain is the transactions between an organization and its suppliers and intermediaries. In this particular case, Cisco outsourced most of the manufacturing and logistics activities as James Crowther, customer business solutions manager said, in order to increase production capacity enough to meet demand. Outsourcing is a business activity subcontracting a process, product design or manufacturing, to a third-party company. Cisco's suppliers not only make all of the components and perform 90% of the sub-assembly work, but they also undertake 55% of the final. By outsourcing production of 70% of its products, Cisco has quadrupled output without building new plants. Furthermore, through Cisco Manufacturing On-line, Cisco has created an extranet application that increases productivity and efficiency in the manufacturing, supply, and logistics functions among globally networked partners. The accomplishment not only increased the outputs but left Cisco free to concentrate on their real strengths: new product development, looking after customer needs and brand management.

Cisco Manufacturing Connection Online (MCO)

Since relationships with suppliers are especially critical in the Economy, Cisco has created an Extract application that leverages productivity and efficiency in the supply function through MCO, which can be viewed as supply chain portal that seamlessly connects Cisco to its contract manufacturers, distributors, and logistics partners. The core of MCO dealing with their supplier is centralizing the process control and as a consequence decentralizing actual execution. There is a three-part strategy to scale its upstream supply chain in a cost-effective manner in MCO:

1. **Auto Test:** To resolve the testing problem, Cisco has installed automated test cells on all Cisco-dedicated supplier production lines using Cisco-developed technology to automatically configure test procedures for each specific customer order so that the quality could be controlled and the cost of deploying a test engineer could be saved. However, although Cisco outsourced much of the physical test, the company retained the intelligence behind the testing.
2. **Direct Fulfillment:** Cisco launched a global direct fulfillment model under which most of the company's manufacturing partners can now ship directly to customers. This will reduce the distribution cost between Cisco and supply chain partners.
3. **Dynamic replenishment:** By direct linking to the suppliers, Cisco could gain real-time access to supplier information so that delivery lead-times, errors and inventory will be cut and the productivity of its employees involved in purchasing will be improved. The purchasing teams can focus on more strategic activities such as partnership and business development.

The implication of increasing outsourcing of core activities is that companies will move towards the virtual organization which leads to a more responsive and flexible company with great market orientation. As Pete Rukavina, Cisco's director of global supply chain management, addressed: "For every Cisco manufacturing employee there are six virtual manufacturing employees who use Cisco processes, are measured against Cisco metrics, and are located around the world."

Traditionally, a new product introduction had been a process in which engineering, procurement, manufacturing and marketing were performed sequentially in time-consuming steps. Cisco has networked these functions in order to extract real benefits with its partners. A perfect example could be car industry where car plants traditionally would be located nearby the raw material factory so that inputs directly from factory will be produced as a result of cars. However, there has been a trend to outsourcing more and more components such as lights, trim and even engine to third party. Just-in-time of Toyota was created based on the outsourcing strategy.

Downstream Issues (Sell-Side)

Downstream supply chain is the transactions between an organization and its customers and intermediaries. There were some potential issues which Cisco has faced in the process of selling products in the past:

- One-third of all faxed orders. Due to the nature of fax, orders will inevitably contain errors sometimes so that it will delay the processing. In addition, 15% of the number of orders required reworking.
- Sundry expenses. Delivering software purchases to its customers on CD by a freight forwarder will generate a cost of delivering.
- New product introduction. Time-to-market of new products is counted in months or years.

Cisco Connection Online is introduced in order to deal with these issues.

Cisco Connection Online (CCO)

Customer Connection Online is essentially a web portal to information stored in Cisco's enterprise resource planning [ERP] databases, legacy systems and client/server systems, and acts as a comprehensive resource for our customers, resellers, suppliers and partners. In fact, it used the Internet as the prime customer contact channel so that customer information and decision-making feeds directly into the supply chain. Technology is vital to supply chain management since managing relationships with customers, suppliers and intermediaries is based on the flow of information and the transactions between the parties. Customers rely on CCO to answer questions, diagnose network problems, and provide solutions and expert assistance worldwide based on four components of CCO:

1. **Market-Place:** It is a virtual shopping center in which customers can purchase items online. It also offers users tools for configure, price, route and submit orders. This function can be used to solve the first problem which is lots of errors contained in fax. With the introduction of Market-place, customers rarely make purchasing mistakes by ordering online. Only 2%ages are required rework.
2. **Status Agent:** It gives Cisco's sales force, as well as direct customers and sales partners, immediate access to critical information about the status of customers' order. The sales force can not only prevent possible billing or shipment problems by accessing order information but also save time such as tracking order status in order to devote to building relationships with customers and seeking new business opportunities.

3. **Customer Service:** It provides nontechnical assistance on a self-help basis for customer requests. No one is better motivated to help the customer than the customers themselves. The self-service model which Cisco is committed is argued to know as raising the customer satisfactory overall.
4. **Technical Assistance and Software Library:** It enables customers and business partners to get online answers to technical questions and download software updates and utilities for Cisco hardware, which saved over US$500,000 per year in freight forwarding charges.

Specifically, the Web gives Cisco both a vehicle through which customers can find out about products and buy them and an automated support system that can reach a larger audience. Modern marketing philosophy requires that organization be committed to customer orientation. It is important that introduce a new product earlier than competitors because customers intend to accept the first new item. In the response of the third problem identified above, Cisco automated the process for gathering product data information, thereby reducing the amount of time required to less than 15 minutes. It is believed that this type of positive impact on time-to-market generated an extra US$388 million in income during 2000.

Furthermore, it is recognized that building strong customer relationships is the key driver to sustainable profitability. CRM is therefore considered to be the most important element within e-business context. Essentially, CRM is an approach to building and sustaining long-term business with customers. It is about customer acquisition, customer retention and customer extension. It is recommended that the first step is to retain existing customer because the costs of acquiring new customers are so high that repeat business is essential. The next step is to acquire new customers on a profitable basis. It is argued that by giving customers tools for self-configuration and turning its back office into the customer's front office could be one of the best ways Cisco do.

Cisco Employee Connection (CEC)

Cisco's ecosystem looks inward as well as outward. Whereas CCO addresses the needs of Cisco customers, partners, suppliers, and employees, Cisco Employee Connection (CEC) is limited to information and services that address the unique needs of individual Cisco employees. In order to improve employee satisfaction and scale its workforce without incurring unnecessary overhead, Cisco re-engineered all its internal and external employee services. Applying the CEC, the following benefits can be provided.

- **Ubiquitous Communications:** Every one of Cisco's employees around the world is connected through the Cisco network.
- **Streamlined Business:** The interactive tools reduce the time that employees spend handling repetitive tasks and streamline routine business process.
- **Integrated Business Systems:** The CEC home page serves as the launching pad, all of information sharing the same navigational tools and a common user interface.

E-Supply Chain (Both Upstream and Downstream Issue)

In today's digital economy, flexibility, adaptation and responsiveness are critical to success. The Internet is the greatest ICT (information and communication technology) tool, and 'integration' is the key to efficiency and success. The company Cisco has opened up its internal information systems to suppliers and other supply chain partners, giving the employees the same access rights to information as Cisco employees, and as a result enabling the Cisco ecosystem to act as a distributed knowledge management network. This networked ecosystem that leverages the collective capabilities of all supply chain partners integrates all supply chain activities so that it achieved successful e-supply chain management. The reasons for that can be described as:

- Firstly, the ecosystem standardizes and streamlines internal processes. The successful ERP system associated with CEC implementation forces Cisco to standardize, restructure and streamline the 'internal' functions. ERP systems enable organizational standardization, including the standardization among different locations belonging to the same enterprise.
- Secondly, the ecosystem streamlines external processes by seamless integration with suppliers and customers in terms of MCO and CCO. Materials and inventory position, product availability, price information, purchase orders and changes, vendor receipt/acceptance, Invoice payments and status reporting information are all visible among partners, including design-related information and sales forecasts
- Thirdly, Cisco has formed strategic alliances and long-term partnerships with suppliers and customers, basing on mutual trust and win-win strategy. Lack of mutual trust and unwillingness to share information among the partners appear to be the greatest obstacles in the way of e-collaboration.

Comparing the Cisco ecosystem with SIMON (Shell Inventory Managed Order Network) which applied by Shell Chemicals, SIMON enables the transfer of responsibility for inventory management from customer to supplier. In other words, there is no need for customer to place an offer since vital inventory will be on customer. Customers pay only for what they consume. The SIMON is so successful in the downstream process that it was then applied to the upstream processes which are acquiring raw materials from supplier. Both Ecosystem and SIMON works in some extent due to the mutual trust and a belief that there are significant benefits to be realized on both sides. The shared information between all parties in the supply chain is also critical to succeed. However, e-business does not always lead to organization success. For instance, Webvan, a top internet grocer based in the US, went bankrupt in 2001, because of poorly implemented e-business and over depending on technology and missed out the customers and inter-organization management.

To sum up, the ability to engage in collaborative planning and making joint decisions with both suppliers and customers are critical components of forming e-supply chain. Moreover, lack of integration between members of a supply chain results in operational inefficiencies that compromise the performance of the supply chain.

SUMMARY

- The electronic purchase and sale of goods and services is known as electronic commerce, or e-commerce.
- E-commerce is the practice of conducting business via the internet and the web. Geographical and other barriers have been overcome by e-commerce companies thanks to technology. But an overwhelming lack of in-person interaction combined with an over-reliance on technology has severely damaged consumer confidence in e-commerce businesses.
- The primary step in developing an e-commerce solution is building and launching an e-commerce website.
- The rise of e-commerce is changing the nature of business. It gives businesses new avenues for market expansion, optimizes internal business processes for more effective delivery of goods and services, draws in and keeps consumers in novel and creative ways, and lowers operating expenses. The way suppliers, workers, and customers interact with one another is changing as a result of e-commerce.
- E-commerce can help even small businesses that offer personal services, like hair and nail salons, by offering a website where customers can purchase related health and beauty products that are typically exclusive to their local clientele.
- Computer tools are beneficial to almost any kind of business; word processors and spreadsheet creators, like Microsoft Word and Excel, have become indispensable office software.
- Data transfer between two different systems can be facilitated with the use of an electronic data interchange tool. This kind of data interchange is subject to a number of regulations and procedures that need to be arranged beforehand.
- M-commerce, or mobile commerce, refers to the purchasing and selling of goods and services via wireless handheld devices, like PDAs and cell phones. M-commerce, sometimes referred to as next-generation e-commerce, allows users to access the Internet without looking for a place to plug in.
- A number of prominent cellular service providers require their users to either consent to this kind of m-commerce or decline to receive the messages.
- A portal is an entrance or door. The World Wide Web and its component webpages are referred to as "online" in this context. A website that serves as a gateway to a variety of resources, including tools, links, and information is known as an online portal, or web portal.
- A collection of software tools called search engines are used to look for information in a particular domain and compile it into a database. Though they can also be created for offline content, like a library catalog, the contents of a personal hard drive, or a catalog of museum collections, this term is most frequently used in reference to Internet search engines, which are created expressly to search the Internet.

- Internet trading has grown significantly in popularity and has greatly aided in the success of many businesses. For instance, trading is the main source of revenue for Internet businesses like eBay and Amazon.com, which have achieved remarkable success in doing so.
- In a large corporation, e-commerce implementation is very challenging. A new area of study called "intra-organizational e-commerce" makes it easier for information to be gathered and shared within organizations so that everyday people's complaints can be quickly resolved.
- E-commerce, an advanced transaction method based on computer networks, has become popular worldwide due to the widespread use of computer networks, communication technology, and the internet.

REVIEW QUESTIONS

1. Explain the need and essential requirements of e-commerce.
2. Write the challenges of e-commerce.
3. What are the elements of e-commerce?
4. Write some features of e-commerce.
5. What so you understand by the electronic data interchange (EDI)?
6. Elaborate the importance of online portal.
7. What is the difference between e-commerce and e-business?
8. Give an overview on the supply chain management role in e-commerce.
9. What is the impact of B2B- electronic data interchange (EDI) on Business?
10. What is the most effective way to promote an e-commerce website?
11. What are the best strategies for dealing with online shopping cart abandonment?
12. What are the social media tools for online sellers?
13. What are the most important metrics for e-commerce companies?

REFERENCES

1. Azad Chowdhury, M. S., Bappi, M. A. U., Imtiaz, M. N., Hoque, S., Islam, S., & Haque, M. S. (2022). The transition of e-commerce industry in Bangladesh: Added concerns & ways of recovery. *International Journal of Economics and Finance, 14*(7), 18. http://dx.doi.org/10.5539/ijef.v14n7p18.
2. Bravo, R., Segura, M. G., Temowo, O., & Samaddar, S. (2022). How does a pandemic disrupt the benefits of e-commerce? A case study of small and medium enterprises in the US. *Journal of Theoretical and Applied Electronic Commerce Research, 17*(2), 522–57. http://dx.doi.org/10.3390/jtaer17020028.
3. Enache, M. C. (2021). Blockchain in e-commerce. *Risk in Contemporary Economy, 1*(1), 254–60. http://dx.doi.org/10.35219/rce20670532118.

4. Gai, S. (2022). *Ecommerce reimagined*. Springer Singapore. http://dx.doi.org/10.1007/978-981-19-0003-7.

5. Heinemann, G. (2020). *B2B eCommerce*. Springer Fachmedien Wiesbaden. http://dx.doi.org/10.1007/978-3-658-27367-5.

6. Kumhar, M. (2022). Ecommerce website. *International Journal for Research in Applied Science and Engineering Technology, 10*(5), 1459–62. http://dx.doi.org/10.22214/ijraset.2022.42447.

7. Lawrence, J. E. (2011). Barriers hindering eCommerce adoption. *International Journal of Technology Diffusion, 2*(2), 47–59. http://dx.doi.org/10.4018/jtd.2011040104.

8. Meier, A., & Stormer, H. (2012). *eBusiness & eCommerce*. Springer Berlin Heidelberg. http://dx.doi.org/10.1007/978-3-642-29802-8.

9. Mohammed, S., Fiaidhi, J., Ramos, C., Kim, T.-H., Fang, W. C., & Abdelzaher, T. (2021). Blockchain in eCommerce. *ACM Transactions on Internet Technology, 21*(1), 11–55. http://dx.doi.org/10.1145/3445788.

10. Peters, K., Albers, S., Asselmann, D., & Schäfers, B. (2009). eCommerce revisited. *Marketing ZFP, 31*(JRM 2), 85–104. http://dx.doi.org/10.15358/0344-1369-2009-jrm-2-85.

11. Singh, S. (2022). Study on impact of e-commerce in Indian economy. *YMER Digital, 21*(05), 658–61. http://dx.doi.org/10.37896/ymer21.05/75.

12. Sugianto, L.-F., & Tojib, D. R. (2007). eCommerce: Portal power. *Monash Business Review, 3*(1), 25. http://dx.doi.org/10.2104/mbr07016.

CHAPTER

7 Networks and Cloud Computing

LEARNING OBJECTIVES

After studying this chapter, you will be able to:

- Understand network fundamentals;
- Explain the internet and World Wide Web;
- Discuss on the internet of things;
- Learn about Cloud computing.

KEY TERMS FROM THIS CHAPTER

Application programming interface
Cloud Data Analytics
Cloud network
Internet of things(IoT)
Platform as a Service (PaaS)
Wide area network
Cloud computing
Cloud Management
Infrastructure as a service
Local area network (LAN)
Software as a service
Wireless access point (WAP)

INTRODUCTION

In the cloud, the network can either facilitate dependability, security, and compliance, or it can act as a barrier that prevents all three. That is the conundrum that many IT workers are currently grappling with. Although cloud computing services can give businesses the flexibility they need to adapt to constantly shifting business needs, IT professionals frequently struggle to get over the worry that something terrible could go wrong. A well-designed network can help overcome these barriers.

A computer network that is housed within or a component of a cloud computing infrastructure is referred to as a cloud network. It is a type of computer network that connects cloud-based and cloud-enabled applications, services, and solutions to one another. A cloud network may be either cloud enabled or cloud based.

The main purpose of a cloud network is to facilitate communication between a cloud computing infrastructure or solution, its related parts, and external users, applications, or services. A cloud network often functions similarly to a traditional computer network, but it is primarily focused on cloud computing in terms of devices, components, and operations. A cloud network, for instance, makes it possible to link a distant user to cloud infrastructure (IaaS) or cloud applications (SaaS). User requests are sent to and received from the remote/backend cloud infrastructure via a web browser or the internet. In a similar vein, network communication between virtual machines is also made possible by cloud networks.

7.1. NETWORK FUNDAMENTALS

In computing, a group of two or more communicative devices is called a network. A network is actually made up of several distinct computer systems connected by wired or wireless connections. The scope can be as small as a single PC sharing out its basic peripherals or as large as global data centers or even the Internet itself. All networks, regardless of size, enable people and/or computers to exchange data and resources. (Rogala, S.M. 2002)

Computer networks serve a number of purposes, some of which include:

- Communications such as email, instant messaging, chat rooms, etc.;
- Shared hardware such as printers and input devices;
- Shared data and information through the use of shared storage devices;
- Shared software, which is achieved by running applications on remote computers.

7.1.1. Defining a Network

A network is a collection of two or more connected devices, such as computers, that share information. Networks facilitate electronic communications, file sharing, and resource sharing. For instance, several computers connected to a network can share a printer or exchange files.

7.1.2. Types of Networks

Two very common types of networks include:

- Local Area Network (LAN)
- Wide Area Network (WAN)

7.1.2.1. Local Area Network

A network that is limited to a small area is called a local area network, or LAN. Usually, it is restricted to a certain location, like a writing lab, school, or building.

Servers and workstations are two general categories for computers that are networked together. Typically, servers are not utilized by people directly; instead, they function constantly to offer services to other computers on the network, as well as to the people who use them. Printing and faxing, hosting software, file sharing and storage, messaging, data storing and retrieval, total access control (security) for the network's resources, and many more services can be offered (Figure 7.1) (Huawei Technologies Co., Ltd. (2023)).

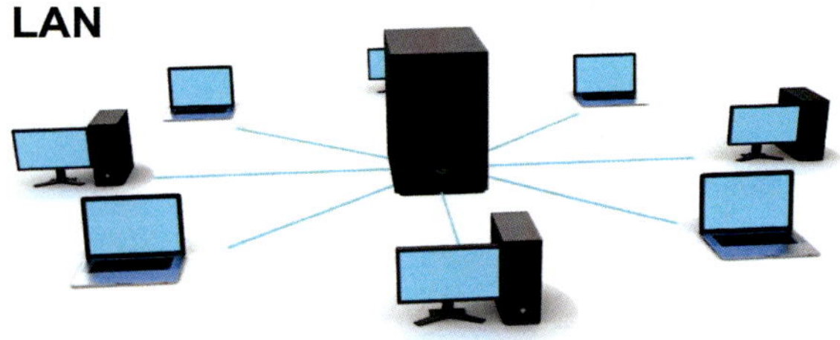

Figure 7.1. *Local area network.*

Source: https://cdn.techterms.com/img/lg/lan_79.jpg.

Workstations get their name from the fact that a human user usually uses them to communicate with the network.

Traditionally, a workstation was defined as either a laptop with an integrated keyboard, display, and touchpad, or a desktop computer with a keyboard, mouse, and display.

Due to their capacity to communicate with networks and make use of network services, tablets and other touch-screen devices, like the iPad and iPhone, are rapidly changing the way we define workstations.

Workstations typically lack the power of servers, though configurations vary depending on requirements. For instance, a collection of servers may be kept out of human sight in a secure location and only reachable via a network. It would be typical for the servers to function in these situations without a dedicated keyboard or display.

However, the cost of the system may increase significantly depending on the capacity and speed of the server's hard drive, main memory, and processor(s). Conversely, a workstation may require a more costly display to meet the demands of its user even though it may not require as much storage or working memory. On a network, every computer needs to be set up properly for its intended use. Computers and servers can be wired or wirelessly connected to one another within a single LAN.

Wireless access points (WAPs) enable wireless connectivity to a wired network. These wireless access points act as a link between networks and PCs. Although in practice a typical WAP may be able to connect far fewer wireless users to a network, theoretically it may be able to connect hundreds or even thousands.

Since cables continue to be the fastest connection type, servers are almost always connected to the network via cables. Static workstations, or desktops, are typically connected to the network via a cable as well. However, with the decreasing cost of wireless adapters, installing workstations in an existing building with inadequate wiring can sometimes be easier and less expensive when using wireless for a desktop.

7.1.2.2. Wide Area Network

Wide Area Networks (WANs) link networks over wider geographical regions, like the globe, Florida, or the US. This kind of global network can be connected via satellite uplinks or dedicated transoceanic cabling.

Schools in Florida can instantly communicate with locations like Tokyo through WANs, all without having to pay exorbitant phone bills. Real-time teleconferences between two users who are separated by half a world and have webcams and microphones on their workstations are possible. A WAN is difficult to use. To link local and metropolitan networks to international communications networks like the Internet, it makes use of multiplexers, bridges, and routers. However, a WAN and a LAN won't seem all that different to users (Figure 7.2).

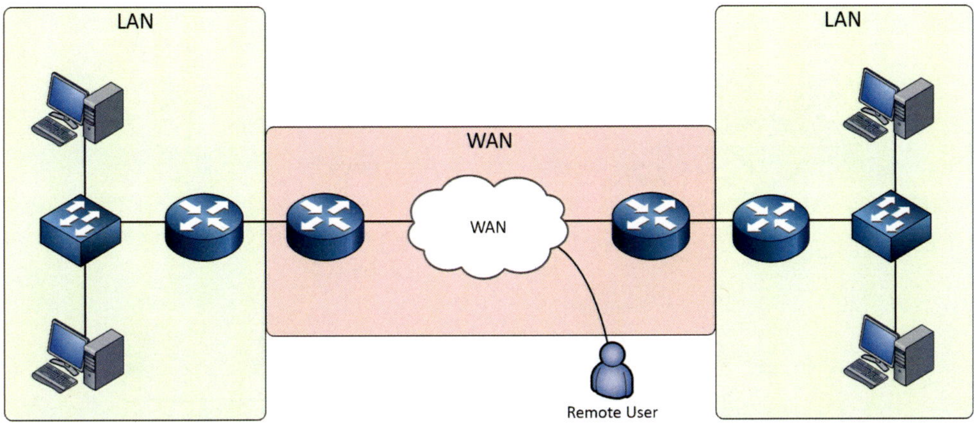

Figure 7.2. *Wide area network.*

Source: https://networklessons.com/wp-content/uploads/2017/01/local-area-network-connected-to-wide-area-network.png.

7.1.2.4 Computer Network Topologies

The relationship between connected devices as represented by a geometric graph is referred to as network topology. In a graph, devices are represented as vertices and the connections between them as edges. It explains the number of connections, their order, and the hierarchy of each device.

Typical topologies comprise the following main types of network topologies to depict the logical or physical architecture of a network.

Networks with Full Mesh Technology, in which every node is interconnected and capable of exchanging data.

Partial mesh networks: these comprise nodes with some connected to other nodes in the network via a full mesh scheme, while other nodes are only connected to one or two other nodes.

- Networks with only two endpoints connected are called point-to-point networks.
- Network fabric: a system of interconnected switches that allows endpoints to communicate with one another and to connect to any other by following a path through a pattern of connections that crisscrosses.
- A tree network is an assembly of two or more interconnected star networks.
- A star network, where each node is linked to a shared central processor.
- A bus is a circuit configuration in which every network device is directly connected to a transmission line. All signals flow through every device in the bus, but each device is uniquely identified and can distinguish between signals that are meant for it (Figure 7.3).

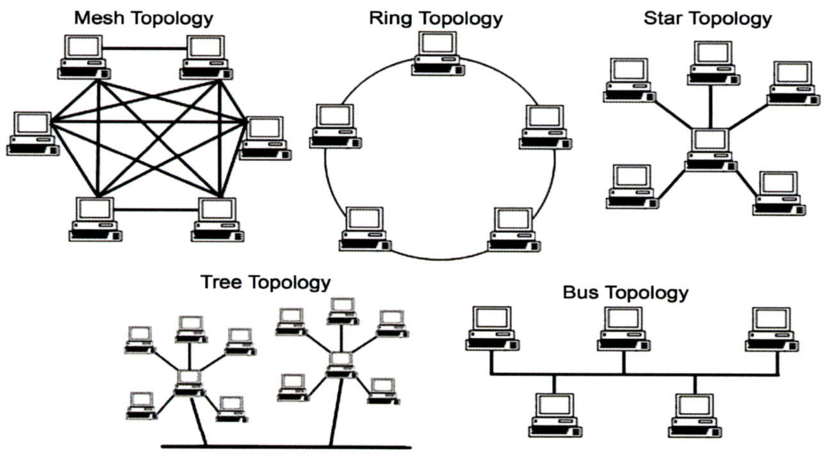

Figure 7.3. *Computer network topologies.*

Source: https://www.computerhope.com/jargon/n/nettopo.gif.

7.1.3. The Importance of Network Standards

To guarantee that hardware and software can cooperate, network standards are crucial. It would be difficult to create a network for information sharing without standards. There are two types of networking standards: formal and de facto (informal).

Governments or industry associations create formal standards. There are formal standards for hardware, data link layer software, network layer software, and other areas. Formal standardization entails a drawn-out process of specification development, decision-making, and industry acceptance.

The American National Standards Institute (ANSI) and the International Organization for Standardization (ISO) are two of the top standardization organizations. The Internet Engineering Task Force (IETF) is the most well-known standards organization in the world. The majority of the Internet is governed by standards set by IETF.

De facto standards comprise the second category of networking standards. Though they lack official support, technology vendors generally support these standards as they arise in the market.

For instance, although it is not officially recognized by any standards body, Microsoft Windows is a de facto standard. Simply put, it is widely acknowledged and accepted.

7.1.4. Network Models

Networks are made simpler by separating everything into layers, each of which is independent of the others and handles a specific task.

From the top layer in one station to the bottom layer, across the channel to the next station, and back up the hierarchy, control is transferred from one layer to the next. A collection of network layers and their interactions are specified by means of network models. The TCP/IP Model and the OSI Network Model are the two most well-known network models.

7.1.4.1. The 7 Layers of the OSI Model

An open standard for all communication systems is called Open System Interconnect, or OSI. A networking framework for implementing protocols in seven layers is defined by the OSI model (Figure 7.4).

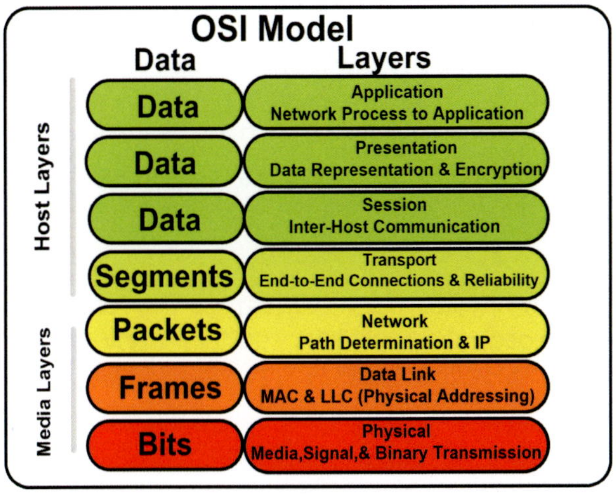

Figure 7.4. *Seven layers of the OSI model.*

Source: http://electricala2z.com/wp-content/uploads/2017/10/osi-model.gif.

7.1.4.1.1. Physical Layer

This layer transmits data through the network at the electrical and mechanical levels, such as an electrical impulse, light, or radio signal. In addition to specifying cables, cards, and other physical components, it offers the hardware necessary for transmitting and receiving data on a carrier. Ethernet, FDDI, B8ZS, and are a few examples. V.35.V.24 RJ45.

7.1.4.1.2. Data Link Layer

Data packets are encoded and decoded into bits at this layer. It provides flow control, frame synchronization, error handling in the physical layer, and knowledge of transmission protocols. The Media Access Control (MAC) layer and the Logical Link Control (LLC) layer are the two sublayers that make up the data link layer. PPP, FDDI, ATM, IEEE 802.5/802.2, IEEE 802.3/802.2, HDLC, and frame relay are a few examples.

7.1.4.1.3. Network Layer

This layer offers routing and switching capabilities, establishing virtual circuits—logical pathways—for data transmission between nodes. This layer handles packet sequencing, error handling, internetworking, packet routing, packet forwarding, and congestion control. IP, IPX, and AppleTalk DDP are a few examples.

7.1.4.1.4. Transport Layer

This layer controls flow and ensures end-to-end error recovery while facilitating transparent data transfer between hosts, or end systems. It guarantees full data transfer. Examples consist of TCP, UDP, and SPX.

7.1.4.1.5. Session Layer

Applications' connections are established, maintained, and ended by this layer. The applications at each end have talks, exchanges, and dialogues that are established, coordinated, and ended by the session layer. NFS, NetBIOS names, RPC, and SQL are a few examples.

7.1.4.1.6. Presentation Layer

This layer offers protection against variations in data representation (e.g., encryption) by converting network format to application format and the other way around. This layer ensures compatibility by formatting and encrypting data before sending it over a network. PICT, TIFF, GIF, ASCII, EBCDIC, JPEG, MPEG, MIDI, and encryption are a few examples.

7.1.4.1.7. Application Layer

The end-user and application processes are supported by this layer. In addition to identifying communication partners, quality of service, user authentication, privacy, and any restrictions on data syntax are also identified. This layer contains only application-specific information. Email, file transfers, and other network software services are provided by this layer's application services. Web browsers, NFS, SNMP, Telnet, HTTP, and FTP are a few examples.

7.1.4.2. The TCP/IP Model

A four-layer reference model is the TCP/IP network model. The top three layers of this model contain all of the TCP/IP protocol suite's protocols.

7.1.4.2.1. Application

Describes application protocols for TCP/IP and the host programs' interface to transport layer services for network usage. Examples of protocols are FTP, TFTP, SNMP, DNS, SMTP, HTTP, Telnet, and FTP.

7.1.4.2.2. Transport

Facilitates the management of communication sessions between host computers specifies the connection's status and service level when sending data. Examples of protocols are TCP, UDP, and RTP.

7.1.4.2.3. Internet

Data is packaged into IP datagrams, which are used to forward datagrams between hosts and across networks. Datagrams contain source and destination address information carries out IP datagram routing. Examples of protocols are ARP, RARP, ICMP, and IP.

7.1.4.2.4. Network Interface

Describes in detail the physical transmission of data over a network, including the electrical signaling of bits by hardware components that interface directly with network media like twisted-pair copper wire, optical fiber, or coaxial cable. Examples of protocols are Ethernet, Token Ring, FDDI, and X.25, RS-232 Frame Relay, v.35. The seven-layer Open Systems Interconnection (OSI) reference model has one or more layers that correspond to each layer of the TCP/IP model.

7.2. THE INTERNET AND WORLD WIDE WEB

The internet is a network system with global connectivity that transmits data over a variety of media types using TCP/IP. Connected by guided, wireless, and fiber-optic technologies, the internet is a global network of exchanges comprising private, public, business, academic, and government networks. (Richard C. Van Sluyters 1997)

Although the terms "internet" and "World Wide Web" are frequently used synonymously, they are not exactly the same. The web is one of the services that is communicated over the internet, whereas the internet refers to the global communication system, including hardware and infrastructure.

A network of HTML-formatted online content accessible through HTTP is called the World Wide Web (WWW). Any linked HTML page that can be viewed online is referred to by this term. When Tim Berners-Lee was a contractor at CERN in 1991, he created the original design for the World Wide Web.

The World Wide Web is most often referred to simply as "the Web."

The Internet is often confused with the World Wide Web, which is actually a part of it. The World Wide Web consists of Web pages, images, videos, and other online content that can be accessed through a Web browser. The Internet, on the other hand, is the infrastructure that allows us to send emails and access the World Wide Web. In its early days, the Web was made up of simple text-based sites created by technically savvy individuals who set up Web servers and learned HTML. Over time, the Web has evolved to include interactive features such as social media and user-generated content that can be easily accessed by people with little to no technical skills.

7.2.1. Internet Facilities

The global telephone network and the Internet are comparable in that they both make it possible to establish two-way connections between sites virtually instantaneously, regardless of location. On the other hand, there are numerous ways we can communicate online, not just over the phone. Most notably, we are not restricted to speaking with others verbally; in many situations, we can access data that is kept on their computers. The following is a description of the fundamental services offered by the Internet: file transfer protocol, email, list servers, USNET/Newsgroups, Internet relay chat, Gopher, and the World Wide Web.

7.2.1.1. E-mail

The most frequently used online tool is email, which is the equivalent of postal mail on the Internet. Emails sent via the Internet can travel thousands of miles before they arrive at their destination. You never play "telephone tag," and you never get a busy signal.

Email programs come with features that let you print, forward, save, and/or reply to messages from other people. Some have sophisticated features that let you attach an image, video, spreadsheet, word processing document, or software program.

7.2.1.2. List Servers

Discussion groups can be formed to exchange information about shared interests thanks to the list server feature.

The most popular list server program, LISTSERV, copies incoming messages sent to the list and distributes them to all subscribers whose email addresses are on the list.

Messages are only sent by subscribers to this group, which the list manager keeps an eye on. When a user, known as the initiator, sends a properly worded email message to a list, the LISTSERV program is automatically prompted to extract the email address of the initiator, add it to the list, and send the initiator a confirmation email along with information about using the list.

7.2.1.3. USNET/Newsgroups

Access to groups on Internet newsgroup servers is typically far less selective than that of list servers. By connecting to a nearby computer that serves as a news server with specialized newsreader software, one can gain unrestricted and free access to thousands of topic-based newsgroups. With the help of this software, users can publish articles or messages to any newsgroup for other users to read and possibly comment on (Figure 7.5).

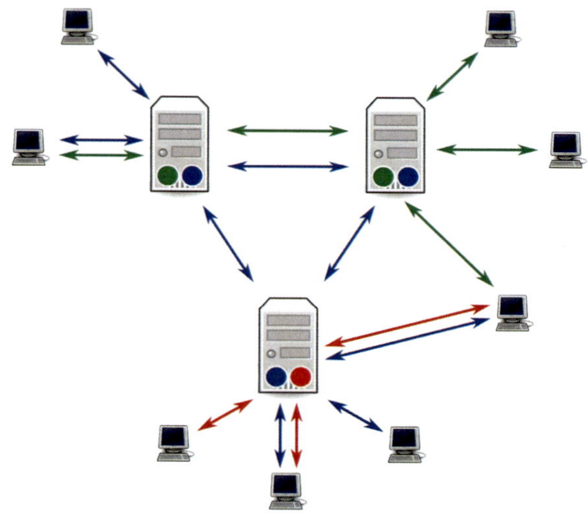

Figure 7.5. *USNET/Newsgroups.*

Source: https://upload.wikimedia.org/wikipedia/commons/thumb/f/f4/Usenet_servers_and_clients.svg/2000px-Usenet_servers_and_clients.svg.png.

7.2.1.4. File Transfer Protocol

Internet users can move software, product upgrades, and other kinds of computer files between computers connected to the Internet by using the File Transfer Protocol feature.

7.2.1.5. Internet Relay Chat

Small groups of people get together in online chat rooms with Internet Relay Chat, and they "talk" to each other by typing messages on their keyboards.

7.2.1.6. Gopher

Named after the golden gopher mascot of the University of Minnesota, the Gopher facility was one of the earliest user-friendly Internet tools for accessing information. Users could easily connect to numerous computers, referred to as "gopher holes," using a menu-driven program. Each gopher hole contained hierarchically organized information, allowing users to click through a list of topics to access text, sound, or images.

7.2.1.7. World Wide Web

For many users, the WWW has come to represent the Internet since it is such a widely used resource. The WWW connects users to websites and was created in 1992 at the European Laboratory for Particle Physics at Cern, Switzerland. The page, akin to this printed page, is the fundamental unit of WWW communication. There are "links" on a Web page that, when clicked, take users to related pages on the same or different websites. The WWW has swiftly taken over as the preferred interface for Internet users thanks to its versatility and ease of use. Users can instantly retrieve detailed information from anywhere in the world through the transmission of text, graphics, audio, and video.

7.2.2. Components of the WWW

The WWW's robust network of links, which enables users to browse related data sets kept on various computers across the Internet, is essential to its success. Any type of data can be accessed from a Web page by clicking on highlighted and/or underlined links that point to other pages thanks to this system of embedding links in the text known as "hypertext." The chosen Web page is automatically accessed by users, even if it is located on a distant computer. The name of the WWW comes from this network of linked pages.

Each Web page has an identifier that is specific to it, called the Uniform Resource Locator (URL). A URL is made up of the name of the computer file that actually contains the Web page as well as the Internet address of the machine that is hosting the page. There are over 500,000 WWW sites on the Internet, and each one could have multiple URLs. Tens of millions of Web pages are the end result!

A unique kind of software known as a "browser" was created so that users could view and retrieve Web pages without having to remember and type the URL every time. A personal computer running a browser program can connect to the Internet and browse the World Wide Web (WWW). Most browsers are free for educators to use and are reasonably priced. With any browser, an Internet user can do the following three things: (1) retrieve Web pages from other computers; (2) display these pages on the user's screen using formatting commands provided by the page author; and (3) activate the Web pages by pointing and clicking on an embedded hypertext link to take the user to the referenced file or URL. Even a computer novice can become accustomed to using a browser in a matter of minutes because they are so simple to use. But the novice user will quickly learn that searching well is essential to finding their way around millions of Web pages. Internet users use WWW software tools known as "search engines" to manage this deluge of information. "

A powerful tool for locating websites with keyword information is a search engine. Web pages, Gopher sites, File Transfer Protocol sites, newsgroup articles, and other content are all scanned by search engines. There are currently a lot of these programs available, and there are subtle differences in their designs. Readers only need to click on the appropriate button on the browser's home page to choose from among the well-known search engines that their browser offers. Typically, users test out a few until they identify which ones are more user-friendly and efficient. Expert Web users usually start a search with a search engine, then navigate the Web by clicking on the hypertext links that are included in the pages that the search engines have located.

7.2.3. Web Programming Languages

A plethora of technologies has surfaced to enable browser-based development. Here, we examine those technologies in an attempt to determine which web programming languages are currently the best. (Ayman Hussien Odeh, 2019)

7.2.3.1. PHP

Because PHP transformed the way internet software could be developed, many of its fans referred to it as the best web programming language available when it first appeared in the mid-1990s. The web was primarily a collection of static content before PHP made it feasible to create dynamic websites, turning it into an interactive platform.

PHP's initial release was twenty years ago, and its popularity has since somewhat declined. There is currently a potent anti-PHP coalition. PHP's ugly design and the fact that simple tasks require a lot of code are the main points of contention.

Whatever you think of PHP, however, it's still the most popular language for web development—even if it's not the greatest one. PHP is an essential language for web developers to know just for that reason.

7.2.3.2. Java

Programmers intended Java to be an all-purpose language. It was never meant specifically for web applications, any more than it was for creating an application for a smartwatch, for example. Although Java wasn't developed exclusively for browser-based development, many people still think it's one of the best web programming languages to learn and work with.

To put it another way, the typical developer is already familiar with Java. Java might work well if you need to create a web application and you don't want the developers—or the people who will eventually have to maintain your code—to learn a new language.

7.2.3.3. Go

Golang, also simply known as Go, is a general-purpose programming language that is easier to use for web applications than Java. It might be just what you're looking for. Go is a robust, extensible language that was released in 2009 and has a vibrant community behind it. It facilitates the development of parallel processing applications for developers. Go has an advantage in this regard if you use it to create high-performing web applications. Although Go is not as well-known as Java, its fan base is probably going to grow.

7.2.3.4. Ruby on Rails

When discussing general-purpose programming languages that are valuable for web development, Ruby on Rails cannot be overlooked. This framework offers a simple solution for developers working with Ruby, a versatile language, to create server-side web applications.

There is a good deal of discussion on whether Ruby and Ruby on Rails are becoming obsolete. However, proponents of the framework will fervently contend that it remains among the top web programming languages for rapidly developing applications. For many years, people have been speculating about Ruby's end, but even though its popularity has declined, it is not going to vanish.

Actually, according to the TIOBE index, which measures programming language popularity, Ruby had made a comeback to the top 10 list in March 2018. Ruby on Rails expertise is a great asset if Ruby is once again in style.

7.2.3.5. Python

Developers can use the scripting language Python in a wide range of situations. Although Python was not intended to be used for web development, web programming can easily be done with it thanks to frameworks like Django. If you'd like, you could also write web apps with plain ol' Python. It is impossible to determine with any degree of objectivity which web programming languages, Python and Django, are the best in technical terms.

Nonetheless, you can argue that Python has a lot of use cases, which is something you can't say about most of the other languages on this list. Put another way, learning Python for web development also means learning a language that can be used for other purposes, like system administration and mobile development.

7.2.3.6. JavaScript (and Node.js)

Another essential language for developing web apps is JavaScript. This is accurate due to the fact that JavaScript is the most popular client-side programming language for websites and that Node.js allows it to be extended to server-side environments.

JavaScript and Node. Python is more extensible than JavaScript. Most likely, you wouldn't use Node JS for system administration, for instance, even though it has been accomplished. When combined, however, these two languages cover almost every programming scenario you could encounter related to the web.

7.2.4. Web Services

Web services are client-server programs that exchange data via the Hypertext Transfer Protocol (HTTP) on the World Wide Web (WWW). Web services, offer a common way for software programs operating on different platforms and frameworks to communicate with one another. Because XML is used, web services have great extensibility and interoperability, and their descriptions can be processed by machines. Complex operations can be accomplished by loosely coupling web services together. Programs that offer basic services can collaborate to offer complex added-value services.

7.2.4.1. Components of Web Services

XML + HTTP is the foundational web services platform. The following elements are used by all common web services:

- SOAP (Simple Object Access Protocol);
- UDDI (Universal Description, Discovery and Integration);
- WSDL (Web Services Description Language).

7.2.4.1.1. SOAP

Originally, SOAP was a component of the specification that also contained Universal Description, Discovery, and Integration (UDDI) and Web Services Description Language (WSDL). It is currently utilized without UDDI or WSDL. SOAP messages are either generated or hardcoded without the use of a repository, as opposed to the repository-based discovery process outlined in the section below on the History of the Web Services Specification. Figure7.6 below depicts the interaction.

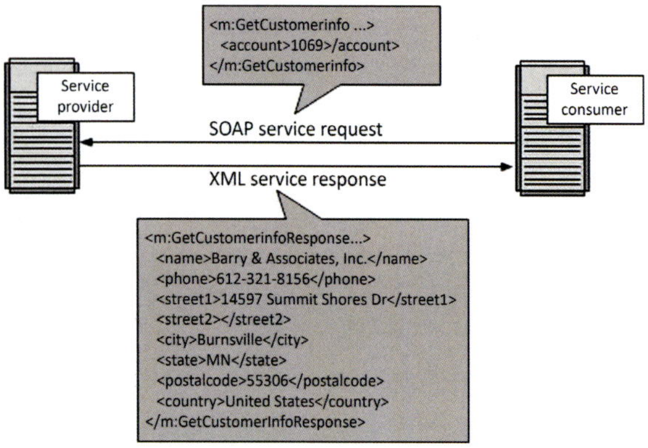

Figure 7.6. *SOAP messages.*

Source: https://www.service-architecture.com/images/web_services/soap_messages.jpg.

SOAP is an XML-based protocol for exchanging information between computers.

- SOAP is a communication protocol.
- SOAP is for communication between applications.
- SOAP is a format for sending messages.
- SOAP is designed to communicate via Internet.
- SOAP is platform independent.
- SOAP is language independent.
- SOAP is simple and extensible.
- SOAP allows you to get around firewalls.
- SOAP will be developed as a W3C standard.

7.2.4.1.2. WSDL

WSDL is an XML-based language for describing web services and how to access them.

- WSDL stands for Web Services Description Language.
- WSDL was developed jointly by Microsoft and IBM.
- WSDL is an XML based protocol for information exchange in decentralized and distributed environments.
- WSDL is the standard format for describing a web service.
- WSDL definition describes how to access a web service and what operations it will perform.
- WSDL is a language for describing how to interface with XML-based services.
- WSDL is an integral part of UDDI, an XML-based worldwide business registry.
- WSDL is the language that UDDI uses.
- WSDL is pronounced as 'wiz-dull' and spelled out as 'W-S-D-L.'

7.2.4.1.3. UDDI

UDDI is an XML-based standard for describing, publishing, and finding web services.

- UDDI stands for Universal Description, Discovery, and Integration.
- UDDI is a specification for a distributed registry of web services.
- UDDI is platform independent, open framework.
- UDDI can communicate via SOAP, CORBA, and Java RMI Protocol.
- UDDI uses WSDL to describe interfaces to web services.
- UDDI is seen with SOAP and WSDL as one of the three foundation standards of web services.

- UDDI is an open industry initiative enabling businesses to discover each other and define how they interact over the Internet.

7.2.4.2. How Does a Web Service Work?

A web service enables communication among various applications by using open standards such as HTML, XML, WSDL, and SOAP. A web service takes the help of:

- XML to tag the data;
- SOAP to transfer a message;
- WSDL to describe the availability of service.

On Solaris, you can create a Java web service that can be accessed from your Windows Visual Basic application.

Additionally, you can use C to create new Windows web services that can be called from a Linux web application that is built using Jakarta Server Pages (JSP).

7.2.4.2.1. Example

Think about a basic order processing and account management system. The accounting staff enters new customer orders and creates new accounts using a client application created with JSP or Visual Basic.

This system's Java-written processing logic runs on a Solaris system that also communicates with a database to hold data.

The steps to perform this operation are as follows –

- The client program bundles the account registration information into a SOAP message.
- This SOAP message is sent to the web service as the body of an HTTP POST request.
- The web service unpacks the SOAP request and converts it into a command that the application can understand.
- The application processes the information as required and responds with a new unique account number for that customer.
- Next, the web service packages the response into another SOAP message, which it sends back to the client program in response to its HTTP request.
- The client program unpacks the SOAP message to obtain the results of the account registration process.

7.3. THE INTERNET OF THINGS

The internet of things, or IoT, is a network of interconnected computing devices, digital and mechanical machines, items, animals, and people that can transfer data over a network without requiring human-to-human or human-to-computer interaction. All of these devices are assigned unique identifiers, or UIDs. (Sandro Nižeti⊠, Petar Šoli⊠, et al., 2020)

The term "thing" refers to any natural or artificial object that can be given an IP address and be able to transmit data over a network. Examples of things that fall under this category include people with implanted heart monitors, farm animals with biochip transponders, cars with built-in sensors that notify the driver when tire pressure is low, and any other type of object.

IoT is being used by businesses across a range of industries to boost productivity, make better decisions, gain a deeper understanding of their clientele, and raise overall company value.

7.3.1. History of IoT

Kevin Ashton, co-founder of the Auto-ID Center at MIT, first mentioned the internet of things in a presentation he made to Procter & Gamble (P&G) in 1999. Wanting to bring radio frequency ID (RFID) to the attention of P&G's senior management, Ashton called his presentation "Internet of Things" to incorporate the cool new trend of 1999: the internet.

Microelectromechanical systems (MEMS), microservices, the internet, and wireless technologies have all come together to form the Internet of Things. The breakdown of silos between information technology (IT) and operational technology (OT) has been facilitated by convergence, allowing unstructured machine-generated data to be analyzed for insights that will lead to improvements.

Even though Ashton introduced the term "internet of things" initially, the concept of interconnected devices—also known as embedded internet and pervasive computing—has been around since the 1970s.

For instance, a Coke machine at Carnegie Mellon University in the early 1980s was the first internet appliance. Should they choose to visit the machine, programmers could use the internet to check on its condition and find out if a cold drink would be waiting for them.

Communication between machines (M2M) gave rise to the Internet of Things (IoT). E. robots interacting with one another face-to-face through a network. M2M describes how to manage and gather data from a device that is connected to the cloud. IoT, a sensor network of billions of smart devices that connects people, systems, and other applications to gather and share data, is taking M2M to the next level. M2M provides the connectivity at the core of the Internet of Things.

Additionally, SCADA (supervisory control and data acquisition) is a class of software application programs for process control, which involves real-time data collection from remote locations to control machinery and conditions. The internet of things is a logical extension of these programs. Both software and hardware are included in SCADA systems. The hardware collects and feeds data into a computer running SCADA software, where it is promptly processed and displayed. Due to the way SCADA has evolved, first-generation IoT systems have evolved from late-generation SCADA systems.

However, it wasn't until the middle of 2010—when the Chinese government, among other things, declared that IoT would be a strategic priority in its five-year plan—that the idea of the IoT ecosystem truly took off.

7.3.2. How IoT works

An Internet of Things ecosystem is made up of web-enabled smart devices that gather, transmit, and act upon data they obtain from their surroundings via embedded processors, sensors, and communication hardware. Connecting to an IoT gateway or other edge device allows IoT devices to share the sensor data they gather, which is then either locally or remotely analyzed. These gadgets occasionally interact with other similar gadgets and respond to the data they exchange. Although people can interact with the devices to set them up, give them instructions, or access the data, the devices do the majority of the work without their help.

The particular Internet of Things applications that are implemented heavily influence the connectivity, networking, and communication protocols utilized with these web-enabled devices.

7.3.3. Applications of the Internet of Things

Industry stands to gain the most from the Internet of Things. Manufacturing has actually taken the lead in this regard, since allowing machines to communicate with one another without the need for human intermediaries has resulted in a significant increase in output across the board. Some factories now essentially operate on their own, with machines communicating with one another to determine what is needed when.

Even though the thought of that specter might give union organizers the chills, it has actually been quite beneficial for the owners of those companies, enabling them to produce more goods at a lower cost. IoT technology is largely to blame for the rise of robots, which will have a significant impact on the labor market over the coming decades (Figure 7.7).

With the exception of the ensuing unemployment, of course, the changes are somewhat less noticeable to the average person, but we can anticipate an increasing number of daily activities to be remotely controlled, typically using a phone. Given that you always have a digital device in your hands and pocket that can broadcast over Wi-Fi, why even bother with a TV remote?

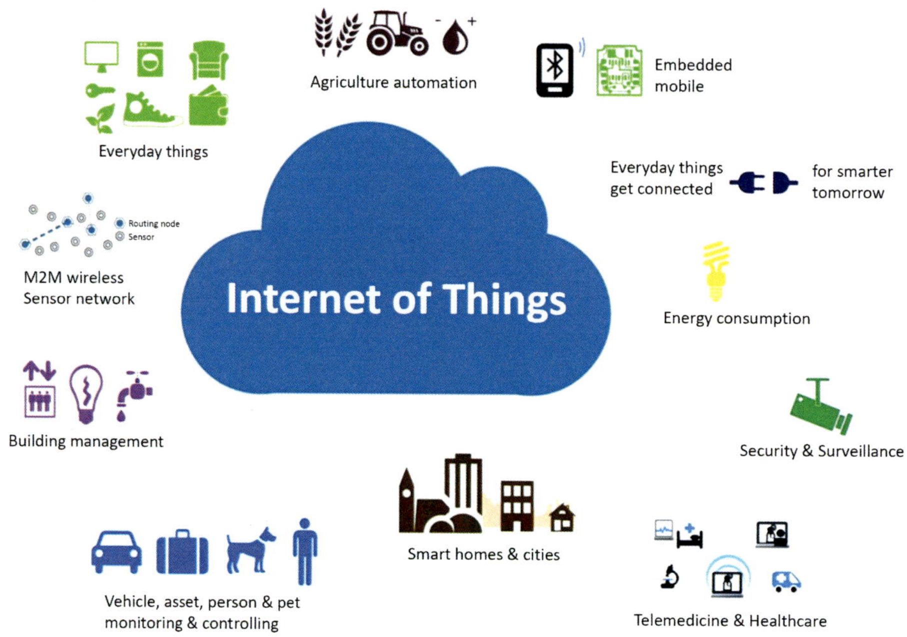

Figure 7.7. *Applications of the Internet of Things.*

Source: https://www.xtendiot.com/wp-content/uploads/2017/09/iot-application-areas.jpg.

Nowadays, control chips are so small that almost anything can be connected to the Internet of Things. All you have to do is come up with a good reason why a table or chair needs a chip, then build it. As automation takes over in the factories, chips are also getting smaller. At the moment, the cutting edge is at a form factor of 10 nanometers, or size, but as you read this, Samsung is working on 8nm processes, which is incredibly small.

That being said, if you find phone-controlled thermostats and memory-enabled refrigerators cool, wait until you see diabetes pumps that can regulate themselves and give you extra insulin when they sense that you've just opened a chocolate bar from the pantry. The possibilities are, as they say, endless. For example, what if a store performed all of its stock taking flawlessly without any human employees?

Almost anyone can assemble an Internet of Things device in their basement because the components are so little and because DIY circuit boards like the Raspberry Pi are so inexpensive, courtesy of the revolution in chip manufacturing. There has been a significant shift in computing and how we engage with the digital world.

7.3.4. Consumer and Enterprise IoT Applications

The internet of things has many practical uses in the real world, from manufacturing and industrial IoT (IIoT) to consumer and enterprise IoT. Applications for IoT are found in many industries, such as energy, telco, automotive, and more.

For instance, in the consumer market, smart homes with connected heating, lighting, and electronic devices as well as smart appliances and thermostats can be remotely controlled from PCs, smartphones, or other mobile devices.

In order to make users' lives easier and more comfortable, wearable devices with sensors and software can gather and analyze user data and communicate that information to other technologies. Additionally, wearables are used in public safety. For instance, they can track the vital signs of firefighters or construction workers at potentially fatal sites, or they can improve the response times of first responders by offering the best routes to a scene.

IoT has several advantages for the healthcare industry, one of which is the capacity to use and analyze generated data to monitor patients more closely. IoT systems are frequently used by hospitals to handle tasks like inventory management for both medical equipment and prescription drugs.

For example, by utilizing sensors to determine the number of people in a room, smart buildings can lower their energy consumption. The temperature can be automatically changed. For instance, sensors may detect that a conference room is full and activate the air conditioner, or they may sense that everyone has left the office and reduce the heat. IoT-based smart farming systems in agriculture can assist in using connected sensors to monitor various agricultural fields' parameters, such as light, temperature, humidity, and soil moisture. Irrigation system automation is another benefit of IoT.

Smart streetlights and smart meters are two examples of IoT sensors and deployments that can help reduce traffic, save energy, monitor and address environmental issues, and enhance sanitation in a smart city.

7.3.5. IoT Security and Privacy Issues

The internet of things uses billions of data points and links billions of devices to the internet, all of which require security.

The increased attack surface of the Internet of Things makes IoT security and privacy top concerns. One of the most well-known recent Internet of Things (IoT) attacks was Mirai, a botnet that compromised domain name server provider Dyn and launched one of the largest distributed denial-of-service (DDoS) attacks ever, taking down numerous websites for an extended period of time. Attackers used weakly secured IoT devices as a means of gaining access to the network.

IoT devices are interconnected, so a hacker only needs to take advantage of one weakness to alter all the data and make it useless. Additionally, manufacturers who fail to update their products on a regular basis or at all expose them to cybercriminals. Furthermore, users of connected devices are frequently prompted to enter personal information, such as names, ages, addresses, phone numbers, and even social media accounts—data that hackers can profit greatly from. But the internet of things isn't just vulnerable to cyberattacks; users are also very concerned about their privacy. For example, manufacturers and distributors of consumer IoT devices may use those devices to acquire and sell user personal information. IoT is risky for vital infrastructure, such as transportation, banking services, and electricity, in addition to leaking personal data.

7.3.6. The Future of IoT

There is no shortage of IoT market estimations. For example:

- Bain & Company expects annual IoT revenue of hardware and software to exceed $450 billion by 2020.
- McKinsey & Company estimates IoT will have an $11.1 trillion impact by 2025.
- IHS Markit believes the number of connected IoT devices will increase 12% annually to reach 125 billion in 2030.
- Gartner assesses that 20.8 billion connected things will be in use by 2020, with total spend on IoT devices and services to reach $3.7 trillion in 2018.

7.4. CLOUD COMPUTING

In contrast to establishing a direct connection to a server, cloud computing is a technique for providing information technology (IT) services in which resources are obtained from the Internet via web-based tools and applications. With cloud-based storage, files can be saved to a remote database instead of being stored on a local or proprietary hard drive. An electronic device can access data and the software needed to run it as long as it is connected to the internet (Figure 7.8). (I. Ahmad, H. Bakht, U. Mohan, 2017)

Figure 7.8. *Cloud computing.*

Source: http://www.net2source.com/wp-content/uploads/2017/10/cloud-computing-1024x855.jpg.

Because the information being accessed is located in the cloud and does not require a user to be in a specific location to access it, the technology is known as cloud computing. With this kind of setup, workers can conduct remote work. Cloud service providers give customers the ability to store files and apps on distant servers and then access all of their data online.

7.4.1. Cloud Computing Basics

A cloud services platform offers quick access to adaptable and affordable IT resources, regardless of whether you are powering apps that distribute images to millions of smartphone users or you are assisting with the vital functions of your company. You can avoid having to invest a lot of money up front in hardware and taking a lot of time to manage it by using cloud computing. Alternatively, you can set up precisely the kind and quantity of computer power you require to run your IT department or power your most recent brilliant idea. You only pay for the resources you actually use, and you can almost instantaneously access as many as you require.

7.4.2. How Does Cloud Computing Work?

A straightforward method of gaining access to servers, storage, databases, and a variety of application services via the Internet is offered by cloud computing. While you provision and use what you need through a web application, a cloud services platform like Amazon Web Services owns and maintains the network-connected hardware needed for these application services.

7.4.3. Cloud Computing Characteristics and Benefits

- **Self-service Provisioning:** Compute resources can be instantly spun up by end users for nearly any kind of workload. This gets rid of the need that IT managers used to have for managing and provisioning compute resources.
- **Elasticity:** Businesses have the flexibility to scale up when computing demands rise and down again when they fall. This removes the requirement for large investments in local infrastructure, which might or might not continue to function.
- **Pay Per Use:** Users can only pay for the workloads and resources they actually use because compute resources are measured down to the lowest possible level.
- **Workload Resilience:** In order to maintain reliable storage and to support users' critical workloads, cloud service providers frequently deploy redundant resources—often across several international regions.
- **Migration Flexibility:** Businesses can automatically or on-demand shift specific workloads to and from the cloud, or between different cloud platforms, to take advantage of new services as they become available or to reduce costs.

7.4.4. Cloud Computing Deployment Models

Cloud computing services can be private, public or hybrid.

Internal users receive private cloud services from a company's data center. This model maintains the management, control, and security typical of local data centers while providing the flexibility and ease of use of the cloud. IT chargeback may or may not be used to bill internal users for services.

Common private cloud technologies and vendors include VMware and OpenStack.

A third-party cloud service provider provides the cloud service via the internet in the public cloud model. While many public cloud services offer long-term commitments, most are sold on an as-needed basis, usually by the minute or hour. Clients only pay for the bandwidth, storage, and CPU cycles that they actually use.

Leading public cloud service providers include Amazon Web Services (AWS), Microsoft Azure, IBM and Google Cloud Platform (Figure 7.9).

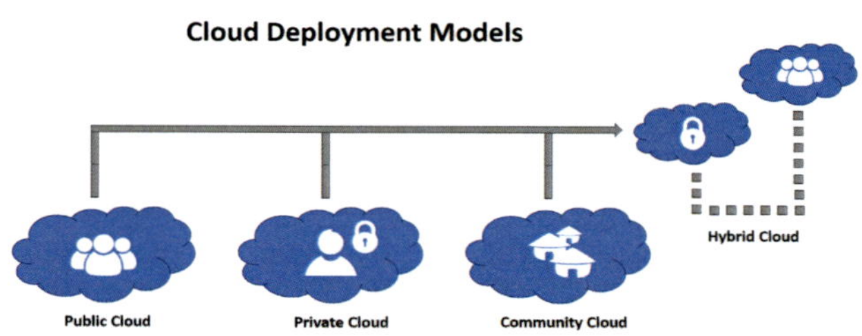

Figure 7.9. *Cloud computing deployment models.*

Source: https://www.uniprint.net/wp-content/uploads/2017/05/Cloud-deployment-structures-diagram.png.pagespeed.ce.vkA8qJuES4.png.

A hybrid cloud combines on-premises private cloud infrastructure with public cloud services, allowing orchestration and automation between the two. Businesses can use the public cloud to manage workload bursts or demand spikes while running sensitive applications or mission-critical workloads on the private cloud. Creating a unified, automated, and scalable environment that leverages the full potential of public cloud infrastructure is the aim of a hybrid cloud, all the while preserving control over mission-critical data.

Furthermore, many organizations are now adopting a multicloud approach, utilizing multiple infrastructure-as-a-service providers. This allows for the seamless movement of applications between different cloud providers, as well as the ability to run applications across multiple cloud platforms simultaneously.

Businesses use multicloud for a variety of reasons. They might take this action, for instance, to reduce the possibility of a cloud service outage or to benefit from a specific provider's more affordable prices. The variations in cloud providers' services and application program interfaces (APIs) can make multicloud implementation and application development difficult. However, as provider services and APIs converge and become more uniform due to industry initiatives like the Open Cloud Computing Interface, multicloud deployments ought to get easier.

7.4.5. Different Types of Cloud Computing

Unlike a microchip or a cell phone, cloud computing is not a single technological component. It is actually a system made up of three main services: platform as a service (PaaS), software as a service (SaaS)+, and infrastructure as a service (IaaS). SaaS and IaaS are predicted to grow at the fastest rates, respectively.

- **Software as a Service (SaaS):** Software as a service (SaaS) involves granting licenses to users. Usually, licenses are offered on an as-needed or pay-as-you-go basis. With 59% of all cloud workloads expected to be SaaS by 2018, this quickly expanding market could present a great investment opportunity, according to a Goldman Sachs report.
- **Infrastructure as a Service (IaaS):** As part of an on-demand service, infrastructure as a service refers to a way to deliver everything via IP-based connectivity, including servers, storage, and operating systems. Customers can obtain these resources through an outsourced, on-demand service, avoiding the need to buy software or servers.
- **Platform as a Service (PaaS):** When it comes to cloud computing, PaaS is thought to be the most intricate of the three tiers. While PaaS and SaaS are similar in certain ways, the main distinction is that PaaS is a platform for developing software that is distributed online, as opposed to software that is delivered online. According to a Forrester analysis, PaaS solutions will bring in $44 billion in revenue by 2020.

7.4.6. Emerging Cloud Technologies and Services

Because cloud providers are in a competitive market, they continuously broaden their offerings to set themselves apart. As a result, public IaaS providers now provide far more than just standard instances for computation and storage. For instance, event-driven computing, also known as serverless computing, is a type of cloud service that carries out particular tasks like database updates and image processing. In conventional cloud deployments, users must create a compute instance and load code into it. The user then selects the duration of the instance's operation and associated cost.

Users don't have to worry about the server or instance aspect of the cloud deployment when using serverless computing; developers just write code, which the cloud provider loads and runs in response to actual events. Users only pay for the quantity of transactions carried out by the function. Serverless computing services include AWS Lambda, Azure Functions, and Google Cloud Functions.

Big data processing, which requires a great deal of computational power for brief periods of time, is another application that public cloud computing excels at. In response, cloud service providers have launched big data offerings, such as Microsoft Azure Data Lake Analytics for processing massive data sets and Google BigQuery for large-scale data warehousing.

Artificial intelligence (AI) and machine learning are two more fields of developing cloud technologies and services. With the use of these technologies, systems can become more intelligent than humans, learn from changes in data, and react in ways that are advantageous to the company. Some examples of these services are Google Cloud Machine Learning Engine, Google Cloud Speech API, Amazon Machine Learning, Amazon Lex, and Amazon Polly.

7.4.7. Cloud Computing Security

Businesses considering cloud adoption still have security as their top priority, particularly when it comes to public cloud adoption. As public clouds are multi-tenant environments, public cloud service providers divide their underlying hardware infrastructure among multiple clients. There must be a great deal of isolation between logical compute resources in this environment. Simultaneously, account login credentials are used to protect access to compute resources and public cloud storage.

For fear of disruptions, loss, or theft, many organizations constrained by intricate regulatory requirements and governance standards are still reluctant to move workloads or data to public clouds. This opposition is, however, waning because data encryption and other identity and access management solutions, along with logical isolation's demonstrated dependability, have increased public cloud security.

7.4.8. Advantages of Cloud Computing

One of the many advantages that cloud-based software has brought to businesses across all industries is the ability to use software from any device through a browser or native app. Consequently, users can effortlessly transfer their files and preferences to different devices. But cloud computing is much more than just having access to files across several devices. Users can access their email on any computer and store files with services like Dropbox and Google Drive thanks to cloud computing services. Users can also back up their files, music, and pictures using cloud computing services, which guarantees that those files will always be accessible in case of a hard drive failure.

Large companies can save a significant amount of money by using cloud computing. Prior to the cloud becoming a practical substitute, businesses had to invest in, build, and maintain expensive infrastructure and information management technology. These days, a company can use lite versions of workstations with lightning fast internet connections, and the employees will interact with the cloud online to create presentations, spreadsheets, and interact with company software, instead of investing millions in massive server centers and complex, global IT departments that require constant upgrades.

People discover that they can free up space on their laptops or desktops by uploading images, documents, and videos to the cloud and then retrieving them whenever it's convenient for them. Furthermore, because software companies can sell their products online rather than through more conventional, tangible methods involving discs or flash drives, the cloud-like structure enables users to upgrade software more quickly. Adobe Systems declared in 2013 that all upcoming iterations of Photoshop and other Creative Suite products would only be accessible via an online subscription. This makes it simple for users to download updates and fixes for their software.

7.4.9. Disadvantages of Cloud Computing

With all of the speed, efficiencies and innovations of cloud computing come risks. Security was initially thought to be a barrier to cloud computing, particularly when it came to private financial and medical data. Although cloud computing services are being compelled by regulations to strengthen their security and compliance protocols, this problem still exists. The news is frequently filled with stories about data breaches at this or that company, wherein private data has been compromised and is now in the hands of malevolent hackers who could erase, alter, or use the data for other purposes (although, in some cases, on-site systems, not cloud-based ones, have been the target of most breaches). Encryption safeguards important data, but the data is lost if the encryption key is misplaced.

Cloud computing companies' servers are susceptible to internal bugs, power outages, and natural disasters. Sadly, cloud computing's geographic reach works both ways: a blackout in California could render users in New York immobile, and a company in Texas could lose its data if its Maine-based provider went down. In the end, managers and staff must adjust to a learning curve, just like with any new technology. However, since numerous users can access and alter data via a single portal, unintentional errors can spread throughout the entire system.

CASE STUDY

CLOUD COMPUTING CASE STUDY OF MCAFEE

McAfee, a global leader in the cybersecurity industry, aimed to significantly enhance the performance and efficiency of its operations, particularly in managing a colossal volume of daily transactions. To achieve this, McAfee turned to Amazon Elastic Block Store (EBS), specifically leveraging the high-performance capabilities of Amazon EBS io2 Block Express volumes.

Challenges

- **Performance Optimization:** McAfee faced challenges in optimizing its operations' performance, especially concerning the management of many daily transactions.
- **Backup Time:** Efficient backup processes were crucial, and McAfee sought ways to streamline and expedite its backup procedures.

Solution

- **Amazon EBS Integration:** McAfee strategically integrated Amazon EBS into its infrastructure, harnessing the capabilities of Amazon EBS io2 Block Express volumes for enhanced performance.
- **High-Performance Storage:** The adoption of io2 Block Express volumes allowed McAfee to leverage high-performance storage, crucial for managing the demanding workload of daily transactions.

Key Achievements

- **Performance Enhancement:** McAfee achieved a substantial 30% improvement in overall performance, optimizing its ability to handle and process 400 million daily transactions.
- **Backup Time Reduction:** The integration of Amazon EBS io2 Block Express volumes resulted in a significant 50% reduction in backup time, streamlining critical backup processes.

Operational Excellence

- **Efficient Data Management:** Amazon EBS provided McAfee with efficient data management capabilities, ensuring that the cybersecurity company could handle daily transactions seamlessly.
- **Reliable Storage:** The high-performance storage offered by io2 Block Express volumes contributed to the reliability and responsiveness of McAfee's operations.

Cost Efficiency

- Optimized Resource Utilization: McAfee optimized resource utilization with Amazon EBS, ensuring that storage resources were allocated efficiently to meet performance demands.
- **Cost-Effective Scalability:** The scalable nature of EBS io2 Block Express volumes allowed McAfee to align costs with actual storage and performance requirements.

Future Optimization

- **Continuous Performance Tuning:** McAfee remains committed to continuous performance tuning, exploring additional AWS services and advancements to further optimize its operations.
- **Exploring Innovations:** The success with Amazon EBS opens the door for McAfee to explore further innovations and integrations within the AWS ecosystem.

CLASS ACTIVITY

BUILDING A NETWORK

In this activity, students are formed into groups of 5–7 and given string so they can connect themselves together to form a computer network.

Students are given several specific networks to form, along with several guidelines for how to best form computer networks. Students are also forced to wrestle with conflicting guidelines in determining the 'best' way to connect together to form a network, and will need to justify why they chose the networks that they did.

Purpose

The physical activity helps provide a memorable experience and personal anchor for the rest of the unit – we can refer to the networks created in this activity to help motivate concepts in later lessons.

In the final challenge for this lesson, it is important to let students wrestle with how to best balance the 3 network guidelines and refine their reasoning and explanation for decisions they made when creating their network.

In this activity, the guidelines are based on the physical impacts of creating a network but towards the end of the unit students will examine the societal and economical impacts for creating computer networks and will again think critically about how to balance several factors from a societal and economic lens.

Activity

1. **Group:** Place students in groups of 5–7. Give each group string according to the following chart:
   - Groups of 5: 10 strings;
   - Groups of 6: 15 strings;
   - Groups of 7: 21 strings.
2. **Do This:** The next activity is guided by the lesson slides. Display the challenge for students and give them a few minutes to form their network using the provided strings. Each new challenge introduces a new guideline they need to follow. These challenges progress in a specific way, with each guideline helping to motivate the next challenge.
   - As a class, read through the rules for all challenges.
   - Challenge #1: Students work in groups to create a network where everyone can speak directly to everyone else.
   - Challenge #2: As a class, read through Guideline A before having students work through the challenge.
   - Challenge #3: As a class, read through Guideline B before having students start work on the challenge.
   - Challenge #4: As a class, read through Guideline C before having students start work on the challenge. Let students know there are many possible answers to this as long as they have a reason for why they created the network that they did.
3. **Discuss:** *Thinking about our 3 guidelines, what is a strength of the network your group created? What is a weakness for the network your group created?*
4. **Discussion Goal:** There are many possible answers to Challenge 4 so it's important for students to think critically about why they made the choices that they did. They can think of Challenge 1 and Challenge 2 as the two extremes – too well connected and not connected enough – and their network finds a balance somewhere in the middle.

You may choose to have groups draw their networks on a sheet of paper and write their responses along with their network drawing. This can help students process their thinking, and can act as an artifact for reference throughout the unit.

Remarks

You've built some interesting networks today. Let's talk a little more about how data moves in these networks. Routing is the process of finding a path from the sender to the receiver. As we have seen, there are many different paths a message might take. How fast that message arrives is determined by bandwidth. In a computing network, the bandwidth is the maximum amount of data that can be sent in a fixed amount of time, usually measured in bits per second. If a message arrives quickly, that may be because of high bandwidth – many bits can be sent per second. If the message arrives slowly, it could be due to low bandwidth.

SUMMARY

- In computing, a group of two or more communicative devices is called a network. A network is actually made up of several distinct computer systems connected by wired or wireless connections.
- Networks facilitate electronic communications, file sharing, and resource sharing. For instance, several computers connected to a network can share a printer or exchange files.
- The relationship between connected devices as represented by a geometric graph is referred to as network topology. In a graph, devices are represented as vertices and the connections between them as edges. It explains the number of connections, their order, and the hierarchy of each device.
- Governments or industry associations create formal standards. There are formal standards for hardware, data link layer software, network layer software, and other areas. Formal standardization entails a drawn-out process of specification development, decision-making, and industry acceptance.
- The internet is a network system with global connectivity that transmits data over a variety of media types using TCP/IP. Connected by guided, wireless, and fiber-optic technologies, the internet is a global network of exchanges comprising private, public, business, academic, and government networks.
- The WWW's robust network of links, which enables users to browse related data sets kept on various computers across the Internet, is essential to its success. Any type of data can be accessed from a Web page by clicking on highlighted and/or underlined links that point to other pages thanks to this system of embedding links in the text known as "hypertext."
- Web services are client-server programs that exchange data via the Hipertext Transfer Protocol (HTTP) on the World Wide Web (WWW). Web services, offer a common way for software programs operating on different platforms and frameworks to communicate with one another.
- The internet of things, or IoT, is a network of interconnected computing devices, digital and mechanical machines, items, animals, and people that can transfer data over a network without requiring human-to-human or human-to-computer interaction. All of these devices are assigned unique identifiers, or UIDs.
- With cloud-based storage, files can be saved to a remote database instead of being stored on a local or proprietary hard drive. An electronic device can access data and the software needed to run it as long as it is connected to the internet.

REVIEW QUESTIONS

1. What is cloud computing? Explain the three main service models: IaaS, PaaS, and SaaS.
2. Describe virtualization. How does it relate to cloud computing?
3. Explain the concept of elasticity in cloud computing. Why is it important?

4. What is a firewall? How does it protect a network?
5. What is a VPN (Virtual Private Network)? How does it enhance security?
6. Describe the process of IP addressing and subnetting. Why is it important?
7. Explain the OSI model. What are the functions of each layer?
8. Explain the concept of network topology. Describe three common types of network topologies.

REFERENCES

1. Ahmad, I., Bakht, H., & Mohan, U. (2017). Cloud computing – A comprehensive definition. *Journal of Computing and Management Studies, 1*(1), 30th January 2017.
2. Alonso, G., Casati, F., Kuno, H., & Machiraju, V. (2003). *Web services: Concepts, architectures, and applications*. Springer Verlag.
3. Barrie, J. M., & Presti, D. E. (1996). The World Wide Web as an instructional tool. *Science, 274*(5286), 371–372. http://science-mag.aaas.org/science/scripts/display/full/274/5286/371.html
4. Huawei Technologies Co., Ltd. (2023). Network fundamentals. In *Data communications and network technologies*. Springer, Singapore. https://doi.org/10.1007/978-981-19-3029-4_1.
5. Nižeti⊠, S., Šoli⊠, P., López-de-Ipiña González-de-Artaza, D., & Patrono, L. (2020). Internet of Things (IoT): Opportunities, issues and challenges towards a smart and sustainable future. *Journal of Cleaner Production, 274*, 122877.
6. Odeh, A. H. (2019). Analytical and comparison study of main web programming languages – ASP and PHP. *TEM Journal, 8*(4), 1517–1522.
7. Rogala, S. M. (2002). Networking fundamentals. In K. J. Dreyer, A. Mehta, & J. H. Thrall (Eds.), *PACS* (pp. 51–63). Springer. https://doi.org/10.1007/978-1-4757-3651-9_4.
8. Van Sluyters, R. C. (1997). Introduction to the internet and World Wide Web. *ILAR Journal, 38*(4), 162–167.

CHAPTER

8 Business Intelligence and Analytics

LEARNING OBJECTIVES

After studying this chapter, you will be able to:

- Focus on basics of business intelligence;
- Understand business intelligence and analytics.

KEY TERMS FROM THIS CHAPTER

Balanced Scorecard (BSC)
Business intelligence (BI)
Data Mining
Enterprise information management
Infographics
Predictive Analytics
Big data analytics
Business performance management
Decision support system
Hadoop
Online analytical processing
Web browser

INTRODUCTION

Business intelligence, or BI, is a collection of procedures, frameworks, and tools that transform unstructured data into insightful knowledge that informs profitable business decisions. It is a collection of tools and services for turning data into knowledge and intelligence that can be put to use. The strategic, tactical, and operational business decisions made by an organization are directly impacted by BI. BI encourages making fact-based decisions based on past data rather than relying solely on intuition or conjecture. BI tools analyze data and produce dashboards, reports, summaries, maps, graphs, and charts in order to give users comprehensive information about the business.

In order to assist organizations in making wise and timely business decisions, business intelligence and analytics, or (BI&A), refers to the technologies, systems, procedures, approaches, and applications used to analyze vast amounts of heterogeneous business data. To convert unstructured data into insightful knowledge that can be utilized at all organizational levels to support business decision-making, a range of BI&A tools are available. These Decision Support Systems (DSS) enable enterprise-wide decision-making by transforming vast amounts of unstructured data into meaningful information through the use of computational power and analytical algorithms. When large amounts of data are presented visually, Visual Business Intelligence, also known as "Data Visualization," enables users to quickly understand the information.

8.1. BASICS OF BUSINESS INTELLIGENCE

Technologies, applications, and procedures for gathering, integrating, analyzing, and presenting business information are collectively referred to as business intelligence (BI). Better business decision-making is the aim of business intelligence. In essence, decision support systems (DSS) powered by data are what business intelligence systems are. Executive information systems, report and query tools, and briefing books can all be referred to as business intelligence at times (Figure 8.1).

Figure 8.1. *Business intelligence.*

Source: *https://www.btelligent.com/fileadmin/_processed_/0/0/csm_business-intelligence_b137e16154.jpg.*

8.1.1. Business Intelligence Versus Data Analytics

Although the term "business intelligence" has been used sporadically since the 1860s, it was formally proposed in 1989 by consultant Howard Dresner as a term for the application of data analysis techniques to support business decision-making processes. Executive information systems and decision support systems, two older, frequently mainframe-based analytical systems, gave rise to what are now known as business intelligence (BI) tools. Sometimes, the terms "business analytics" and "business intelligence" are used interchangeably; in other instances, "business analytics" is used more widely to refer to both BI and advanced analytics, or more narrowly to refer to advanced data analytics.

8.1.2. Importance of Business Intelligence Tools or Software Solutions

Business intelligence systems, which typically use data collected into a data warehouse or data mart and occasionally work from operational data, provide historical, present, and predictive views of business operations. Statistical data mining, visualization, reporting, and interactive "slice-and-dice" pivot-table analyzes are all supported by software components. Applications address a wide range of business data sources, including sales, production, finances, and more, for uses such as business performance management. Benchmarking is the process of gathering information about other businesses in the same industry.

8.1.3. Types of BI Tools

Ad hoc analytics and querying, enterprise reporting, online analytical processing (OLAP), mobile BI, real-time BI, operational BI, cloud and software-as-a-service BI, open source BI, collaborative BI, and location intelligence are just a few of the many data analysis applications that are combined into business intelligence. BI technology also comprises tools for creating BI dashboards and performance scorecards, which present visualized data on business metrics and key performance indicators in an understandable manner, as well as data visualization software for creating charts and other infographics.

Recently, data visualization tools have taken center stage in contemporary business intelligence. The technology was initially defined by a few prominent vendors, but more conventional BI vendors have since followed in their footsteps. These days, almost all of the major BI tools have visual data discovery features. Advanced analytics techniques like data mining, predictive analytics, text mining, statistical analysis, and big data analytics may also be included in business intelligence programs. However, while BI teams are in charge of more basic business data querying and analysis, advanced analytics projects are frequently carried out and managed by independent teams of data scientists, statisticians, predictive modelers, and other knowledgeable analytics professionals. Typically, business intelligence data is kept in smaller data marts or data warehouses that house subsets of an organization's data. Furthermore, Hadoop systems are being used more and more in business intelligence (BI) architectures as landing pads or repositories for BI and analytics data, particularly unstructured data, log files, sensor data, and other big data types. To guarantee that users are analyzing accurate and consistent data, raw data from various source systems needs to be combined, cleaned, and integrated using data integration and data quality tools before it is used in BI applications.

8.1.4. Business Intelligence Trends

Organizations are now beginning to realize that content and data should be managed as an integrated enterprise rather than as distinct components of information management. Business intelligence and enterprise content management are combined through enterprise information management. Organizations are currently shifting toward operational business intelligence, which is uncontested by vendors and currently underserved. There is currently a paradigm shift that is aimed at bringing business intelligence to the bottom of the pyramid with a focus on self-service business intelligence. Traditionally, business intelligence vendors have only targeted the top of the pyramid.

8.1.5. Self-Service Business Intelligence (SSBI)

Business systems and data analytics that provide business end users with access to an organization's information without requiring direct IT intervention are referred to as self-service business intelligence (SSBI). End users can do more with their data thanks to self-service business intelligence, even if they lack technical expertise. These solutions are typically designed to be user-friendly and adaptable, enabling end users to conduct independent data analysis, decision-making, planning, and forecasting. Businesses like PARIS Technologies have adopted a strategy to make business intelligence a simple tool to integrate with other end-user tools like Web browsers, Microsoft Excel, Access, and other vendors.

8.1.6. BI for Big Data

Big data systems are increasingly using BI platforms as their front-end interfaces. Flexible back ends are a common feature of modern BI software, allowing users to connect to a variety of data sources. The tools are a good fit for big data architectures because of this and their straightforward user interfaces. Users can create a unified view of their diverse data by connecting to a variety of data sources, such as cloud platforms, Hadoop systems, NoSQL databases, and more traditional data warehouses. Instead of the usual approach where only highly specialized data architects have access to data, using BI as a big data front end allows a large number of potential users to become involved because the tools are usually fairly simple.

8.1.6.1. Examples of Business Intelligence System used in Practice

8.1.6.1.1. Example 1

Information that could be entered into a product database could be entered into an Online Transaction Processing (OLTP) system.

- Add a product line;
- Change a product price (Figure 8.2).

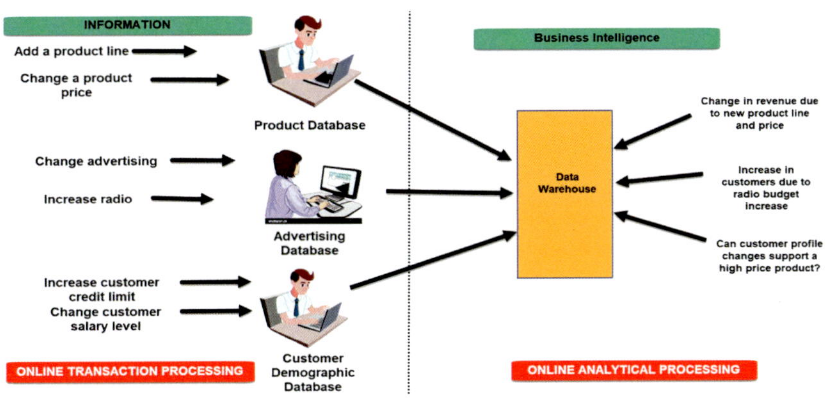

Figure 8.2. *Business intelligence system used in practice.*

Source: https://www.guru99.com/images/1/022218_0435_WhatisBusin2.png.

Accordingly, a query for the product subject area in a business intelligence system could ask whether adding a new product line or changing the price of an existing product increased sales.

An executable OLTP system query is present in an advertising database.

- Changed in advertisement options;
- Increase radio budget.

Accordingly, the number of new clients added as a result of the modification in the radio budget could be queried in the BI system. Data feedable would be in an OLTP system that deals with customer demographic databases.

- Increase customer credit limit;
- Change in customer salary level.

Similarly, can customer profile changes support higher product price? is an executable OLAP system query.

8.1.6.1.2. Example 2

A hotel owner can obtain statistical data on average occupancy and room rate by using BI analytical applications. Finding the total revenue made per room is helpful.

To determine its competitive position in different markets, it also gathers data from customer surveys and market share statistics from each hotel.

By examining these patterns on an annual, monthly, and daily basis, management is able to provide room rental discounts.

8.1.6.1.3. Example 3

Branch managers have access to BI applications through a bank. It assists branch managers in identifying the most lucrative clients and the clients they ought to focus on.

Information technology workers are relieved of the responsibility of producing analytical reports for the departments through the use of BI tools. Employees in the department now have access to a more comprehensive data source.

8.1.7. Four Types of BI Users

The four main users of the business intelligence system are listed below:

- **The Professional Data Analyst:** A statistician who constantly needs to delve deeply into data is a data analyst. Their BI system gives them new insights to create innovative business plans.
- **The IT users:** The BI infrastructure is largely maintained by the IT user as well.
- **The Head of the Company:** By increasing their company's operational efficiency, the CEO or CXO can boost profits.
- **The Business Users:** Users of business intelligence are dispersed throughout the organization. Business users can be divided into two categories.
  - Casual business intelligence user;
  - The power user.

The distinction between the two is that a power user can work with large, complex data sets, whereas a casual user will typically use dashboards to assess smaller, pre-defined data sets.

8.1.8. Advantages of Business Intelligence

Here are some of the advantages of using Business Intelligence System:

- **Boost Productivity:** Businesses can save a tonne of time and resources by creating reports with just one click using a BI program. Additionally, it enables workers to complete their tasks more productively.

- **To Improve Visibility:** Additionally, BI helps to increase these processes' visibility and make it possible to pinpoint any areas that require attention.
- **Fix Accountability:** The organization's accountability is assigned by the BI system because someone has to take responsibility and ownership for the organization's performance in relation to its goals.
- **It Gives a Bird's Eye View:** BI systems, with their typical dashboards and scorecards, also assist organizations' decision makers by providing an overall overview.
- **It Streamlines Business Processes:** All of the complexity related to business processes is eliminated by BI. By providing benchmarking, computer modeling, predictive analysis, and other techniques, it also automates analytics.
- **It Allows for Easy Analytics:** The use of BI software has become more accessible, enabling even non-technical and non-analyst users to swiftly gather and process data. This enables the many people to harness the power of analytics.

8.1.9. BI System Disadvantages

Here are some of the disadvantages of using Business Intelligence System:

- **Cost:** Costs associated with business intelligence can affect both small and medium-sized businesses. Using this kind of system for standard business transactions could be costly.
- **Complexity:** Another disadvantage of BI is the complexity of implementing a data warehouse. It can be so intricate that it can make it challenging for businesses to adapt their techniques.
- **Limited Use:** Like all improved technologies, BI was initially developed with wealthy firms' purchasing power in mind. For many small and medium-sized businesses, the BI system is therefore still too expensive.
- **Time Consuming Implementation:** The complete implementation of a data warehousing system takes approximately 1.5 years. It takes a lot of time as a result.

8.2. BUSINESS INTELLIGENCE AND ANALYTICS

The infrastructure, tools, applications, and other resources that come together to produce data and insights—which in turn help businesses make decisions, find opportunities for revenue, and assess performance—are collectively referred to as business intelligence (BI) and analytics.

The two main advantages of BI and analytics are speed and agility, which let companies process multiple data streams more quickly with an easy-to-use dashboard. The information that is produced can be used to track performance in real time and spot trends and opportunities. Better business decisions are made possible by BI and analytics by giving users and stakeholders access to these in-depth forecasts and insights. Data is no longer restricted to a single department or location thanks to BI and analytics, which also foster transparency and visibility across siloed networks both inside and outside of an organization. Additionally, the same data is instantly accessible to all offices and departments.

When combined, deeper insight and understanding of a company's place in the market allow businesses to make more proactive decisions, particularly regarding organizational effectiveness, changing market conditions, and customer needs. This gives them a competitive advantage.

Analytics and business intelligence (BI) are essential elements of data-driven decision-making in enterprises, although they complement one another in different ways and have somewhat distinct functions.

- **Business Intelligence (BI):** BI encompasses the procedures, equipment, and technologies needed to transform unprocessed data into useful insights for commercial endeavors. Its main areas of concentration are diagnostic and descriptive analytics, answering questions such as "What happened?" and "Why did it happen?" Key features of BI include:

– **Data Integration:** Collecting information from various sources and combining it into a single format so that it can be examined.

– **Data Warehousing:** Organizing and centrally storing vast amounts of structured data to facilitate easy access and analysis.

– **Reporting and Dashboards:** Facilitating decision-making by presenting summarized data in aesthetically pleasing formats such as dashboards, graphs, and charts.

- **Ad Hoc Querying:** Enabling interactive data exploration by letting users ask questions on the fly and getting answers right away.
- **Alerts and Notifications:** Notifying interested parties of any noteworthy events or changes found in the data.

BI is useful for keeping an eye on historical trends, tracking key performance indicators (KPIs), and giving executives a thorough picture of how well their company is performing.

- **Analytics:** Conversely, analytics is a more comprehensive collection of methods designed to draw conclusions from data in order to inform decisions and actions in the future. Prescriptive, diagnostic, predictive, and descriptive analytics are all included:
  - **Descriptive Analytics:** looking through previous data to comprehend past performance and spot patterns or trends.
  - **Diagnostic Analytics:** looking into the causes of previous results or occurrences, frequently using root cause analysis.
  - **Predictive Analytics:** utilizing machine learning models and statistical algorithms to predict future trends and results from past data.
  - **Prescriptive Analytics:** utilizing insights from predictive analytics to make recommendations for actions that will maximize future results.

Beyond simple reporting, analytics can offer deeper insights, predict future events, and recommend proactive strategies for development and growth.

- **Integration and Synergy:** Together, BI and analytics can improve an organization's capacity for making decisions. Analytics builds upon BI's foundation to produce actionable insights and propel strategic initiatives. BI establishes the foundation by gathering and organizing data. Businesses may obtain a thorough grasp of their operations and take proactive measures to address opportunities and problems by combining BI tools with advanced analytics capabilities.

In conclusion, analytics broadens the scope by combining predictive and prescriptive capabilities to guide future strategies and actions, whereas business intelligence (BI) concentrates on historical and real-time data analysis to support daily operations and reporting. When combined, they create a potent framework for using data inside businesses as a strategic asset.

8.2.1. Business Intelligence Architecture

A framework for data organization, information management, and technological components used in the construction of business intelligence systems for reporting and data analytics is known as business intelligence architecture. The data sources that company executives and other business stakeholders must access and analyze in order to satisfy their business requirements are included in the data components of a BI architecture. A few crucial factors in the process of choosing a source are data quality, data currency, and data detail level. A business intelligence architecture must include information from both internal and external sources in addition to both structured and unstructured data.

8.2.2. BI&A Evolution: Key Characteristics and Capabilities

Since the 1950s, scientists studying artificial intelligence have used the term intelligence. It wasn't until the 1990s that the term "business intelligence" gained traction in the IT and business communities. Business analytics was first presented as the primary analytical element of business intelligence (BI) in the late 2000s. The terms "big data" and "big data analytics" have more recently been used to characterize data sets and analytical methods in applications that require sophisticated and one-of-a-kind technologies for data management, storage, analysis, and visualization because they are so large (ranging from terabytes to exabytes) and complex (ranging from sensor to social media data) (Figure 8.3).

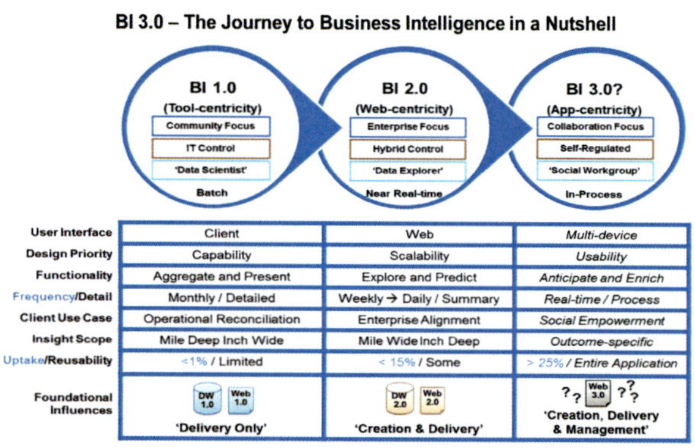

Figure 8.3. *Defining business intelligence 3.0.*

Source: https://www.capgemini.com/wp-content/uploads/2017/07/BI-3.01.png.

8.2.2.1. BI&A 1.0

The field of database management is where BI&A, as a data-centric approach, originated. A multitude of technologies are used extensively for data extraction, collection, and analysis. Industry-wide adoption of BI&A technologies and applications can be categorized as BI&A 1.0, where an organization's data is primarily structured, gathered via a variety of legacy systems, and frequently kept in relational database management systems (RDBMS) that are sold commercially. Developed in the 1970s and 1980s, statistical methods and data mining techniques form the foundation of the analytical techniques commonly employed in these systems, which gained popularity in the 1990s. (Chaudhuri et al., 2011; Turban et al., 2008).

Data warehousing and management are regarded as the cornerstones of BI&A 1.0. To convert and integrate enterprise-specific data, data mart design and extraction, transformation, and load (ETL) tools are critical. Key data attributes are explored through database queries, online analytical processing (OLAP), and reporting tools built around clear, uncomplicated graphics. A range of performance metrics can be analyzed and visualized with the use of scorecards and dashboards in business performance management (BPM). Apart from the aforementioned well-established functions of business reporting, numerous business applications employ statistical analysis and data mining techniques for association analysis, data segmentation and clustering, classification and regression analysis, anomaly detection, and predictive modeling. The majority of these analytical and data processing technologies are already included in the top commercial business intelligence platforms that are provided by well-known IT companies like SAP, IBM, Microsoft, and Oracle.

The following eight features—reporting, dashboards, ad hoc queries, search-based BI, OLAP, interactive visualization, scorecards, predictive modeling, and data mining—

are among the 13 that are thought to be necessary for BI platforms. Based on the Gartner BI Hype Cycle analysis for emerging BI technologies, a few BI&A 1.0 areas—data mining workbench, column-based DBMS, in-memory DBMS, and real-time decision tools—are still actively being developed. Database management systems, data mining, and multivariate statistics are just a few examples of the organized courses that are frequently included in academic curricula for computer science (CS) and information systems (IS).

8.2.2.2. BI&A 2.0

The Internet and the Web have presented opportunities for novel data collection and analytical research and development since the early 2000s. Web search engines like Google and Yahoo as well as e-commerce sites like Amazon and eBay are examples of HTTP-based Web 1.0 systems that enable businesses to display their brands online and communicate with clients directly. Their detailed and IP-specific user search and interaction logs, which are seamlessly collected through cookies and server logs, have become a new gold mine for understanding customers' needs and identifying new business opportunities, in addition to translating their traditional RDBMS-based product information and business contents online. A new and exciting era of business intelligence and business analytics (BI) has been brought about by web intelligence, web analytics, and the user-generated content gathered through Web 2.0-based social and crowd-sourcing systems. In the 2000s, BI research focused on text and web analytics for unstructured web contents. (Doan et al., 2011)

Through various text and web mining techniques, a vast amount of information about companies, industries, products, and customers can be gathered from the web and organized and visualized. Web analytics tools like Google Analytics can provide a trail of a user's online activities and reveal the user's browsing and purchasing patterns by analyzing customer clickstream data logs. Web analytics can be used for a variety of tasks, including product placement optimization, web site design, customer transaction analysis, market structure analysis, and product recommendations. A wealth of user-generated content has also been produced by the numerous Web 2.0 applications that were developed after 2004. These applications include forums, online groups, web blogs, social networking sites, social multimedia sites (for images and videos), virtual worlds, and social games. Not only can Web 2.0 applications record celebrity gossip, everyday event references, and socio-political sentiments expressed in these media, but they can also effectively collect a large amount of timely feedback and opinions from a diverse customer base for various business types.

Instead of the conventional business-to-customer, one-way "marketing," many marketing researchers think that social media analytics offer businesses a special chance to treat the market as a "conversation" between businesses and customers. Future BI&A 2.0 systems will need to incorporate seasoned and scalable text mining techniques, in contrast to BI&A 1.0 technologies that are already incorporated into commercial enterprise IT systems, e.g., DBMS-based BI&A 1.0 systems for information extraction, topic identification, opinion mining, question-answering, web mining, social network analysis, and spatial-temporal analysis. There are currently no advanced text analytics for unstructured content taken into account in the 13 capabilities of the Gartner BI platforms, with the exception of basic query and search capabilities. Nonetheless, a number of them—including content/text analytics, natural language question answering, and information semantic services—are mentioned in the Gartner BI Hype Cycle. To address the need for technical training, new IS and CS courses in text mining and web mining have been developed.

8.2.2.3. BI&A 3.0

A new research opportunity in BI&A 3.0 is emerging, while web-based BI&A 2.0 has drawn active research from academia and industry. For the first time in 2011, there were more mobile phones and tablets (roughly 480 million units) than laptops and PCs (roughly 380 million units).

The same article predicted that by 2020, there will be 10 billion mobile devices connected to the internet, despite the fact that there were more than one billion PCs in use in 2008. From travel advisories to multiplayer games, mobile devices like the iPad, iPhone, and other smartphones, along with their entire ecosystems of downloadable applications, are revolutionizing a variety of societal sectors, including government, healthcare, education, and entertainment.

The "Internet of Things," which is made up of various sensor-based Internet-enabled gadgets with radio tags, barcodes, and RFID, is creating exciting new avenues for creative application. For the remainder of the 2010s, there will be special research opportunities and challenges due to the capacity of such mobile and Internet-enabled devices to support highly mobile, location-aware, person-centered, and context-relevant operations and transactions. Promising research areas include mobile interface design, visualization, and HCI (human–computer interaction).

The underlying mobile analytics and location and context-aware techniques for gathering, processing, analyzing, and visualizing such large-scale and fluid mobile and sensor data are still unknown, despite the apparent arrival of the Web 3.0 (mobile and sensor-based) era.

In the near future, no integrated, commercial BI&A 3.0 systems are anticipated. The majority of academic studies on mobile BI are still in their infancy. Mobile BI is one of the new technologies that has the potential to seriously disrupt the BI market, according to the Gartner BI Hype Cycle analysis, despite not being part of the core capabilities of the current BI platform.

Table 8.1 lists the salient features of BI&A 1.0, 2.0, and 3.0 in relation to the Gartner BI platforms core capabilities and hype cycle. The uncertainty surrounding BI&A 3.0 offers the IS community another distinctive research avenue.

High-impact BI&A research and development, for both industry and academia, is expected to flourish in the 2010s. Industry and the business community have already made significant strides toward BI&A adoption. In order to have significant and enduring effects on science and society, the IS community must overcome special obstacles and seize special opportunities. Future directions, curricula, and action plans for IS research and education programs must be carefully considered, ranging from BI&A 1.0 to 3.0.

Table 8.1. *BI&A Evolution: Key Characteristics and Capabilities*

	Key Characteristics	Gartner BI Platforms Core Capabilities	Gartner Hype Cycle
BI&A 1.0	*DBMS-based, structured content* • *RDBMS & data warehousing* • *ETL & OLAP* • *Dashboards & scorecards* • *Data mining & statistical analysis*	• *Ad hoc query & search-based BI* • *Reporting, dashboards & scorecards* • *OLAP* • *Interactive visualization* • *Predictive modeling & data mining*	• *Column-based DBMS* • *In-memory DBMS* • *Real-time decision* • *Data mining workbenches*
BI&A 2.0	*Web-based, unstructured content* • *Information retrieval and extraction* • *Opinion mining* • *Question answering* • *Web analytics and web intelligence* • *Social media analytics* • *Social network analysis* • *Spatial-temporal analysis*		• *Information semantic* *services* • *Natural language question* *answering* • *Content & text analytics*
BI&A 3.0	*Mobile and sensor-based content* • *Location-aware analysis* • *Person-centered analysis* • *Context-relevant analysis* • *Mobile visualization & HCI*		• *Mobile BI*

Source: https://www.jstor.org/stable/41703503.

8.2.3. BI&A Research Framework: Foundational Technologies and Emerging Research in Analytics

The BI&A industry and the research community are very excited about the prospects presented by the aforementioned high-impact and emerging applications. While industry concentrates on integrated and scalable systems and their implementations for various applications across various organizations, academia must keep pushing the boundaries of analytics technology.

Five key technical areas can be used to categorize emerging opportunities in analytics research: (big) data analytics, text analytics, web analytics, network analytics, and mobile analytics. These areas can all be used to support BI&A 1.0, 2.0, and 3.0. These five topic areas have been categorized in a way that aims to draw attention to the salient features of each; that being said, some of these areas may make use of comparable underlying technologies. We outline the established and well-developed foundational technologies for each analytics field and recommend a few key areas for future research (*see* Table 8.2).

Table 8.2. *BI&A Research Framework: Foundational Technologies and Emerging Research in Analytics*

	(Big) Data Analytics	Text Analytics	Web Analytics	Network Analytics	Mobile Analytics
Foundational Technologies	• *RDBMS* • *data warehousing* • *ETL* • *OLAP* • *BPM* • *data mining* • *clustering* • *regression* • *classification* • *association analysis* • *anomaly detection* • *neural networks* • *genetic algorithms* • *multivariate statistical analysis* • *optimization* • *heuristic search*	• *information retrieval* • *document representation* • *query processing* • *relevance feedback* • *user models* • *search engines* • *enterprise search systems*	• *information retrieval* • *computational linguistics* • *search engines* • *web crawling* • *web site ranking* • *search log analysis* • *recommender systems* • *web services* • *mashups*	• *bibliometric analysis* • *citation network* • *co-authorship network* • *social network theories* • *network metrics and topology* • *mathematical network models* • *network visualization*	• *web services* • *smartphone platforms*

Emerging Research	*• statistical machine learning • sequential and temporal mining • spatial mining • mining high-speed data streams and sensor data • process mining • privacy-preserving data mining • network mining • web mining • column-based DBMS • in-memory DBMS • parallel DBMS • cloud computing • Hadoop • MapReduce*	*• statistical NLP • information extraction • topic models • question-answering systems • opinion mining • sentiment/ affect analysis • web stylometric analysis • multilingual analysis • text visualization • multimedia IR • mobile IR • Hadoop • MapReduce*	*• cloud services • cloud computing • social search and mining • reputation systems • social media analytics • web visualization • web-based auctions • internet monetization • social marketing • web privacy/ security*	*• link mining • community detection • dynamic network modeling • agent-based modeling • social influence and information diffusion models • ERGMs • virtual communities • criminal/ dark networks • social/ political analysis • trust and reputation*	*• mobile web services • mobile pervasive apps • mobile sensing apps • mobile social innovation • mobile social networking • mobile visualization/ HCI • personalization and behavioral modeling • gamification • mobile advertising and marketing*

Source: https://www.jstor.org/stable/41703503.

8.2.3.1. (Big) Data Analytics

The term "data analytics" describes BI&A technologies that primarily rely on statistical analysis and data mining. As previously indicated, the majority of these methods depend on the established commercial technologies of data warehousing, ETL, OLAP, BPM, and relational database management systems. Researchers from the database, algorithm, and artificial intelligence communities have been creating different data mining algorithms since the late 1980s. Based on expert nominations, citation counts, and community surveys, the top 10 data mining algorithms were determined for the

IEEE 2006 International Conference on Data Mining (ICDM). PageRank, AdaBoost, kNN (k-nearest neighbors), CART, k-means, SVM (support vector machine), Apriori, EM (expectation maximization), CART, and AdaBoost are the algorithms in order of ranking. Classification, clustering, regression, association analysis, and network analysis are all covered by these algorithms. Commercial and open source data mining systems have integrated the majority of these well-known data mining algorithms. The success of data mining in various applications has also been attributed to other developments like neural networks for classification/prediction and clustering and genetic algorithms for optimization and machine learning.

For BI&A, two additional data analytics techniques that are frequently taught in business schools are also essential. Multivariate statistical analysis, which is based on statistical theories and models, includes analytical methods that have been effectively applied in a variety of business applications, including discriminant analysis, factor analysis, regression, and clustering. Heuristic search and optimization techniques, which originated in the field of management science, are also appropriate for certain BI&A issues like web crawling and spidering and database feature selection. The majority of these methods are covered in business school curricula. (Chaudhuri et al., 2011).

Data analytics is still a hot topic for research because of the community's combined success in data mining and statistical analysis. Applications for data, text, and web analytics have made use of statistical machine learning, which is frequently founded on strong mathematical models and potent algorithms. Methods like Bayesian networks, Hidden Markov models, support vector machines, reinforcement learning, and ensemble models are a few examples of these. Other cutting-edge data analytics methods, such as sequential/temporal mining, spatial mining, data mining for high-speed data streams, and sensor data, investigate and take advantage of distinctive data features. Research on privacy-preserving data mining is just getting started as a result of growing concerns about privacy in various e-commerce, e-government, and healthcare applications. While some of these strategies are process-driven and specify how data can be accessed and used, many of these data-driven strategies rely on different forms of anonymization. Process mining is a new research area that has emerged in the last ten years that focuses on the analysis of processes using event data. The availability of event logs in a variety of industries (such as supply chains and healthcare) along with new methods for process discovery and conformance checking have made process mining feasible. The fascinating research in network analytics and web analytics that is presented below was also aided by network data and web content.

Apart from the ongoing scholarly investigations into data analytics, there has also been significant buzz from industry research and development, particularly concerning big data analytics for semi-structured content. Semi-structured data may require ad hoc and one-time extraction, parsing, processing, indexing, and analytics in a scalable and distributed MapReduce or Hadoop environment, in contrast to structured data that can be handled repeatedly through an RDBMS. Hugely parallel, large-scale data access has been praised for MapReduce as a revolutionary new platform. Hadoop is a Java-based software framework for distributed processing of data-intensive transformation and analytics, partly inspired by MapReduce. Hadoop has been embraced by the top three commercial database providers, Microsoft, IBM, and Oracle, some of which are housed in cloud infrastructures. For business analytics, the open-source Apache Hadoop platform has also become increasingly popular. This includes Chukwa for data collection, HBase for distributed data storage, Hive for ad hoc querying and data summarization, and Mahout for data mining.

8.2.3.2. Text Analytics

Textual content, such as corporate documents, web pages, and social media content, makes up a sizable amount of the unstructured content that an organization gathers. The academic fields of computational linguistics and information retrieval are the foundation of text analytics.

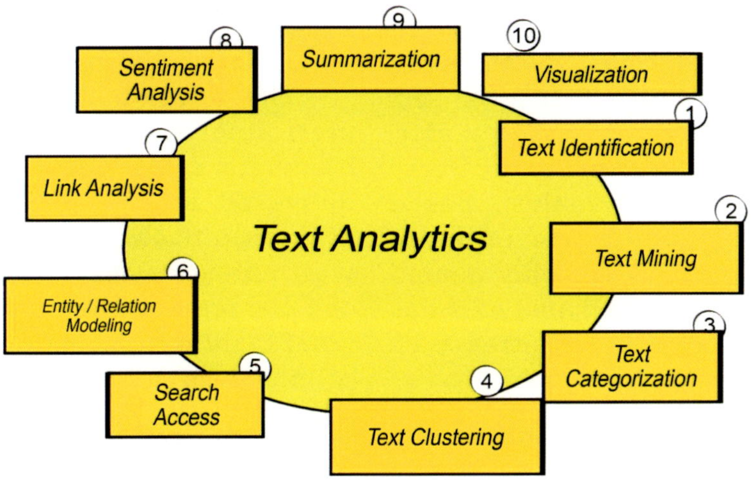

Figure 8.4. *Text analytics.*

Source: http://oralhistory.eu/images/tech/textanalytics.png.

Document representation and query processing serve as the cornerstones for the development of the vector-space, Boolean, and probabilistic retrieval models in information retrieval. These models, in turn, served as the inspiration for the creation of contemporary digital libraries, search engines, and enterprise search systems (Salton 1989). Statistical natural language processing (NLP) methods for part-of-speech-tagging (POST), word sense disambiguation, lexical acquisition, and probabilistic context-free grammars have gained importance in computational linguistics as text representation methods. To improve search performance, user models and relevance feedback are just as crucial as document and query representations (Figure 8.4).

Search engines have developed into sophisticated commercial systems since the early 1990s. These systems now include analytics for search logs, efficient inverted indexing, quick and distributed crawling, and inlink-based page ranking. A large number of these fundamental text processing and indexing methods are used in BI&A 1.0's text-based enterprise search and document management systems.

8.2.3.3. Web Analytics

Within BI&A, web analytics has become a vibrant area of research during the last ten years. Web analytics presents special analytical opportunities and challenges, building on the information retrieval and natural language processing (NLP) models in text analytics and the data mining and statistical analysis foundations in data analytics. Specialized Internet-based technologies for web site crawling/spidering, web page updating, web site ranking, and search log analysis have been developed in part thanks to HTTP/HTML-based hyperlinked web sites, related web search engines, and directory systems for finding web content. Subsequently, active research in recommender systems has emerged from web log analysis based on customer transactions. However, since web services and Web 2.0 systems gained traction in the mid-2000s, web analytics has grown even more fascinating. (Bettencourt et al., 2006)

Web services, which are based on XML and Internet protocols (HTTP, SMTP), provide a novel approach to integrating and reusing legacy or third-party systems. AJAX (asynchronous JavaScript + XML) for data interchange and dynamic display, RSS (really simple syndication) for news "pushing," REST (representational state transfer) for invoking remote services, JSON (JavaScript object notation) for lightweight data-interchange, and other new types of web services and their corresponding APIs (application programming interface) make it easier for developers to integrate diverse content from various web-enabled systems. These simple programming models facilitate multimedia content "mashups," data syndication, and notifications (e.g., Flickr, YouTube, Google Maps) from various online sources—a procedure that is comparable to BI&A 1.0's ETL (extraction, transformation, and load) process. The majority of online retailers have made their product and user content accessible through robust APIs. For instance, developers can access the Amazon Elastic Compute Cloud (EC2) for processing capacity, the product catalog, user reviews, site ranking, and historical pricing through Amazon Web Services. In a similar vein, Google's web APIs support GData (for Calendar, Gmail, etc.), Map API, and AJAX search), Google App Engine for cloud computing resources, and Google Translate. For BI&A 2.0 research, web services and APIs continue to offer an exciting stream of new data sources.

The development of cloud computing platforms and services, which include hardware, system software, and applications delivered as services over the Internet, is a significant emerging component in web analytics research. Cloud computing can be provided as software as a service (SaaS), infrastructure as a service (IaaS), or platform as a service (PaaS), and is based on service oriented architecture (SOA), server virtualization, and utility computing. Currently, only a small number of top IT vendors are equipped to support cloud-based high-end, high-throughput BI&A applications. For instance, users can rent virtual computers on Amazon Elastic Compute Cloud (EC2) to run their own software. Online storage web service is offered by its Simple Storage Service (S3). A platform for creating and hosting web applications with a Python or Java foundation is offered by Google App Engine. Google Bigtable is employed for the storage of backend data. The Windows Azure platform from Microsoft offers cloud services like SQL Azure and SharePoint in addition to supporting the execution of .Net framework applications. For BI&A researchers, the industry-leading web and cloud services present particular difficulties in terms of data processing, analytics, and collection.

8.2.3.4. Network Analytics

New computational models for online community and social network analysis are included in the emerging field of network analytics, which developed from the previous citation-based bibliometric analysis. Citation networks and co-authorship networks, which are based on bibliometric analysis, have been used for a long time to study the dissemination of knowledge and the impact of science. One useful illustration of a citation metric is the h-index. With the help of computer scientists, mathematicians, and sociologists, network science has advanced quickly since the early 2000s. To better understand the characteristics and relationships of networks, a variety of social network theories, network metrics, topology, and mathematical models have been developed, including, structural holes, structural balance; random network, small-world network, scale-free network; centrality, betweenness, cliques, and pathways.

8.2.3.5. Mobile Analytics

According to respondents to a recent IBM technology trends survey, mobile computing is the second most "in demand" area for software development. It is an effective way to reach a large number of users and can boost the productivity and efficiency of an organization's workforce. According to the Gartner BI Hype Cycle analysis, mobile BI is another emerging technology that has the potential to significantly upend the BI market. The market for mobile advertisements is predicted to grow rapidly, from an estimated $2.6 billion in 2012 to $10.8 billion in 2016, according to eMarketer. (Snider 2012)

As more and more businesses create applications, mobile computing presents a way for IT professionals to advance their careers. Since 2010, Android has maintained its position as the leading mobile platform thanks to its sizable and expanding global install base. Because of its significantly shorter learning curve and availability as an open source platform built on Java and XML, Android is very popular among IT professionals. Of those surveyed by IBM, 70% said they planned to use Android for their mobile development, compared to 49% who planned to use iOS and 35% who planned to use Windows 7. These smart devices have made it possible to gather highly personalized, context-aware, location-specific, and fine-grained data, which has created new opportunities for cutting edge BI&A. A new direction for BI&A research is provided by the distinct apps ecosystem created by the community of volunteer mobile app developers, in addition to the benefits of hardware and content. As of August 2012, there were more than 500,000 apps available in the Apple App Store alone, covering practically every possible category. The quantity of Android apps also approached 500,000 at that same time. Mobile apps are starting to see a wide range of revenue models emerge, from paid or free but ad-supported apps to mobile gamification, which rewards users (e.g., users, or staff) through awarding contributions. According to the IBM survey, businesses are thinking about enterprise apps, industry-specific apps, e-commerce apps, and social apps (in that order) for mobile BI.

The lightweight programming models used in modern web services, such as HTML, XML, CSS, Ajax, Flash, and J2E, along with the advancing mobile development platforms like Android and iOS, have greatly helped in the quick evolution of mobile web services. These mobile web services, including HTML5, Mobile Ajax, Mobile Flash, and J2ME, are being used in a variety of mobile applications, from disaster management to healthcare support. There is a growing focus on mobile analytics research, with advancements in areas like mobile sensing apps that are location-aware and activity-sensitive, mobile social innovation for m-health and m-learning, mobile social networking and crowd-sourcing, mobile visualization/HCI, as well as personalization and behavioral modeling for mobile apps. Additionally, research is being done on social, behavioral, and economic models related to gamification, mobile advertising, and social marketing, which could potentially shape the future of BI&A 3.0 systems.

8.2.4. Implications of BI&A as Capability Monitoring

8.2.4.1. Capability-focused Design of BI&A

The dynamic capability perspective of BI&A suggests that monitoring capabilities within an organization should be targeted towards specific organizational abilities, while also considering both internal and external environments. This presents challenges for BI&A architecture as it needs to balance these conflicting demands. The five elements of BI&A discussed here provide possible strategies for designing BI&A architecture. Centralizing the management of data collection from both internal and external sources, as well as identifying discrepancies in these environments, can lead to synergistic advantages. However, detecting issues and requesting changes requires expertise and focus on specific capabilities.

The importance of focusing on specific BI&A activities brings up the issue of how resources are allocated. It is widely understood that enhancing capabilities can be costly and should be done strategically. Simply having a dynamic capability without utilizing it can be a burden without any rewards. Conversely, constantly seeking opportunities to change in order to exercise dynamic capabilities can lead to expenses and disruptions that outweigh the benefits. Therefore, when deciding how to allocate resources for BI&A, it is important to consider the potential need for changing capabilities, as well as the costs and advantages of making those changes.

8.2.4.2. Assessment of BI&A Success

The capability dynamization view proposes that the main focus of BI&A is to generate requests for changes in current capabilities. This contrasts with traditional views of BI&A, which emphasize the goal of providing managerial insights. According to this perspective, the success of BI&A efforts should be evaluated based on the number of change requests made, the action taken on those requests, and the outcomes of the resulting changes. To achieve this, it is essential to track how change requests are implemented and whether they lead to positive or negative results, and integrate this feedback into the BI&A process. Exploring the role of feedback in managing BI&A activities represents a promising avenue for future research.

8.2.4.3. Alignment with Change Management

The suggested perspective of BI&A as a capability monitoring tool suggests that change requests are put into action. However, implementing these changes is not simple and requires strong change management skills, known as adaptive agility. This highlights the importance of closely aligning BI&A with organizational change management practices. Business Process Management (BPM) has become a comprehensive approach to enhancing business value by improving organizational efficiency and adaptability. BPM is linked to an organization's ability to successfully carry out changes, which complements the use of BI&A for enhancing capabilities. While process analytics and mining are recognized as crucial components of both BI&A and BPM, further research on the intersection of the two is needed.

8.2.5. The Key Advantages of Business Intelligence and Analytics

Businesses can make adjustments and take the required actions to increase efficiency across their operations with the aid of business intelligence solutions. In order to serve its best interests, an organization may also recognize new business opportunities and grow in response. Tools for business intelligence software are heavily reliant on quickly developing technologies, such as data mining, big data, and predictive analytics. To assist organizations in determining their business intelligence needs, a large number of technology consultants offer specialized business intelligence tools, technology consulting, and implementation support along with extensive industry expertise. The main benefits of utilizing business intelligence tools are outlined below:

8.2.5.1. Faster Decision Making

Key executives play a crucial role in determining the direction and strategy of a business. Without the use of business intelligence solutions, this decision-making process often relies heavily on assumptions. The lack of detailed reports and analysis means that executives may have to make decisions based on limited information, such as sales figures and market demand. Business intelligence eliminates this uncertainty by providing real-time production stats and customer feedback for different product lines, supported by concrete data. Additionally, predictive BI techniques allow for scenario analysis to understand the potential impact of decisions on the company's future. This wealth of information offers key insights and a broader perspective, allowing for quicker decision-making when it matters most.

8.2.5.2. Real-time Performance Measurement

Business intelligence tools carefully examine vast volumes of data produced by an organization in real time for a variety of performance metrics, including productivity, sales numbers, and business-related marketing expenses. This facilitates communication between business units and upper management regarding the performance and status of various key organizational components. Business executives can also use it to identify and seize market opportunities.

8.2.5.3. Improved Reporting Speed

BI users are able to quickly access organized and interactive reports that present large amounts of raw data in a readable format. This saves time by eliminating the need to manually sift through data or print multiple reports.

8.2.5.4. Greater Insights into Customer Behavior

Business intelligence can use sales figures and customer feedback to provide valuable insights into customer preferences and needs.

For example, in the IT industry, customer information can be analyzed to understand how customers are responding to the design of software products like Google Chrome and Microsoft Windows. By continuously monitoring and updating products based on this feedback, companies can better meet customer demands. Analyzing this information can also help companies identify customer buying patterns and needs, allowing them to make informed decisions to retain and expand their customer base.

8.2.5.5. Identify New Business Opportunities

Business intelligence can assist in identifying customer touch points where multiple products from the same company are purchased individually. These touch points present new opportunities for businesses to sell bundled products as a single integrated package in order to retain and expand their customer base. By utilizing business intelligence, companies can uncover previously unnoticed opportunities and maximize profits.

8.2.6. Role of Organizations in Making BI Projects a Success

To ensure that BI solutions are easily adopted and that an organization gets the most out of their investment in BI, they should implement the following two crucial changes:

8.2.6.1. Operational Changes

Some businesses have become more profitable and highly efficient thanks to business intelligence. But even though BI is a very strong tool, it cannot be effectively used in the absence of sufficient data. The quantity and caliber of data that a company has on hand is essential to a business intelligence project's success. An organization must make a number of adjustments to its operations before starting a business intelligence project. Some of these adjustments include replacing outdated reporting methods with more up-to-date ones, mandating that the entire company use a particular standard for reporting and data storage, ensuring that data access is available in every area of business operations, and pinpointing the precise areas where business intelligence is required.

8.2.6.2. Usability Support

For a business intelligence tool to be successful, it must also have extensive usability support. The ease with which a user can access and add data to the system is referred to as usability. The quality of business operations should be enhanced by the integration of analytics software and business intelligence. This is only feasible if all stakeholders in the business, including customers and employees, have an intuitive interface that allows them to input the required data into the business intelligence system. BI needs to be integrated into the company's work culture and made as seamless as possible with all of the current procedures and guidelines. This will significantly enhance a BI system's output and performance. When business intelligence is utilized correctly, it can greatly enhance operational efficiency. By partnering with a skilled technology consultant, a robust BI system can be seamlessly integrated into the organization's infrastructure. Additionally, standardized procedures should be established for data storage and record-keeping. To fully realize the benefits of a BI system, the organization must ensure proper selection and implementation, smooth integration, and full engagement of key stakeholders.

CASE STUDY

UNDERSTANDING THE ROOT CAUSES OF ORDER DELIVERY RELATED ISSUES IN THE RETAIL INDUSTRY

Business Overview

Nowadays retailers tend to create value, strengthen trust and enrich the customer experience by offering on-time and fast delivery services. Our client is a leading manufacturer in fluid system connection technology in Germany and they wanted to understand the root cause of common order and delivery issues and enable decision-making by identifying gaps. They lacked a strong platform to drive analytics use cases for customer growth and retention.

Objectives

Since the company's core business is dealing with providing sales and services for its products, any error or delay could cause a negative impact on its credibility. Nowadays customers are more likely to hold retailers responsible for delays. We identified that they faced many problems in understanding their orders, shipment, and delivery.

Prowesstics's Data Warehouse and reporting solutions focused on

- The areas of delayed orders and delivery reliabilities.
- Latest start time, and the promised delivery time.
- Issues in complex data acquisition processes and different data access protocols.

To solve this, they wanted a systematic approach to the analysis method; a way to handle a complex system with a global point to identifying the suitable data model aligned to their business objectives and then building a core data store that can provide generalized and automated solutions for all their analytics needs.

The Solution- Established A Centralized Approach

After analyzing, we provide the customer with the view that the problem caused by the order delay is based on dimensions such as sales products, sales territory, sales partner, and shipping partner.

We've implemented a centralized approach through

- Discovery;
- Analysis;
- Development;

- Deployment – encompassing data engineering and data science.

We have examined the data quality and understood the multiple factors (supply, demand, and time) that affect order delivery. Examining the data quality, in turn, improves confidence in data, eradicates errors, and lowers the risk.

The Outcome

- On-Time Delivery Performance Improved;
- Our approach helped them to find below metrics:
  - Improve on-time delivery;
  - Reduces complaints related to delivery issues;
  - Increases their CRR (customer retention rate).
- *Customer retention analytics not only help them to avoid losing customers and also help to build the loyalty that encourages them to return to purchase your product or services over and over to maximize their potential growth. Positive results showed that order delay was reduced, and as a result, on-time delivery performance improved.*

CLASS ACTIVITY

CLOUD COMPUTING

Step 1: Individually – Review the Following Narrative

The Owl Business School recently suffered from some negative PR as a result of a malicious hacking incident. In an effort to improve customer relations and proactively connect with all its customers, the Owl Business School would like to implement a CRM. You have been assigned the role of selecting the top 3 CRM solutions in the marketplace and presenting it to the Senior Provost Office (SPO) Leadership team so they can decide on the final CRM solution to implement. It is critical that the top three CRM solutions you pick meet the features and requirements for acceptance at the Owl Business School.

Step 2: Class Discussion

Determine the CRM requirements for the Owl Business School after speaking with the Dean (Instructor). Some questions to consider: Budget? In-House Development Versus Outsourced? Cloud Versus On Premise? Backup of Data? Recovery of Data? Reporting and Analytics? Number of Users? Recurring Versus One-Time Cost? Maintenance? Support? Talent? Features? Security? Data Privacy? Other questions?

Step 3: Class Discussion

Document some of the pros and cons between a cloud solution Versus an on premise solution.

Cloud	**On Premise**
Pros	*Pros*
Cons	*Cons*

Step 4: Class Discussion

Review the Gartner Magic Quadrant for the CRM Customer Engagement Center. Use this chart to determine some leading CRM vendor solutions in the marketplace.

SUMMARY

- Technologies, applications, and procedures for gathering, integrating, analyzing, and presenting business information are collectively referred to as business intelligence (BI). Better business decision-making is the aim of business intelligence.
- Business intelligence systems, which typically use data collected into a data warehouse or data mart and occasionally work from operational data, provide historical, present, and predictive views of business operations. Statistical data mining, visualization, reporting, and interactive "slice-and-dice" pivot-table analyzes are all supported by software components.
- Ad hoc analytics and querying, enterprise reporting, online analytical processing (OLAP), mobile BI, real-time BI, operational BI, cloud and software-as-a-service BI, open source BI, collaborative BI, and location intelligence are just a few of the many data analysis applications that are combined into business intelligence.
- Business systems and data analytics that provide business end users with access to an organization's information without requiring direct IT intervention are referred to as self-service business intelligence (SSBI).
- Big data systems are increasingly using BI platforms as their front-end interfaces. Flexible back ends are a common feature of modern BI software, allowing users to connect to a variety of data sources. The tools are a good fit for big data architectures because of this and their straightforward user interfaces.
- The infrastructure, tools, applications, and other resources that come together to produce data and insights—which in turn help businesses make decisions, find opportunities for revenue, and assess performance—are collectively referred to as business intelligence (BI) and analytics.
- A framework for data organization, information management, and technological components used in the construction of business intelligence systems for reporting and data analytics is known as business intelligence architecture.
- Tools for business intelligence software are heavily reliant on quickly developing technologies, such as data mining, big data, and predictive analytics. To assist organizations in determining their business intelligence needs, a large number of technology consultants offer specialized business intelligence tools, technology consulting, and implementation support along with extensive industry expertise.

REVIEW QUESTIONS

1. What is data mining? How does it contribute to BI?
2. Describe OLAP (Online Analytical Processing) and its role in BI.
3. Describe the main components of a BI system.
4. What are the main techniques used in predictive analytics?
5. What are the ethical considerations in business analytics?
6. Discuss the role of big data in business analytics.

REFERENCES

1. Beck, C. (2020). Business intelligence. *Manufacturing Management, 2020*(1), 34–35. http://dx.doi.org/10.12968/s2514-9768(22)90109-7.
2. Chamoni, P., & Linden, M. (2011). Business intelligence. *WiSt – Wirtschaftswissenschaftliches Studium, 40*(6), 276–281. http://dx.doi.org/10.15358/0340-1650-2011-6-276.
3. Chandrasekhar, S. (2005). Business intelligence. *Asia Pacific Business Review, 1*(1), 84–88. http://dx.doi.org/10.1177/097324700500100110.
4. Chaudhuri, S., Dayal, U., & Narasayya, V. (2011). An overview of business intelligence technology. *Communications of the ACM, 54*(8), 88–98. https://doi.org/10.1145/1978542.1978562.
5. Doan, A., Ramakrishnan, R., & Halevy, A. Y. (2011). Crowdsourcing systems on the world-wide web. *Communications of the ACM, 54*(4), 86–96. https://doi.org/10.1145/1924421.1924442.
6. Grünwald, M., & Taubner, D. (2009). Business intelligence. *Informatik-Spektrum, 32*(5), 398–403. http://dx.doi.org/10.1007/s00287-009-0374-1.
7. Herring, J. P. (1993). Business intelligence. *Journal of Business Strategy, 14*(3), 10–12. http://dx.doi.org/10.1108/eb039552.
8. Post, G. V., & Kagan, A. (2012). Business intelligence. *International Journal of Business Intelligence Research, 3*(3), 16–28. http://dx.doi.org/10.4018/jbir.2012070102.
9. Quijada, C. A. (2020). Business intelligence. *Realidad Empresarial*(9), 45–48. http://dx.doi.org/10.5377/reuca.v0i9.10068.
10. Reinkemeyer, L., Gallenberger, M., Beria, M., Müller, U., & Hahn, T. (2018). Business intelligence. *Digitale Welt, 3*(1), 44–52. http://dx.doi.org/10.1007/s42354-019-0149-z.
11. Skyrius, R. (2021). *Business intelligence*. Springer International Publishing. http://dx.doi.org/10.1007/978-3-030-67032-0.
12. Turban, E., Sharda, R., Aronson, J. E., & King, D. (2008). *Business intelligence: A managerial approach*. Pearson Prentice Hall. ISBN: 9780132347617.
13. Werther, I. (2013). *Business intelligence*. Carl Hanser Verlag GmbH & Co. KG. http://dx.doi.org/10.3139/9783446436350.
14. Yermish, I., Miori, V., Yi, J., Malhotra, R., & Klimberg, R. (2010). Business plus intelligence plus technology equals business intelligence. *International Journal of Business Intelligence Research, 1*(1), 48–63. http://dx.doi.org/10.4018/jbir.2010071704.

CHAPTER

9 Security of Information

LEARNING OBJECTIVES

After studying this chapter, you will be able to:

- Understand security management and control;
- Explain internet worked security;
- Discuss about encryption;
- Explain firewalls;
- Know virus protection;
- Learn e-mail monitoring;
- Identify security code;
- Describe biometric security;
- Focus on cybercrime & cyber security.

KEY TERMS FROM THIS CHAPTER

Access Control
Cybersecurity
Encryption
Firewall
Malware
Security
Computer Virus
E-Commerce
Encryption
Information Security
Packet Filter
Security Biometric

INTRODUCTION

Protecting information from unauthorized access is essential for maintaining the availability, privacy, and integrity of data. While information security typically refers to enhancing computer security measures, it also encompasses safeguarding various types of sensitive data, including personal documents and confidential information. Although no security system is completely fail-safe, implementing fundamental security measures is crucial for effective information security. One of the primary steps in bolstering information security is utilizing passwords. This method restricts access to authorized individuals, minimizing the risk of unauthorized access. However, passwords are not infallible, as hacking tools can swiftly crack simple codes within seconds. Carelessness, such as failing to log out of a public computer or using easily guessable passwords like "password" or "1234," can also compromise the security of sensitive information.

Users should avoid using easily guessed password combinations, like birthdays or family names, and instead create passwords that combine capital and lowercase letters, numbers, and symbols to make access as secure as possible. Passwords should not be written down on paper that is placed next to the computer. Instead, users should create unique passwords for each account. A computer user might want to think about changing their password every few months for increased security (Figure 9.1).

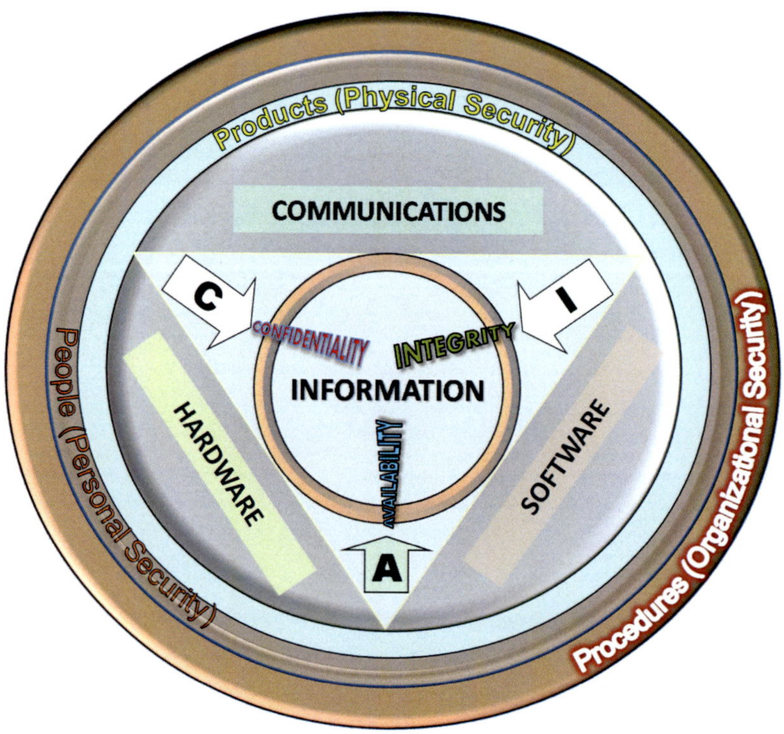

Figure 9.1. *Information security management.*

Source: https://cvgstrategy.com/wp-content/uploads/2019/11/1200px-CIAJMK1209-500x490.png.

Three crucial security principles for information on the internet are confidentiality, integrity, and availability, while principles relating to the users of the information include authentication, authorization, and nonrepudiation. When unauthorized individuals read or copy information, it leads to a loss of confidentiality, which is especially critical for sensitive data such as research findings, medical records, and corporate strategies. Legal obligations to protect privacy may be required in certain industries such as banking, healthcare, and tax collection.

Information can be compromised when accessed through insecure networks, resulting in a loss of integrity where unauthorized modifications are made. Integrity is essential for maintaining the accuracy and security of critical data used in financial transactions and safety-critical systems. Likewise, when information becomes inaccessible or is erased altogether, it leads to a loss of availability, preventing authorized users from accessing necessary information. Availability is crucial for service-focused businesses that rely on timely and accurate information for operations such as flight scheduling and inventory management.

Anyone whose business or education depends on a network connection should be aware of the network's availability. A denial of service occurs when users are unable to access the network or particular services offered on it. Organizations utilize authorization and authentication to ensure that information is only accessible to those who can be trusted with it. Verifying that a user is who they say they are is known as authentication. This evidence could be something the user possesses (like a "smartcard"), something they know (like a password), or something that verifies their identity (like a fingerprint). Determining whether a specific user (or computer system) has the authority to perform a specific task, like reading a file or running a program, is the process of authorization. Authorization and authentication are interdependent. Before performing any action that they are permitted to do, users must first authenticate themselves. When the authentication method is unchallengeable—that is, when the user cannot subsequently deny carrying out the action—security is strong.

This is referred to as nonrepudiation. These principles of information security also pertain to information security, meaning that internet users seek assurance that their actions cannot be denied.

- They can trust the information they use;
- The information they are responsible for will be shared only in the manner that They expect;
- The information will be available when they need it;
- The systems they use will process information in a timely and trustworthy manner.

Furthermore, information assurance covers various types of systems such as large-scale distributed systems, control systems, and embedded systems. It includes systems that consist of hardware, software, and human components. The technologies in information assurance focus on preventing system intrusions and protecting information from compromises.

9.1. SECURITY MANAGEMENT AND CONTROL

Modern information systems are intricate collections of technological components (i.e., people, and processes that come together to give organizations the capacity to quickly process, store, and transmit information in order to support a variety of missions and business operations. (Amanda M. Y. Chu, and Mike K. P. So 2020)

Because of how much businesses now rely on these information systems to carry out regular, significant, and vital missions and business operations, the security of the underlying systems is essential to the organization's success. A crucial task that can have a significant impact on an organization's assets and operations as well as the welfare of individuals is choosing the right security controls for an information system. 10 Security controls are the operational, technical, and managerial precautions or defenses that are mandated for an information system in order to preserve the availability, confidentiality, integrity, and non-repudiation of the system and its data. After security controls are implemented in an information system, they are evaluated to provide the data required to ascertain their overall effectiveness. This is the measure of how well the controls are applied, how well they function as intended, and how well they meet the system's security requirements. Determining the risk that using the information system poses to the organization's operations and assets, to individuals, to other organizations, and to the country requires an understanding of the overall efficacy of the security controls implemented in the system and its operating environment.

The following people have developed the guidelines to assist the federal government in achieving more secure information systems:

- Facilitating repeatable, comparable, and more consistent evaluations of security measures with repeatable outcomes.
- Helping to conduct more affordable evaluations of security measures that play a role in determining the overall effectiveness of controls.
- Encouraging a deeper comprehension of the dangers posed to organizational operations, assets, individuals, other organizations, and the nation due to the operation and utilization of federal information systems.
- Providing organizational officials with more comprehensive, dependable, and trustworthy information to support risk management choices, reciprocity of assessment outcomes, information exchange, and FISMA compliance.

This complies with the Federal Information Security Management Act (FISMA) and surpasses the information security standards set for executive agencies. These guidelines apply to all federal information systems, excluding national security systems defined in 44 U.S.C., Section 3542. They have been designed from a technical standpoint to align with guidelines for national security systems and can be used for such systems with approval from federal officials. State, local, and tribal governments, as well as private sector organizations, are encouraged to utilize these guidelines as needed. Companies use this in conjunction with an authorized security plan to create a workable security assessment plan that generates and gathers the data required to assess the efficacy of the security measures implemented in the information system. This was created to give organizations the ability to customize and add to the basic assessment processes offered. The security assessment plan starts with the assessment procedures and uses them as input. Organizations consider available data regarding the security controls to be evaluated when creating efficient security assessment plans (e.g., outcomes of risk assessments conducted by organizations, hardware, software, or firmware dependencies unique to a given platform, and any evaluation processes required as a result of organization-specific controls.

Three factors determine the rigor, intensity, and scope of the assessment as well as the choice of appropriate assessment procedures:

- The security categorization of the information system;
- The assurance requirements that the organization intends to meet in determining the overall effectiveness of the security controls; and
- The selection of security controls as identified in the approved security plan.

Rather than creating security, the assessment process is an information-gathering activity. By applying the findings of risk assessments, taking into account the quality and maturity of the organization's risk management procedures, and utilizing the concepts' flexibility, organizations can decide how to implement this crucial component of their information security program in the most economical way possible. An organization can use the data generated by security control assessments to:

- Recognize possible issues or deficiencies in the organization's execution of the Risk Management Framework.
- Determine the shortcomings and weaknesses of the information system.
- Give top priority to decisions on risk mitigation and the corresponding activities for risk mitigation.
- Verify that the information system's deficiencies and vulnerabilities have been addressed.
- Encourage ongoing monitoring and situational awareness regarding information security.
- Facilitate security authorization decisions; and
- Inform budgetary decisions and the capital investment process.

It is not expected of organizations to utilize every assessment object and method included in the assessment procedures for the related security controls implemented in or carried over from organizational information systems. Instead, organizations are naturally flexible enough to decide how much work is required for a given assessment (e.g., which evaluation techniques and items are thought to be most helpful in producing the intended outcomes). This decision is made based on what will achieve the assessment goals most efficiently and with enough assurance to back up the subsequent assessment of the resulting mission or business risk.

9.2. INTERNET WORKED SECURITY

With the expansion of international e-commerce, more and more people are growing accustomed to transacting money online. Naturally, this has resulted in an increase in cybercrime, or illegal activity conducted online. (Qi Jing, Athanasios Vasilakos, et al., 2014)

Originally carried out by people with actual insider knowledge of companies, cybercrime has evolved into an anonymous attack that is frequently supported by organized crime. Cybercriminals use a variety of techniques, such as malware, phishing scams, and spam, to further their objectives. The following describes a few of these examples.

9.2.1. Spam

Bulk unsolicited electronic messages are referred to as "spam." Although email is the most common medium for spam, text messages, short message services (SMS), computer instant messages (IM), and phone calls are also becoming more and more common ways to use it. In addition to frequently directing the recipient to an external website, spam emails can also be used as a platform for phishing scams and the spread of malware (see the sections that follow). In this way, spam is also being utilized more frequently by the previously mentioned "rogue" or no-prescription pharmacies. Spam is widely used. According to a recent report from MessageLabs Intelligence, the global ratio of spam in email traffic is 75.8%, or one out of every 1.33 emails received. With a 29% increase in spam percentage from the previous month, the Russian Federation emerged as the nation with the highest spam rate globally, at 82%.

Spam messages, although inefficient, are a low-risk method used by cybercriminals. A study on spamming in 2008 found that spammers typically only get one response for every 12.5 million emails they send. Despite the dismal response rate, spammers are still able to make a profit, although it is not as much as some believe. This profit may be attributed to identity theft and a more targeted approach to spam, focusing on consumer groups more likely to engage with and buy from spam emails, such as those with certain medical conditions or social issues like obesity.

As a subset of spam, pharmaceutical spam is highly prevalent. Indeed, according to experts in Internet security, "Pharmaceutical spam" makes up more than 65% of all spam. The "Canadian Pharmacy" is the most often featured brand in pharmaceutical spam; nonetheless, other websites that are comparable, like the "United Pharmacy" or the "Indian Pharmacy," are starting to show up more regularly. The Spamhaus Project is one of the best-organized efforts to ban spam to date. Spamhaus is a global non-profit organization with headquarters in London, United Kingdom, and Geneva, Switzerland. It publishes the Register of Known Spam Operations (ROKSO) and keeps multiple spam blocking databases. Additionally, Spamhaus collaborates with a number of law enforcement agencies and cybercrimes units, such as the National Cyber-Forensics and Training Alliance (United States), Australia Communication and Media Authority, Independent Authority of Posts and Telecommunications (Netherlands), and Scotland Yard Computer Crime Unit (United Kingdom).

Notably, Spamhaus has been recognized for their efforts with several awards from both governmental bodies (e.g., United States' Federal Bureau of Investigation, or FBI), as well as the media (e.g., Virus Bulletin Award for the most significant contribution over the previous ten years to the fight against spam).

9.2.2. Viruses and Malware

The phrase "wide range of software" with "malicious or fraudulent intent" is known as malware.

Malware includes things like Trojan horses, worms, spyware, fake adware, scareware, and computer viruses. MessageLabs Intelligence estimated in a recent report that one in every 290,1 emails sent globally contained malware. South Africa had the highest percentage of malware detected, with one out of every 81.8 emails containing malware; further country-specific data can be found in (Table 9.1).

Most remarkably, attachments in the portable document format (PDF) have become the preferred attack vector for targeted attacks, with a 12.4% increase in usage between 2009 and 2010. The fact that PDFs are one of the most widely used formats for electronic document sharing and that most people view them as trustworthy file types puts cybercriminals at an advantage.

Table 9.1. *Malware Rates by Country*

Country	Malware ratio (per e-mail)
South Africa	1 in 81.8
United Kingdom	1 in 139.0
Canada	1 in 328.8
Australia	1 in 365.8
Germany	1 in 393.1
Denmark	1 in 451.1
China, Hong Kong SAR	1 in 455.3
China	1 in 457.0
United States	1 in 713.6
Singapore	1 in 828.9
The Netherlands	1 in 910.4
Japan	1 in 1331

Source: https://iris.who.int/bitstream/handle/10665/44782/9789241564397_eng.pdf?sequence=1&isAllowed=y.

Nonetheless, it is very simple to hide harmful software in PDF files. These potentially harmful programs might be spyware, which keeps an eye on users while they browse the web in order to show adverts or send advertising money to the program's developer. In addition to being used for theft and fraud, spyware can also be used to steal private information such as passwords, health insurance details, credit card numbers, and bank account numbers. Using the "Zeus" crimeware toolkit, over 100 cybercriminals and money mules were apprehended in 2010 for stealing US$70 million from bank accounts. Similar to this, complete medical identity theft is on the rise, and phishing and spyware can hasten the process, particularly as more patient data is stored digitally in personal and open-system electronic health records.

The Office of the National Coordinator (ONC) for Health Information Technology in the United States released a report in 2009 addressing the role of health information technology in combating medical identity theft. In developing countries, internet users are at a heightened risk of viruses and malware due to the high cost of operating system licenses and antivirus software. This vulnerability is exacerbated by a prevalence of piracy and a lack of network security. According to the Organization for Economic Co-Operation and Development (OECD) Task Force on Spam, the cost of a basic Windows OS and antivirus program can equal a month's salary in developing economies. As a result, many computer owners turn to cheaper (often pirated) software that leaves their machines susceptible to viruses and difficult to update.

9.2.3. Phishing Scams

Phishing scams entail email messages that purport to be from reputable, well-known companies or organizations, but are actually fraudulent attempts to steal your identity. Either the sender is directed to a website where they are tricked into providing personal information, or the sender is asked to send private information, like passwords, bank account numbers, medical insurance registry numbers, and credit card details, via email. Like a fisherman, the cybercriminals send out emails like bait, knowing that some people will be duped into biting even though the majority will ignore them. Phishing schemes frequently use rogue online pharmacies as their online front. The website presents a convincing "storefront" for the sale of various lifestyle drugs; however, upon placing an order, the buyer's money and credit card details are stolen by cybercriminals who never plan to fulfill the order. The prevalence of phishing has increased to the point where 1 in 216,767 emails may be related to a phishing scheme. South Africa was the nation most frequently targeted, with phishing rates estimated at one in 32.5 emails.

9.3. ENCRYPTION

In order to provide privacy, encryption refers to algorithmic schemes that transform plain text into cipher text or an unintelligible form. By using a "key," the recipient of the encrypted text can decrypt it and restore it to its original plain text format. The algorithm's trigger mechanism is crucial. Encryption was mostly used by the military and was not commonly used by the general public until the invention of the Internet. Even the typical householder is far more aware of it these days thanks to online marketing, banking, healthcare, and other services. When a web browser is connected to a secure server—identified by an address that starts with https—it will initiate text encryption automatically (Pronika and Tyagi, 2021).

When the text arrives, the server decrypts it, but because the information is transferred between computers, anyone "listening in" will only see unintelligible gibberish if they intercept the transmission. Not all encryption techniques are trustworthy; there are numerous varieties. Strong encryption can be cracked with the same computing power that creates weak schemes. Although 128-bit encryption is currently the norm, 64-bit encryption was once thought to be fairly strong. This will surely change in the future. Even though browsers encrypt data by default when they connect to a secure website, many users also opt to encrypt email correspondence. Programs that have interfaces or plug-ins for well-known email clients make it simple to do this. The most well-known of these is called Pretty Good Privacy (PGP), a lowly moniker for an extremely potent encryption program that is used on military hardware. PGP enables the encryption of personal files and folders in addition to email messages.

It is also possible to encrypt a whole drive or volume. The drive must be "mounted" with a unique decryption key in order to be used. The drive can be read and used normally in this state. When it's done, the drive is dismounted and goes back to being encrypted, making it unreadable for snoops, Trojan horses, spyware, and intruders. Certain individuals decide to store sensitive data, such as financial programs, on encrypted drives. Symmetric and asymmetric encryption schemes are distinguished from one another. A predetermined key that is shared by the sender and the recipient is the basis for symmetric key algorithms like Blowfish, AES, and DES. Text can be encrypted and decrypted using this key. A user is given a "key pair" (a public key and a private key) in asymmetric encryption schemes like Diffie-Hellman and RSA. Text that is to be sent to the public key owner can be encrypted using the public key, which is made available online for use by senders. The only person who can decrypt hypertext once it has been encrypted is the owner of the private key for that key pair. The two keys collaborating with one another is the foundation of this algorithm. Because the decryption key can be kept secret, asymmetric encryption is thought to be one level safer than symmetric encryption. Although data is private when encrypted well, it is not always secure.

Usually, certificates or digital signatures are used to complete this online. With more people becoming aware of how public the Internet, email, and instant messaging are, encryption will surely gain traction. Without it, data transferred over the Internet is not only open to almost anybody to intercept and read, but it is also frequently kept for years on servers that are susceptible to theft or other security breaches. It is a goal worth working toward for all of these reasons.

9.3.1. Encryption Key

Numerous encryption schemes exist, but not all of them are safe. With today's computer power, simple algorithms can be readily cracked, and the decryption process itself has another flaw. If someone has the password or key, even the most secure algorithms will decrypt. A single password can be used to encrypt and decrypt data in symmetric encryption schemes. When the encryption key is provided, the drive can be "mounted" so that users can work in an unencrypted state and then, once their work is done, return it to cipher. The employed algorithms are thought to be extremely safe; one of them was chosen to be the Advanced Encryption Standard (AES) utilized by the U.S. government for keeping information that is top secret and classified.

Public asymmetric encryption schemes also employ very safe algorithms that operate on a distinct encrypting and decrypting mechanism. A key pair is what this software uses to access two keys. The first is the public key, which is unrestricted and can be distributed to anyone as long as it is used for encryption. The private key, which is not shared, is the other key. Anything encrypted with the public key must be decrypted using the private key. Software with asymmetric encryption is frequently used to secure email and instant chats. One of the many encryption programs available can be installed by users, and the program will create a key pair for them. You can share the encryption key, also known as the public key of the key pair, with other people who are using an encryption program that works with yours. Once someone has obtained the public key, they are able to communicate with the owner of the key via encrypted messages. Even the author is unable to decrypt a message once it has been encrypted. The algorithms used in the encryption process rely on a key pair, and the encryption process itself can only be decrypted using the private key of that particular key pair. After that, the mail or message is delivered to the public key owner. Before decrypting, the private key will ask for a passphrase when it receives the mail. Software will enable a user to store the passphrase locally so that messages can be automatically decrypted, but for optimal security, this passphrase should be entered manually. Because the key that initiates decryption is not shared, asymmetric encryption is thought to be more secure than symmetric encryption.

9.4. FIREWALLS

An organization's computer network is secured by a firewall, which is a system of hardware and software. It filters all data packets entering or leaving the network since it is typically deployed at every point of contact between the network and the external Internet. It is standard procedure to allow outgoing data packets to flow through unhindered while filtering incoming packets based on a predetermined set of rules, known as the rule base. The firewall allows a data packet that matches a rule in the rule base to flow through and onto the network; the other packets are rejected by the firewall because they are deemed dangerous for the network (Abie, 2000). Any hardware (or software) used to restrict or filter traffic flow is called a firewall. Usually installed on the edge of the network, firewalls work by identifying zones that are trusted and untrusted (Figure 9.2).

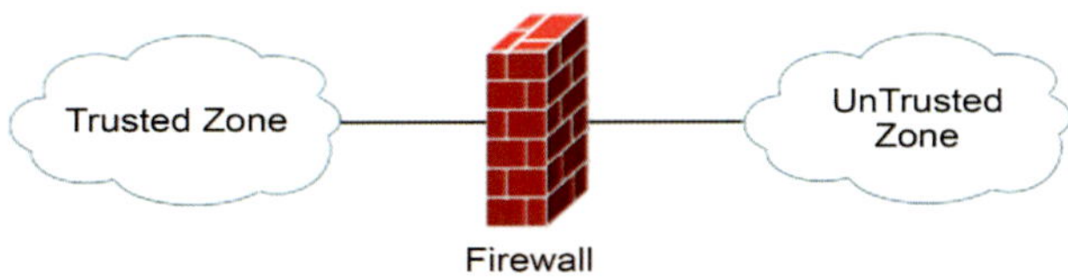

Figure 9.2. *A firewall.*

Source: https://d3i71xaburhd42.cloudfront.net/d779d9c83a9aee4d5d52ef12cf4ec3dc2abf396d/1-Figure1-1.png.

Without any specific configuration, the majority of firewalls will allow traffic from the trusted zone to the untrusted zone. Traffic from the untrusted zone to the trusted zone needs to be specifically allowed, though. Therefore, any traffic from the untrusted to trusted zone that is not specifically allowed will be implicitly denied (most firewall systems by default). A firewall is not restricted to just two zones; it can have several "less trusted" zones as well, which are also known as Demilitarized Zones (DMZs) (Figure 9.3).

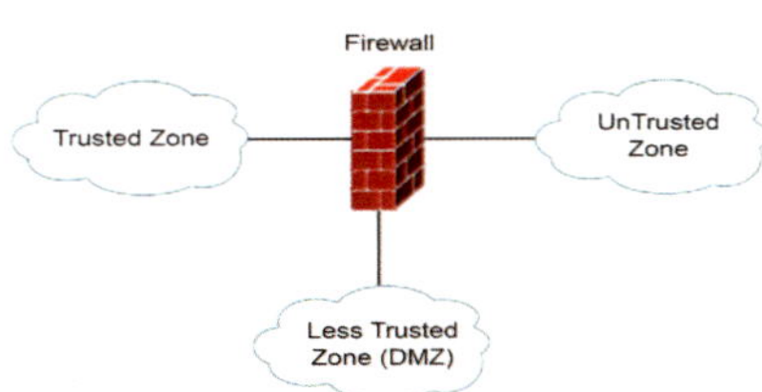

Figure 9.3. *Firewall protection.*

Source: https://routeralley.com/guides/intro_firewalls.pdf.

A security level, which can be a number or even a color, is assigned to each firewall interface in order to control the trust value of each zone. As an illustration, the Trusted Zone in the above diagram might have a security value of 100, the Less Trusted Zone, 75, and the Untrusted Zone, 0. Traffic from a higher security zone to a lower security zone is (usually) permitted by default, whereas traffic from a lower security zone to a higher security zone needs permission in writing.

Firewalls perform the following services:

- Packet Filtering;
- Stateful Packet Inspection;
- Proxying;
- Network Address Translation (NAT).

9.4.1. The Packet Filter

The static packet filter is expanded upon by the packet filter. The packet filter looks at the data packet's network header and a portion of the transport header. It verifies the network header's source and destination IP addresses. Additionally, it verifies the source and destination port numbers in the transport header, as well as the data packet's transport protocol (TCP or UDP). The packet filter additionally keeps track of a table of connection streams known as the Connection Bypass table in order to provide state awareness. A unique connection stream is formed by all data packets having the same source and destination IP addresses, port numbers, and transport layer protocols (TCP or UDP). Each packet is linked to its connection stream by means of a packet filter. The packet filter examines the incoming packet's connection stream against the list of connection streams it keeps in the connection bypass table when a data packet reaches it. The data packet is permitted to enter the network without undergoing any additional inspection if it is discovered to arrive on a connection stream that has already been encountered (for which a record has already been made in the table). It gets around all later filter rules.

The data packet is first checked in accordance with the static packet filtering rules if it comes on an unknown connection stream. The packet filter only permits a data packet to enter the network if it is determined to be acceptable in accordance with those guidelines. In addition, the packet filter simultaneously creates an entry in the connection bypass table that corresponds to the data packet's connection stream. This enables all incoming packets on that connection stream to pass through all filtering rules and enter the network. To put it simply, the packet filter knows the difference between an established connection and a new one. One of the main functions of firewalls is packet filtering. A multitude of criteria can be used to filter (allow or deny) packets.

- Source address;
- Destination address;
- Protocol Type (IP, TCP, UDP, ICMP, ESP, etc.);
- Source Port;
- Destination Port.

Therefore, the structure of a packet filter can be represented as:

Connection Bypass Table

+

Static Packet Filter

9.4.2. The Connection Filter

Prior to permitting a packet to enter the network, the Connection Filter verifies the validity of the connection. It looks at the data packet's network header and transport header. The connection filter looks at specific network fields and the packet's transport headers when a packet reaches it. The following fields are looked at in the network header:

- Source IP address;
- Destination IP address.

The fields examined within the transport header are:

- Source Port number;
- Destination port number.

The connection filter for TCP connections looks at the sequence numbers involved in the TCP handshaking process, as well as the SYN and ACK flags, in addition to the fields mentioned above. This aids in the connection filter's ability to confirm the legitimacy of the new connection. For the aforementioned reason, the connection filter keeps track of a Connection Verification table. An entry details the flags' current condition (i.e., sequence number of the most recent packet to arrive in the connection stream, as well as the SYN and ACK flags. Consequently, the connection filter's structure can be written as follows:

Packet Filter

+

Connection Verification Table

9.4.3. The Application Filter

Before sending packets inside the firewall, the Application Filter is a firewall that examines the payload's structure and content.

Since the application filter looks through all of the data, it needs to break the link between the external host (e.g., a client asking to establish a connection) and the internal host (e.g., a server answering the request for connection).

The network header, transport header, and application header of the data packet are all examined by the application filter. The application filter examines a data packet's content by using proxies. All that this proxy does is watch the connections going through the filter and search for anomalies in them. Only the packets created by services (like HTTP and FTP) whose proxies are operating on it would be permitted through the application filter.

9.5. VIRUS PROTECTION

Any software intended to corrupt data on a computer system or network is referred to as a computer virus. Documents, images, apps, and—worst of all—system files that are essential to the computer system's correct operation could be among the data that is impacted. (Muchelule Yusuf Wanjala and Neyole Misiko Jacob, 2017)

A computer virus is created by a malicious programmer and can be transmitted through email, floppy disks, or downloaded software. This program can secretly enter a computer system and infect it by changing or installing files or residing in the memory. While some viruses may be harmless, others can cause serious damage and may even erase data. Viruses spread through various means, including network connections, email, shared folders, and removable media like flash drives and CDs. Once a computer is infected, the virus works to spread itself to other systems, similar to how viruses impact human health.

People occasionally distinguish viruses based on the means by which they propagate. Viruses known as worms replicate themselves and spread over networks and email. Trojan horses are seemingly trustworthy computer programs that are specifically made to interfere with your computer usage or use it for purposes you did not intend.

A computer virus only affects your computer's software—it doesn't harm the hardware. If, in the worst situation, a virus takes over your computer and does irreversible damage, you can still recover your system by wiping the hard drive and reinstalling your operating system (Windows 95, Windows 98, etc.). Naturally, this is a painful solution because you lose all of your data! There are better ways to avoid this. First, a more thorough explanation of the primary virus types is provided here:

- **Trojan Horses:** The term "Trojan Horse" is well-suited for a malicious type of software known for its harmful capabilities. While technically not classified as a virus, a Trojan horse poses a significant threat that should not be overlooked. For a Trojan Horse to carry out its harmful actions, it must first be installed on a computer. This can be done by someone physically accessing the computer, such as in an office setting, or more commonly through the unsuspecting download and installation of seemingly innocent software. Similar to the soldiers hidden within the legendary wooden horse, a Trojan Horse can discreetly attach itself to another program and install itself on the computer without the user's knowledge when the program is installed.
- **Key-logger Programs:** Which log every keystroke on a keyboard and store the data in a log file, are a common component of Trojan Horses. The sender of the Trojan horse is then contacted via email with this log file each time someone accesses the Internet. Everything that is typed, including phone numbers, passwords, credit card numbers, emails, and letters. are all recorded and obtained by the hacker, thereby compromising privacy to the fullest extent.

- **Worms:** They are able to reproduce and spread on their own without human interaction. They can be programmed to self-replicate and infect other computers through email. Unlike viruses that spread from file to file, worms spread from computer to computer, allowing them to rapidly infect systems without human assistance. Unwanted emails with worm attachments can lead to the worm spreading throughout a computer once opened. Worms that can replicate and email themselves to multiple recipients have caused email servers to crash in the past due to the high volume of traffic.
- **Zombies:** On your computer, zombies might dormantly exist for a very long time. Typically, hackers use these programmers to launch a coordinated attack on a system, in which they activate a zombie to support their attack on a network or system. Zombies by themselves typically don't cause any harm, but having them on your computer is obviously undesirable. Similar to numerous other virus types, they are typically spread via email.

The most important guideline is to always be on the lookout for unsolicited emails, particularly those that seem "unsavory," like those that contain pornographic content. It is not advisable to open any executable .EXE files unless the sources are reliable.

Downloaded programs with entertaining or helpful promises are another source of viruses. Always be cautious when installing software and make sure the company has the right credentials. Be extremely cautious when using downloaded "Warez" (illegal pirated software), as this is another source. Make a backup of all crucial files and programs on CD ROMs, zip disks, or floppies. In the worst case scenario, at least your entire body of work won't be erased from your hard drive.

9.5.1. Anti-Virus Software

Only one kind of computer user—those without an Internet connection, those who don't share floppy or zip disks—needs anti-virus software installed.

It may also help if they reside in a remote log cabin. For the remainder of us, it would be best to get some good software right away. There are numerous brands at competitive pricing. Each performs comparable tasks to varying degrees of effectiveness. Antivirus software lives in the computer's active memory and takes over to warn users when there is an active virus on the system. The software will either quarantine the file or offer you the option to safely delete it if it is unable to repair the infected file (Figure 9.4).

Figure 9.4. *Anti-virus software.*

Source: https://5.imimg.com/data5/SELLER/Default/2022/12/IX/HT/VU/164210537/antivirus-protection-500x500.jpg.

Additionally, CD ROMs, zip disks, floppy disks, and hard drives can all be scanned with antivirus software. It can also be used to scan email attachments.

9.5.2. Personal Firewall

Firewall technology is not new; most LAN and Internet servers have had it for a long time. The availability of firewall technology on a smaller scale for individuals using a single computer linked to the Internet is what's new. A firewall is something you might want to consider purchasing if you are concerned about your online security and privacy, even though it isn't as urgently necessary as antivirus software (Figure 9.5).

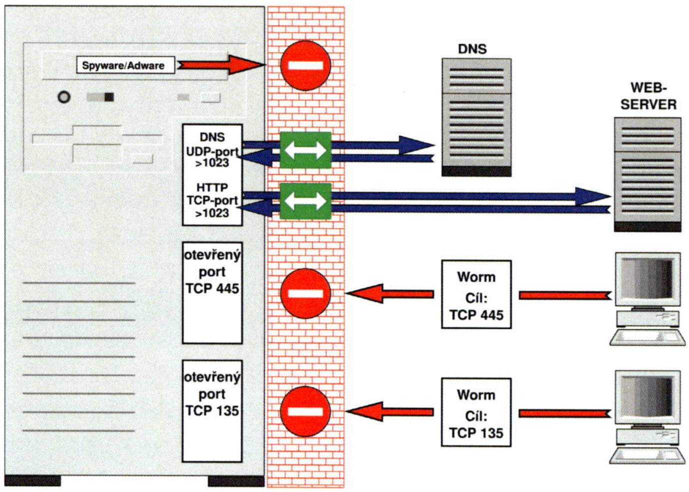

Figure 9.5. *Personal firewall.*

Source: https://en.wikipedia.org/wiki/File:Personal_firewall.svg.

A safe barrier that separates your computer from the outside world is created by firewall software. It keeps an eye on all traffic coming into and going out of your computer and determines if it's typical Internet usage or an unwelcome security risk. A firewall makes it appear to a hacker that your computer is not there, or is very difficult to find. Firewalls also offer extra security against Trojan horses because they prevent the key-log file from being sent to its intended recipient without authorization and notify you when a Trojan horse tries to do so.

Firewall software comes in a variety of brands, just like antivirus software. These days, a lot of businesses provide firewall and anti-virus software in one package at a discounted cost, which usually ends up being very good value for peace of mind.

9.6. E-MAIL MONITORING

Because email servers can be a single point of failure in an email environment, email monitoring tools usually concentrate on the health of email servers. Email monitoring tools have the ability to monitor the state of the server that hosts the email serving application as well as the application itself. In complex network environments, email monitoring aids email administrators in maintaining email flow (Snyder and Cornetto, 2009)

Businesses depend on effective communication, and your email system is crucial for keeping everything running smoothly. Email monitoring is an essential service for your business, as many important communications happen between your company and its partners, customers, suppliers, and employees. Any delay in email transmission can lead to help desk tickets, especially when users expect quick responses and time is critical.

Email sender and recipient issues can result in missed opportunities. Amazing insights about your business can also be obtained through email, such as who interacts with whom, when you actually respond, and which clients appear to require more care than usual. It is essential to be aware of what is happening with your email correspondence. These are nine justifications for setting up email monitoring:

- Find out quickly what or who is taking up all of your disk space. While email monitoring can reveal the reason and the names of the worst offenders, server monitoring can only indicate when a volume is nearing its capacity. Email monitoring can assist you in getting users back in line with company policy and best practices, whether teams are exchanging files via email or someone is sharing a video file.
- Organize the communications both inside and outside of your company. Occasionally, it matters more to whom than it does who sends the majority of the emails. The ability to promptly and accurately report on the important channels of communication makes it possible for someone else to quickly catch up, regardless of turnover or the absence of a key employee.
- Verify SLAs. Both your help desk and your customer service representatives are accountable to your service level agreements and owe customers—internal or external—a prompt response to their questions. Email monitoring will make it simple for you to determine what needs to be improved or to verify that SLAs are being met.
- Find those anomalies. SLAs are important, but sometimes it can be difficult to meet them when a small number of users require more care and attention than is typical. You can address training or provide additional services to those who require extra attention by using email monitoring to identify them.
- Assist in making sure that tasks are completed. Like many privileges, using company email for personal purposes is probably allowed, but it can also be

abused. Users who spend a little too much time on personal email can be identified by email monitoring, allowing you to take action before it becomes a problem.

- Verify whether email archiving is necessary. Email hoarders can be quickly and easily identified, with email monitoring able to provide information about the individual, the amount of emails being hoarded, and the age of the emails. Creating email retention policies and sizing your email archiving solution is made simple by this data.
- Find sinkhole accounts fast. Mailboxes that are still accepting emails but are not actively monitored can be found in almost every email system. You can locate these through email monitoring, preventing the loss of important communications, such as customer emails and notifications.
- Assist in preserving professionalism. Email managers can address standards of communication with their department when needed by using email monitoring to identify inappropriate or slang language in emails.
- Defend the intellectual property you own. You want to make sure that your email system is not leaking data, regardless of why users are forwarding company email to their personal accounts in the first place. This could be because they are doing so to read email on their personal devices or to build up a cache of important information to take with them when they change jobs. Employ email monitoring to identify and block users who send large amounts of emails off-site, ensuring that your intellectual property is protected.

9.7. SECURITY CODE

Presently found on the front of American Express cards and the majority of Visa, MasterCard, JCB, Switch, and Solo cards' backs is a significant new addition to Internet security. This new code, which consists of three or four digits, offers a cryptographic verification of the data embossed on the card. The security code aids in confirming that the credit cardholder and the credit/debit card account holder are the real owners of the credit card used for the online order. To utilize the security code, you must physically possess the card; it is not included in the magnetic stripe information or displayed on sales receipts or billing statements. The security code is only printed on the card (Yilmaz and Ulusoy, 2022). Standard credit card readers do not scan card security codes because they are not raised. The card holder is the only one who can theoretically see these numbers. Help the merchant confirm that the order is being placed by the card holder when you give them your card security code. Furthermore, it is forbidden for retailers to store a customer's security code in any form. The security code may only be retained by merchants for the duration required to bill orders.

9.8. BIOMETRIC SECURITY

The science of identifying a person by their physical attributes, such as their fingerprints, eyes, or hands, is known as security biometrics. Products utilized in this system include fingerprint readers and retinal scanners. When thinking about security biometrics, one should aim for physical attributes that are hard to fake or intentionally alter, remain stable over time, and exhibit consistency (Faundez-Zanuy, 2006).

The use of security biometrics has given rise to a number of ethical questions, some of which are as follows:

- Certain biometric techniques are invasive, like retinal scans.
- The collection of biometric data, such as fingerprints, is typically connected to illegal activity.
- When big organizations like the military or police collect the information, you might feel as though your privacy and dignity have been violated.
- You may feel embarrassed if you are rejected by a public sensor.
- Without your knowledge or consent, your movements could be tracked by automated facial recognition technology used in public areas.

Two of the most common queries regarding security biometrics that have been brought up are as follows:

- How will data be stored and safeguarded?
- Who will have access to information?

And then there's the never-ending debate over the most effective biometric security method. There is no one technique that performs data collection better than the others; all have their own advantages, some being less intrusive, some being extremely difficult to forge, and some that can be completed without your knowledge. These are a few biometric identification techniques you can employ; ultimately, it all depends on what best suits your requirements.

- **Face Recognition Biometrics Security:** Since it can be carried out without the subject knowing they are being scanned, this is one of the most adaptable techniques. The distance between the eyes, nose width, cheekbone position, jaw line, and chin, to mention a few, are among the features of every person's face that this system examines.
- **Fingerprint Identification:** All of your fingerprints are unique and stay the same throughout your life. Due to the requirement for clean hands and the possibility of fingerprint injuries preventing accurate identification, this may not work in industrial settings.
- **Hand Geometry Biometrics Security:** This requires no clean conditions, can operate in challenging environments, and only requires a small dataset. It is frequently utilized in industrial settings and is not regarded as intrusive.
- **Retina Scan:** As far as is known, the pattern of blood vessels at the back of the eye is completely unique and never changes, and there is simply no way to replicate a retina. The drawback is that a thorough scan requires roughly 15 seconds of focused attention, but military and government installations still use this method as standard.
- **Iris Scan:** While it might be challenging for small children or the elderly, this is also extremely hard to replicate and remains constant throughout your lifetime.
- **Signature Biometrics Security:** This kind of security is not physically invasive and is simple to gather.
- **Voice Analysis:** Even though it is simpler to fabricate using a tape recording, this biometric security method can be carried out covertly; it cannot be carried out by attempting to mimic the voice of another person.

9.9. CYBERCRIME AND CYBER SECURITY

Any illegal activity involving a computer, networked device, or network is referred to as cybercrime. While the majority of cybercrimes are committed with the intention of making money for the perpetrators, some are committed specifically to harm or disable computers or devices, while others use networks or computers to disseminate malware, illicit data, images, or other materials. A few cybercrimes combine the two, i.e., aim to infect target computers with viruses, which subsequently spread to additional devices and occasionally whole networks (Tuli et al., 2022).

The financial impact of cybercrime is one of its main effects. Cybercrime can include a wide range of profit-driven criminal activities, such as ransomware attacks, identity theft, credit card fraud, and email and internet fraud. Cybercriminals may target corporate data and private personal information for theft and resale.

9.9.1. Defining Cybercrime

According to the U.S. Department of Justice, cybercrime falls into three categories: crimes where the computer is used as a weapon, like launching a denial-of-service (DoS) attack; crimes where the computer is used as an accessory to a crime, like using a computer to store illegally obtained data; and crimes where the computer is the target, like using it to gain network access.

The United States is a signatory to the Council of Europe Convention on Cybercrime, which defines cybercrime as a broad range of malicious activities, such as copyright violations, illegal data interception, and system interferences that jeopardize network availability and integrity. Additional types of cybercrime include soliciting, producing, possessing, or distributing child pornography, as well as selling illicit goods like drugs, weapons, or counterfeit goods.

Because it is now possible to commit a cybercrime without having to be physically present, the volume and pace of such crimes have increased due to the widespread availability of internet connectivity. The speed, ease of use, anonymity, and global reach of the internet facilitate the commission of hate crimes like bullying and stalking as well as computer-based variants of financial crimes like ransomware, fraud, and money laundering.

Cybercrime can be committed by highly organized international criminal groups, which may include competent developers and other experts in the field, or by individuals or small groups with relatively low technical skill. Cybercriminals frequently opt to operate in nations with lax or nonexistent cybercrime laws in order to further decrease the likelihood of being discovered and prosecuted.

9.9.2. Origins of Cybercrime

Though it may seem unlikely, the word "hack" was not originally connected to computers or cybercrime. The phrase was first used in the 1960s by MIT students who were passionate about model trains to refer to the process of changing a process or product to change how it normally functions or to solve an issue. Hacking, to put it simply, is the act of altering specific features without completely reprogramming the device. A hacker is someone who devises a cunning solution to a product's issue or looks for a simple way to enhance its functionality.

But in the 1970s, a phenomenon known as phreaking—where tech-savvy individuals attempted to undermine early computerized phone systems—came to mix hacking with malicious intent. These so-called "phreakers" figured out the right codes and tones to get free long distance service.

In order to figure out how to take advantage of the system, they conducted numerous experiments on early telephone hardware, pretended to be operators, and combed through Bell Telephone Company trash to uncover confidential information. This kind of criminal activity was difficult for law enforcement to deal with, partly because there was a lack of legislation to support criminal prosecution and a shortage of investigators knowledgeable about the technology being hacked. These incidents demonstrated that criminal activity could occur on computer systems, and that as technology advanced, so did criminal activity.

Cybercrime had become a well-established means of gaining control over and destroying computer systems, obtaining information, and stealing millions of dollars by the mid-1980s.

The Federal Computer Fraud and Abuse Act, which was passed in 1986 in response to the need for action, made damaging computer activity a felony crime with jail time and fines. Cybercrime has expanded and changed since then. Criminals can be anything from lone hackers to intricate networks of agents operating together to state-sponsored international attacks. There are always going to be threats in an increasingly connected world. With more and more devices being connected annually, along with the growing Internet of Things industry, there are plenty of opportunities for cybercrime for the resourceful and bold hacker.

9.9.3. How Cybercrime Works

Cybercriminals carry out their cyberattacks using a variety of attack vectors, and they are always looking for new ways to accomplish their objectives without being discovered and apprehended. Cybercriminals have been known to employ the following frequent attack types:

- Systems and networks are frequently brought down by distributed denial of service (DDoS) attacks. This kind of attack overwhelms a network's capacity to reply to connection requests, turning the network's own communications protocol against it. DoS attacks can be used to divert the target organization's attention from another attack or exploit being carried out concurrently, but they can also be carried out maliciously or as part of a cyberextortion scheme.

- Malware is used to infect networks and systems in order to cause harm to the system or its users, such as corrupting software, hardware, or data stored on the system. Similar techniques are used in ransomware attacks, but the malware encrypts or locks up victim computers until a ransom is paid.
- Phishing campaigns are used to gain access to corporate networks by tricking employees into opening attachments or clicking on links in bogus emails. This allows the intruders to infect their systems with malware or viruses, which is then transferred to the company's networks via the users' systems.
- By installing key sniffer software, utilizing brute force attacks, or taking advantage of software or hardware vulnerabilities that could reveal the victim's credentials, cybercriminals can carry out credential attacks, in which their goal is to guess or steal user IDs and passwords for the victim's systems or personal accounts.
- Cybercriminals may also try to take over a website in order to alter or remove content or gain unauthorized access to or alter databases. A hacker could be able to access and tamper with records or gain unauthorized access to data, such as customer passwords, credit card numbers, personally identifiable information (PII), trade secrets, intellectual property, and other sensitive information, by, for instance, inserting malicious code into a website using an SQL injection exploit.

Although malware and other software are frequently used by cybercriminals to carry out their operations, social engineering is frequently a crucial part of the execution of the majority of cybercrimes. Phishing emails play a significant role in many forms of cybercrime, but they are particularly important in targeted attacks like business email compromise (BEC), where the attacker uses email to pretend to be a business owner in an attempt to persuade staff members to pay fake invoices.

9.9.4. Types of Cybercrime

Numerous types of cybercrimes exist, with the primary goal for attackers typically being financial gain. However, the methods used by cybercriminals to receive payment can vary widely.

- Cyberextortion is a criminal act that involves threatening an attack on a system and demanding money to prevent it. One example of cyberextortion is a ransomware attack, where the attacker infiltrates an organization's systems, encrypts important files, and demands payment in cryptocurrency, like bitcoin, to unlock the data.

Scripts are used in cryptojacking attacks to mine cryptocurrency inside browsers without the user's knowledge or permission. Installing cryptocurrency mining software on the victim's computer may be one way to carry out such attacks. However, a lot of attacks rely on JavaScript code that performs in-browser mining as long as the user has a tab or window open on the malicious website; this means that no malware needs to be installed because the in-browser mining code is executed when the affected page is loaded.

Identity theft happens when someone gains access to a computer and steals personal data from the user. This information can then be used by the attacker to obtain access to bank or other accounts or to steal the victim's identity. On darknet markets, identity information is bought and sold by cybercriminals who offer financial accounts along with other kinds of accounts such as webmail, online auctions, video and audio streaming, and more. Identity thieves also frequently target personal health information.

When hackers breach a retailer's system to obtain a customer's credit card and/or banking information, credit card fraud happens. On darknet markets, where hackers who have taken large amounts of credit cards make money by selling them to less experienced cybercriminals who make money by using credit card fraud against individual accounts, stolen payment cards can be purchased and sold in large quantities.

Cyberextortion known as ransomware occurs when malware infects the victim's device, making it impossible for the owner to use it or access the data stored on it. The victim must pay the hacker a ransom in order to get back access to the device or data. Unintentionally downloading ransomware can happen when you open a contaminated email attachment, go to a hacked website, or click on a pop-up advertisement.

Cybercriminals engage in cyberespionage when they breach systems or networks in order to obtain private data that is owned by a government or other entity. Cyberespionage activities can include any kind of cyberattack to collect, alter, or destroy data as well as using network-connected devices, such as webcams or closed-circuit TV (CCTV) cameras, to spy on a targeted individual or groups and monitor communications, such as email, text messages, and instant messages. Attacks can be driven by ideology or by profit.

9.9.5. The State of Cybercrime Today

Three out of every four respondents to a recent US State of Cybercrime Survey reported having detected a security event in the previous year, but many organizations also report suffering from technology debt, which is estimated to be worth over $1 trillion. This indicates that organizations are effectively allocating their IT budgets to the development of new business technologies while letting their IT infrastructure become outdated to the point where it is unable to perform security functions.

Common security deficiencies have been found in organizations most susceptible cybercrime:

- Reactive or unplanned cybersecurity spending;
- No assessments of the security capabilities of their third-party providers;
- Lack of understanding and/or assessment of supply-chain risks;
- Inadequate or nonexistent mobile device management and security;
- Insider threats and risk not adequately addressed;
- Lack of thorough employee security and awareness training.

The rate at which cybercrime is growing is geometric in spite of these obstacles. An average of 900 phishing attempts have been found per financial institution, and over 9,000 attempts have been found per technology company. Phishing websites are also imitating all of the leading names in technology. Along with Dropbox, Google, Apple, Facebook, and Yahoo are all potential targets for phishing attempts. Phishing websites have the ability to trick users into uploading their files to fraudulent accounts.

The average daily launch rate of malicious IPs is 85,000, meaning that 65% of all URLs globally have an average reputation score. It is an international project with significant hubs in Asia, the United States, and Russia. As a result, users have a thirty percent chance in a year of becoming victims of a zero-day phishing attack.

Cybercrime is not limited to desktop computers alone; in recent years, mobile devices have become more and more common, bringing viruses, malware, and phishing scams with them. In particular, a wide range of malware thrives on the Android platform due to its open marketplace. According to a recent survey, 72% of all OS apps were thought to be unwelcome, malicious, or suspicious, with Trojans accounting for the majority of threats.

While external cybercrime is a serious issue, numerous experts concur that internal attacks present an even bigger risk to businesses and organizations because they access sensitive data through employment. Strong employee awareness and security training can help reduce insider risk, but the sad truth is that many organizations don't even offer this kind of training. IT policy violations are often precursors to insider cybercrime risk; being aware of and scrutinizing these trends can help prevent crimes that would otherwise go undetected until after the fact.

Data indicates that many decision makers at organizations do not fully comprehend the scope or gravity of threats, do not think they are in danger, or have grown numb to the warnings. Why does this behavior persist among organizations? Businesses that have experienced cybercrime over the course of a year typically take security more seriously, and for good reason. Companies with more than a thousand workers also take cybercrime more seriously and have more internal and external risk mitigation procedures in place.

9.9.6. Impact

In 2014, there was a 176% increase in attacks on American businesses and organizations, resulting in 138 successful attacks every week. These attacks are becoming harder to resolve, with the global average time to detect an attack being 170 days, the longest average time being 259 days, and the average time to resolve an incident being 45 days. Cybercrime affects nearly every industry in the US, with the energy & utilities and defense industries experiencing the highest annual costs.

Cybercrime can harm citizens in a variety of ways and poses a threat to the vital infrastructure of governments and businesses worldwide. Cybercrime is thought to have cost the world economy hundreds of billions of dollars, and sadly, there is no indication that it will stop.

Cybercrime impact can take many forms, including

- Direct financial loss;
- Damage to company and brand reputation;
- Loss of sensitive data and intellectual property;
- Mitigation and recovery costs;
- Regulatory penalties;
- Customer compensation;
- SLA breaches;
- Job loss.

9.9.7. Cyber Security

Information and other communication systems can be safeguarded against unauthorized use, modification, exploitation, and even theft through the potential activity of cyber security.

Cybersecurity, on the other hand, is a well-thought-out method to safeguard computers, networks, various applications, private information, etc., from unwanted entry.

High security is required for all types of data, whether they are corporate, personal, or government. Nevertheless, some data are owned by banks, defense research and development organizations, government defense systems, etc. are extremely private, and even a tiny bit of carelessness with these data could have serious consequences for the entire country. As a result, very high security is required for such data.

9.9.7.1. How to Secure Data?

Let us now discuss how to secure data. In order to make your security system strong, you need to pay attention to the following:

- Security Architecture;
- Network Diagram;
- Security Assessment Procedure;
- Security Policies;
- Risk Management Policy;
- Backup and Restore Procedures;
- Disaster Recovery Plan;
- Risk Assessment Procedures.

Having a comprehensive plan that covers all of the aforementioned points will enable you to better secure your data and recover it in the event of an issue.

9.9.8. How can Cybercrime be Prevented?

MSPs confront a particular difficulty in the fight against cybercrime: in addition to making sure their clients' endpoints are safe, they also need to protect their own servers, systems, and gadgets. Thus, in order to maximize efficiency and safeguard their users at the same time, they need to have quick, efficient, and deployable antivirus and anti-malware tools in place.

Additionally, MSPs must ensure that user endpoints and servers have the necessary disaster recovery and backup systems in place in case an unthinkable cybercrime attack occurs. Systems must be ready, safe, and easily restorable in case a user clicks on a phishing link and releases malicious code. Downtime can ruin a business and harm an MSP's reputation and clientele.

These days, MSPs do more than just protect SMB computers. With the proliferation of devices, including tablets and smartphones, there is a growing need for mobile device management (MDM) to make sure that password policies are followed, anti-malware tools are updated, and viruses are prevented. SMBs want their MSP to be at the forefront of the fight against cybercrime so they can concentrate on growing their business. This expectation is growing.

CASE STUDY

CHATTER CYBER SECURITY

Company Overview

Fledgling social media platform, 'Chatter' launched in September 2017. Its main users are 13-21 year olds. Users can:

- Share photos and post status updates;
- Send messages via a private chat;
- Play games with other users, and make in-app purchases.

Their head office is in Birmingham, and they employ 30 people. All staff members have a staff pass to enter the building, and have a company iPhone and laptop. All staff have received an email outlining the best practice for cyber security but this was not read by everyone and staff have not undertaken any mandatory training.

Your Challenge

Recently, Chatter had a minor cyber security threat. They are therefore looking to improve their cyber security and are looking for a cyber security specialist to help.

PwC are in competition with other firms to be selected by Chatter to help them. You are part of the PwC Cyber Team who will have to pitch our proposal to Chatter for how we could resolve their cyber security threats. In your teams, you will have to prepare a pitch to Chatter that outlines:

1. Chatter's cyber risks – which one of these do you think Chatter should focus on first?
2. Which team you think Chatter needs to help them improve their Cyber Security and why.

Chatter's Recent Cyber Security Incident

A staff member left their laptop on the train while commuting home. The laptop was picked up by someone and they were able to gain access to it.

Fortunately, the member of staff had reported it missing and the laptop was remotely wiped. Chatter cannot be sure if any data was accessed before the laptop was remotely wiped.

Important Government Regulations

GDPR – General Data Protection Regulation

As of Spring 2018, changes to GDPR came into force, designed to better protect consumer and personal data. Any organization holding data must:

- Gain consent from the consumer to process their data;
- Anonymise the data collected to protect privacy;
- Provide data breach notifications;
- Safely handle the transfer of data across borders. Transferring data outside Europe. The GDPR imposes restrictions on the transfer of personal data outside the European Union, to third-party countries or international organizations, to ensure that the level of protection of individuals afforded by the GDPR is not undermined;
- Require certain companies to appoint a data protection officer to oversee GDPR compliance.

If these rules are not followed, then companies face hefty fines of up to €20million.

PwC's Cyber Security Teams

Core Advisory

We help organizations from all sectors operate securely in the digital world. Our expertise enables clients to resist, detect and respond to cyber-attacks. Our Core Advisory team works globally to support clients across the public, private and financial sectors, helping them to understand and reduce their cyber risks. Some of the services offered to clients include:

- Assessing and measuring their exposure to cyber security risk;
- Developing a strategy and vision for tackling cyber security;
- Designing and implementing the secure IT systems a client needs to be secure;
- Designing and putting in place security training and awareness programmes;
- Gaining experience of security operations and incident response.

Ethical Hackers

The ethical hacking team will work within the boundaries defined to legally penetrate the company with their permission. This exercise is designed to help companies understand their technical security weaknesses, to provide specific recommendations to clients to help them keep hackers out.

- Ethical hacking to expose vulnerabilities in client IT systems;

- Identifying and monitoring malicious activity on client networks;
- Actively tracking and disrupting cyber threat actors and seeking out new ones;
- Investigating networks which attackers have compromised and removing threat actors.

Crisis Team

Cyber crisis team help companies prepare for, respond to and recover from a cyber-security crisis. A crisis may include events that prevent the business from operating. This team works with their people, to define these plans or understand what work has already been done to prepare for these types of events. The team also facilitate exercises to help companies test their approach, helping the team to practice for real events and can turn up to help you 'steady the ship' when under attack.

Benefits of this service include:

- Help companies consider what they would do when under attack. The team may help simulate this and ensure non-technical members of staff know how to respond.
- Help companies to understand and develop key access controls to their critical systems and assets during a crisis or active cyber threat.
- Helping the company to 'steady the ship' when under attack.

Cyber Threat Team

This team tracks and gathers information on cyber threats across the globe that could target the industry or type of company. The team uses various methods to gain a well-rounded view of the company's threat landscape, and can help them to understand those that could be motivated to attack the company.

- Threat intelligence – look into political situations and try and detect threat actors, e.g., hacking groups.
- Track and gather intelligence to share with companies.
- Analyze the virus and malware used for information.

Identity and Access Management

Companies often grant access to information and assets to staff even if it is not relevant to that member of staff's role. It is important for companies to follow the principle of least privilege – only granting access to the systems necessary for each member of staff's role. This helps to reduce the risk of attackers gaining access to critical systems by compromising a less protected user account used in another area in the business. If all user accounts only have access to what they need, this should help contain compromises to their area of origin, to help prevent them from spreading throughout the business.

- Help companies to understand who in their company has access to what information
- Help them to improve their governance and management of their access granted throughout the business.

CLASS ACTIVITY

ROLE PLAYING EXERCISE

Have students role-play different cyber security scenarios and practice their responses.

- **Benefit:** Helps students practice responding to different cyber security scenarios, which can be useful in real-life situations.

SUMMARY

- Modern information systems are intricate collections of technological components (i.e., people, and processes that come together to give organizations the capacity to quickly process, store, and transmit information in order to support a variety of missions and business operations.
- With the expansion of international e-commerce, more and more people are growing accustomed to transacting money online. Naturally, this has resulted in an increase in cybercrime, or illegal activity conducted online.
- With the expansion of international e-commerce, more and more people are growing accustomed to transacting money online. Naturally, this has resulted in an increase in cybercrime, or illegal activity conducted online.
- Any hardware (or software) used to restrict or filter traffic flow is called a firewall. Usually installed on the edge of the network, firewalls work by identifying zones that are trusted and untrusted.
- A computer virus is created by a malicious programmer and can be transmitted through email, floppy disks, or downloaded software. This program can secretly enter a computer system and infect it by changing or installing files or residing in the memory. While some viruses may be harmless, others can cause serious damage and may even erase data.
- Businesses rely heavily on communications, and the heart that keeps that blood pumping is your email system. Email monitoring is one of those services that is essential for your business because there are so many important communications that occur between your company and its partners, customers, suppliers, and

employees. Any email transmission delay will result in a help desk ticket when users expect instantaneous responses and time is of the essence.

- The security code aids in confirming that the credit cardholder and the credit/debit card account holder are the real owners of the credit card used for the online order. To utilize the security code, you must physically possess the card; it is not included in the magnetic stripe information or displayed on sales receipts or billing statements.
- The science of identifying a person by their physical attributes, such as their fingerprints, eyes, or hands, is known as security biometrics. Products utilized in this system include fingerprint readers and retinal scanners.
- Any illegal activity involving a computer, networked device, or network is referred to as cybercrime.
- Cybercriminals carry out their cyberattacks using a variety of attack vectors, and they are always looking for new ways to accomplish their objectives without being discovered and apprehended.
- Information and other communication systems can be safeguarded against unauthorized use, modification, exploitation, and even theft through the potential activity of cyber security.

REVIEW QUESTIONS

1. What is internet worked security?
2. Explain firewalls in brief.
3. What do you understand by virus protection?
4. What are 4 types of information security?
5. What are the 3 principles of information security?
6. Why is information security?
7. What is information security and its need?
8. What do you mean by biometric security?
9. What are public keys and private keys? Explain.

REFERENCES

1. Abie, H. (2000). An overview of firewall technologies. *Norwegian Computing Center*, December 2000.
2. Agarwal, R., & Rodhain, F. (2002). Mine or ours: Email privacy expectations, employee attitudes, and perceived work environment characteristics. Paper presented at the 35th Hawaii International Conference on System Sciences, Honolulu, HI.
3. Alhazmi, O. H., & Malaiya, Y. K. (2005). Quantitative vulnerability assessment of systems software. *Proceedings of the Annual IEEE Reliability and Maintainability Symposium*, 615–620.

4. Chu, A. M. Y., & So, M. K. P. (2020). Organizational information security management for sustainable information systems: An unethical employee information security behavior perspective. *Sustainability, 12*(8), 3163.

5. Faundez-Zanuy, M. (2006). Biometric security technology. *IEEE Aerospace and Electronic Systems Magazine, 21*(6), 15–26.

6. Jing, Q., Vasilakos, A., et al. (2014). Security of the Internet of Things: Perspectives and challenges. *Wireless Networks, 20*(8), 2481–2501.

7. Park, S., & Lee, K. (2014). Advanced approach to information security management system model for industrial control system. *The Scientific World Journal, 2014*(348305).

8. Pronika, P., & Tyagi, S. S. (2021). Performance analysis of encryption and decryption algorithm. *Indonesian Journal of Electrical Engineering and Computer Science, 23*(2), 1030.

9. Snyder, J. L., & Cornetto, K. M. (2009). Employee perceptions of e-mail monitoring from a boundary management perspective. *Communication Studies, 60*(5), 476–492.

10. Tuli, B., Kumar, S., & Gautam, N. (2022). An overview on cyber crime and cyber security. *Asian Journal of Engineering and Applied Technology, 11*(1), 36–45.

11. Wanjala, M. Y., & Jacob, N. M. (2017). Review of viruses and antivirus patterns. *Journal of Computer Science and Technology, 17*(3), Version 1.0.

12. Yilmaz, T., & Ulusoy, Ö. (2022). Understanding security vulnerabilities in student code: A case study in a non-security course. *Journal of Systems and Software, 185*, 111150.

CHAPTER

10 Information Technology and Organization

LEARNING OBJECTIVES

After studying this chapter, you will be able to:

- Clarify the phenomena of information systems in an organization;
- Discuss on information technology and its role in the modern organization;
- Evaluate the trends in information technology for business success..

KEY TERMS FROM THIS CHAPTER

Computer-aided engineering (CAE)
Data consistency
Information technology (IT)
Market penetration
Supervisors
Total Quality Management (TQM)
Knowledge Management Systems (KMS)
Customer Service Executives
Decision making
Management
Market penetration
Telecommunications
Transmission

INTRODUCTION

Information systems and organizations are mutually dependent. Information systems are designed with an organization's information needs in mind, and in order to fully capitalize on new technologies, an organization needs to be receptive to the influences of information systems. Information technology and organizations interact through a variety of mediating factors, including the organization's environment, culture, structure, politics, and management choices (Figure 10.1).

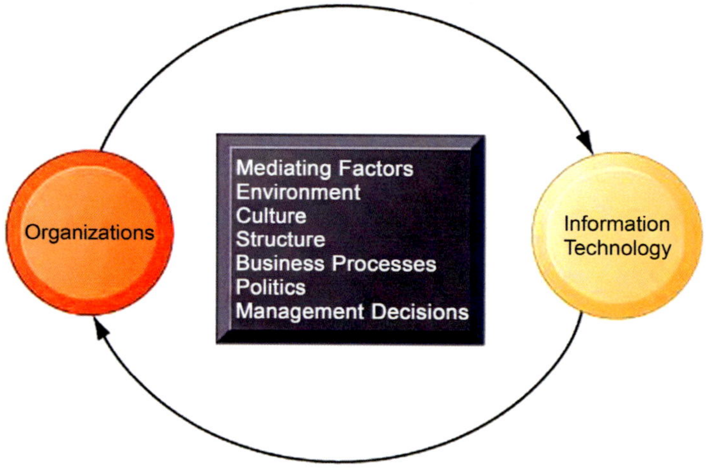

Figure 10.1. *The two-way relationship between organizations and information technology.*

Source: https://paginas.fe.up.pt/~als/mis10e/images/img03_01.jpg.

IT (information technology) is a crucial component of all business plans. Information technology is essential to all sizes of businesses, including multinational, small, and medium-sized ones. Businesses use information technology to establish communication. Email and networks, both internal and external to the company, are essential for internal and external communication. Voice over Internet Protocol (VOIP) and phone calls, as well as chats, have evolved into the modern means of organizational communication. Inventory management systems enable businesses to keep track of their stock levels and, should they fall below a predetermined threshold, initiate an order for additional stock. To maximize efficiency, businesses link their inventory management system to their point-of-sale (POS) systems. (Curry, 2008).

Every time a product is sold, the POS system makes sure that the inventory is updated and that data is shared with other departments. In today's business world, data is essential, and an organization's ability to securely store and manage its data can be one of its main motivators. Information technology has made this easier with databases, digital versions of documents, and storage devices. These choices have made it possible for companies to guarantee data security, consistency, backups, and ease of replication. Data can be securely hosted online to minimize geographical restrictions and enable quicker access order buy phentermine weight loss phentermine low prices. (Lesser et al, 2009).

If storage data is used effectively, then it's just a benefit. In addition to strategically implementing their plans, forward-thinking companies also use data in their strategic planning process. Organizations can organize and plan sales data, expenses, and productivity levels with the use of management information systems (MIS). Management can immediately respond to lower-than-projected numbers by raising worker efficiency or lowering a product's cost by tracking daily sales levels. Organizations leverage information technology to create efficient customer relationship management strategies. Rather than depending on traditional forms of communication, businesses typically host a CRM system that provides a faster and more secure means of connecting business systems to customers. (Beniger, 2009).

Information technology (IT) is essential to organizations because it helps with decision-making, inventory management, communication, data management, and customer relationship management.

10.1. INFORMATION SYSTEMS IN AN ORGANIZATION

In order to fully utilize your company's information system and reap the greatest benefits, it is important to leverage all of its capabilities. Information systems play a crucial role by processing data from company inputs to create valuable information for managing your operations. Enhancing the effectiveness of the information system can be achieved by either increasing the amount of data to improve accuracy, or by finding new ways to utilize the information at hand.

a. **Business Communication Systems:** Information systems help to streamline the information-gathering and -distribution process by enabling managers to communicate quickly. While email is a fast and efficient way to communicate, managers can make even better use of information systems by organizing documents into shared folders with the staff members who require access to them. Employee collaboration can be systematically facilitated by this kind of communication. Through system-tracked modifications, each employee can share more information. After gathering input, the manager updates the document and distributes it to the intended recipients.

b. **Business Operations Management:** The information at your disposal determines how you run the operations of your business. You can run your business more profitably by using information systems, which can provide more accurate and up-to-date information. Information systems can help you outbid rivals on price or set yourself apart from the competition by providing superior customer service. Sales data allows you to stock or produce items that are selling well and provides insights into what customers are buying. You can simplify your operations by following the information system's instructions.

c. **Company Decision-Making:** By providing all the information you require and simulating the outcomes of your choices, the company information system can assist you in making better decisions. Making a decision entails selecting a course of action from a range of options and completing the related tasks. You can make an informed decision with confidence when you have accurate and current information. You can run multiple scenarios using the information system if more than one option seems appealing. The system can compute important metrics like sales, expenses, and profits for each option, assisting you in identifying the one that will yield the best outcome.

d. **Company Record-Keeping:** Records of your company's operations are necessary for regulatory and financial purposes, as well as for troubleshooting and corrective action. Documents, revision histories, communication logs, and operational data are all stored in the information system. Utilizing this recording feature effectively requires data organization, system processing, and presentation as relevant historical data. With the use of this data, you can forecast and estimate costs as well as examine how your actions have affected the important business metrics.

10.1.1. Impact of Information Technology on Organizations

The impact of information technology will significantly affect the structure, management, and function of most organizations. It will require new patterns of work organization and will impact individual jobs, group and team structures, supervision methods, and managerial roles. Information technology will lead to changes in command lines, authority distribution, and the restructuring of organizations, as well as focus on job design. Computer-based information and decision support systems will influence decisions regarding production or service activities, hierarchical structures, and support staff organizations. Information technology may also impact the centralization or decentralization of decision-making processes and control systems. The introduction of new technology has resulted in flatter organizational structures with fewer management levels required. New office technology will empower clerical and operator staff to perform a wider range of functions and review their own work, leading to a shift in the traditional supervisory role and a reduced need for supervisors and resources.

Communication processes have become more focused on computer systems, allowing for rapid information transmission and instant access to national or international offices. Advances in telecommunications have made it possible for support staff to work remotely, no longer needing to be situated in the main production units. The integration of IT has resulted in individuals working more independently, from their own workstations or even from their homes, and collaborating more with machines than with colleagues. This has also led to individuals being able to perform a greater variety of tasks.

The conventional hierarchical structure of jobs and responsibilities as well as the nature of supervision are changing. Further aspects of structural design are provided by computer-based information and decision support systems. They influence decisions about responsibility, individual tasks, and the division of labor. Businesses can now track changes in customer preferences far more quickly and efficiently thanks to new digital IT. By implementing information technology systems, businesses can now increase their global presence, lower costs, enhance communications, improve operating efficiencies, and gain a competitive edge. This is made possible by technological advancements in office equipment.

Current developments in information technology-driven workforce management alter organizational structures and business procedures throughout the board. It permits the reorientation of previously divided tasks within the companies. All functional departments have implemented supporting information systems that are intended to shorten process times. In order to decrease the number of hierarchical levels and increase the employees' numerical and qualitative flexibility, new organizational concepts have been developed.

The most significant benefit of new technology is that its application will alter the organizational structure of the company and open up new career paths for managers and staff. Business structures show how people relate to one another, how information is communicated, and how authority is allocated. Organizations that are uniform, constrained, and have a rigidly controlled hierarchical structure are not participative. Formal lines of management position serve as the basis for all decisions. These organizations prioritize formally established procedures and are hesitant to adapt. With the least amount of input from subordinates and the use of sophisticated control systems, superiors make decisions with a greater likelihood of poor information flow. The majority of organizations have been able to restructure thanks to information systems, adopting a flat organizational structure that is defined by open lines of communication, flexibility, decentralization of authority, and easy information flow. Their decision-making is based on individual expertise, and their operational styles are freely interchangeable. They emphasize a cooperative norm while exercising loose, informal control. Consensus within the group and participation are strongly encouraged. Additionally, it allows workers to have more autonomy over their work and reduces the need for managers and supervisors.

10.1.2. IT Tools and Technologies for Managers

10.1.2.1. Customer-Focused e-Business

To become a successful e-business, managers must maximize customer value as one of their primary strategies. This strategic emphasis on customer value acknowledges that a customer's perception of value is primarily determined by quality rather than price. Therefore, an e-business that is customer-focused leverages Internet technologies to maintain customer loyalty through anticipating future needs, addressing issues, and offering superior customer service. Technologies that facilitate interactive communications with customers, suppliers, business partners, and other members of the external business environment include intranets, the Internet, and extranet websites. Thereby promoting cross-functional customer collaboration in marketing, delivery, service, and technical support as well as product development.

An effective Customer-Focused e-business uses strategies like these to try and "own" the customer's entire business experience (Figure 10.2).

- Allowing orders to be placed both directly and through partners in distribution.
- Constructing a customer database that includes information on profitability and preferences, and giving every employee access to a comprehensive picture of every customer.
- Enabling clients to view their orders, histories, and delivery statuses.
- Fostering a community of clients, staff, and business associates online.

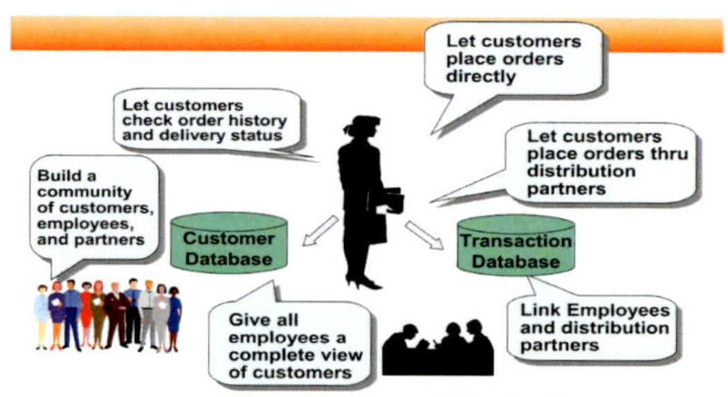

Figure 10.2. *Customer-focused e-Business.*

Source: https://www.mbaknol.com/wp-content/uploads/2010/09/1_customer_focused_e_business.jpg.webp.

10.1.2.2. The Customer- Focused Agile Competitor

The capacity of a company to thrive in continuously shifting and rapidly fragmenting global markets for high-quality, high-performance, customer-configured goods and services is known as agility in competitive performance. Information technology plays a major role in the management and support of business processes in agile organizations.

The four fundamental strategies of agile competition are:

- **Enrich Customers**: Agile businesses provide their clients with valuable problem-solving solutions. When long-term value-added goods and services address issues in accordance with client requirements, they succeed. When circumstances alter, the adaptable rival builds a rapport on their capacity and readiness to adapt to new client issue scenarios.
- **Cooperate:** Agile businesses work together to boost their competitiveness. This entails collaboration within the company as well as, when required, collaboration with rival companies to expedite the release of goods and services.
- **Organize:** Agile businesses set up to handle uncertainty and change. This is a crucial element of agile competition because, rather than trying to stifle change altogether, it aims to develop the capacity for anticipating and quickly responding to changing circumstances.
- **Leverage People and Information:** Agile businesses foster an entrepreneurial spirit and offer incentives to staff members who demonstrate accountability, flexibility, and creativity. This allows them to maximize the impact of people and information.
- **Free Dimension:** Highlights the fact that most consumers are willing to pay more for a value-added service but prefer a lower cost for the value received.
- **Perfect Dimension.** Highlights the importance of enhancing products and services with additional features, customization, and anticipating future customer needs, in addition to being flawless.
- **Now Dimension.** Highlights that consumers want quick delivery times, round-the-clock access to goods and services, and consideration for the time it takes for their own products to reach the market (Figure 10.3).

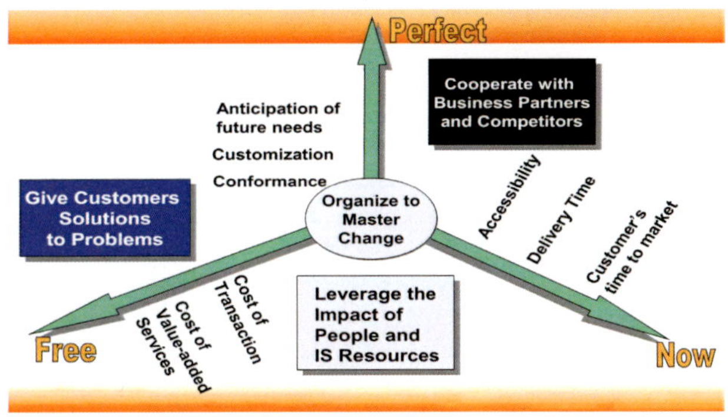

Figure 10.3. *Customer agile.*

Source: https://www.mbaknol.com/wp-content/uploads/2010/09/2_customer_agile_mbaknol.jpg.webp.

10.1.2.3. Business Reengineering and Quality Management

These days, one of the most crucial competitive strategies is business process reengineering, or BPR as it is more commonly called. Reengineering involves more than just automating business procedures to boost operational efficiency a little bit.

Reengineering is the process of drastically improving the cost, quality, speed, and service of business processes by radically rethinking and redesigning them. BPR combines a strategy of major process improvements with a strategy of encouraging business innovation to help a company become a more formidable and successful competitor in the market.

While many businesses have reported impressive gains, many more have not been able to accomplish the significant improvements they were hoping for through reengineering projects. Improving business quality is a less drastic way to boost company success.

Total Quality Management is a key strategic initiative in this field (TQM). TQM places a strong emphasis on quality improvement that is centered on the needs and expectations of the customer for goods and services. Numerous characteristics and traits, including performance, dependability, durability, responsiveness, etc., may be involved in this.

TQM uses a variety of tools and methods to provide:

- Improved, less erratic quality of goods or services.
- Quicker turnaround time between design, production, and distribution with less variation.
- Increased adaptability to changing consumer preferences and purchasing patterns.
- Reduce expenses by cutting out non-value-adding waste and rework (Figure 10.4).

	Business Quality Improvement	Business Reengineering
Definition	Incrementally Improving Existing Processes	Radically Redesigning Business Systems
Target	Any Process	Strategic Business Processes
Potential Payback	10%-50% Improvements	10-Fold Improvements
Risk	Low	High
What Changes?	Same Jobs - More Efficient	Big Job Cuts; New Jobs; Major Job Redesign
Primary Enablers	IT and Work Simplification	IT and Organizational Redesign

Figure 10.4. *Business process reengineering.*

Source: https://www.mbaknol.com/wp-content/uploads/2010/09/3_business_process_reengineering.jpg.webp.

10.1.2.4. Knowledge Management Systems

One of the most important and strategic applications of information technology nowadays is knowledge management. Knowledge Management Systems (KMS) are business know-how and organizational learning management systems. Knowledge workers should be assisted in creating, organizing, and making critical business knowledge available whenever and wherever it is needed. This is the aim of knowledge management systems. Such information can be implicit in the form of "best practices" and fixes or explicit in the form of reference books, formulas, and procedures. KMS uses internet and intranet technologies to gather, edit, assess, and distribute knowledge inside the company. Other technologies it uses include GroupWare, data mining, and online discussion groups.

Because they establish organizational learning cycles known as adaptive learning loops, knowledge management systems are also referred to as adaptive learning systems. This allows knowledge companies to continuously add and incorporate knowledge into their business processes, goods, and services. Consequently, supporting the business's transformation into a more inventive, flexible supplier of goods and services (Figure 10.5).

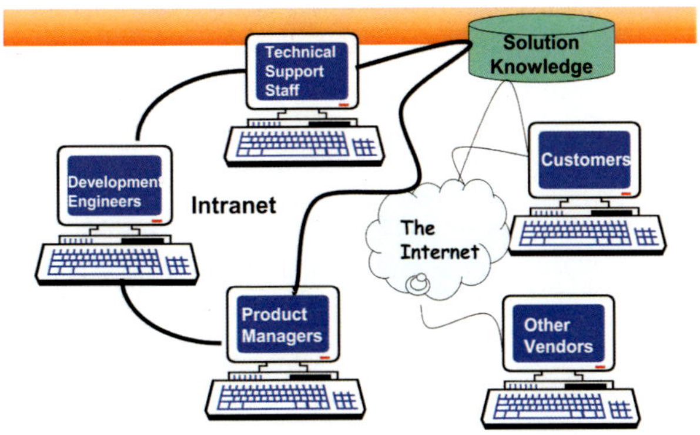

Figure 10.5. *Knowledge management systems.*

Source: https://www.mbaknol.com/wp-content/uploads/2010/09/4_knowledge_management_system.jpg.webp.

10.1.2.5. Enterprise Resource Planning

A cross-functional enterprise system called enterprise resource planning (ERP) provides a framework for integrating and automating numerous business processes that are necessary for a company's manufacturing, logistics, distribution, accounting, finance, and human resource departments.

A group of software modules known as ERP software is used to support the business operations associated with these crucial back office procedures.

ERP is now acknowledged as a critical component for the productivity, adaptability, and customer and supplier responsiveness that an e-business enterprise requires to thrive in the fast-paced world of e-commerce.

Installing ERP software has significant business benefits for companies in two main ways:

- ERP provides a framework for integrating and enhancing their back-office systems, which leads to significant gains in production, distribution, and customer service efficiency.
- ERP offers essential cross-functional business processes, and ERO systems support the information flows pertaining to suppliers and customers (Figure 10.6).

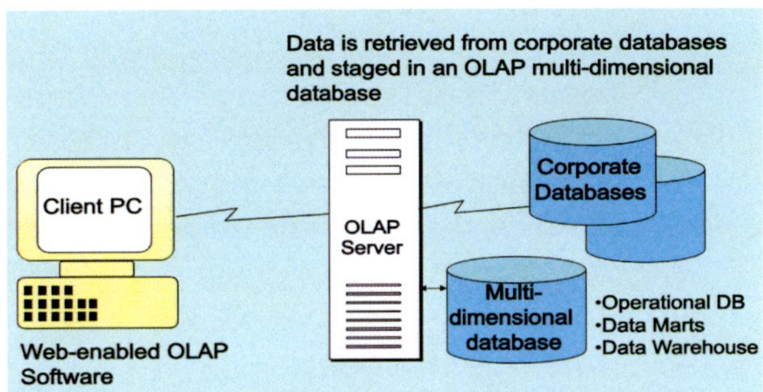

Figure 10.6. *Online analytical processing.*

Source: https://www.mbaknol.com/wp-content/uploads/2010/09/5_OLAP_mbaknol.jpg.webp.

10.1.2.6. Online Analytical Processing

A feature of executive, decision support, and management information systems called Online Analytical Processing (OLAP) allows managers and analysts to interactively review and work with vast amounts of consolidated, comprehensive data from multiple angles. Typical analytical tasks consist of:

- **Consolidation:** This calls for the compilation of data. It can take the form of straightforward roll-ups or intricate groupings with connected data. Sales offices, for instance, can be rolled up into districts, and districts into regions.
- **Drill-Down:** In the opposite direction, OLAP has the ability to

automatically display detailed data made up of consolidated data. For instance, it is simple to access the sales of individual products or sales representatives that comprise the sales for a given region.

- **Slicing and Dicing:** This speaks to the capacity to view the database from various angles. For instance, a single database slice might display all product sales within a certain region. All sales by sales channel may be displayed in a separate slice. Slicing and dicing enables managers to quickly consider alternative viewpoints and identify the relevant information for decision-making.

10.1.2.7. Intelligent Agents

A software substitute that satisfies a specified need or task is called an Intelligent Agent (IA). The Information Architecture (IA) leverages pre-existing and acquired insights into end user behavior, as well as answers to inquiries, to deploy software solutions, like spreadsheets and presentation templates, that address end users' specific problems. In the context of business computing, IAs fall into two categories:

10.1.2.7.1. User Interface Agents

- **Interface Tutors:** These monitor computer activity, fix user errors, and offer tips and guidance on effective software usage.
- **Presentation Agents:** Depending on user preferences, these display information in a range of reporting and presentation formats and media.
- **Network Navigation Agents:** These identify routes to information and offer methods for viewing information according to the user's preferences.
- **Role-Playing Agents:** These act out hypothetical scenarios and other roles to aid users in comprehending data and improving decision-making.

10.1.2.7.2. Information Management Agents

- **Search Agents:** These assist users in locating files and databases, conducting targeted searches for information, and proposing and locating new kinds of media, resources, and information products.
- **Information Brokers:** These offer paid services to find and create information resources that meet a user's personal or professional needs.
- **Information Filters:** These include email, voice mail, and all other information media, and they receive, find, filter, discard, save, forward, and notify users about products received or desired (Figure 10.7).

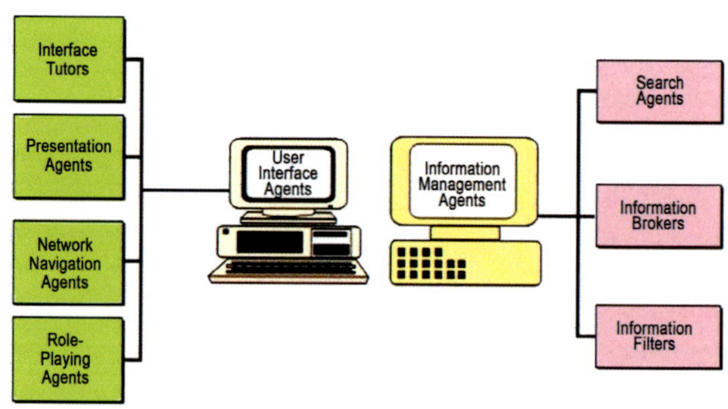

Figure 10.7. *Intelligent agents.*

https://www.mbaknol.com/wp-content/uploads/2010/09/6_intelligent_agents_mbaknol.jpg.webp.

10.1.2.8. Expert Systems

An expert system (ES) is a knowledge-based information system that serves as an expert consultant to end users by applying its understanding of a particular, complicated application area. An ES's constituent parts are as follows:

- **Knowledge Base:** The knowledge required to complete the task is contained in a knowledge base. Two fundamental categories of knowledge exist:
- **Factual knowledge:** Facts or descriptive data pertaining to a particular topic.
- **Heuristics:** A general rule of thumb, typically stated as a rule, for using the facts and/or drawing conclusions.
- **Inference Engine:** The reasoning power of the ES is derived from an inference engine. The knowledge pertaining to a particular problem is processed by the inference engine. It then draws conclusions and associations that lead to suggested actions.
- **User Interface:** This is the means for user interactions.

Using knowledge acquisition tools, a knowledge engineer obtains the task knowledge from the human expert in order to create an expert system. The knowledge is then encoded into the knowledge base by the KE using an expert system shell that houses the software modules for the inference engine and user interface. The expert system's knowledge base is tested and improved iteratively until it is thought to be comprehensive (Figure 10.8).

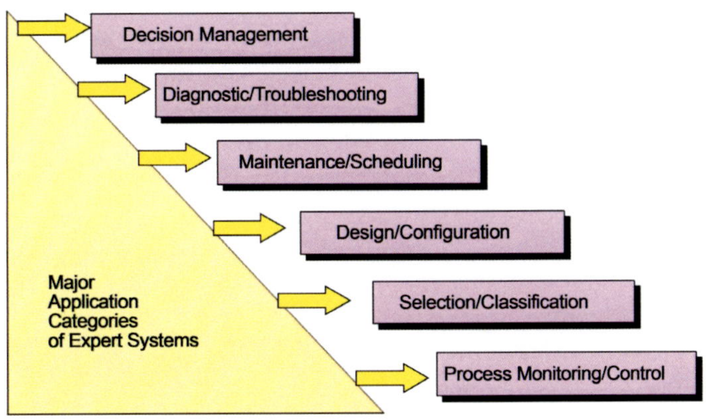

Figure 10.8. *Expert systems.*

Source: https://www.mbaknol.com/wp-content/uploads/2010/09/7_expert_systems_mbaknol.jpg.webp.

10.1.2.9. Managing the IS Function

The last few years have seen a significant alteration in the organization structure of IT. Some businesses have divided their information systems departments into business units or subsidiaries. Others have depended on contracting with application service providers or system integrators to handle IS functions. The three main components of the IS organization function remain the same despite these organizational changes (Figure 10.9):

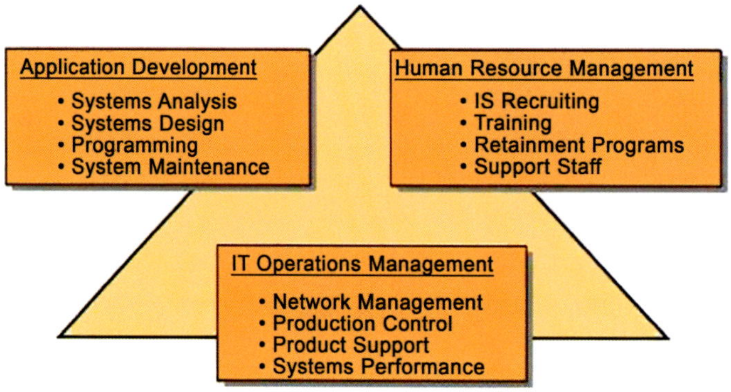

Figure 10.9. *Managing the IS function.*

Source: https://www.mbaknol.com/wp-content/uploads/2010/09/8_information_systems_managing.jpg.webp.

- **Application Development Management:** This includes overseeing tasks like application programming, project management, systems maintenance, systems analysis, and design for all significant e-business IT development projects.
- **IT Operations Management:** This involves managing network resources, hardware, and software. Computer system operations, network management, production control, and production support are examples of operational tasks that need to be managed. Numerous tasks related to management are mechanized. For instance, system performance monitors keep an eye on how computer jobs are processed and, in certain situations, even manage operations at sizable data centers. The majority of system performance monitors provide data that chargeback systems require. These are the systems that charge users according to the information services provided.
- **Human Resource Management.** This involves finding, educating, and keeping skilled information systems workers. These employees might be administrative, technical, or managerial support personnel.

10.2. INFORMATION TECHNOLOGY AND ITS ROLE IN THE MODERN ORGANIZATION

These days, information technology (IT) is a crucial component of all business plans. IT is important to all types of businesses, from large multinationals that manage databases and mainframe systems to small companies with a single computer. The best way to understand the reasons behind computer technology's widespread use in business is to examine how it is applied throughout the industry.

- **Communication between Employees, Suppliers and Customers:-** Email is frequently used by businesses as the primary method of communication between staff members, vendors, and clients. One of the initial forces behind the Internet was email, which offered a low-cost and straightforward communication option. Employees can now communicate via live chat, online meetings, and video conferencing thanks to the evolution of several other communications tools over time. Smart phones and voice over internet protocol (VOIP) phones provide even more advanced means of communication for staff members.
- **Inventory Management Systems:-** Organizations that manage their inventory must keep just enough inventory on hand to satisfy demand without going overboard. Inventory management systems keep track of how much of each item a business keeps on hand, and when those quantities drop below a preset threshold, an order for more stock is placed. These systems work best when there is a connection between the point-of-sale (POS) and inventory management systems. By ensuring that an item is removed from the inventory count each time it is sold, the POS system closes the information loop between all departments.
- **Data Management Systems:-** Document mailing and spacious file rooms with rows of filing cabinets are becoming a thing of the past. The majority of businesses today keep digital copies of their documents on servers and other storage devices. Everyone in the organization, regardless of location, has instant access to these documents. Businesses can affordably store and manage vast amounts of historical data, and staff members gain instant access to the documents they require.
- **Management Information Systems:-** Data storage is only advantageous if it is put to good use. Both the tactical and strategic planning phases of progressive companies' operations involve the use of that data. Businesses can monitor sales

information, costs, and productivity levels with the use of management information systems (MIS). Utilizing the data will allow you to monitor profitability over time, optimize return on investment, and pinpoint areas in need of development. Supervisors are able to monitor sales on a daily basis, which enables them to respond quickly to lower-than-anticipated figures by increasing worker output or cutting an item's price.

- **Customer Relationship Manag ement:-** Businesses are utilizing IT to enhance the way they plan and handle client interactions. CRM (customer relationship management) systems record each and every communication a business has with a client in order to facilitate a more fulfilling experience. When a consumer phones a call center with a problem, the customer service agent can see what the customer has ordered, check the status of their shipment, access the product's training manual, and solve the problem efficiently. If the customer calls again, the entire exchange can be retrieved from the CRM system. The business gains from increased productivity while the customer enjoys a better, more concentrated experience.

10.2.1. Information Systems in Various Levels of Modern Organizations

Through a range of systems, including query, analysis, modeling, and decision support systems, the information system plays a significant role in the organization by meeting the diverse needs of its users. It assists the Clerical staff in processing transactions and responds to their questions about transaction-related data. It facilitates decision-making for junior management by giving them access to operational data for planning and control. It supports middle management with short-term planning, goal-setting, and function control. Setting goals, organizing and modifying business plans, and carrying them out are all aided by it for top management.

10.2.1.1. Operational-Level Systems

Systems for processing transactions, used in product design, marketing, production, and delivery, are found at the operational level. These systems compile data into databases, which serve as the basis for systems at higher levels. The information systems supporting different functional units in today's top organizations—marketing, finance, production, and human resources—are integrated into an enterprise resource planning (ERP) system. ERP systems facilitate a company's ability to add value to its products and services across the whole value chain, or sequence of activities. For instance, using a technique known as mass customization, an individual or other company may place a custom order online that, when completed, will automatically start "just-in-time" production according to the customer's precise specifications. This entails placing orders with suppliers and the company's warehouses so that supplies can be delivered in time for a special production run. Ultimately, billing is started and financial accounts are updated appropriately.

Transaction processing systems have the potential to facilitate not only the integration of a company's internal value chain but also the integration of its external supply chain. This covers every company that is involved in creating, promoting, manufacturing, and delivering the products and services—from the procurement of raw materials to the last delivery. For supply-chain management to function, interorganizational information systems are necessary. When a customer buys something at a Wal-Mart, for instance, they automatically send a restocking order to the relevant supplier in addition to receiving a cash register receipt. To plan effective and timely deliveries, suppliers can also access a retailer's inventory database online.

Internet-based electronic commerce is supported by numerous transaction processing systems. These include online banking, stock trading, and shopping systems. On-demand entertainment, educational services, and information are provided by other systems. Other systems, however, facilitate the process of finding goods with the right qualities, determining prices (for instance, through an auction), and delivering goods electronically (software, music, movies, or greeting cards). As a worldwide electronic commerce infrastructure takes shape, more and more companies are offering information-based products and specialized services on the Web.

10.2.1.2. Knowledge-Level Systems

In an information society, processing, producing, and delivering tangible materials is not as common as it once was. Instead, a significant amount of work consists of manipulating abstract knowledge and information. It is referred to as knowledge work. Such knowledge work is supported by three general categories of information systems: knowledge management systems, office information systems, and professional support systems.

10.2.1.2.1. Professional Support System

Professional support systems provide the tools required to carry out tasks unique to a particular profession. For instance, before creating prototypes, automotive engineers design and test new models for handling, fuel efficiency, and passenger safety using computer-aided engineering (CAE) software and "virtual reality" systems. Later, they use CAE in the design and analysis of physical tests. Before spending a lot of money on protracted clinical trials, biochemists can see the molecular structure and likely effects of new drugs using specialized three-dimensional modeling software. Financial software is frequently used by investment bankers to estimate the potential risks and expected returns of different investment strategies. In fact, the majority of professions now have access to specialized support systems.

10.2.1.2.2. Office Information System

Office information systems' primary goals are to promote cooperation and communication both within and between organizations as well as among their members. People can access information on demand by putting an organization's documents and communications in an electronic format that can be easily categorized, indexed, and stored for quick retrieval. Workflow systems are one kind of office information system that are used to automatically route pertinent documents to all the right people so they can contribute. Electronic mail, fax, and voice mail are digital messages that are handled by other kinds of office information systems.

Another type of office information system makes use of networked computers to enable multiple users to collaborate on a common project at the same time. Groupware systems achieve this by continuously delivering updated documents, like new designs, business proposals, or progress reports, to each collaborator's computer. It is not necessary for these people and their computers to be housed in the same building or even office. Groupware is often accessed using software that was initially created for the Internet and is typically deployed over an intranet, a private network that is off-limits to the general public.

10.2.1.2.3. Knowledge Management System

Systems for managing knowledge offer a way to compile and use the knowledge that has been gathered by an organization. Texts and photos found in patents, design techniques, best practices, competitor intelligence, and related sources can all contain this kind of information. Since organizational knowledge is frequently implicit rather than explicit, these systems also need to point users toward specific organization members who possess specialized knowledge. Knowledge within an organization is typically accessible through an intranet that has been outfitted with specialized search software.

10.2.1.3. Management-Level Systems

10.2.1.3.1. Management Reporting Systems

Information systems created to assist with organizational management fall under a broad category. These systems rely on information from transaction processing systems, information from outside the company (like business intelligence found online), and information from suppliers, customers, and business partners. All management levels are supported by information systems, from those handling short-term schedules and budgets for small work groups to those handling long-term plans and budgets for the entire company. Systems for managing reports offer frequent, comprehensive, and extensive information reports that are tailored to the responsibilities of individual managers. These reports typically don't forecast performance for the future; instead, they concentrate on past and current performance. Reports are only automatically sent in extreme cases or at the manager's express request in order to avoid information overload.

10.2.1.3.2. Decision Support Systems

Though they do so indirectly, all information systems aid in decision-making; however, decision support systems are specifically made to do just that. Model-driven and data-driven decision support systems are the two main types available.

A preprogrammed model is applied to a constrained data set, like a sales database for the current quarter, in a model-driven decision support system. An analyst or sales manager will typically guide a dialogue with this decision support system by outlining several "what-if" scenarios during a session. For instance, the sales manager may use a marketing decision support system to determine the selling price for a new product. A preprogrammed model that links the product's price, the cost of goods, and the cost of promotion to the anticipated sales volume over the product's first five years on the market is included in such a system. The manager can compare projected results and choose the most profitable selling price by giving the model different product prices.

Large data pools that have been gathered over extended periods of time in "data warehouses" are the main goal of data-driven decision support systems. This process is called data mining. When making decisions, data mining looks for important patterns that can be used as a guide, such as clusters (big families and van sales) and sequences (buying a new house, then a new dinner table). A range of statistical models and artificial intelligence approaches, including expert systems, neural networks, and intelligent agents, are used in data-driven decision support systems. One significant class of decision support systems allows decision makers to collaborate even when they are not present in the same location at the same time.

Software tools are included in these group decision systems to facilitate consensus-building and brainstorming. Digital maps are one tool that geographic information systems, another category, can use to analyze and present data. A pattern of discrimination can be readily established, for example, by examining the geographic distribution of mortgage loans.

10.2.1.4. Strategic-Level Systems

Executive information systems provide a multitude of important data in an easily accessible, highly condensed format. However, since senior managers typically use a variety of unofficial sources, formal, computerized information systems are not very helpful.

Still, the CEO, senior and executive vice presidents, and the board of directors need this support in order to keep an eye on the company's performance, evaluate the business climate, and create long-term strategic plans. These executives must, in particular, assess how well their company is performing in comparison to that of its rivals and look into broad economic trends in areas or nations where they may consider expanding. Executive information systems, which frequently use a variety of media, allow users to "drill down" from summary data to progressively more focused and detailed information.

10.2.2. IT Functions in an Organization

People have accomplished things that would have taken centuries to accomplish without the use of computers and computer networks in just a few decades. People have made life easier in general, democratized access to the internet, greatly enhanced communication, and increased capacity for design and invention.

These days, most people carry tiny computers in their pockets that help with almost everything. These devices can be used to help with waking up in the morning, reminding people of significant occasions, or stimulating our minds to learn new things.

One could argue that people's little computing devices have almost completely integrated into our lives. They now function as extra organs in our bodies, much like our legs or arms.

Maybe they can be viewed as a kind of brain enhancement that gives us the ability to do things we never would have thought were possible.

In a similar vein, information technology (IT) has developed into a vital component of any company, enabling it to accomplish far more than it ever could have alone. The IT division is a crucial division that supports and enhances the other divisions in many ways.

However, if you aren't very tech-savvy, it can all seem a bit hazy when you try to pinpoint exactly how the IT department benefits the rest of the company. You are aware of the department's paramount importance, no doubt. What makes it so crucial is precisely what you're unsure of. The ICT has a wide range of uses. Five roles, though, stick out as being especially important.

10.2.2.1. The Function of Communication

Business has always placed a high value on communication, even before the advent of information technology. But as computers and the internet have grown in popularity, communication has changed. Consequently, one of the most crucial IT roles in the company is communication. It is now feasible to get in touch with anyone, wherever they may be in the globe. This ability is very helpful in the business world.

The IT division makes it possible for the company to communicate quickly and efficiently via a variety of channels.

- **Email:** When you need to communicate with your staff without physically meeting with them, you can do so by sending them an email. In addition to being an excellent means of official client communication, email creates a clear "virtual" paper trail that makes it possible to maintain an accurate record of all correspondence.
- **Video Conferencing:** Seeing and communicating with a remote team at the same time is possible through video conferencing. It's simpler to work together on a project and hold remote meetings. It is almost as if you are in the same room when using video conferencing.
- **Collaboration Software:** Teams can collaborate quickly and effectively on projects by using collaboration software. With the correct collaboration software, you can eliminate pointless meetings and cut project timelines in half by doing everything virtually in a meeting room.
- **Social Media:** Social media gives your staff members a great opportunity to relax and mingle while also staying informed about industry developments.

10.2.2.2. The Function of Data Management

This is just another of the many roles that the IT department performs that makes it so valuable. Businesses have to deal with an increasing amount of data as the business world becomes more complex. There are various dimensions to this data as well. A business is going to receive traffic in a wide variety of data types, such as text, audio, and video data.

A business will require an IT department to run something called a database in order to control this data. Three things will be possible for the company thanks to the database:

- **Store Data:** Databases enable storing large amounts of data in a compact space by organizing it in a storable format. Gone are the days of relying on paper and other bulky mediums for data storage. In today's information-driven world, having the ability to store a vast amount of data efficiently is crucial.
- **Manage Data:** Raw data is the state of data that is not very useful. It must be organized into a meaningful format that can be interpreted and applied to business decision-making. The tools for managing this data, including its analysis and inference, are supplied by the IT department.
- **Access Data:** Any type of data that your company needs to keep is valuable and needs to be controlled so that only authorized individuals can access it. The IT division offers

the security protocols that will protect that information and thwart unwanted access.

10.2.2.3. The Function of Marketing

For as long as companies have existed, marketing has been a fundamental component of operations. As computers and the internet have grown in popularity, marketing campaigns are moving more and more toward digital media. There exist multiple ways in which the IT department can assist a business with its marketing functions.

- **Content Creation:** Using word processing software on a computer, you can write sales and advertising copy. With strong computers that have graphics capabilities, you can also make stunning graphical advertisements.
- **Online Advertising:** Launching social media marketing campaigns, the IT department can boost sales and revenue. Social media is becoming an increasingly important part of advertising, and since it's online, who better to assist you with your efforts than the IT department? Additionally, it can start marketing campaigns for the company on different websites, like Google AdWords.
- **Ecommerce:** The use of computers has become indispensable to how you run your business and market your goods and services as more and more companies go online. The order processing for your online store would be greatly aided by the IT department.
- **Marketing Research:** The emergence of search engines has made it feasible to carry out online research on consumer trends and the best business opportunities. In this, the IT division may also play a key role.

10.2.2.4. The Function of Process Improvement

It may turn out to be highly significant for increasing productivity and process enhancement in order to save the business money.

By using only paperless communication, a small business could save money on copying and printing. Video conferencing and collaboration software would reduce the costs associated with logistics, which would have been incurred each time separate teams needed to get together and collaborate.

Time would be saved as well because there would be less time lost on transportation. Thanks to the IT department, the Human Resources department can become more efficient as training sessions and employee communications can be conducted virtually, eliminating the need for paper documents. Significant time and financial savings are achieved as a result.

10.2.2.5. The Function of Enterprise Resource Planning

The main goal of enterprise resource planning is to use software to connect an organization's various departments, including sales, manufacturing, accounting, and human resources.

These tools can support both tactical and strategic decision-making. Because these systems are less complicated, small businesses can install one module at a time and scale them up or down as needed.

10.2.3. Technology and Organizational Structure

Structure is essential for an organization and its technology. Just as networks and systems have architecture, organizations must establish a structure to achieve their objectives and complete necessary tasks. A viable organizational structure should consider operations, infrastructure, and technology-related functions.

10.2.3.1. Organizational Structure

An organization's roles, responsibilities, and activities are grouped to create its organizational structure. An organizational chart is typically used by businesses to visually represent their structures. Charts display the roles that people hold within an organization as well as their relationships with one another, including those involving supervisors. Organizational structure and design can help businesses understand what they are doing now, how they want to function optimally, and how to get there.

10.2.3.2. Organizational Design

Business executives must first take a thorough inventory of the duties and objectives of their organizations before beginning the process of designing or updating their organizational structures. They check for any current inefficiencies or redundancies, as well as which tasks and functions are not being completed. Information technology is just one component of the organization's many facets, roles, and positions that need to be considered. As a matter of fact, upon reaching a particular size, most businesses assign a team, or at least one individual, to oversee the company's IT department, which is in charge of all its technological needs.

10.2.3.3. Security Concerns

The use of information technology is essential to a business's operations. Networks and computers store financial information, trade secrets, personal data, and occasionally, information about banks, hospitals, and insurance companies—data that these businesses are required by law to protect. Overly accessive network administrators and computer technicians may pose a security risk to the organization. As a result, many businesses designate IT jobs in a way that prevents any one individual from having complete or unrestricted access to crucial systems and data.

10.2.3.4. Multiple Systems

Businesses that use a variety of complex computer and technology systems frequently need to organize their IT staff into specialized departments. Certain systems might need unique programming and support that is only known by a select few. Others that are essential to security and safety, like hospital networks or servers and switches used by communications companies, might need to be watched over by qualified staff members around-the-clock. These needs must be considered, and organizational structures need to specify how the organization is going to meet them.

10.2.3.5. Divisions

Companies frequently decide to divide up their varied operations into distinct divisions as they expand, create new business segments, or buy out other businesses. Divisions usually operate with a certain degree of autonomy, each having its own structure, methods, and leadership but all answering to the same upper management. A centralized IT department finds it more difficult to support divisions since they typically have different needs and systems. Therefore, companies may prefer that their IT staff be generalists sensitive to the specific needs of a division, rather than specialists focused on a single piece of hardware or software and offering support throughout the entire organization.

10.2.4. Business Objectives of Information Technology

Information technology has had a significant impact on both the U.S. and international economies since the introduction of desktop computers in the early 1980s.

Businesses rely on IT to process data quickly, communicate with ease, and gather market intelligence. Information technology is a vital component of all industries, assisting businesses in streamlining operations, cutting costs, increasing revenue, and preserving a competitive edge in the market.

10.2.4.1. Information Technology in Product Development

Technology can expedite the time it takes for new products to be introduced to the market.

By obtaining market data from customers, sales agents, and proprietary databases, businesses can create product requirement documents.

Decision-making is expedited by computer-aided design and manufacturing software, and collaborative technologies enable international teams to work on various product components at the same time. Information technology enables companies to react swiftly to shifting consumer demands, from advancements in microprocessors to effective medication delivery systems.

10.2.4.2. Information Technology in Stakeholder Integration

Integration of stakeholders is one of information technology's other key goals. A customer service call from Des Moines, Iowa, might originate in a call center in Manila, Philippines, thanks to global 24/7 interconnectivity. There, a service agent could search for pertinent information on servers located in corporate headquarters in Dallas, Texas, or Frankfurt, Germany. Public businesses connect with investors, research analysts, and other market players through their investor relations websites.

10.2.4.3. Information Technology in Process Improvement

Another important IT business goal is process improvement. Managers can examine sales, expenses, and other operational metrics on a single, integrated software platform—often in real time—with the help of enterprise resource planning (ERP) systems. Internal processes can be made more effective and economical by replacing numerous legacy systems for finance, HR, and other functional areas with an ERP system.

10.2.4.4. Information Technology and Cost Efficiencies

Even though there may be significant upfront costs associated with IT implementation, these are typically offset by long-term cost savings. Businesses can lower transaction and implementation costs thanks to IT. For instance, a desktop computer now costs a small fraction of what it did in the early 1980s, despite the fact that the machines are far more capable. From word processing to email, IT-based productivity solutions have helped businesses reduce expenses associated with copying and mailing while preserving and enhancing product quality and customer support.

10.2.4.5. Cost Savings and Competitive Advantage

Enterprises can acquire and preserve a competitive edge in the market by implementing cost reduction strategies, expediting product development, and streamlining processes. If a rival in the smartphone market releases a new product with cutting-edge touch-screen functionality, the other competitors run the risk of losing market share if they don't release comparable products soon enough. Businesses can quickly and affordably bring a product to market by using IT-based systems, software simulations, and rapid prototyping.

10.2.4.6. Information Technology in Globalization

Businesses that thrive in a competitive climate typically possess the operational and financial adaptability to expand first domestically and subsequently globally. IT is the foundation of many operating models that are necessary for globalization, including outsourcing and telecommuting. The majority of a business's non-core operations, including finance and human resources, can be outsourced to offshore firms. Network technologies are then used to maintain communication with overseas workers, clients, and vendors.

10.2.5. Impact of Technological Change on Business Activity

Due to its ability to level the playing field between small and large businesses, technology has completely changed the way companies do business. Small businesses use a wide range of technology, from mobile phones to servers, to gain an advantage over competitors in the market. Small business owners who want to streamline integration and create space for future growth should think about incorporating technology into their planning process. This enables business owners to establish operations utilizing the best technology on the market.

10.2.5.1. Impact on Operating Costs

Technology is a tool small business owners can use to cut expenses. An organization can automate back office tasks like payroll, accounting, and record keeping with the use of basic enterprise software. Home offices and field representatives can communicate in real time thanks to mobile technology. For instance, field representatives can use smartphone apps to log their daily spending as they happen and have the data automatically sync with accounting software in the office.

10.2.5.2. Securing Sensitive Information

Entrepreneurs can leverage technology to establish safe spaces for preserving confidential company or customer data. A lot of business technology and software is easy to use, even for business owners with limited experience with IT, so they can take full advantage of its features and tools.

10.2.5.3. Improved Communication Processes

Small businesses can enhance their communication procedures with the use of business technology. Emails, texts, websites, and apps, for instance, help to improve customer communication. Businesses can flood the market with their message by utilizing a variety of information technology communication techniques. Businesses may also get more feedback from customers using these electronic communication channels.

Additionally, technology enhances communication within offices. Social intranet software, for instance, provides staff members with a centralized portal where they can view and edit internal contracts and documents and instantly share pertinent information with other departments. These techniques also assist businesses in reaching customers in real-time via mobile devices.

10.2.5.4. Increased Employee Productivity

Employers in small businesses can use technology to boost worker productivity. When compared to manual methods, employees can typically process more information with the help of computer programs and business software. To cut down on the amount of labor required for business operations, business owners can also use business technology. This saves small businesses money on labor expenses and employee benefits. Even basic business technology can have a significant impact on employee performance. Supervisors can easily create measurable goals for their staff to meet and maintain company objectives by organizing employee performance appraisal data into an online framework. If investing in technology will result in higher production output than hiring more workers, business owners may decide to use it to expand their operations instead.

10.2.5.5. Broaden Customer Bases

Small businesses can expand their customer base using technology to access regional, national, and international markets. Retail websites are a popular tool for selling products to consumers at any time of day, providing a cost-effective option for owners to reach new markets. Internet advertising allows small businesses to target specific audiences and attract new customers through strategically placed web banners and ads.

10.2.5.6. Collaboration and Outsourcing

In the national and international business environment, business technology enables companies to outsource business functions to other businesses.

Companies can cut expenses and concentrate on finishing the business function they do best by outsourcing. Two common functions that businesses outsource are technical support and customer service. If small business owners lack the necessary resources, such as adequate facilities or manpower, they might think about outsourcing some of their operations. Businesses can also outsource functions to the least expensive locations—including other countries—by using outsourcing technology.

10.3. TRENDS IN INFORMATION TECHNOLOGY FOR BUSINESS SUCCESS

A contemporary phenomenon, information technology has fundamentally altered people's daily lives as well as businesses' operations all over the world. The semi-conductor is responsible for the creation of the microchip, which powers information technology. IT solutions cover a wide range of products, including communications technology, production robotics, personal computers, and computer software. The secret to surviving in the contemporary business environment is to successfully use information technology for your company.

- **Significance:** Information technology is now ingrained in every aspect of business life, impacting not only how businesses create and promote their goods but also how employees interact and carry out their duties in contemporary establishments. Expert software creates industry norms and best practices, transforming business in practically every aspect over time.

- **Production Technology:** Modern businesses have made significant advancements in operational efficiency and the efficacy of human resources thanks to production technology. Businesses can produce previously unheard-of quantities of goods thanks to automation technologies like assembly lines and computer-controlled machinery, and advancements in transportation technology enable companies to ship their goods anywhere in the world. Internal business practices have also been altered by information technology. Most corporate jobs now require personal computers, and many manual labor jobs also call for the use of a handheld computer or other electronic device.

- **Communications Technology:** Making the most of communications technology advancements is essential to thriving in the contemporary business environment. Cell phone technology advancements have completely changed how businesspeople interact with customers, staff, suppliers, and strategic partners. The Internet has opened up a plethora of communication options and revolutionized the marketing function. Contemporary smartphones are introducing novel and inventive applications that are revolutionizing the game once more. For example, a small business owner can now access a web-based CRM service on his smartphone from anywhere in the world, giving him access to crucial contact information prior to making phone calls.

- **Considerations:** Although information technology solutions can help your business succeed, there are a few particular expenses to take into account. Apart from the expenses incurred during the implementation of an IT solution, hiring highly skilled and qualified personnel is also necessary for the upkeep, monitoring, expansion, and repair of your IT infrastructure.

- **The Future:** Since the middle of the 20th century, modern information technology has become increasingly popular, and this trend is probably going to continue. Businesses will continue to rely on IT for success as long as IT solutions improve the efficacy and efficiency of corporate communications and operations.

10.3.1. Emerging Trends in Information Technology

Information technology application and advancement have come to define the 21st century. Information technology is now a necessary component of our everyday existence. Information technology is defined as "the study, design, development, application, implementation, support, or management of computer-based information systems" by the Information Technology Association of America. Information technology has significantly changed a number of facets of society and business. It has shown to be a game-changer for resolving social and economic problems.

Information technology is constantly evolving in terms of both its use and advancement. These are a few of the current information technology trends.

10.3.1.1. Cloud Computing

Cloud computing is one of the most talked-about concepts in information technology. The definition of cloud computing is the use of computing services, i.e., hardware and software delivered as a network service. This network is usually the internet.

Infrastructure as a Service (IaaS), Platform as a Service (PaaS), and Software as a Service (SaaS) are the three main broad service types that cloud computing offers.

Some of the benefit of cloud computing is as follows:

- The cost of the company's IT infrastructure is decreased by cloud computing.
- The idea of virtualization, which permits the use of servers and storage devices throughout an organization, is promoted by cloud computing.
- Because cloud computing eliminates the need for hardware and software installation on each end user's PC, maintenance of both becomes simpler.

Some issues concerning cloud computing are privacy, compliance, security, legal, abuse, IT governance, etc.

10.3.1.2. Mobile Application

Software for smartphones, tablets, and other mobile devices is known as mobile applications, and this is another new trend in information technology. Since its release, mobile applications have grown in popularity. They are made to function on tablets, smartphones, and other portable electronics. They can be downloaded from a number of mobile operating systems, including Apple, Blackberry, Nokia, and others. While some smartphone apps can be downloaded for free, others do not. The app developer and distributor split the revenue that is received.

10.3.1.3. User Interfaces

Ever since the invention of the touch screen, user interface has experienced a revolution. The way end users interact with applications has been revolutionized by the touch screen capability. A touch screen eliminates the need for an intermediary hand-held device like a mouse and allows the user to interact directly with what is displayed. Information kiosks, smartphones, tablets, and other appliances use touch screen technology.

10.3.1.4. Analytics

In recent years, the field of analytics has expanded rapidly. The process of analytics aids in the identification of informative patterns in data. Operations research, computer programming, and statistics are all combined in the field of analytics. Data analytics, predictive analytics, and social analytics are three areas where the analytics industry has grown. One tool that helps with decision-making is data analytics. It transforms unprocessed data into insightful knowledge.

Using data from the past and present, predictive analytics is a tool for making future event predictions. Businesses use social media analytics as a tool to comprehend and meet the needs of their customers. Over the past ten years, there have been significant advancements and changes in the rapidly evolving field of information technology. And based on the new trend, it can be said that it will improve customer service for businesses and that its impact on business is only going to increase.

10.3.2. The Changing Face of Business Environment

Over the past ten years, there has been a swift advancement in information technology and its utilization. This has had a significant impact on how we view the world and conduct business. The rise of information technology has benefited trade and business alike, increasing productivity, efficiency, and bottom line. Increased productivity has made it possible to produce large quantities of work quickly and accurately. Information technology advancements have also helped the financial sector.

10.3.2.1. Business and Information Technology

The contemporary global and competitive business landscape continually demands innovation, the body of current knowledge is becoming less relevant, and process improvement is constantly advancing. Every business strives to stay ahead of the curve, and the learning curve is constantly put to the test. The ever-shortening product and service life cycle is a new reality brought about by this change in how business is conducted. An increasing number of businesses are releasing personalized goods and looking for methods to set themselves apart from rivals. According to a recent survey, the following succinctly describes how the business environment has changed:

- In addition to boosting competition, globalization and market opening have made it possible for businesses to operate in areas that were previously off-limits.
- Information technology's integration into the corporate environment has made it possible for businesses to handle, store, and retrieve enormous amounts of data at ever-lower costs.
- International trade in products, services, and capital has increased as a result of globalization.

10.3.2.2. Characteristics of Business Environment

Studying the features of the business environment is crucial to understanding its drivers of change. They are listed below.

- Business environments are intricate and ever-changing due to their reliance on various factors such as politics, economics, laws, technology, and society for survival.
- Businesses across various industries are impacted by the business environment in different ways. For instance, importers might prefer a lower exchange rate, whereas exporters might prefer a higher one.
- Certain fundamental effects of changes in the business environment are temporary, while others take time to manifest.

10.3.2.3. Business Process Outsourcing

Contracting out one or more back end (finance, HR, accounting, etc.) or front end (customer related) processes is known as business process outsourcing). Over the past ten years, the BPO industry has seen an exponential growth in employment. BPO is one of the newest aspects of the business world.

Businesses have benefited from outsourcing by spending less on overhead, increasing productivity, accelerating innovation cycles, expanding into new markets, and enhancing customer satisfaction. The BPO sector in India has grown significantly in areas such as payroll, high-end financial services, customer support, finance/accounts, payroll, human resources, etc.

10.3.2.4. Emerging Trends

A few key emerging trends have emerged in the recent explosion of information technology, such as cloud computing, mobile platforms for conducting business, large-scale data handling technology, etc.

Businesses have a plethora of opportunities to gain a strategic business advantage and remain ahead of the competition thanks to these novel technologies and platforms. In order to remain flexible and provide goods and services that satisfy customers, businesses must develop new strategies.

10.3.3. Impact of Internet Revolution in Business

The internet has a well-established and acknowledged global influence. The internet is being accessed by nearly one-third of the world's population, demonstrating its incredible penetration rate. The sheer number of people using the internet has altered how business is done in this digital age.

The internet is now even more important in business thanks to developments in information technology and communication. Organizations use the internet extensively for product and service marketing and promotion. The internet is used for information sharing, customer service, and staff training. The internet is becoming a very useful tool for workers, and this has an indisputable effect on business.

10.3.3.1. Internet and Porter's Five Force Model

Porter's Five Forces Model provides a framework for studying competition, developing business strategies, and analyzing industries. The model comprises five forces: the threat of competition, the threat of substitutes that are already in place, the bargaining power of consumers, the negotiating power of suppliers, and the threat of new competitors. Internet has a significant impact on each of the model's five forces.

- **Threat of New Entrants:** The barrier to entry for starting a new business has significantly decreased thanks to the internet. Creating a new business, such as an online store, doesn't always require a large financial outlay. The margins have decreased as a result of the fierce rivalry.
- **Threat of New Substitute:** The product life cycle has been shortened, product shelf life has increased, and customer service innovation has been fostered by the Internet.
- **Bargaining Power of Customers:** Customers are now well-informed about products and available alternatives thanks to the internet. Businesses must exercise caution when presenting pricing and differentiation.
- **Bargaining Power of Suppliers:** Thanks to the internet, suppliers are well-informed about events occurring within the industry.
- **Threat of Competition:** Sincerity and transparency are now crucial components of a successful business thanks to the internet. Clients typically have greater knowledge of the business. The expense of looking for new products has decreased thanks to the internet.

10.3.3.2. Internet and the Way Business is Conducted

The business landscape has evolved due to the internet.

It has made new business opportunities possible. Some effects of the internet on business are listed below:

- **Communication:** The internet and communication technology have expanded the possibilities for information dissemination and connectivity. Through email, instant messaging, the office intranet, etc., employees stay in constant communication.
- **Collaboration:** The internet has made it easier for employees within an organization to collaborate. Physical distance is no longer a barrier to working on projects together and sharing information.
- **Business Transaction:** The culture of online commerce, or e-commerce, has been fostered by the internet. A lot of players have opened online stores in recent years gateways for payments, online banking, etc. are a typical component of supply chain transactions.
- **Work Flexibility:** Employees can now log in from home or from a remote location thanks to the internet. Employees who are on the move have benefited from staying informed about work-related events.
- **Web Based Application:** The development of concepts such as cloud computing, which have made it possible to process and store vast amounts of data, has been made possible by the internet. The internet has assisted the business in lowering its infrastructure costs.

Thus, both positively and negatively, the internet has had a significant impact on how business is conducted. Many businesses, like post offices, have become obsolete due to the internet problems with online security, such as identity theft and hacking represent a continual risk to internet users.

10.3.4. Internal Technology Framework

The product life cycle is shrinking in this era of rapid technology and relentless innovation. Businesses face unyielding pressure to distinguish themselves from the competition and captivate customers. To navigate the tides of change in this dynamic landscape, a robust internal network is essential for organizational success.

The McKinsey 7S framework is one tool available for conducting analysis to evaluate an organization's effectiveness in achieving strategic goals.

The 7S model is used to analyze and recommend areas for improvement within the organization, assess the impact of changing strategy, and ensure internal alignment with each merger and acquisition.

The seven components that make up the 7S framework influence how effective an organization is. These seven elements include staff, management style, employee skills, shared values, IT systems, organizational structure, and strategy. These seven elements can be broadly divided into two categories: shared values, skills, style, and staff; and hard elements, such as strategy, structure, and systems. The above-highlighted "hard" elements are those that management can directly influence. Soft factors are influenced by internal culture and are not directly under management's authority.

The 7 factors as per the framework can be defined as follows:

- **Strategy:** It is described as an action plan that strives to achieve the goal established by the organization.
- **Structure:** It is described as the organization-employee interaction designed to achieve a specific goal.
- **Systems:** It is described as information systems that an organization has invested in order to achieve a specific goal.
- **Staff:** It is defined as workers employed by the organization.
- **Style:** It is described as the strategy used by the leadership to communicate with staff members, vendors, and clients.
- **Skills:** It is described as traits shared by workers who are connected to the company.
- **Shared Values:** It serves as the hub of the entire 7S framework. It is a concept that an organization has chosen to use in order to accomplish its goal.

The fundamental tenet of the 7S framework is that all seven components must be in harmony and mutual balance for an organization to achieve its goals. The model is used to determine which of the seven components needs to be balanced in order to support organizational change.

The 7S framework is useful in pinpointing the issues that are impeding an organization's ability to grow. In the digital age, technology and technology-driven information systems both revolutionize how organizations meet their goals. Businesses are shifting in the direction of cloud computing, automation, etc. As a result, technology now serves as the organization's central nervous system.

The 7S framework can be used by businesses in any industry. It is a leading model for assessing the efficacy of organizations. The organization's strategy is always changing in this demanding environment. In a situation like this, it is crucial for the organization to reflect on its seven components in order to pinpoint the issue impeding its progress.

An organization can determine how it fits into the current strategy by using the 7S framework.

The challenge for the CIO is to help the organization achieve its goal by leveraging technology.

10.3.5. Alignment of Technology and Corporate Planning

Information technology is crucial to an organization's success in the digital age. In our globalized world, technology gives us an advantage. Businesses compete not only with other local businesses but also with foreign businesses. In this kind of situation, it's critical that the business makes technology investments that complement its overarching business plan. This necessitates developing a technology strategy.

10.3.5.1. Technology Strategy Formulation

Aligning technology strategy with the organization's overarching plan is discussed in technology strategy formulation. This is where the Chief Information Officer's role becomes important. Both a short- and long-term vision for technological advancement should be held by the CIO. The CIO should connect organizational strategy with the implications of technological advancement. The executive leadership must be informed in a clear and concise manner of how technology affects the organization.

The following topics are central to the CIO and CEO's alignment:

- CIO responsibilities and participation in the organization's overall strategy development.
- The availability of financial resources for technology investments.
- Previous outcomes of technology and organizational strategy alignment.
- External business conditions.

10.3.5.1.1. Planning

Corporate strategy and technology alignment are significantly influenced by corporate planning. The CEO and CIO should ideally have the same planning horizon. On the other hand, it appears that the CIO and CEO have different visions for everything from strategy to execution. This presents the idea of lead time planning. In certain organizations, the technology planning horizon and execution do not align with the strategy execution. By the time the technology strategy is put into practice, the system has advanced more, losing its competitive advantage. In the case mentioned above, businesses stop being proactive and start acting reactively. Businesses must adapt to the challenges posed by trend-setters and market leaders. A solid rapport between the CIO and the CEO guarantees that the organization gains knowledge of the technological obstacles and how they affect the organization as a whole.

10.3.5.1.2. Organizational Structure

Organizations must make sure that their organizational structure is adaptable and agile in order to handle technological advancements. They ought to be sufficiently effective and efficient to handle shifting market demands. Flexible and adaptable technology systems must be developed and maintained by organizations. Businesses can use three different kinds of technology infrastructure for knowledge management, data warehousing, and enterprise resource planning (ERP). ERP, Data Warehousing, and Knowledge Management offer the organization cutting edge in all three areas.

10.3.5.1.3. Organizational Systems

Organizations strategically invest in technology based on their current needs, future requirements, and potential to gain a competitive advantage. Technology systems can be categorized into three groups based on their lifecycle: new systems, mature systems, and declining systems. New systems feature cutting-edge technology that gives organizations a competitive edge. However, as time passes, more companies adopt similar systems and technology, diminishing the competitive advantage. Eventually, systems and technology become obsolete and are phased out due to declining usage.

Organizations' executive leadership must oversee new system ranges in order to maintain a competitive edge. But this calls for a significant financial commitment and a clear understanding of the state of technology in the future. As a result, organizations must tread carefully when investing in new technology and retiring outdated ones.

10.3.6. Information Technology and Business Intelligence

The commercial world underwent a significant transformation after the 1990s. Organizations from all industry sectors have begun utilizing information technologies in an effort to increase profitability and productivity. Businesses began to use the internet, telecommunications, mainframes, and PCs in addition to the products and services they provided to customers. This procedure is now the cornerstone of information technology evolution. The information technology industry has seen a sharp rise in investments. The US economy is currently experiencing expansion and has seen remarkable growth in its Gross Domestic Product over the last few years. Low inflation and a rise in the need for labor have both occurred. This lack of price increase has also confounded a lot of economists. According to conventional theories, price pressures are more likely to occur whenever the economy expands and the unemployment rate decreases.

The process of using productive inputs to produce output is known as "productivity." Effective use of all input resources, including labor, machinery, and materials, can improve cost control and enable businesses to charge end customers a fair price for their goods and services. Organizations can boost productivity by fusing cutting-edge information technology with business tactics. A business strategy takes into account a number of factors, including target market identification, customer preferences, and process management for the production and delivery of goods and services to the final consumer. Business executives and decision-makers can create a variety of business strategies based on economic theories thanks to information technology. This is accomplished by providing information to decision-makers and staff members across the board in an organization. The managers can readily analyze the following operations by implementing efficient IT. They're as follows:

- Production;
- Marketing/advertising;
- Customer relationship management;
- Distribution;
- Finance;
- Human Resource;
- Telecomm and network processes.

Information technology is already helping organizations become more efficient in their business operations. Information technology has also seen significant advancements, such as increases in computer speed and memory. This has consequently made room for powerful, cutting-edge software applications. The internet is enhanced by the most recent advancements in telecommunications technology. An organization's information pulse is now a vast information network created by the combination of all these technologies.

The term "business intelligence" (BI) describes the methods and instruments used to transform unprocessed data into information that is both meaningful and practical. These methods are used to manage vast amounts of unstructured data in order to find and develop new business opportunities.

Facilitating the user's interpretation of data is the primary goal of business intelligence.

Through the use of business intelligence tools, organizations can obtain a competitive edge in the market and long-term stability. When unstructured or raw data is converted into value-added information, people in an organization across all categories have a greater understanding of business. Decision-makers use these data to put different business strategies based on economic theory into practice. Additionally, resources are easily managed to meet the needs of the final customer.

Common functions of BI are:

1. Reporting;
2. Online analytical processing;
3. Analytics;
4. Data mining;
5. Process mining;
6. Business performance management;
7. Predictive analysis; and
8. Prescriptive analysis.

10.3.7. Information Technology as Driving Force for Innovation

Information technology has advanced significantly over the past 20 years. The way that business is conducted has changed as a result of information technology advancements. Innovation is one of the most remarkable aspects of information technology. Innovation in processes, services, and products has been fueled by information technology.

10.3.7.1. Innovation in Last Decades

It has made possible things that were only thought of as possibilities for fiction novels in the past. The miniaturization of electronic circuits made possible by information technology has led to the portability of many products, including phones and computers. Due to its affordability, information technology has aided in the advancement of communication technology. Mobile phone penetration is higher than it has ever been, with more coverage and ever-lower costs. With the advancement of high-memory storage devices, the idea of big data has come to pass.

10.3.7.2. Function of Information Technology

Information technology is a network of interconnected devices that transform data into meaningful and usable information. Thus, innovation in information technology is centered on six main functions. These are the six main functions:

- **Capture:** Its definition is the process of obtaining data in a way that allows for additional manipulation. Information can be entered using a keyboard, mouse, picture, etc.

- **Transmit:** It is described as a procedure that transfers captured data from one system to another. This system may exist inside or outside of the same geographic area. Radio, TV, email, phone, fax, etc. are a few examples.
- **Store:** It is described as a procedure that allows for the safe and secure storage of collected data that can be retrieved as needed. For instance, USB, hard drives, etc.
- **Retrieval:** It is described as a procedure that enables the retrieval of stored data when needed. For instance, a hard drive, RAM, USB, etc.
- **Manipulation:** It is described as a procedure that enables the transformation of information that has been recorded and stored. This transformation could take the form of a data arrangement, computation, display, etc. Take computer software, for instance.
- **Display:** It is described as an information-projecting process. For instance, a printer, computer screen, etc.

10.3.7.3. Innovation and Information Technology

There are roughly six functions that have been developed and evolved in information technology over the last 20 years. The six functions have resulted in innovation propelled by information technology. Several noteworthy advancements have been made, including the following.

- **Portability:** Information technology advancements have made it possible for all electronic devices to be portable.
- **Speed:** The speed at which computation is done today is faster than it was for earlier supercomputer generations.
- **Miniaturization:** Another innovation is the development of information systems and handheld computing devices, such as the GPS, iPad, and Smartphone.
- **Connectivity:** Communication capabilities have changed as a result of information technology.
- **Entertainment:** Multimedia and digital information have proliferated enormously.
- **User Interface:** The way people interact with computers has evolved as a result of information technology advancements. With the invention of the touch screen, computing has become interactive and intuitive.

The aforementioned examples make it abundantly clear that development and information technology are the main forces behind modern innovation.

10.3.8. Managing Technology in Operations Management

Over the past ten years or so, technology has transformed the way businesses operate. The introduction of technology to operation management has raised organizational productivity. Over time, the focus of technology and operation management has shifted from product development to the design, administration, and enhancement of operating systems and procedures. Through the use of technology in operation management, businesses are now able to focus on customization, standardize and improve quality, cut costs, enhance the delivery process, and increase customer value.

10.3.8.1. Integration of Technology with Production System

The implementation of technology in an organization boosts efficiency and enhances productivity. Despite these benefits, integrating technology into the production system is a challenging and intricate process that requires following specific steps:

- **Technology Acquisition:** Acquired technology should be approved after a thorough cost-benefit analysis and should be in line with the organization's overall goals.
- **Technology Integration:** Technology has an impact on every facet of production labor, capital, and client. As a result, a strong plan for integrating technology is necessary.
- **Technology Verification:** After technology is integrated, it's critical to assess whether it's being fully utilized and providing operational effectiveness.

10.3.8.2. Technology in Manufacturing and Design

The use of technology in the customization of goods and services is growing. Computer use and related electronic systems are essential to today's industrial and service sectors. The following categories can be used to broadly classify current techniques:

- **Computer-Aided Design (CAD):** Through the use of very high accuracy CAD, it is possible to link two more complex design components, increasing productivity.
- **Computer-Aided Manufacturing System (CAM):** Computerized numerically controlled machines are utilized because they provide the highest level of accuracy possible. Precision is vital to the operation of all machines.
- **Standard for the Exchange of Product Data:** Product design is communicated between CAM and CAM in three dimensions, as the name implies. The Standard for the Exchange of Product Data facilitates neutral file exchange and allows product sharing throughout the whole life cycle.

10.3.8.2.1. Software Systems in Manufacturing

To integrate manufacturing and operations with other organizational business functions, a variety of software systems are available. Enterprise resource planning (ERP), supply chain management (SCM), new product development (NPD), and customer relationship management (CRM) are a few examples of popular software programs. Using a single software platform, enterprise resource planning, or ERP, connects all business operations, including finance, marketing, manufacturing, and human resources. The ERP solution's primary advantages are that it decreases database errors while simultaneously providing customers with value through expedited delivery and order fulfillment.

10.3.8.2.2. Automation in Production and Operations

Automation streamlines the manufacturing process by minimizing manual tasks, boosting efficiency, and minimizing mistakes, resulting in cost savings through economies of scale. However, there are drawbacks to automation including potential job loss, expensive maintenance costs, and significant upfront investment. It is crucial to carefully consider the organization's objectives before implementing automation to ensure its suitability for the specific situation.

10.3.8.2.3. Challenges

Technology has the potential to enable changes in production management and operations. However, there may be challenges associated with using technology in all areas, including high initial investment costs, high maintenance costs, and poor management.

10.3.9. Leveraging Information Technology for Leadership

Technology is among the most significant elements that has altered every business's landscape. Organizations have used systems, connectivity, and the unimagined possibilities offered by the internet and communications to strive toward not only expanding their global empires but also developing novel and impactful methods of interacting with their clientele and delivering exceptional value and performance. Businesses that are leaders in their industry set themselves apart from the competition, and knowing what makes them unique helps us develop and aspire to be leaders ourselves. You will first and foremost notice that these organizations are fully dedicated to giving their clients faultless, effective, and hassle-free service. Second, they look for ways to continuously improve their internal innovation and business processes in order to reduce costs and pass the savings and benefits along to their clients. Thirdly, these organizations use technology to advance the two agenda items listed above.

Consider your credit card company, your preferred car rental company, your regular airline, or even the chain of hotels you stay at when traveling. They make sure to get to know you better, comprehend your needs, pay attention to your requirements, and make sure you have a pleasant and hassle-free transaction or service with them. You would have to take the time and effort to fill out your personal details into their database only once.

It just takes a few minutes to submit a request through Hertz's system whenever you want to rent a car. You'll be pleasantly surprised to learn that they are aware of your preferences and will see to it that the appropriate vehicle is delivered to the city of your choosing. Your hotel reservation system makes sure that the airport customer service representative has access to your information and handles all other logistics, freeing you up to enjoy and feel good.

These businesses are utilizing technology systems to streamline their operations. By using cutting-edge technology like handheld scanners and mobile devices, customer service representatives can quickly access guest information, understand their needs, and efficiently execute their tasks. This enables seamless and instantaneous communication and action through technology and systems.

The in-warding supervisor at the store is already aware of every detail about the incoming stock, including the color, model, size, and containerization plan of the truck, down to the last piece of apparel. They also know where that specific shirt is stocked in which box when the supplier's truck leaves the warehouse to arrive at Wal-Mart. The system suggests a few brands and alternatives that you might find interesting when you try to search for an item on the Home Depot website. The system also makes recommendations for products you might want to buy but forgot to because it records and analyzes your past purchasing behavior. People's love for Home Depot's online ordering is understandable.

Why do customers love purchasing music, books, and other items from Amazon?

Because the company is constantly making an investment to learn about your preferences and tastes in order to provide you with more value and help you narrow down your search by suggesting books based on your interests, letting you write reviews, and providing book previews, among other things. They make your online shopping and browsing more valuable and meaningful by utilizing systems and technology. They are always working to enhance the features and capabilities of their system so that you can have a more valuable and rich experience, spend less time searching or entering a lot of data, etc. After making a few purchases on Amazon, it's possible that you will grow accustomed to using them exclusively because you will feel as though you are familiar with the platform that Amazon and its system are aware of your needs and preferences, and that using them is easy and efficient. Some people develop an addiction to the Amazon system because they log in frequently to check out the newest releases and to read or write reviews. The technology makes a difference in each of the aforementioned situations. Companies that are leaders in their industry have fully realized the potential of information technology and used it as the foundation for their entire business strategy.

10.3.10. Information Security Threats in Organizations and Ensuring Prevention and Recovery

Having extensive IT infrastructure and software/hardware assets has become standard in modern organizations. Every organization, regardless of size, requires an IT backbone to function. IT is essential for ensuring competitive advantage and conducting business transactions. However, simply having an IT system is not enough to guarantee success. It is crucial for organizations to implement well-designed Information Security protocols and procedures to protect their IT assets from internal and external threats.

In fact, as IT becomes more widespread, so do the various threats it poses. These include external hacking, internal actors—including employees—stealing private and confidential information, cyberattacks that expose the IT infrastructure to financial risk, and—above all—the constant risk of these bad actors gaining access to organizational IT systems and taking actions that could jeopardize the organizations' ability to conduct business. Both internal and external threats are mentioned above. It is commonly recognized that external threats arise when hackers and cybercriminals exploit weaknesses and vulnerabilities in IT systems and infrastructure. However, it is equally important to acknowledge that internal threats can be equally dangerous as external ones.

In fact, there has been a growing trend in recent years for internal actors within organizations to assist cybercriminals by giving them inside knowledge and specifics about the IT infrastructure and organizational systems. Furthermore, it has been discovered that insiders are frequently the ones who allow outside hackers to enter an organization's IT systems, cause havoc, and cause chaos.

However, it is important to acknowledge the threats posed by hackers who aim to infiltrate IT systems for personal gain or to gain a competitive advantage. The involvement of competitors and other entities in cyber-attacks has become increasingly common, raising concerns among Information Security professionals. Additionally, countries and their intelligence agencies have also begun engaging in cyber hacking activities, targeting rival organizations to inflict damage and economic losses. This behavior is particularly prevalent in the rivalry between the United States, China, and Russia, with hackers supported by commercial and national security interests attacking systems to disrupt business operations and cause financial and reputational harm.

Because of all these factors, IS professionals in companies need to make sure that their hardware, software, and IT assets are protected as well as their systems are foolproof in order to protect them from these numerous threats. It is true that organizations and IS departments frequently install firewalls and restrict access to their systems from outside sources due to the numerous threats that exist in cyberspace. This is also the reason that a lot of businesses have recently implemented measures to limit their employees' internet usage in order to prevent them from leaving "digital footprints" in cyberspace that hostile hackers and cybercriminals could use against them. The rising rate of identity theft and phishing, which is much more dangerous when it affects managers' and senior executives' accounts in addition to the leadership in their companies, is another issue that worries IS professionals.

Identity theft and phishing can result in financial losses for individuals and organizations. However, when senior employees are targeted, the potential damage to the organization's objectives is significant due to the sensitive information they possess. This has led information systems professionals to emphasize the need for secure systems tailored specifically for managers and senior leaders, with more advanced security measures in place. To address these concerns, IT professionals are implementing dedicated and isolated internet access for high-level employees, in contrast to the generic access provided to lower-level staff.

Lastly, as they say, offense is the best form of defense and prevention is better than cure. Therefore, IS professionals would be well advised to take proactive measures to prevent cyber breaches rather than respond to them. They should also adopt aggressive postures against potential hackers and malicious insiders rather than waiting to respond to breaches or hacking incidents. Moreover, it is also true that commonplace actions like writing down passwords on unguarded papers can result in intrusions into information systems. Furthermore, although it may seem that hacking only occurs "out there," a significant breach can originate from something as simple as visiting a website with lax security measures. In conclusion, it's important to keep in mind that oversight and negligence are the main causes of information security risks, so it makes sense to take precautions against them.

CASE STUDY

ON INFORMATION TECHNOLOGY MANAGEMENT: FRITO-LAY'S LONG-TERM IT PLAN

Because the rate of technological change is so rapid, most people see IT through the narrow lens of short-term, silver-bullet solutions. IT vendors want you to believe that their important new technologies will blow away what has come before. You can't blame a salesperson for trying to sell, or CIOs for having a queasy buy-or-lose feeling, but this attitude is precisely the opposite of the one companies should be taking. We would argue that because the winds of change affect IT more than any other area of the organization, IT benefits most from a long-term, disciplined, strategic view, and a square focus on achieving the company's most fundamental goals. For example, Frito Lay's strategic goal has always been to make, move, and sell tasty, fresh snack food as rapidly and efficiently as possible. That goal hasn't changed since 1930s, when founder Herman Lay ran his business from his Atlanta kitchen and one delivery truck. He bought and cooked the potatoes. He delivered the chips to the stores. He collected the money and knew all his customers. He balanced the books and did his own quality assurance. Herman Lay knew how to conduct the perfect "sense and respond" e-business before such a thing ever existed, for he held real-time customer, accounting, and inventory information all in one place—his head! After years of spectacular growth, the company became progressively distracted from this simple business model. By the early 1980s, the company's sales force had swelled to 10,000, and information grew harder and harder to manage. The company's old batch-based data processing systems were all driven by paper forms that took 12 weeks to print and distribute to the sales force. All sales transactions were recorded by hand; reams of disparate data were transferred to the company's mainframe computers. Much was lost in the process of setting up a dozen different functional organizations and a variety of databases, none of which communicated with each other. This modus operandi made it impossible to change prices quickly or develop new regional promotions, streamline production, or improve inventory management. It was as if Herman Lay's company had suffered a spinal cord injury, with the brain and body no longer connected. At the same time, the company was seeing the rise of strong regional competitors. The leaders realized that if trends continued as they were, its overall revenues would fall significantly by early 1990s.

Mike Jordan, who took over as CEO of Frito Lay in 1983, decided to tackle the problem. He reconstructed the company as a hybrid organization that was neither totally centralized nor decentralized. His goal was to teach the company to "walk and chew the gum at the same time," as he put it, by separating the company's two competitive advantages: the purchasing, production, and distribution leverages of a national powerhouse, and the local resources that gave the company regional speed and agility. All this led to an organizational design that kept purchasing, manufacturing, distribution, systems, accounting, and R&D as the centralized platform, leaving the decentralized sales and marketing organizations to launch their store-by-store and street-by-street offensives. Having identified the company's strategy, Jordan then developed a long-term renewal (as opposed to "rip and replace") plan. An executive committee- comprised of CEO, CFO, CIO, and two executive vice presidents- outlined a shift from paper to a risky, emerging handheld technology for the sales people on the street, as well as transformation from batch accounting to online operational systems. The goal was to digitally reconnect the company's nervous system. Equipped with the cool new handhelds, the sales force would be able to manage price, inventory, and customer changes in real time and connect to supply pipeline. The handheld computers would also establish a technological "beach-head"- one sufficiently important to keep business's attention and achieve fast operating results. Paying for all this, of course, would not be easy. The journey would take from 1984 to 1988, at a huge cost (at the time): $40 million for the handhelds and about $ 100 million for databases and core systems. Some of the executive committee balked, arguing that efficiencies gained by the technology would be lost by the sales people working fewer hours. But the company had no choice but to revitalize its regional sales, and though the systems overhaul would be costly, staying put would be even costlier. To fund the new computers, Jordan set up a long term, ongoing funding mechanism designed to keep IT spending both predictable and fairly stable from year to year. To get things rolling, each sales region had to commit to a reduction in selling expenses from 22 cents on the dollar to 21 cents within a year of the handhelds' installation. The savings would be achieved by increasing sales at constant cost, reducing costs, or a combination of two. The scheme worked; with the new system in place, the company saved between 30,000 to 50,000 hours of paperwork per week. By 1988, savings resulting from better control over sales data came to more than 4 40 million per year—savings that in turn funded the renewal of the core data systems. Frito Lay was able to cut the number of its distribution centers, reduce stale product by 50%, and increase its domestic revenues from $ 3 billion in 1986 to $ 4.2 billion by 1989. Today, Frito lay continues to be the dominant player in the snack-food industry. Frito Lay's technology story received a lot of press at the time, mostly because the handheld technology was sexy. But notice what the story was really about: it was about executing Herman Lay's original, real-time business experience—feeling the money jingling in the pocket and seeing the inventory in the truck!

CLASS ACTIVITY

DIGITAL FIELD TRIPS

An increasingly popular, useful, and cost-effective tool for teachers searching for new ways to use technology in the classroom is taking digital field trips. Google Streetview and other similar apps allow you to virtually explore parks, forests, and even national and international landmarks from the comfort of your classroom. Virtually experience the view from the Statue of Liberty or hike through the Grand Canyon to get students excited to learn about a location or subject and extend learning beyond the page.

SUMMARY

- In order to fully utilize your company's information system and reap the greatest benefits, it is important to leverage all of its capabilities. Information systems play a crucial role by processing data from company inputs to create valuable information for managing your operations.
- The impact of information technology will significantly affect the structure, management, and function of most organizations. It will require new patterns of work organization and will impact individual jobs, group and team structures, supervision methods, and managerial roles.
- IT is important to all types of businesses, from large multinationals that manage databases and mainframe systems to small companies with a single computer.
- Through a range of systems, including query, analysis, modeling, and decision support systems, the information system plays a significant role in the organization by meeting the diverse needs of its users. It assists the Clerical staff in processing transactions and responds to their questions about transaction-related data.
- Systems for processing transactions, used in product design, marketing, production, and delivery, are found at the operational level. These systems compile data into databases, which serve as the basis for systems at higher levels.
- In an information society, processing, producing, and delivering tangible materials is not as common as it once was. Instead, a significant amount of work consists of manipulating abstract knowledge and information. It is referred to as knowledge work.
- Information systems created to assist with organizational management fall under a broad category. These systems rely on information from transaction processing systems, information from outside the company (like business intelligence found online), and information from suppliers, customers, and business partners.
- Executive information systems provide a multitude of important data in an easily accessible, highly condensed format. However, since senior managers typically use a variety of unofficial sources, formal, computerized information systems are not very helpful.
- Structure is necessary for an organization and its technology. An organization has architecture, just like the networks and systems you use for information technology do. Businesses set themselves up to best accomplish their objectives and complete all of their required tasks. An organizational structure must consider the operations, infrastructure, and functions related to technology if it is to be truly viable.
- Due to its ability to level the playing field between small and large businesses, technology has completely changed the way companies do business. Small businesses use a wide range of technology, from mobile phones to servers, to gain an advantage over competitors in the market.

- A contemporary phenomenon, information technology has fundamentally altered people's daily lives as well as businesses' operations all over the world. The semi-conductor is responsible for the creation of the microchip, which powers information technology.
- The product life cycle is getting shorter in this day of advanced technology and constant innovation. Businesses are under constant pressure to set themselves apart from the competition and win over customers. To handle any kind of change in such a business environment, an effective internal organization network is crucial.
- The internet has a well-established and acknowledged global influence. The internet is being accessed by nearly one-third of the world's population, demonstrating its incredible penetration rate. The sheer number of people using the internet has altered how business is done in this digital age. The internet is now even more important in business thanks to developments in information technology and communication.

REVIEW QUESTIONS

1. Determine the various IT tools and technologies for managers.
2. How to define the role of information systems in various levels of modern organizations?
3. Examine the IT functions in an organization.
4. Write the relationship between technology and organizational structure.
5. What are the business objectives of information technology?

REFERENCES

1. Beniger, J. (2009). *The control revolution: Technological and economic origins of the information society*. Harvard University Press.
2. Bidgoli, H. (2004). *The internet encyclopedia* (Vol. 1, p. 707). John Wiley & Sons, Inc.
3. Curry, M. (2008). *Digital places: Living with geographic information technologies*. Routledge.
4. Ettlie, J., Perotti, V., Joseph, D., & Cotteleer, M. (2005). Strategic predictors of successful enterprise system deployment. *International Journal of Operations and Production Management, 25*, 953–972.
5. Goksoy, A., Ozsoy, B., & Vayvay, O. (2012). Business process reengineering: Strategic tool for managing organizational change—An application in a multinational company. *International Journal of Business and Management,* 7(2), 89–112. https://doi.org/10.5539/ijbm.v7n2p89.
6. Joshi, G. (2013). *Management information systems* (p. 328). Oxford University Press.
7. Kawalek, P., & Wood-Harper, T. (2002). The finding of thorns: User participation in ES implementation. *Data Base, 33*(1), 13–22.

8. Laudon, K. C., & Laudon, J. P. (2009). *Management information systems: Managing the digital firm* (11th ed., p. 164). Prentice Hall/CourseSmart.
9. Laudon, K., & Laudon, J. (2010). *Management information systems: Managing the digital firm* (11th ed.). Pearson Prentice Hall.
10. Lesser, E., Fontaine, M., & Slusher, J. (2009). *Knowledge and communities*. Routledge.
11. Lim, E., Pan, S. L., & Tan, C. W. (2005). Managing user acceptance towards ERP systems—Understanding the dissonance between user expectations and managerial policies. *European Journal of Information Systems, 14*, 135–149.
12. Lorenzo, O., & Kawalek, P. (2004). A model of enterprise systems infusion. *Proceedings of the European Operations Management Association (EurOMA) Conference*, INSEAD, France.
13. Lorenzo, O., Kawalek, P., & Wood-Harper, T. (2005). Embedding the enterprise systems into the enterprise: A model of corporate diffusion. *Communications of the Association for Information Systems, 15*, 609–641.

Index

O

P

Q

R

FSC
www.fsc.org
MIX
Papier | Fördert
gute Waldnutzung
FSC® C083411

Kolibri 360 GmbH
Ferdinand-Jühlke-Straße 7
99095 Erfurt, Deutschland
produktsicherheit@kolibri360.de